THE WRITER'S WORKPLACE

Building College Writing Skills

SIXTH EDITION

SANDRA SCARRY
Formerly with the Office of Academic Affairs, City University of New York

JOHN SCARRY
Hostos Community College, City University of New York

HEINLE & HEINLE
THOMSON LEARNING™

Australia Canada Mexico Singapore Spain United Kingdom United States

HEINLE & HEINLE
THOMSON LEARNING™

The Writer's Workplace/Sixth Edition
Sandra Scarry • John Scarry

Publisher: Earl McPeek
Acquisitions Editor: Stephen Dalphin
Developmental Editor: Michell Phifer
Production Editor: Linda McMillan
Market Manager: John Meyers

Compositor: Publications Development
Project Editor: Joyce Fink
Art Director: Garry Harman
Cover Photo: Tony Stone/Justus Hardin Photog.
Printer: RR Donnelley & Sons

Printed in the United States of America.
4 5 6 7 8 9 10 06 05 04 03

For more information contact Heinle & Heinle, 25 Thomson Place, Boston, Massachusetts 02210 USA, or you can visit our Internet site at http://www.heinle.com

ISBN: 0-15-505920-3
Library of Congress Catalog Card Number: 2001012345

THE WRITER'S WORKPLACE

Sixth Edition

For Our Students

What shall I do this year?
What shall I become?
What shall I learn—truly learn and know that I have learned
by the time I look at these pages next year?

Lorraine Hansberry
Journal entry of August 23, 1962*

*From *To Be Young, Gifted and Black,* adapted by Robert Nemiroff (Englewood Cliffs, NJ: Prentice-Hall, 1969).

Preface

OVERVIEW

The Writer's Workplace, Sixth Edition, offers a **complete** writing program for students who need additional preparation to do college-level work. Each chapter in the book helps student writers understand a single aspect of the writing process. As students explore each element that goes into making an effective piece of writing, they will enjoy the book's engaging tone, find interesting content, feel the helpfulness of a step-by-step approach, and be rewarded with a wealth of challenging material.

The book is also a **flexible** resource for both teacher and student. Instructors may start to work in almost any chapter, depending on the needs of a particular class. Students may be encouraged to do some of the work on their own, especially those exercises that review grammar topics. Instructors will be able to choose from among the rhetorical modes in the sections devoted to paragraph and essay development which ones they wish to focus on in any particular semester. For those who wish to assign more readings, the additional readings at the back of the book will be appreciated. Finally, since writing is a process, many opportunities for revising and editing student essays can be found throughout the book, as well as opportunities for many other collaborative activities. Whatever vision an instructor or writing faculty has for a school's writing classes, *The Writer's Workplace* will be a pleasure to use and will provide a solid resource for students.

An important goal of this book is to engage students in many activities that involve **collaborative learning.** Group activities, designed to encourage critical thinking and appreciation for the ideas of others, are contained in the Working Together feature that ends each chapter. Themes in these sections are often work-related, a recognition that students have an interest in career issues. Each chapter also gives suggestions for **exploration on the Internet** because students in writing classes must have many opportunities to develop their computer skills, an area of technology that in today's world is increasingly linked to both college and on-the-job writing.

While the book always keeps its emphasis on mastering basic writing skills, *The Writer's Workplace* never forgets the importance of **student creativity** throughout every stage of the writing process. As teachers and students of writing who have used previous editions know, *The Writer's Workplace* is a rich resource, one that can be used with confidence and success throughout the semester.

THE ORGANIZATION OF *THE WRITER'S WORKPLACE*

Part I Looking at the Whole

This section introduces the college writer to the writing process, focusing on short activities that immediately involve the student in a variety of prewriting activities. Considerations of the elements of good writing, such as *unity* and *coherence,* are also introduced.

Part II Creating Effective Sentences

Section two will take students through a number of grammar topics with one goal in mind, to give them a sound understanding of the difference between a complete sentence and a fragment or run-on. Instructors will find this sentence building section one of the most comprehensive and thoughtful treatments available, with multiple exercises on each topic that give every student ample opportunity to succeed. Furthermore, most of the exercises are written in continuous discourse; that is, all the sentences are based on material related to a particular subject. This will make for greater student interest in the content as students learn the fundamental skills for writing clear and complete sentences.

Part III Understanding the Power of Words

The ability to make correct word choices includes a range of skills, from knowing the difference between *its* and *it's,* to an understanding of why using the slang word *kid* to mean *child* is considered inappropriate in formal writing. This part of the book is made up of enjoyable but challenging lessons on how to use precise, appropriate language. After doing the work of this section, students will have a heightened awareness of the impact of word choice on the construction of a piece of writing.

Part IV Creating Effective Paragraphs

Many teachers who have used earlier editions of *The Writer's Workplace* describe this section as the heart of the book. They see it as central to their work because it is here that students explore the several ways they can develop the paragraphs that eventually lead to the construction of a successful college essay. The directions for learning each mode are very specific, while the model paragraphs inspire student writers to search for their own specific details as they incorporate the rhetorical modes into their writing. As teachers of composition realize, students produce their most effective writing when they understand both the objective discipline of the writing process as well as the challenge of giving clear expression to their own individual thoughts.

Part V Structuring the College Essay

The goal of most writing programs is to give each student an understanding of how to construct an essay that contains a clear thesis statement, includes fully developed support paragraphs, and leads to a logical conclusion. This section of the book builds on the student's grasp of sentence mechanics and paragraph development, skills taught in the preceding sections, and then adds the more demanding requirements of a longer piece of writing: the organization of material, the thesis statement and introduction, transitions between ideas, the development of paragraphs, the use of outside sources, and the arrival at an appropriate conclusion. This section concludes with one of the most challenging assignments in writing: composing the persuasive essay, a mode of composition that demands careful logic and critical thinking.

Appendices

Students may be referred to several parts of the appendices for further study. These sections will be especially helpful to ESL students. Students will find an alphabetical list of the irregular verbs, definitions and examples of the parts of speech, a comprehensive explanation of spelling issues, and a listing of all the transitional expressions presented in different chapters of the book.

The "Working Together" Activities
The Working Together activity that ends every chapter offers a variety of activities to encourage student participation in the collaborative learning process. Announced by a lively illustration and brief, provocative text, each *Working Together* asks students to brainstorm, plan, or write about issues of importance in the world of school and of society. Interesting real-life writing activities such as producing a résumé, taking a survey, or analyzing a newspaper editorial are the focus points for group discussion and the planning of written responses.

NEW TO THIS EDITION

- Previews now begin each chapter to help students stay on target as they learn the basic concepts and terms presented in each chapter.
- Part I has two new chapters. The first chapter focuses on prewriting techniques while giving students several opportunities to practice those techniques. The second chapter concentrates on the basic elements of good writing and provides activities for work on such crucial skills as *unity* and *coherence*.
- The need for college writers to master computer literacy has led to the wide range of computer activities included in the new edition. Through guided suggestions and listings of specific sources, students are encouraged to explore writing-related topics using the World Wide Web.
- Chapter 15 now focuses entirely on the skill of editing by guiding students in the revision of several student paragraphs and essays.
- Chapter 18, "Developing Paragraphs: Illustration," is new to this edition.
- Two appendices have been added to provide the student with basic spelling rules and a list of all the transitional words and phrases given throughout the book.
- Several new model paragraphs and essays have been added to inspire ideas for discussion and writing on current topics as well as supply outstanding examples of modes of development.

ANCILLARY MATERIALS

Instructor's Resource Manual
Exercise and Test Book
Writer's Resources CD-ROM

ACKNOWLEDGMENTS

We are deeply grateful to all those individuals in our lives who make it possible to work on such an extensive and ongoing project as this textbook. First of all, we wish to thank J'laine Robnolt for her constant generosity of spirit as she so willingly has shared her talents, her perceptions, and her student's essays with us. We also thank our daughter Siobhán who graciously assisted us whenever asked. Her wonderful insights and ongoing contributions to the textbook are a source of continual appreciation. We consider ourselves blessed by these and other family members, friends, colleagues, and students whose faith in our work keeps us ever involved and excited in the hope of producing the ideal composition textbook.

We would like to thank the following reviewers for their encouragement and expertise: Marilyn Curall, Valencia Community College; Enoch Jordan, Norfolk State University; Mimi Markus, Broward Community College; Susan Matheny, Pasco-Hernando Community College; James Steven Mullis, Central Piedmont Community College; Sharon Race, South Plains College; Kokila Ravi, Morehouse College; Thera Woodard, Valencia Community College; and Ong Wooi-Chin, Long Beach City College.

Finally, we are indebted to the team at Harcourt for their continued enthusiasm for our work. The ease with which this edition has evolved is largely thanks to their care and helpfulness. We thank Sandra Lord, permission editor, for her tireless work on so many details. We are also grateful to Joyce Fink, our project editor, whose cheerful attentiveness we quickly came to depend on. We would also like to thank Linda McMillan, production manager, and Garry Harman, art director, for their contributions to making the final book. For Michell Phifer, our developmental editor, we express our greatest admiration. Her intelligence, good humor, patience, complete professionalism, and encouraging guidance made our job so much easier than it might otherwise have been. Finally, we wish to give our very special thanks to Steve Dalphin for his faith in our vision for this new edition.

Contents

RHETORICAL LIST OF PARAGRAPHS AND ESSAYS

The following symbols are used: one paragraph ¶
two or more paragraphs ¶'s
complete essay E

PART I AN INVITATION TO WRITING

Part I invites you to explore the beginning stages of the writing process and examine the essential elements of any effective piece of writing. Begin your work in this writing course with the kind of spirit that spells success.

- **Begin with a positive attitude**

You know more than you think. You have unique life experiences, and your ideas are worth writing about. Fortunately, writing is a skill that can be developed. No matter what your present skills are, practice can greatly help you improve those skills.

- **Be receptive to new techniques and approaches**

As a student beginning this course, you undoubtedly have not yet explored all the various techniques for getting your ideas on paper, and you may still have to learn how to use other people's ideas in your writing. Be willing to experiment with the techniques given in this section of the book. Once you practice these proven techniques, you will feel a new confidence as you tackle your own writing assignments.

- **Actively reach out and welcome help from others**

When we learn new skills,we are not expected to figure out everything by ourselves. Most students need help getting started, and since learning styles are different, students need to explore whatever methods work best for them. At every stage of the process, writers need each other to brainstorm, to read and comment on drafts, and to help revise, edit, and proofread each other's work. Part I of this book will help you extend your own thinking as you work beyond your first thoughts on a topic.

- **Respect the ideas of others**

Communication goes two ways. In the process of exploring and expressing our ideas, we must be open to other points of view, whether they come from our instructors, our classmates, or from our own reading. We can debate opposing ideas without criticizing the people who hold those ideas.

- **Finally, practice, practice, practice**

This means being willing to put in the time with thoughtful and earnest effort.

Chapter 1 Gathering Ideas for Writing

Preview

In this first chapter, you will learn about several prewriting techniques that students and professional writers use in order to generate ideas and gather material for their own writing.

- Journal writing
- Focused freewriting
- Brainstorming, clustering, and outlining
- Conducting interviews and surveys/questionnaires
- Taking notes: Direct quotation, summarizing, paraphrasing

Overview of the Writing Process

The following chart shows the stages a writer goes through in order to produce a finished piece of writing. Writers may differ slightly in how they approach a task, but for most of us, all of the following steps are necessary.

THE WRITING PROCESS

Prewriting Stages

1. Choose the topic and consider what aspect of that topic interests you.
2. Gather ideas, using prewriting techniques.

Writing and Revising

3. Compose a first draft and then set it aside for a period of time.
4. Reread your first draft, and if possible, ask the instructor or classmates for input.
5. Revise the first draft by adding, cutting, and moving material. Continue to revise and produce new drafts until satisfied.

Proofreading

6. Proofread the final copy, looking especially for typographical errors, misspellings, and omitted words.

Beginning to Write: Caring about Your Topic

Whether you are writing a college paper or a report on the job, your belief in the importance of your topic and confidence in your own ideas are major factors in your success as a writer. Sometimes a college writing assignment can seem as though it has little or no relevance beyond achieving a passing grade. In this course, however, you should consider each assignment as an opportunity to do the following:

- discover that you have ideas worth expressing
- explore topics that you care about
- incorporate the ideas of others into your own work

Prewriting Techniques: The First Step in the Writing Process

Prewriting, the earliest stage of the writing process, uses various techniques to put ideas into words.

Very few writers ever sit down and start writing immediately. In order to produce effective work, most writers begin by using a variety of strategies called *prewriting techniques*. These techniques help writers generate ideas and gather material about topics that are of interest to them or that they are required to write about for their work. Prewriting techniques are a way to explore and give some order to what might otherwise be a confusing hodgepodge of different thoughts on a topic. These techniques reassure every writer who feels the stress of looking at a blank page or an empty computer screen, knowing it has to be filled. Not only will the writer have material to write about, but he or she can also plan how to develop that material: what the major ideas will be, what the order of those ideas will be, and what specific details will be used. The rest of this chapter will describe these prewriting techniques and give opportunities to practice them.

EXPLORING ONLINE

See http://www.urich.edu/~writing/wweb.html at the University of Richmond Writing Center Web site for more prewriting techniques.

For more information on the writing process, visit http://www.usc.edu/dept/LAS/writing/tools/process.html

I. Journal Writing

Journal writing is a record of thoughts, opinions, observations or reactions to everyday experiences, kept on a regular basis.

A great many people keep a diary or journal at some point in their lives. Keeping a journal shows that a person feels the need to make a record of day-to-day events, or wishes to put down on paper some important thoughts, reactions, or opinions on what is happening in life. What makes the private journal especially helpful is that the writer does not have to worry about making a mistake or being misunderstood. The journal writer does not have to worry about handwriting or how thoughts are organized since the writer is the only person who will be reading the pages of that journal. A journal allows a person to be totally honest and write about anything he or she wishes.

You may have kept your own journal at one time, or one of your college instructors may have required a journal as part of a semester's work. Work included in a journal may even have been a consideration in the final grade for a course. Instructors who make a journal part of their semester's assignments realize that such writing gives students valuable practice in setting thoughts down on paper on a regular basis. Over a period of time, journals help students grow as writers and add to their overall success in college.

If you keep a journal, you might want to record events that happen around you, focus on problems you are trying to solve, or note your private reactions to the people you know. Until you actually put your thoughts into words, you may not be fully aware of all your feelings and opinions. Most writers are surprised and pleased with the results of their personal explorations in writing.

EXPLORING ONLINE

A journal can be a book with a lock and key, a notebook, or a file on your hard drive or diskette. Go to http://207.158.243.119/html/tips.html for tips on getting the most out of your journal writing.

Entry from *The Diary of Latoya Hunter*

Journals are especially popular during adolescence, partly because these years are usually a time of uncertainty when young people try to discover themselves as individuals.

The following selection is from the published diary of a junior high school student, Latoya Hunter, who kept a journal when she was only twelve years of age. The diary reports on her growing need for independence and her changing perceptions of the world around her.

> Today my friend Isabelle had a fit in her house. It was because of her mother. She's never home and she expects Isabelle to stay by herself. Today she was extra late because she was out with her boyfriend. Isabelle was really mad. She called her father and told him she wanted to live with him because her mother only cared about one person—her boyfriend. She was so upset. She was throwing things all over the place and crying. I never saw her like that before. It was really sad to see. I felt bad when I had to leave her all by herself. I hope she and her mother work it out but all mothers are the same. They think that you're young and shouldn't have an opinion. It's really hard to communicate with my parents. They'll listen to me but that's about it. They hardly take me seriously and it's because of my age. It's like discrimination! If you do speak your mind, you end up getting beaten. The real pain doesn't come from the belt though, it comes from inside. That's the worst pain you could ever feel.

EXPLORING ONLINE

Anne Frank was a young diarist who went into hiding during the Nazi occupation of the Netherlands. You can read her story and excerpts from her famous diary at http://www.annefrank.nl/eng/diary/diary.html Compare one of Anne Frank's entries to Latoya Hunter's. What differences in style, observation, and perspective do you notice?

ACTIVITY 1 **Writing a Journal Entry of Your Own**

In the selection you have just read, Latoya Hunter sadly overhears a friend going through an emotional crisis. Latoya uses her journal to explore her own feelings about parent–child relationships and to express what she thinks are some of the common failings of parents.

Write a journal entry of your own. Use your writing to report on an incident in which you were successful (or unsuccessful) in communicating with someone you know. The person could be a family member or someone from outside your family. Looking back on the incident, what contributed to the success or failure of that communication? What part did each person play that led to the final outcome?

EXPLORING ONLINE

Journals are important for businesspeople also. See the Veech Business Journal Pages at http://www.ate.co.nz/journal/ for the definition and goal of a business journal and techniques to get you started.

II. Focused Freewriting

Focused freewriting offers another way to explore writing topics. With this technique, the writer keeps on writing for a certain period of time and does not stop, no matter what. The goal of this technique is to put words on paper, and even if nothing new comes to mind, the writer keeps going by repeating a particular idea over again. This approach is one way to free a writer from what is often called "writer's block," that moment in the writing process when a person runs out of words and becomes paralyzed in front of the blank page or computer screen.

Focused freewriting is a prewriting technique in which the writer explores a topic by writing for a certain period of time without stopping, even if it means repeating the same ideas.

Here, for example, is what one young man wrote when he was asked to write for five minutes on the topic of *keeping a journal:*

```
I'm supposed to write about journal writing. I've never
kept a journal so how can I say anything about it? But I
broke into my younger sister's diary once and found out
about a boy she had kissed. It was one of those diaries
with those little keys and I ruined the lock. She didn't
speak to me for over a month and my parents were mad at
me. I thought it was funny at the time. After that she
didn't keep a diary anymore. So now what should I say?
Now what should I say? I don't really know. I guess I
might keep a journal to keep track of important things
that happen to me, like the day my dad came home with a
used car for me—now that was really cool. Of course, it
had a lot of problems that we had to fix over the next
year little by little, but that was really an awesome
day.
```

EXPLORING ONLINE FOR ESL STUDENTS

If English is not your first language, prewrite in your first language, and translate later. This will prevent you from limiting yourself to only the words and concepts that you can easily express in English. For more ideas, see Dave's ESL Cafe at http://www.eslcafe.com

ACTIVITY 2 **Focused Freewriting**

In this exercise you will consider the topic *My attitude toward writing* as an opportunity to practice focused freewriting. Write for at least five minutes without stopping, making sure that you keep going even if you feel you have nothing to say. Do not stop, even if you have to repeat some thoughts over and over.

COMPUTER PREWRITING TECHNIQUES

- Try "blind freewriting." Turn off your monitor as you key in your thoughts. This method prevents the writer from worrying about spelling and punctuation. The blank screen can sometimes be as intimidating as the blank page.
- Speak aloud your thoughts into voice recognition software.
- Perform an Internet search on your topic.
- Visit a threaded discussion group or chat room on your topic.

III. Brainstorming, Clustering (Also Called Mapping), and Outlining

Journal writing and *focused freewriting* are two methods of getting words down on paper during the early stages of the writing process. Other approaches are also useful to help the writer get started. Of all the prewriting techniques, perhaps the most widely used is brainstorming.

Brainstorming is an exercise in free association. You allow a phrase or thought to lead you from one thought to the next until you can't think of anything else. Many writers find it very liberating to do this because it is not necessary to worry about the thoughts being useful or in any particular order. The main goal is to jot down everything while your mind explores different paths. Later, you can sort the items on your list, putting them into groups or eliminating an item if it no longer fits. Unless the writer can do outside research, brainstorming is probably the best way to discover ideas for writing.

Brainstorming is a prewriting technique that uses free association to create a list of whatever words, phrases, or ideas come to mind on a given topic. It can be done alone or in a group.

Looking at a Student Brainstorming List

- **Below is an example of a student's first brainstorming list on the topic of *parent/teen communication.***

```
Problems talking with my own father
  Calls me immature sometimes
  Occasionally shouts
  Too tense
  Seems overly critical
Stacy's father
  Seems to have a sense of humor about everything, not so
    serious, easygoing
Guidance counselor
  Always calm, no hurry, always listens
What prevents a good talk with a parent?
  person's voice—loud, soft, angry, calm
  namecalling, put downs
  words can hurt
  bad language
  no eye contact
  authoritarian/controlling
  monopolizing the conversation
  tense/rigid
  withdrawal/the silent treatment
  teens can act worse than parents: disrespectful and
    rude
  rushed, not listening
  frowning, glaring, body language
  rigid, won't consider any other viewpoint
  sarcastic
```

- **Below, the student arranges the material taken from the brainstorming list:**

Once a writer has a brainstorming list, the next step is to think how the items might be grouped. At this point, the writer may cross out some items that do not seem to fit, include one item with another, and in general, consider how to organize the material. Here is how the student reorganized the initial brainstorming list:

```
   Advice to Parents: How to Communicate with Your Teen
Choose your words carefully
  do not call people names
  do not belittle them—use example of my father
  do not use bad language
  do not be disrespectful
```

```
    do not be mean or sarcastic
    do not use the silent treatment or monopolize the talk
  Listen to the way you sound, your tone, your attitude
    watch the volume of your voice—use example of Stacy's
      father
    wait until you have calmed down so you do not sound
      angry and tense
    don't sound rushed and hurried as if you have no time
      to listen
    don't sound too controlling
  Take a look at your body language
    work at being calm and relaxed
    do not withdraw; if possible give the person a hug or a
      pat on the shoulder
    no physical abuse: pushing, shoving, slapping
    what is your facial expression? (frowning, glaring,
      smirking, no eye contact)
```

Clustering is another method of gathering ideas during the prewriting stage. Clustering is very similar to brainstorming, except that when you cluster, you produce a visual map of your ideas rather than a list. You begin by placing a key idea (usually a single word or phrase) in the center of the page. Then you jot down other words and phrases that come to mind as you think about this key idea. As you work, you draw lines or branches to connect the items to each other.

> **Clustering** is the mapping of whatever comes to mind when you think about a topic. Variations of clustering are called ***webbing*** or ***branching.***
> (see example on page 11)

Outlining is the most formal method of organizing prewriting ideas. It is more difficult than the other prewriting techniques in that it usually comes after a good bit of brainstorming and rearranging of ideas. In a formal outline you must distinguish between major points and supporting details and put them in the order of your presentation of ideas. Since organization and order are important in outlining, there are rules for the outline so that you can tell by looking at it which ideas are major and which ideas are supporting details. In the sample outline that follows, notice the use of capital Roman numerals for major points, indented capital letters for details, and Arabic numbers if there are still further details that fall under the secondary points.

> **Outlining,** the most formal method of organizing prewriting ideas, distinguishes between major points and supporting details by using numerals and letters to show the organization of the planned piece of writing.
> (see example on page 11)

- **Here is how the writer might have explored his topic using a cluster technique.**

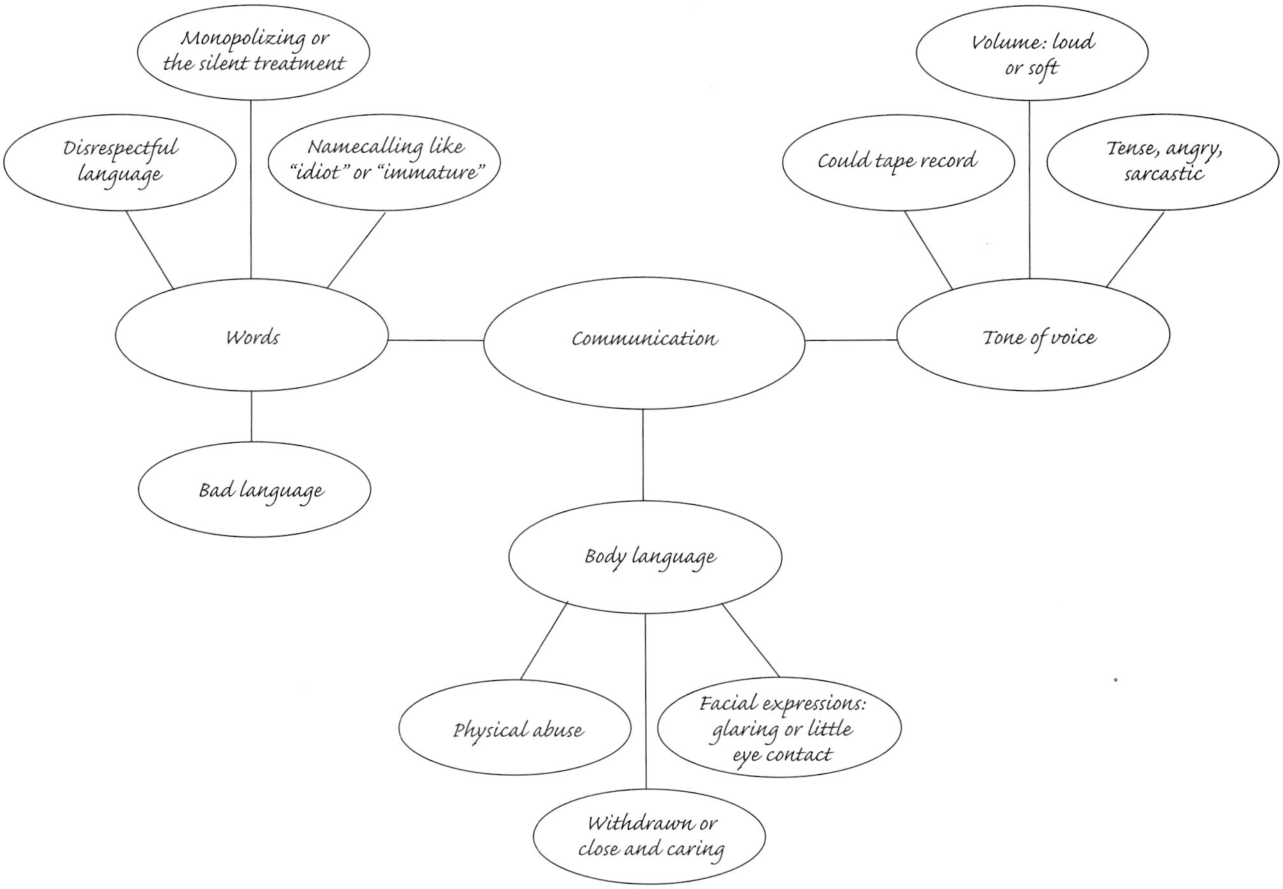

- **Here is what a student outline of this material might look like:**

Advice to Parents: How to Communicate with Your Teen

I. Introduction
   Topic Sentence: *Parents need to consider their words, tone, and body language when they talk to their teens.*
II. Choose your words carefully.
   A. Do not call people names.
      1. My father calls me "immature."
      2. Parents sometimes use words like "idiot."
   B. Do not use bad language.
   C. Do not be disrespectful.
   D. Do not monopolize the conversation.
   E. Do not use the silent treatment.
III. Listen to your tone.
   A. Wait until you have calmed down so you do not sound angry and tense.
   B. Watch the volume of your voice.
      1. Stacy's father speaks softly.
      2. Stacy's father speaks reassuringly.
   C. Taping a conversation would reveal tone.

IV. Take a look at your body language.
   A. Watch out for your facial expression.
      1. Are you glaring?
      2. Are you full of rage?
   B. Make eye contact.
   C. Do not withdraw; if possible give the person a hug or hold their hand.
   D. Physical abuse is never appropriate.
V. Conclusion
   Parents who think about these three factors of communication will be able to avoid a lot of pain and heartache.

- **Now we are ready to see the student essay that evolved from the initial brainstorming list. Notice the writer is not bound to follow the brainstorming list or the outline word for word. Notice that as the student wrote, a certain creative flow occurred.**

Advice to Parents: How to Communicate with Your Teens

When parents and teens cannot sit down and talk together, parents should take a long hard look at themselves to see if part of the blame might lie with themselves. Parents need to consider three factors: the words they choose, the tone of voice they use, and the message their body language gives.

One usually thinks of words as being at the center of communication, and of course, words are important. The wrong words can unintentionally put people in a bad mood. Parents very often belittle their children or call them names. My father, for example, sometimes uses the word "immature" to describe me when I make a mistake. I feel put down. It would probably be better if he would talk with me about the situation and explain why he thinks I made a bad choice. After all, I am only nineteen. I'm not totally mature yet. I've heard parents call their children "idiots" and even worse. Name-calling only makes teens angry and defensive. It's hard after being attacked to feel open to any discussion at all. I've heard teens and parents use bad language and speak disrespectfully to each other. Speaking in the heat of the moment, people often say things they really don't mean, but when they calm down, it's too late to take the words back. The harm is done. Then there is the parent who monopolizes the discussion, giving the teen no opportunity to explain his or her position. Finally there is the complete opposite of the wrong words, and that is no words at all. Have you ever experienced the silent treatment, no words at all? With this approach, everyone feels terrible and there is no chance to work out a problem.

A parent's tone of voice is a second factor in communicating with a teenager. Something said in a tense, harsh, or angry voice creates unnecessary bad feelings. The same words said with a firm but soft and reassuring voice can make for a completely different conversation. Even the volume of a person's voice can make a tremendous difference when people talk. My friend Stacy, for example, has a lot of disagreements with her father, but I have never heard their disagreements turn into angry arguments. Her father is from another country where people speak very softly. His voice is so calm and soft that I suppose this is one reason why Stacy never seems to get angry with him. He also uses a lot of humor, and they can laugh about her occasional outrageous behavior. I think it would be a good idea for some parents to tape themselves when they are talking with their teenagers. They might be very surprised to hear their tone. They might then have a better understanding of why their teenagers suddenly become upset or withdrawn.

I also wish some parents could see themselves when they are talking to their teens. Their body language really screams, "I am angry at you!" Facial expressions can be glaring or even full of rage. In order to communicate with your teen, you need to make eye contact and if possible even give an affectionate hug or hold the teen's hand; in other words, let your body language say that you care about them even though you have a serious concern about their behavior. Obviously, any kind of physical abuse is never appropriate. Slapping, hitting, or punching is absolutely unacceptable. If you cannot control your teen without physical restraint, you need to seek outside help.

If only parents would think of the three factors of words, tone, and body language the next time they faced a conflict with their teens. Much needless pain and unhappiness could be avoided, and many problems would be more quickly solved.

ACTIVITY 3 **Using Brainstorming or Clustering for a Topic of Your Own**

Use either brainstorming or clustering to develop your ideas on one of the following topics:

- communicating with teachers and classmates
- communicating on the cell phone
- communicating on the internet (e-mail and chat rooms)

Create your brainstorm list or cluster on a separate sheet of paper.

IV. Conducting Interviews and Surveys/Questionnaires

Interviews

Journal writing, focused freewriting, and brainstorming are all techniques that can be used to explore your own thoughts and ideas. Often, however, a writer needs to go further and obtain information from outside sources. An excellent way to obtain such information is to conduct an interview or prepare and distribute a survey or questionnaire. News reporters, marketing people, social workers, and government workers are only a few of the people who use these techniques in their everyday work.

Interviews are useful in certain situations. Speaking to a single individual can lead to information that you might not be able to get any other way. For example, you might want to do an interview with an older family member in order to preserve stories of your family's past. You might want to talk to someone in a certain career to learn if that line of work would be of interest to you. If you were considering a career in law, for example, speaking to a lawyer in your community might be more revealing than reading about the legal profession in a book. An interview is also an excellent way to find out information on very current topics, material you might have trouble finding in the library.

The secret of a good interview lies in what happens before the interview. You must take the time to prepare properly. First of all, make an appointment with the person you are interviewing. Let that person know how long the interview will take. If you intend to bring a tape recorder, be sure to ask for permission in advance. It is important for the person being interviewed to know what to expect so he or she can be relaxed and in a receptive frame of mind. Most importantly, the interviewer should always have a number of questions prepared beforehand. Few interviews go well without some structure and a sense of direction. When you prepare your questions, compose them in such a way that the answers require some thought. You do not want to ask questions that can be answered with a simple yes or no; such replies are not very useful because they do not encourage any in-depth discussion of the answer. This is not to say that every question must be asked in the order in which it was prepared; an interviewer is not restricted to a fixed set of questions. An interview can often take an interesting and unexpected turn with a single good question that leads to a surprising exploration of a subject.

ACTIVITY 4 **Preparing Questions for an Interview**

The following five pairs of sentences could have been used in an interview in which a person was trying to learn about a lawyer's work. In each case, check which question would more likely lead to a thoughtful interview response.

1. ______ What is a typical day at work like?

______ How many hours a day do you work?

2. ______ How much do you earn in a year?

______ What is the range of salary that a person could expect to earn as a lawyer?

3. ______ What kind of law do you practice?

______ What are the different areas of law practice, and how did you choose which one you wanted to practice?

4. ______ What is the most important case you have ever had?

______ Have you ever had an important case?

5. ______ Do you ever have a bad day?

______ What are some of your greatest challenges and how do you handle them?

EXPLORING ONLINE

Interviewing can be conducted on the Internet by accessing the Web site of an expert on your topic, posting questions on a bulletin board, or e-mailing a group of people you have deemed appropriate for your research.

Surveys/Questionnaires

Taking a survey is an especially helpful prewriting technique when you want to write about a certain group's attitudes, practices, or experiences. For instance, you could do a survey on your classmates' attitudes toward binge drinking, your family's attitude about how to share the household chores, or your community's attitude about the need for a teen center. The survey or questionnaire is somewhat like an interview in that the person conducting it prepares a set of questions. The interview is conducted one-to-one, and the conversation has great flexibility. The survey, on the other hand, is usually written. A number of participants agree to fill out answers to a set of questions. They may or may not complete the survey in your presence. What you will get will be the briefest answers to your questions, no more, no less. Obviously, you will be in trouble if you realize later on that you should have asked different questions. Therefore, in a survey, most of the work lies in the preparation of the questions and in experiments with different ways of presenting questions so as to get the best answers. Unlike the interview, you may want to ask questions that can be answered with a *yes* or a *no*. You may also want to ask questions that call for precise facts and figures. Here are a few other considerations:

1. **Will people give their names, or will the survey be anonymous?**
2. **How will the surveys be returned? Will you give people a deadline and collect the surveys yourself, or will you give them a self-addressed stamped envelope so they can mail the survey to you when they are finished?**
3. **Be prepared: Some people may not answer the survey at all. If it is too long or too complicated, people may decide they don't have time to do it. After all, most people volunteer to answer a survey, and they will be doing this one as a favor to you.**
4. **The more responses there are to a survey, the more valid the results of that survey will be. For example, if you want to know the attitudes of your class toward journal writing, the closer you come to having 100 percent of the class fill out your survey, the more valid your survey will be.**
5. **How will you tally the answers? Will the results be presented as a chart, or will you write a report in which you explain the results?**

ACTIVITY 5

Composing Questions for a Survey

Several serious problems on college campuses today concern the use of alcohol. Underage drinking, binge drinking, drunken fights, and vandalism of school property are some of the issues college administrations face. Compose five questions that could be included in a survey of your classmates in order to determine their drinking habits. Construct each question so that it asks for personal experience, not a person's opinion about what other students are doing.

Example: Which of the following best describes how often you have an alcoholic drink?

a) never
b) only on holidays and other special occasions
c) two or three times a month
d) once or twice a week
e) three or more times a week
f) every day

1. ______________________________

____

____

____

2. ______________________________

____

____

____

3. ______________________________

____

____

____

4. ______________________________

____

____

____

5. ______________________________

____

____

____

V. Note Taking

In doing research, whether conducting an interview, listening to a lecture, reading an article in a library periodical, or searching on the Internet, a student needs to be good at taking notes. Taking notes is not always a simple task because it involves judgment about what will be needed later on (perhaps for a paper or a test). Some people try to write down everything; others do not write down enough. Still others have trouble distinguishing between major points and minor details. Learning to take good notes is one of the most important skills a college student should master. Depending on how the information is going to be used, notetaking can be done any one of three ways: *direct quotation, paraphrasing,* and *summarizing.*

Imagine a student is writing a paper on the subject of *the social problems of adolescence.* The student finds the following paragraphs in the book *Fatherless America: Confronting Our Most Urgent Social Problem* by David Blankenhorn.

> The United States is becoming an increasingly fatherless society. A generation ago, a child could reasonably expect to grow up with his or her father. Today, a child can reasonably expect not to. Fatherlessness is approaching a rough parity with fatherhood as a defining feature of childhood.
>
> This astonishing fact is reflected in many statistics, but here are the two most important: Tonight, about 40 percent of U.S. children will go to sleep in homes in which their fathers do not live. More than half of our children are likely to spend a significant portion of childhood living apart from their fathers. Never before in this country have so many children been voluntarily abandoned by their fathers. Never before have so many children grown up without knowing what it means to have a father.
>
> Fatherlessness is the most harmful demographic trend of this generation. It is the leading cause of the decline in the well-being of children. It is also the engine driving our most urgent social problems, from crime to adolescent pregnancy to domestic violence. Yet, despite its scale and social consequences, fatherlessness is frequently ignored or denied. . . .

Study the examples below to see how the student used the three different types of note taking in order to extract ideas from this passage.

Direct Quotation

This method is appropriate for information that is so carefully constructed and important that the student records the exact words so the passage can be quoted later on to support the student's own points.

> **Direct quotation** entails using quotation marks around the exact words of another writer.

The example below shows how a student selected one sentence in the paragraph as a possible quote for the paper.

```
fatherlessness                              Blankenhorn, p. 1
"Tonight, about 40 percent of U.S. children will go to
sleep in homes in which their fathers do not live."
```

Paraphrasing

This method is used when the research material seems important enough for each idea to be recorded. In this case, the student will compose new sentences to restate each idea in his or her own words. Paraphrasing demands a great deal of skill because a writer has to have extensive control of language in order to restate ideas using different words or different sentence structures.

Paraphrasing entails using your own words to restate each idea from the text of another writer.

Sentence from text:

> Fatherlessness is approaching a rough parity with fatherhood as a defining feature of childhood.

Here is how the student paraphrased this sentence:

```
fatherlessness                          Blankenhorn, p. 1
We are soon reaching the point when childhood is just as
easily described as growing up without a father as with a
father.
```

Summarizing

This method of note taking is used when the student wants to reduce the material to a single main idea. A chapter might be reduced to a paragraph, or a paragraph might be reduced to a sentence. Summarizing is a skill that depends on a student's ability to grasp the main ideas as he or she reads.

Summarizing involves using your own words to restate only the main ideas from the text of another writer.

Here is how the student summarized the third paragraph:

```
fatherlessness                          Blankenhorn, p. 1
Growing up without a father is the most harmful change to
this generation of American children; sadly, little is
being said or done about it.
```

ACTIVITY 6

Taking Notes on a Text

Below is a paragraph on the subject of drunk driving. After you have read it, follow the instructions for taking notes.

> Nationally, the confidence of the drunk driver remains almost unshaken. Amazingly, four out of every ten drivers admit to driving while under the influence of alcohol, while 10 percent of all drivers on weekend nights can be legally defined as intoxicated. There are good reasons for this, one of which is brought out by a recent report from the National Transportation

Safety Board. It found that only one in 2,000 who drive while intoxicated will be pulled over. And even with the most thorough police control and rigorous administration, it doesn't rise to more than one in 200. Yet, all too often, those who do escape arrest do not live to get home. Every year, about 25,000 do not, including 4,000 teens.

1. Write a summary for the paragraph. Remember you will be reducing the paragraph to one or two sentences and focusing on the main idea.

____

____

____

____

2. Paraphrase the last sentence.

____

____

____

3. Write a sentence in which you directly quote words taken from the paragraph.

____

____

____

EXPLORING ONLINE

Direct quotation—http://www.richmond.edu/~writing/wweb/dq.html

Paraphrasing—http://www.richmond.edu/~writing/wweb/paraphrs.html

Summarizing—http://www.clearcf.uvic.ca/writersguide/Pages/summariesTOC.html

WORKING TOGETHER

CONDUCTING AN INTERVIEW: INTRODUCING A CLASSMATE

Choose a partner for this activity. Each of you will interview the other, taking no more than ten or fifteen minutes for each interview. The following questions will serve as your guide, but ask additional questions if they occur to you. Use the lines provided after each question to record the answers you are given.

Suggested Questions for Your Interview

1. Did you come to college immediately after high school, or did you do something else before deciding to continue school?

2. What made you decide to go to college?

3. What major subject or what field of study do you plan to follow?

4. What would you like to be doing five years from now?

5. What do you think will be the greatest challenge as you work toward your goal?

____

____

____

6. What has been the most enjoyable part of going to college so far?

____

____

____

7. What has been the least enjoyable part of going to college so far?

____

____

____

After you and your classmates have interviewed each other, use the answers you have gathered to compose a paragraph that could introduce that person to the entire class.

Online Activity

Are you a good listener? Good interviewers are excellent listeners. Go to http://facetofacematters.com/pages/qlistenc.htm, and take the "Rate Your Listening" quiz. Compare notes with classmates.

Portfolio Suggestion

Place your interview in your portfolio. In future writing tasks, consider using the interview approach as a technique for gathering material that can be transformed quite easily into an essay. Remember that people who write for a living, newspaper and magazine writers for example, depend heavily on interviews for their material.

Chapter 2 The Elements of Good Writing

Preview

When a piece of writing is effective, all of the following elements have come together:

- The **subject** has been carefully chosen.
- The writer has been clear about the **purpose** of the writing.
- The writing has been directed toward a specific **audience.**
- A consistent **voice** has been maintained throughout the piece.
- All parts of the work relate to the central theme, resulting in **unity.**
- Readers are easily able to follow the writer's logic, giving **coherence** to the piece.

The Subject: What the Writing Is About

The subject of a piece of writing can also be called the *topic* or the *central theme*. The subject can be chosen by the writer or assigned by someone else. We've all heard the student who complains, "I don't have anything to say." Not true! It may be that the student hasn't yet developed the skill to put ideas into writing, but we all know more than we think we do. We all know about our families, our homes, our friends, our opinions, our experiences. We have childhood memories, interests, activities we participate in, and dreams. Writers need to tap into these life experiences and life lessons to find topics that interest them when they write. We also need to remember we can gather more information by consulting others. Even with an assigned topic, a writer can often find an aspect of the subject that is of interest. For example, on the subject of *binge drinking in college,* a writer might choose to narrow the subject to one of the following aspects:

Tell a personal story:	The story of my friend Tom who flunked out of college last semester
Provide statistical information:	The facts about drinking on college campuses
Discuss the effects:	The effects of binge drinking on college campuses
Explain how to do something:	How to avoid substance abuse in college
Take a stand on an issue:	The need for colleges to enforce the laws for underage drinking

ACTIVITY 1

Choosing an Aspect of a Subject

Give five possible approaches a writer might take, given the topic of *working while going to college.*

1. ______________________________
2. ______________________________
3. ______________________________
4. ______________________________
5. ______________________________

Purpose: The Writer's Intention

When a student hands in a writing assignment for a course, that student's purpose may be primarily to get a good grade. A worker may produce a written document with the purpose of getting ahead in a job. This is not what we mean by *purpose.* In writing, *purpose* is what the piece of writing itself is intended to accomplish, apart from any other personal aims of the writer.

What Are the Main Purposes for Writing?

1. Entertainment

A writer may want to entertain an audience. One way to do this is by telling a good story. We all remember how as children it was so much fun when someone would read us a story. We were being entertained. Most of the stories we see on television are shown for the purpose of entertainment. The novels we buy in bookstores were written to entertain us. What we call *narrative writing* (the telling of stories) is mostly in this category of writing for the purpose of entertainment.

2. Information—Presentation of facts

Most of the writing you will do in college and in your future career will be informational in nature. In school, you will take written tests and write papers to explain what you know about a certain subject; at work, you might find yourself explaining why your company's profits have diminished or increased. These explanations in formal writing can be developed in more than one way, depending on the type of information required. The methods of development which you will learn in this book include the following:

- Illustration (giving examples)
- Process (explaining how to do something)
- Comparison and contrast
- Cause and effect
- Definition and analysis
- Classification (putting material into mutually exclusive groups)

3. Persuasion or argumentation

Persuasive writing, or argumentation, tries to convince the reader to agree with the writer's point of view on a topic. In our daily lives, the newspaper editorial is the most common example of persuasive writing. Such writing gives facts and examples and uses logical reasoning to support the writer's claim. An argument seeks to change the reader's mind or confirm beliefs already there. Often, the conclusion pleads for a plan of action to be taken.

ACTIVITY 2 **Understanding Purpose in Writing**

If your instructor told you that your assignment was to write an essay on some aspect of technology, each person in the class would most likely choose a slightly different topic. Below are five different topics concerned with some aspect of technology. For each topic, indicate what the writer's possible purpose (entertainment, information, or persuasion) could be.

Topic	Purpose
1. the cost of fax machines	____________
2. my cell phone nightmare	____________
3. the meaning of *compound interest*	____________
4. how to send a message by e-mail	____________
5. why our company should expand now	____________

Audience: A Writer's Intended Readers

Effective writers make an effort to know something about their audience so that the audience will be receptive to the ideas. Several important questions need to be asked. For example, what do the readers already know about the subject? What are their attitudes toward the subject? Will they be in agreement with the writer's point of view? Will they be of similar age or gender? Will they have a similar level of education? Will they have interests, tastes, or political points of view that agree? Any number of factors could be important in determining how a writer chooses words and presents ideas.

For example, consider the age factor. If the readers are small children, the vocabulary and ideas of the piece will have to be age appropriate. Consider another factor, the readers' level of education. If the readers are professionals who want to increase their knowledge in a certain field, the use of slang or dialect will obviously be out of place; the writer will be expected to know and use the terminology of that field. Finally, consider the readers' attitudes. If the subject is a very sensitive one, a writer certainly will not want to joke about it.

ACTIVITY 3 **Subject, Audience, and Purpose**

Below are five possible writing subjects. In each case, choose a specific audience and imagine the writer's purpose. An example is done for you.

Subject	Audience	Purpose
Description of two history courses	College students	Information to help students make course selections
1. Instructions for CPR (cardiopulmonary resuscitation)	____________	____________

2. A proposal for a group home for emotionally disturbed adults in a neighborhood ______ ______
3. Description of features on a new model computer ______ ______
4. A letter to a local newspaper about a civilian police review board ______ ______
5. My so-called job ______ ______

Voice: How a Writer's Attitude Is Revealed

It is very difficult for a writer to be objective; writing almost always reveals conscious or unconscious attitudes. The *voice* of the writer comes through the text by the words that are chosen and by the strategies that are used. In general, we can think of *voice* as revealing two different attitudes:

1. **An attitude toward the subject matter:** A politician might speak *passionately* about a subject. The comic writer could be *humorous* or *sarcastic* about a subject. The critic could reveal a *lighthearted* or *judgmental* attitude.
2. **An attitude toward the audience:** The writer's attitude toward the audience ranges from the very formal, such as an expert presenting a research paper in an academic journal, to less formal, for example, a student writing a friendly and casual letter to a classmate.

The skilled writer learns how to choose an appropriate and consistent voice, depending on the purpose of the writing. Cooking instructions on a box of rice, for example, are probably almost completely voiceless, with no indication of a writer's personality. The reporting of a news event should also be without any apparent voice, but sometimes the writer's personal attitude sneaks in by a word choice that carries a positive or negative connotation. Sometimes an attitude is revealed by the choice of which facts are included and which facts are left out. In general, writing that seeks to inform is usually more objective than writing that seeks to entertain or persuade.

Another way a writer expresses voice is by the choice of a personal pronoun used throughout the piece. A writer chooses a pronoun that fits the subject and the audience. If you were writing a chemistry lab report, the third person *(he, she, it,* or *they)* would be most appropriate. The third person is the most formal and objective choice. If you were writing a book about how to arrange flowers, you might want to address readers in the second person *(you)*. The second person is less formal and speaks directly to the readers. If you were writing a story about your own childhood, you would most likely choose the first person *(I* or *we)*. When you use the first person, you are being the most informal, and you also reveal the most about your personality. The choice of which personal pronoun to use is determined by the level of formality that is most appropriate between you and your audience.

Two additional points about voice need to be kept in mind. The first point is the importance of being consistent. Do not change your writing voice without a very clear reason for doing so. In other words, if you begin by addressing your readers with *you,* do not switch to *we* later on in the same piece of writing. The second point is to be sincere. Do not try to be someone you are not. For instance, taking words from a thesaurus is not a good idea since these words could easily be used in the wrong way, and they would nearly always sound a little out of place compared to the rest of your writing. If you are a writer of English as a second language, you have to be especially careful about this since your vocabulary may be limited. This may also mean that you need more complete understanding of words and their shades of meaning.

Formal Writing: Voice Is in the Third Person *(he, she, it,* or *they)*

In formal writing, where there is a distance between the writer and the reader, the *third person* is generally used. This is the writing you would use for most college-level work as well as job-related work. Read the paragraph that follows in order to study the writer's use of the third person. Notice that each use of the third person has been italicized.

> Many *families* feel lost trying to make sense of cyberspace. *They* become frustrated trying to find specific information such as the image of a skeleton for a child's science paper. *They* worry that a preteen daughter may not be safe when she is chatting with classmates online. Most *parents* are unsure how to navigate the Web. The millions of pages of information on the Net can make locating useful and enjoyable stops seem more like work than play. How should *families* choose among them? Six exceptional Web destinations described below will eliminate this uncertainty. As a group, these Web sites offer useful advice *parents* need and provide fun features *children* want.

Less Formal Writing: Voice Is in the Second Person *(you, your)*

Here is the same material written in a less formal voice, one that uses the second person (you), and more casual language. This choice of voice is effective in giving instructions and speaking directly to the reader. Notice that each use of the second person is italicized.

> Is *your* family lost in cyberspace? *You* know the feeling. Maybe it's the rush of frustration that comes after *your* son says he needs an image of a skeleton for a science paper but he can't find one on the Internet—and neither can *you.* Or perhaps it's that twinge of anxiety as *your* preteen daughter announces she wants to chat with classmates online, but *you* are not sure how she can do it safely. If *you* are unsure how to navigate the Web, *you* are not alone. The millions of pages of information on the Net can make locating useful and enjoyable stops seem more work than play. How can *you* choose among them? Consider the six terrific Web destinations described below. As a group, they offer the useful advice *you* need along with the fun features *your* children want.

ACTIVITY 4

Voice: Rewriting a Paragraph Using First Person Singular (I)

Use the same material found in the two paragraphs you have just read to compose a new paragraph using the first person *(I)*. Since this is the least formal voice, you can adopt a more personal and casual tone using language you feel is appropriate.

____

____

____

____

____

____

____

____

____

____

____

____

Unity: All Parts Relate to the Central Theme

In a good piece of writing every sentence serves the central theme, with every detail directly related to the main idea. All of the parts go together to make up a whole. The result is a sense of oneness or wholeness, so that by the end of the piece, the writing feels complete, and the reader has no trouble grasping the writer's main point.

ACTIVITY 5

Editing Student Writing for Unity

The following paragraph lacks unity because some sentences do not contribute to the main idea. As you read the paragraph, cross out all the parts that do not contribute to the unity of the piece.

> Many parents fear the time when their children reach adolescence. When that time does come, some parents are afraid to give their children freedom to make choices. These same parents do not admit that their children have any ideas or feelings that are valid. Many adults like to look back on their own childhoods. Pets are often remembered fondly. Conflicts between parents and children are bound to develop. Some conflicts, of course, are a sign of healthy development within the family. Psychologists say that parents should not be fearful when teenagers challenge their authority. Challenging authority is a normal part of the maturing process. Adults without children have none of these concerns. The need for privacy is also a normal emotion during adolescence and should be respected and not feared. On the other hand, when the right moment comes along and a teenager wants to talk, parents should not miss the chance. Sometimes teenagers and their younger brothers and sisters fight continuously over the most trivial things. Most important of all is the need for parents to be sensitive to the feelings of their teenagers. Remember, adolescence does not last for a lifetime, but hopefully a good relationship between parent and child will last!

Coherence: Clear and Logical Progression of Thought

A piece of writing needs careful organization of all its parts so that one idea leads logically to the next. To help all the parts relate to one another, writers use three important techniques: *repetition of key words, careful pronoun reference,* and *transitional expressions.*

All writers must continually work to achieve coherence. Even professional writers find themselves working on more than one draft because they see room for improvement as they move from one idea, one sentence, or one paragraph to the next. If something is unclear or lacks logical sequence, they have the skills to revise the writing. In this course, you too will be working on coherence in many of the chapters of the book. The piece of writing below will give you an overview of how the three techniques (repetition of key words, careful pronoun reference, and transitional expressions) contribute to the coherence of a text.

Here is a paragraph from an essay on the major movements in Western art:

> Instead of looking at major themes and design elements of Western art through individual masterpieces, an easier approach is to look at it through time. Different movements in Western art spawned specific styles, for a period of time. Then the world saw the emergence of a new style, which either built upon the last style or emerged as a reaction to it. Within these different movements, we can see distinct artistic styles, elements, and motifs. Often these disappear for hundreds of years, only to resurface when a new movement starts. Therefore, the simplest way of getting a handle on Western art is to understand the major movements in art.

Repetition of Key Words

When we study this paragraph, it quickly becomes apparent that key words are repeated as the piece moves from sentence to sentence: the subject *Western art* appears three times; the idea that we need to look at art by the *movements* in *time* is made clear by two uses of the word *time* and four uses of the word *movement.* The word *style* or *styles* appears four times.

Careful Use of Pronouns

Coherence is also achieved by the careful use of pronouns. In the above paragraph, look at the word *it* in the first sentence, *it* in the third sentence, and *these* in the fourth sentence. An arrow shows the noun to which each pronoun refers. Too many pronouns could be confusing, but failing to use pronouns would mean repeating the key words too many times.

Use of Transitional Expressions

Finally, coherence is achieved by the use of transitions, words and expressions that show how ideas relate to each other. Turn to Appendix D at the back of this book to see the listing of several of these words and expressions.

The two transitions used in this piece clearly move the reader forward to the next idea. One of the most common transitions of all is the word *then,* used to begin the third sentence. It signals the movement to the next idea or to the next event in a series of events. Toward the end of the paragraph the transition *therefore* signals that the following sentence will state the result of the information given so far.

ACTIVITY 6

Studying a Text for Coherence

Read the following paragraph in order to discover the techniques used by the writer to achieve coherence. Find (1) two examples of the repetition of key words, (2) two examples of pronoun reference, and (3) one example of a transitional word or expression. Label each of the examples that you find. (If necessary, refer to Appendix D for the list of transitional words and expressions.)

> There are, if you believe a recent study by Inktomi and the NEC Research Institute (www.inktomi.com/webmap), one billion Web pages currently online and accessible to the public. These pages are not numbered. They are not organized. They do not come with a table of contents or an index. It's as if people around the world took all their books and magazines, ripped out all the pages and dumped them into one gigantic pile. And in the past five years, that pile has grown bigger and bigger and bigger. So how do you find your way through this maze of information? Search engines. As with any technology, some very smart people are devising new search engines for the Internet, based on the lessons of the previous generation. With names like Google, Fast Search and Northern Light, these search engines may be dark horses, but they may also be your best bet for actually finding what you need quickly on the Web.

EXPLORING ONLINE

Audience—http://www.dc.peachnet.edu/~shale/humanities/composition/handouts/audience.html

Unity and Coherence—http://www.uottawa.ca/academic/arts/writcent/hypergrammar/parunif.html

Transitional Words and Phrases—http://www.richmond.edu/~writing/wweb/trans1.html

Voice—http://www.richmond.edu/~writing/wweb/voice.html

WORKING TOGETHER

TAKING A SURVEY: STUDENT ATTITUDES ABOUT WRITING

A writer can obtain information for an essay in a number of different ways. One very good way is to gather material by conducting a survey, using a group of people who have something in common. For this exercise, you will participate in a survey of the students in your class. This survey will question students to discover their attitudes and experiences with writing. The members of your class may add their own questions, or they may change the questions suggested here.

Use the following procedure:

1. Remove the survey page from your textbook.
2. Put your name or an assigned number in the top right-hand corner of the survey for purposes of identification.
3. Answer the survey questions as completely and honestly as possible.
4. Select two persons who will collect all the surveys and lead the class in tallying the information. One person can read off the responses; the other person can put the information on a blackboard where everyone can view the information and take notes.

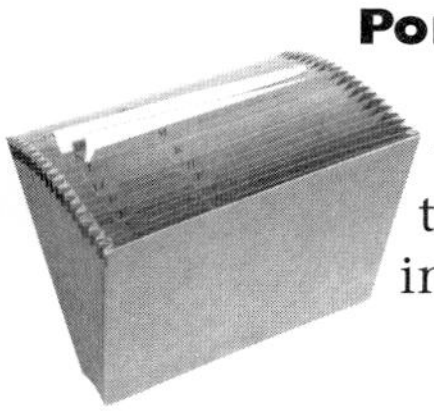

Portfolio Suggestion

With the information gathered from the survey, compose an essay that describes the attitudes and experiences of your classmates when it comes to writing. Keep this essay, as well as the survey results, in your portfolio. You may want to use these survey results for other writing in the future.

Online Activity

Go to http://www.survey.net and take two of the surveys on the site. Pay close attention to the types of questions that are asked. After you have reviewed the survey results, decide whether the surveys are thorough, valuable, and/or slanted. Discuss your opinions in small groups.

continued on next page

STUDENT SURVEY

1. Where do you do your best writing—in the library, at home, or someplace else? What makes some places better than others?

____

____

____

____

____

____

2. Is a certain time of day better for you than other times? When do you concentrate the best?

____

3. How long can you write with concentration before you have to take a break?

____

4. What fears do you have when you write?

____

5. What do you believe is your major weakness as a writer?

____

6. Are you comfortable using a computer to compose?

____

7. In high school, how many of your classes included writing opportunities? How often did you write?

____

8. Keeping in mind that most people today use a telephone to keep in touch, how often do you find yourself writing a letter?

____

9. Which of the following best describes your feeling about writing at this point in your school career?

_____ I enjoy writing most of the time.

_____ I occasionally like to write.

_____ I usually do not like to write.

_____ I don't have any opinion about writing at all.

10. What could be the **purpose** of an essay that would use the responses to this survey?

____

____

____

PART II CREATING EFFECTIVE SENTENCES

Students in many college writing classrooms want to fill in the gaps left from their earlier school experiences. For example, these students want their writing corrected very closely, beginning with sentence level errors. For these corrections to have any lasting effect, however, the student writers must be familiar with some basic terms and concepts. Learning these terms and understanding sentence structure will give every student the confidence needed to work with the written word. In addition, whether drafting or revising, editing or proofreading, students will have the full benefit of help from instructors or peers after everyone has agreed on the definitions of basic terms. Part II of this book will provide the needed foundation for a solid understanding of this part of the writing process. When student writers are in control of this material, revising any paper, especially the paper that has been returned with correction symbols, will be a helpful learning experience.

Chapter 3 Finding Subjects and Verbs in Simple Sentences

We express our ideas in more than one way. When we respond to someone with a gesture such as the shake of our head, we are expressing an idea. When we make a comment by saying a single word such as "cool," we are expressing an idea, this time more verbally. The shake of the head means either *yes* or *no,* and the use of the word *cool* is a current slang expression meaning approval of some kind. Speaking informally with friends gives us the advantage of having our tones and gestures understood. When we express ourselves in written form, however, our words must be more deliberate and more precise. As writers, we need to express ourselves in complete sentences so that our ideas will be fully understood. This need for completeness means that every writing student must be clear as to what makes up a sentence.

Preview

This chapter establishes what is essential in constructing the basic sentence. The most basic sentence in English is called the *simple sentence. Simple* in this case does not mean *easy,* but it does mean that the sentence has only *one subject/verb group.* This chapter helps you practice finding subjects and verbs in simple sentences. You will also learn about (or review) the many key terms you need to know in order to discuss and edit sentence level problems in your writing. When you finish this chapter, you should be able to do the following:

Find the **subject** of a simple sentence
- with noun subjects
- with pronoun subjects
- with adjectives as modifiers of nouns and pronouns
- with compound subjects
- with prepositional phrases
- with hidden subjects

Find the **verb** of a simple sentence by recognizing three classes of verbs
- action verbs
- linking verbs
- helping verbs

Identify **parts of speech** in a simple sentence
- noun
- pronoun
- adjective
- preposition
- verb
- adverb

Identify the following **phrases**
- prepositional phrase
- appositive phrase
- infinitive phrase

Key Terms

Complete sentence
Noun
Pronoun
Adjective
Compound subject
Prepositional phrase
Appositive phrase
Action verb
Linking verb
Helping verb (also called auxiliary verb)
Adverb

Rule

- The subject of a sentence is never found within a prepositional phrase or an appositive phrase.

Charts

Four types of pronouns
List of common prepositions
List of common prepositional combinations
Sample list of action verbs
List of common linking verbs
List of common helping verbs

What Is a Complete Sentence?

A **complete sentence** is a group of words that contains a subject, a verb, and also expresses a complete thought. For example, the **simple sentence** is one type of complete sentence, and it has only one subject/verb group.

Simple sentence: Avon lifts weights.

Note: The words ***Avon lifts*** would not make up a complete sentence. Although the group of words has a subject and a verb, the thought is not complete. Avon lifts what? Some verbs, such as ***lift,*** usually require an object.

How Do You Find the Subject of a Sentence?

For most simple sentences, you can find the subject by keeping in mind the following five points:

- **In a sentence, the *subject* usually answers the question, "Who or what is the sentence about?"**

Practice.......... In the following sentences, find the subject by asking yourself, "Who or what is the sentence about?"

1. The gym seemed noisier than usual.

2. The coach was shouting last minute instructions.

3. He expected total concentration.

4. The cheerleaders were warming up.

5. People were beginning to fill the bleachers.

- **The *subject* often occurs early in the sentence.**

Review each of the five sentences above and notice that in each case, the subject occurred early in the sentence.

- **The *subject* of a sentence is usually a *noun* or a *pronoun.***

Nouns

A **noun** is a word that names persons, places, or things. A noun can function as a subject, an object, or a possessive in a sentence.

Subject: *Avon* lifts weights.
Object: The coach trained *Avon.*
Possessive: *Avon's* coach always arrives early.

Nouns can be categorized in two different ways:

1. common nouns or proper nouns

Most nouns in English are *common nouns.* They are not capitalized.
Proper nouns name particular persons, places, or things. They are always capitalized.

Common Nouns	Proper Nouns
aunt	Aunt Mary
country	Nigeria
watch	Timex

2. concrete nouns or abstract nouns

A second way to categorize nouns is to identify them as *concrete* or *abstract* nouns. Concrete nouns are all the things we can see or touch, such as *desk, car,* or *friend.* Abstract nouns are the things we cannot see or touch, such as *justice, honesty,* or *friendship.*

Concrete Nouns	Abstract Nouns
face	loneliness
people	patriotism
jewelry	beauty

Practice.......... Underline every noun in each of the sentences below.

1. The morning of June twenty-seventh was clear and sunny.

2. The flowers were blossoming profusely and the grass was richly green.

3. The people of the village began to gather in the square.

4. The lottery was conducted by Mr. Sommers.

5. The jovial man had time and energy to devote to civic activities.

Pronouns

A **pronoun** is a word used to take the place of a noun. Just like a noun, a pronoun can be used as the subject, the object, or in some cases as a way to show possession.

> ***Subject:*** *He* lifts weights
> ***Object:*** The coach trained *him.*
> ***Possessive:*** *His* coach always arrives early.

Pronouns can also be categorized or divided into groups: *personal, relative, demonstrative,* or *indefinite.* The following chart categorizes pronouns into these four major groups.

PRONOUNS

1. Personal Pronouns	Subjective		Objective		Possessive	
	Singular	*Plural*	*Singular*	*Plural*	*Singular*	*Plural*
1st person	I	we	me	us	my (mine)	our (ours)
2nd person	you	you	you	you	your (yours)	your (yours)
3rd person	he she it	they	him her it	them	his (his) her (hers) its (its)	their (theirs)

2. Relative Pronouns (can introduce noun clauses and adjective clauses)	3. Demonstrative Pronouns (can point out the antecedent)	4. Indefinite Pronouns (refer to nonspecific persons or things)			
who, whom, whose	this	*Singular*			
which	that everyone	someone	anyone	no one	
that	these	everybody	somebody	anybody	nobody
what	those	everything	something	anything	nothing
whoever		each	another	either	neither
whichever		*Singular* or *Plural* (depending on meaning)			
whatever		all	more	none	
		any	most	some	
		Plural			
		both	few	many	several

Practice.......... In each of the sentences below, replace the underlined word or words with a pronoun.

1. The crowd arrived early. ____________
2. The crowd's voices filled the gym. ____________
3. All eyes were on Coach Johnson. ____________

4. Coach Johnson had not lost a game yet this season. ____________

5. Steven and I found the best seats in the front row. ____________

6. Not one person could predict the outcome. ____________

- **Noun or pronoun subjects in a sentence can be modified by *adjectives.***

> An **adjective** is a word that modifies (describes or limits) a noun or a pronoun. Adjectives usually come directly in front of the nouns they modify, but they can also appear later in the sentence and refer back to the noun or pronoun.
>
> *young* Avon
>
> He is young.

Practice.......... Identify the adjectives in each of the following sentences.

1. The swimmer was confident.

2. Her long and arduous training would soon pay off.

3. Several meters remained to reach the finish line.

4. Suddenly, she felt a terrible cramp in one leg.

5. A disappointing defeat would be the result.

- **The subject of a sentence can be *compound.***

> A **compound subject** is made up of two or more nouns or pronouns joined together by *and, or, either/or,* or *neither/nor.*
>
> *Avon and his coach* lift weights.

Practice.......... Identify the compound subjects in each of the following sentences.

1. Exercise and diet are the secrets to good health.

2. Mothers and fathers should help their children establish healthy lifestyles.

3. Unfortunately, biological factors or environmental factors could cause health problems.

Practice.......... The following sentences illustrate the different kinds of subjects you will encounter in this chapter. Examine each sentence and decide who or what each sentence is about. Underline the word you believe is the subject of each sentence. Then, on the lines to the right, indicate the kind of subject (for example, *concrete noun* or *personal pronoun*) you have underlined. Be as specific as possible.

1. The young child played. ____________
2. Young Helen Keller played. ____________
3. She played. ____________
4. The park grew chilly. ____________
5. The leaves stirred. ____________
6. A thought suddenly struck her. ____________
7. Her parents and teacher would be waiting. ____________

Note: Not every noun or pronoun in a sentence is necessarily the subject of a verb. Nouns and pronouns function as subjects and as objects. In the following sentence, which noun is the subject and which noun is the object?

Helen drank the water.

If you chose *Helen* as the subject and *water* as the object, you were correct.

In the exercises that follow, you will have the opportunity to practice finding subjects and verbs. Refer back to the definitions, charts, and examples as often as needed.

EXERCISE 1 **Finding the Subject of a Sentence**

Underline the subject in each of the following sentences. An example is done for you.

The loudspeaker blared.

1. The train stopped.
2. Steven Laye had arrived.
3. He was afraid.
4. Everything looked so strange.
5. The fearful man held his bag tightly.
6. The tunnel led up to the street.
7. Buses and cars choked the avenues.
8. People rushed everywhere.
9. The noise gave him a headache.
10. Loneliness filled his heart.

EXERCISE 2 **Finding the Subject of a Sentence**

Underline the subject in each of the following sentences.

1. The road twisted and turned.
2. A young boy hurried along briskly.
3. He carried an important message.
4. A red-winged blackbird flew overhead.

5. Dark clouds and a sudden wind surprised him.
6. His family would be elated.
7. Someone was raking the leaves.
8. His father called out his name.
9. The old man tore open the envelope.
10. The message was brief.

EXERCISE 3 **Finding the Subject of a Sentence**

Underline the subject in each of the following sentences.

1. The Chicago World's Fair opened.
2. Americans had never seen anything like it.
3. Architects had designed a gleaming white city.
4. The buildings and grounds were unique.
5. George Ferris designed an enormous wheel 264 feet high.
6. It could carry sixty passengers per car.
7. The inventor George Westinghouse designed the fair's electric motors and even the electric lights.
8. Other fair inventors included Thomas Edison and Alexander Graham Bell.
9. All played an important part.
10. The future seemed bright.

EXERCISE 4 **Composing Your Own Sentences**

Create ten sentences using a variety of subjects. If you wish, you may use the suggested nouns and pronouns given below.

a) proper noun:	Tiger Woods
b) common noun:	golfer
c) abstract noun:	skill
d) compound subject:	trainer and friend
e) pronoun:	he

Exchange your sentences with those of another classmate. For each sentence your classmate has written, underline the subject and identify it to show you understand the various terms.

How Do You Find the Subject in Sentences with Prepositional Phrases?

The sentences in Exercises 1 and 2 were short and basic. If we wrote only sentences of that type, our writing would sound choppy. Complex ideas would be difficult to express. One way to expand a simple sentence is to add one or more prepositional phrases.

Example:

He put his suitcase on the seat.

On is a preposition.
Seat is a noun used as the object of the preposition.
On the seat is the prepositional phrase.

A **prepositional phrase** is a group of words containing a preposition and an object of the preposition along with any modifiers. Prepositional phrases contain nouns or pronouns, but these nouns or pronouns are *never* the subject of the sentence.

In sentences with prepositional phrases, the subject may be difficult to spot. What is the subject of the following sentence?

In the young man's apartment, books covered the walls.

In the sentence above, what is the prepositional phrase? Who or what is the sentence about? To avoid making the mistake of thinking that a noun in the prepositional phrase could be the subject, a good practice is to cross out the prepositional phrase.

~~In the young man's apartment~~, books covered the walls.

With the entire prepositional phrase crossed out, it becomes clear that the subject of the sentence has to be the noun *books*.

The subject of a sentence is *never* found within the prepositional phrase.

If you memorize the prepositions in the following lists, you will easily be able to spot prepositional phrases in sentences.

COMMON PREPOSITIONS

about	behind	except	on	toward
above	below	for	onto	under
across	beneath	from	out	underneath
after	beside	in	outside	unlike
against	between	inside	over	until
along	beyond	into	past	up
among	by	like	since	upon
around	despite	near	through	with
at	down	of	throughout	within
before	during	off	to	without

In addition to these common prepositions, English has a number of prepositional combinations that also function as prepositions.

COMMON PREPOSITIONAL COMBINATIONS		
ahead of	in addition to	in reference to
at the time of	in between	in regard to
because of	in care of	in search of
by means of	in case of	in spite of
except for	in common with	instead of
for fear of	in contrast to	on account of
for the purpose of	in the course of	similar to
for the sake of	in exchange for	

EXERCISE 5 **Creating Sentences with Prepositional Phrases**

Use each of the following ten prepositions to create a prepositional phrase. Then write a sentence containing that prepositional phrase. An example follows:

Preposition: *between*

Prepositional Phrase: between the two barns

Sentence: Between the two barns, the old Buick lay rusting.

Notice that when a prepositional phrase begins a sentence, a comma usually follows that prepositional phrase. (Sometimes, if the prepositional phrase is short, the comma is omitted.)

1. Preposition: *in*

Prepositional Phrase: ______________________

Sentence: ______________________

____

2. Preposition: *with*

Prepositional Phrase: ______________________

Sentence: ______________________

____

3. Preposition: *of*

Prepositional Phrase: ______________________

Sentence: ______________________

____

4. Preposition: *from*

Prepositional Phrase: ______________________________

Sentence: ______________________________

____

5. Preposition: *during*

Prepositional Phrase: ______________________________

Sentence: ______________________________

____

6. Preposition: *by*

Prepositional Phrase: ______________________________

Sentence: ______________________________

____

7. Preposition: *for*

Prepositional Phrase: ______________________________

Sentence: ______________________________

____

8. Preposition: *through*

Prepositional Phrase: ______________________________

Sentence: ______________________________

____

9. Preposition: *on*

Prepositional Phrase: ______________________________

Sentence: ______________________________

____

10. Preposition: *beside*

Prepositional Phrase: ______________________________

Sentence: ______________________________

____

EXERCISE 6 **Finding Subjects in Sentences with Prepositional Phrases**

Remember that you will never find the subject of a sentence within a prepositional phrase. In each of the following sentences, cross out any prepositional phrases. Then underline the subject of each sentence. An example follows:

~~On the circus grounds~~, Lisa wandered ~~among the elephants, horses, and camels~~.

1. Young people in the circus search for travel, adventure, danger, and romance.

2. After a few weeks of pulling cages and sleeping on hay, most of these people get tired of the circus and go back home.
3. The art of clowning, for instance, is very serious work.
4. Today, a circus clown must graduate from Clown College in Venice, Florida.
5. The staff of Clown College looks across the country for applicants.
6. Admission to the college is not easy.
7. Only sixty people out of three thousand applicants are admitted.
8. After ten weeks of training, graduation ceremonies are held.
9. At the ceremony, the clown graduate must perform for three continuous hours.
10. In the past, clowns were not so carefully trained.

EXERCISE 7 **Finding Subjects in Sentences Containing Prepositional Phrases**

Remember that you will never find the subject of a sentence within a prepositional phrase. In each of the following sentences, cross out any prepositional phrases. Then underline the subject of each sentence. An example follows:

~~Throughout the 1990s~~, memoirs were being sold ~~in ever increasing numbers~~.

1. The essay became very popular as a form of writing in the early eighteenth century in England.
2. Famous essayists of that time included Joseph Addison, Richard Steele, and Jonathan Swift.
3. Now, essay writing, one of the most powerful and provocative of all literary forms, is enjoying a rebirth.
4. For example, many of today's newspapers and magazines are carrying more personal stories.
5. With the increasing use of the Internet, personal writing is finding another way to become part of the mainstream again.
6. On the Internet, people have found ways to show their interest in the thoughts and experiences of others.
7. The Internet is the ideal place for experiencing the modern personal essay.
8. On a growing number of Web sites, Internet users can share their personal stories on subjects ranging from love to finances.
9. Unlike centuries ago, ordinary people today have the chance to communicate their thoughts to enormous numbers of people all over the world.
10. From the earliest childhood memory to the joys and pains of growing old, every life is full of fascinating stories.

What Are the Other Problems in Finding Subjects?

Sentences with a Change in the Normal Subject Position

Some sentences begin with words that indicate that a question is being asked. Such words as *why, where, how,* and *when* signal to the reader that a question will follow. Such opening words are not the subjects. The subjects will be found later on in these sentences. The following sentences begin with question words:

Why is *he* going away?

How did *he* find his sister in the city?

Notice that in each case the subject is not found in the opening part of the sentence. By answering questions or changing the question into a statement, the subject is easier to spot.

He is going away . . .

He found his sister . . .

Using *There* or *Here*

Such words as *there* or *here* can never be the subjects of sentences.

There is a new teacher in the department.

Here comes the woman now.

Who or what is this first sentence about? This sentence is about a teacher. *Teacher* is the subject of the sentence. Who or what is the second sentence about? This sentence is about a woman. *Woman* is the subject of the second sentence.

Commands

Sometimes a sentence contains a verb that gives an order:

Go to Chicago.

Help your sister.

In sentences that give orders, the subject *you* is not written down but *you* is understood to be the subject of that sentence. This is the only case where the subject of a sentence may be left out.

Sentences That Contain Appositive Phrases

An **appositive phrase** is a group of words that gives us extra information about a noun in a sentence.

For example:

Martin Johnson, the retired salesman, sat at his desk.

In this sentence, the words *the retired salesman* make up the appositive phrase because they give you extra information about Martin Johnson. Notice that commas separate the appositive phrase from the rest of the sentence. If you leave out the appositive phrase when you read this sentence, the thought will still be complete:

> Martin Johnson sat at his desk.

Now the subject is clear: *Martin Johnson.*

> The subject of a sentence is *never* found within an appositive phrase.

EXERCISE 8

Finding Hidden Subjects

Each of the following sentences contains an example of a special problem in finding the subject of a sentence. First cross out any prepositional phrases or appositive phrases. Then underline the subject of each sentence. An example follows:

> ~~In every car of the crowded train~~, passengers settled down ~~for the night~~.

1. In the speeding train, the child slept.
2. The motion of the railroad cars was relaxing.
3. The child's mother, a tired and discouraged widow, put a coat under the child's head for a pillow.
4. Outside the window, towns and cities sped by in the night.
5. Sometimes you could look into people's living rooms.
6. There was a silence in the train.
7. Why did these people travel at night?
8. In most cases, children will rest quietly at night.
9. The woman with a young child and heavy bags had a difficult time.
10. On the platform, an elderly man anxiously waited for the first sight of his grandson.

EXERCISE 9

Finding Hidden Subjects

Each of the following sentences contains an example of a special problem in finding the subject of a sentence. First cross out any prepositional phrases or appositive phrases. Then underline the subject of each sentence. An example follows:

> Disney World, ~~the dream of every child~~, is a favorite destination ~~for family vacations~~.

1. There is a fantasy playland in the state of Florida.
2. Look at a map to find this child's paradise.
3. Orlando, the location of Disney World, is the place.

4. Where else can people see toddlers and grownups shaking hands with Mickey Mouse and Minnie Mouse?
5. In Disney World, everyone is surrounded by living cartoon favorites.
6. At breakfast, lunch, and dinner, you might shake hands with Pluto, Donald Duck, and Goofy.
7. The cleanliness of the place also impresses most families.
8. During the day, there are scores of attractions and activities.
9. Would your parents like to enjoy the cooler and less crowded evening activities?
10. In Disney World, it is hard to tell the children from the adults.

EXERCISE 10 **Finding Hidden Subjects**

Each of the following sentences contains an example of a special problem in finding the subject of a sentence. First cross out any prepositional phrases or appositive phrases. Then underline the subject of each sentence. An example follows:

> ~~In the attic of most houses~~, boxes ~~of forgotten toys and old clothes~~ could be tossed out.

1. How can you get rid of all those unwanted items in your apartment or home?
2. Hold a garage sale!
3. Bob L. Berko, author of "Holding Garage Sales for Fun and Profit," warns of the difficulties in having your own sale.
4. In addition to the dragging of everything up or down stairs, garage sales require careful planning and skillful dealings with people.
5. Why are some garage sales more successful than others?
6. Here are some tried and true methods for garage sale success.
7. Advertise and carefully price all items ahead of time.
8. Improve the chances of a sale by separating the items into categories.
9. Of course, the best items should go in the most visible spot.
10. There is a treasure for someone in all your junk.

How Do You Find the Verb of a Sentence?

Verbs tell time. Use this fact as a way to test a word to see if it is used as a verb in a sentence. If you can change a word into either the present, past, or future tense in a sentence, then that word is used as a verb. Use the sentence below as a model.

Present tense: Today, the woman *dances.*

Hint: Change the time to the past by beginning the sentence with *Yesterday.*

Past tense: Yesterday, the woman *danced*.

Hint: Change the time to the future by beginning the sentence with *Tomorrow*.

Future tense: Tomorrow, the woman *will dance*.

Three Classes of Verbs

- Action Verbs

An **action verb** tells us what the subject is doing and when the action occurs.

The woman *studied* ballet.

What was the woman doing?	studying
What is the time of the action?	past (*-ed* is the past tense ending)

ACTION VERBS

Most verbs are *action verbs*. Here are a few examples:

arrive	learn	open	watch
leave	forget	write	fly
enjoy	help	speak	catch
despise	make	teach	wait

EXERCISE 11 **Finding Action Verbs**

Each of the following sentences contains an action verb. Find the action verb by first underlining the subject of the sentence. Then circle the verb (the word that tells what the subject is doing). Cross out any prepositional phrases. Note also the time of the action: past, present, or future. An example follows:

Many <u>people</u> (begin) hobbies ~~in childhood~~.

1. Collectors enjoy the search for unusual items.
2. Some people collect very strange objects.
3. A collection, like odd rocks or unique automobiles, gives a person some individuality.
4. One man saves the fortunes from fortune cookies.
5. A group in Michigan often trades spark plugs.
6. People in Texas gather many types of barbed wire.
7. One person in New York keeps handouts from the street.

8. Arthur Fiedler hung hundreds of fire hats on pegs around his study.
9. Tom Bloom finds "inspected by" tickets in the pockets of new clothes.
10. Collections entertain us from childhood to old age.

EXERCISE 12 **Finding Action Verbs**

Each of the following sentences contains an action verb. First, cross out any prepositional phrases. Then underline the subject. Finally, circle the verb. Note that each verb you circle has a tense. Is the action in the past, present, or future? An example follows:

~~With the rise of literacy~~, the demand ~~for reading glasses~~ increased.

1. In ancient Rome, the emperor Nero gazed at gladiators in combat through a large emerald.
2. The Chinese manufactured sunglasses seven hundred years ago.
3. Monks carved from quartz the first magnifying glasses for reading.
4. They needed to see the tiny handwriting of manuscripts.
5. In the fourteenth century, with the rise of the Venetian glass industry, glass lenses replaced quartz lenses.
6. The invention of the printing press in the 1450's spread books to the common man.
7. In London in 1728, a man invented a pair of glasses with metal pieces and hinges to keep the glasses secure.
8. George Washington bought a pair of these new glasses.
9. By 1939, movie producers in Hollywood devised colored contact lenses for special effects in horror movies.
10. In 1948 an American technician developed the first pair of modern contact lenses.

• Linking Verbs

A **linking verb** is a verb that links the subject of a sentence to one or more words that describe or identify the subject.

For example:

The child is a constant dreamer.

She seems distracted.

We feel sympathetic.

In each of these examples, the verb links the subject to a word that identifies or describes the subject. In the first example, the verb *is* links *child* with *dreamer*. The verb *seems* links the pronoun *she* with *distracted*. Finally, in the third example, the verb *feel* links the pronoun *we* with *sympathetic*.

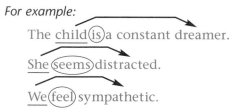

COMMON LINKING VERBS	
act	feel
appear	grow
be (am, is, are, was, were, have been)	look
	seem
become	taste

EXERCISE 13

Finding Linking Verbs

Each of the following sentences contains a linking verb. Find the linking verb by first underlining the subject of the sentence. Then draw an arrow to the word or words that identify or describe the subject. Finally, circle the linking verb. An example follows:

Dreams are very important for many cultures.

1. My dream last night was wonderful.
2. I had become middle-aged.
3. In a sunlit kitchen with a book in hand, I appeared relaxed and happy.
4. The house was empty and quiet.
5. In the morning light, the kitchen felt cozy.
6. The brewing coffee smelled delicious.
7. The bacon never tasted better.
8. I looked peaceful.
9. I seemed to have grown calmer.
10. I felt satisfied with life.

EXERCISE 14

Finding Linking Verbs

Each of the following sentences contains a linking verb. Find the linking verb by first underlining the subject of the sentence. Then draw an arrow to the word or words that identify or describe the subject. Finally, circle the linking verb. An example follows:

Surprises can be fun.

1. We were anxious to make the evening a success.
2. The apartment looked empty.
3. Everyone remained quiet.
4. Martha turned red at the sound of "Surprise!"
5. She seemed surprised.
6. The music sounded wonderful.
7. The food smelled delicious.

8. All of her presents were lovely.

9. The birthday party was a complete success.

10. Everyone appeared pleased with the evening.

- **Helping Verbs (Also Called Auxiliary Verbs)**

Some verbs can be used to help the main verb express a special meaning or a particular time.

Helping Verbs	Time Expressed by Helping Verbs
He *is sleeping.*	right now
He *might sleep.*	maybe now or in the future
He *should sleep.*	ought to, now or in the future
He *could have been sleeping.*	maybe in the past

COMMON HELPING VERBS

can, could
may, might must
shall, should
will, would
forms of the irregular verbs *be, do,* and *have*

Remember that *be, do,* and *have* are also used as the main verbs of sentences. In such cases, *be* is a linking verb while *do* and *have* are action verbs. All the other helping verbs are usually used only as helping verbs.

Adverbs are words that can modify verbs, adjectives, or other adverbs.

Watch out for adverbs that may come in between the helping verb and the main verb.

In the following sentence, the word *often* is an adverb coming between the verb phrase *can frighten.* For a list of common adverbs, see Appendix A: Parts of Speech (p. 565).

Dreams can often frighten young children.

EXERCISE 15 **Finding Helping Verbs**

Each of the following sentences contains a helping verb in addition to the main verb. In each sentence, first cross out any prepositional phrases and underline the subject. Then circle the entire verb phrase. An example follows:

In some writing classes, students must keep a diary of their work.

1. A diary could be simple or elaborate.

2. In a journal, a person can safely express true feelings without fear of criticism by family or friends.

3. Well kept diaries have helped to give people insight into the motivations for their actions and have also been a help in dealing with change.

4. Diaries do improve a person's powers of observation to look inwardly at one's own feelings as well as to look outwardly at actual happenings.

5. You will be able to capture your memories.

6. Important, too, would be the development of a writing style and the improvement of language skills.

7. A journal might awaken your imagination.

8. It may unexpectedly bring pleasure and satisfaction.

9. Keener observations will add to the joys of life.

10. You should seriously consider the purchase of one of those lovely fabric-bound notebooks.

EXERCISE 16

Finding Helping Verbs

Each of the following sentences contains a helping verb. In each sentence, first cross out any prepositional phrases and underline the subject. Then circle the entire verb phrase. An example follows:

~~In this country~~, daycare has become an important issue.

1. How do you start a child care center?

2. First, notices can be put in local churches and supermarkets.

3. Then, you should also use word-of-mouth among your friends.

4. Many parents will need infant care during the day, after-school care, or evening and weekend care.

5. With luck, a nearby doctor may be willing to help with the local health laws and legal requirements.

6. Of course, the licensing laws in your state must be thoroughly researched.

7. Unfortunately, you could have trouble finding a low rent place for your center.

8. Any child care center will depend on its ever-widening good reputation.

9. In good day-care centers, parents are never excluded from meetings or planning sessions.

10. Finally, the center must be more interested in the character of its teachers than in the teachers' degrees.

EXPLORING ONLINE FOR ESL STUDENTS

Test your English fluency at

http://www.edunet.com/english/practice/test-ces.html

Parts of Speech

In this chapter you have learned how most of the words in the English language function. These categories for words are called *parts of speech.* You have learned to recognize and understand the functioning of *nouns, pronouns, adjectives, verbs, adverbs,* and *prepositions.* (In later chapters you will learn how the *conjunction* functions.) You can review your understanding of these parts of speech as you practice identifying them in the exercises provided here. You may also refer to Appendix A (at the back of the book) for a quick summary whenever you want to refresh your memory.

EXERCISE 17 **Identifying Parts of Speech**

In the sentences below, identify the part of speech for each underlined word. Choose from the following list:

a. noun	c. adjective	e. adverb
b. pronoun	d. verb	f. preposition

_______________ **1.** Chubby Checker taught the world how to twist.

_______________ **2.** Dick Clark, host of American Bandstand, decided he liked "The Twist" and showcased it.

_______________ **3.** The song shot up to number one on the pop charts in September of 1960.

_______________ **4.** Twisting became the biggest teenage fad.

_______________ **5.** At first, it was considered strictly kid stuff.

_______________ **6.** Then it became respectable among older groups.

_______________ **7.** Liz Taylor and Richard Burton were seen twisting in the fashionable night spots of Rome.

_______________ **8.** The dance set the pace for a decade.

_______________ **9.** The "beautiful people" were seen breathlessly twisting at the Peppermint Lounge in New York.

_______________ **10.** The 60s were going to be a reckless and unruly time.

EXERCISE 18 **Identifying Parts of Speech**

In the sentences below, identify the part of speech for each underlined word. Choose from the following list:

a. noun	c. adjective	e. adverb
b. pronoun	d. verb	f. preposition

_______________ **1.** "The Grand Ole Opry" is a famous radio program.

_______________ **2.** It began more than seventy years ago in Nashville, Tennessee.

_______________ **3.** By the 1930's, the program was the best source of country music on the radio.

_______________ **4.** In 1943, the program could be heard in every home in the nation.

_______________ **5.** Many people traveled to Nashville.

__________ **6.** They wanted to see the performers for themselves.

__________ **7.** The existing old concert hall, poorly constructed in the nineteenth century, was not an ideal place for modern audiences.

__________ **8.** Television came in during the 1950s, and with it the demand for a new hall.

__________ **9.** Now the Nashville hall is modern and air-conditioned.

__________ **10.** Three million people visit Nashville every year.

EXERCISE 19 **Identifying Parts of Speech**

In the sentences below, identify the part of speech for each underlined word. Choose from the following list:

a. noun	c. adjective	e. adverb
b. pronoun	d. verb	f. preposition

__________ **1.** The people of the country of Mali, in Africa,

__________ **2.** built a mosque out of mud bricks. The Great

__________ **3.** Mosque in the town of Djenne was built

__________ **4.** by the Mali people sometime between A.D. 1100 and

__________ **5.** 1300. Most of the leaders of Mali at that time

__________ **6.** were Muslims. Djenne became a center of Islamic

__________ **7.** learning. When the leader Konboro converted to

__________ **8.** Islam, he asked a holy man, “How may I please God?”

__________ **9.** The holy man said, “Build a mosque. The people

__________ **10.** will bless your name for centuries.”

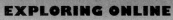

EXPLORING ONLINE

For fun while learning parts of speech, particularly subjects and verbs, go to http://www.funbrain.com/grammar/, and feed the Grammar Gorillas.

Mastery and Editing Tests

TEST 1 **Finding Subjects and Verbs in Simple Sentences**

In each of the following sentences, cross out any prepositional phrases or appositive phrases. Then underline the subject and circle the complete verb. An example follows:

The main street ~~of Corning, New York,~~ (has been) beautifully (renovated).

1. Older people today may recall the main street of their home town as a wonderful place forty or fifty years ago.
2. Why can't we have these old main streets back again?
3. In 1970, the National Trust for Historical Preservation began a program to bring new life to the nation's downtown areas.
4. Cities and villages needed new attitudes toward downtown areas.
5. Some local planners began a program to revitalize main streets.
6. One of the most important challenges was to convince businesspeople to repair old buildings.
7. Towns quickly saw the value of making changes.
8. Citizens understood the advantages of a comfortable downtown.
9. Now many towns gladly sponsor special events and parades.
10. Will the tradition of personal service return to the American main street?

TEST 2 **Finding Subjects and Verbs in Simple Sentences**

In each of the sentences in the following paragraph, cross out any prepositional or appositive phrases. Then underline the subject and circle the complete verb.

Go West! Western Australia, one of the remaining great boom areas of the world, comprises one-third of the Australian continent. Why did people by the tens of thousands go to western Australia in the late 1800s? In 1894, Leslie Robert Menzies jumped off his camel and landed in a pile of gold nuggets. In less than two hours, this man gathered over a million dollars in gold. He eventually took six tons of gold to the bank by wheelbarrow! Kalgoorlie and Boulder, the two boomtowns that grew up there, boast of the richest golden mile in the world. With all the gold seekers, this surface gold did not last very long. Now the only bands of rich ore lie more than 4,000 feet down under the ground. There are many ghost towns with their empty iron houses and run-down chicken coops.

TEST 3 **Student Writing: Finding Subjects and Verbs in Simple Sentences**

In each of the sentences in the following paragraph, cross out any prepositional or appositive phrases. Then underline the subject and circle the complete verb.

~~In the field of writing~~, practice (is) important ~~for growth~~.

A certain amount of stress can be a good thing. In many cases, stress motivates us. When does stress become distress? Your own self-awareness is the best place to start. Have there been changes in your sleep or appetite? Are you using alcohol or drugs to excess? Anxious people feel trapped by pressure and disappointment. There is usually help from your family and friends. Many can offer you their observations and advice. Clinical depression, a more serious condition, usually responds well to the right combination of psychotherapy and medicine.

EXPLORING ONLINE

Test your knowledge of grammar with the online grammar quiz (answers provided): http://www.grammarbook.com/tests/grammar/graTest.html.

WORKING TOGETHER

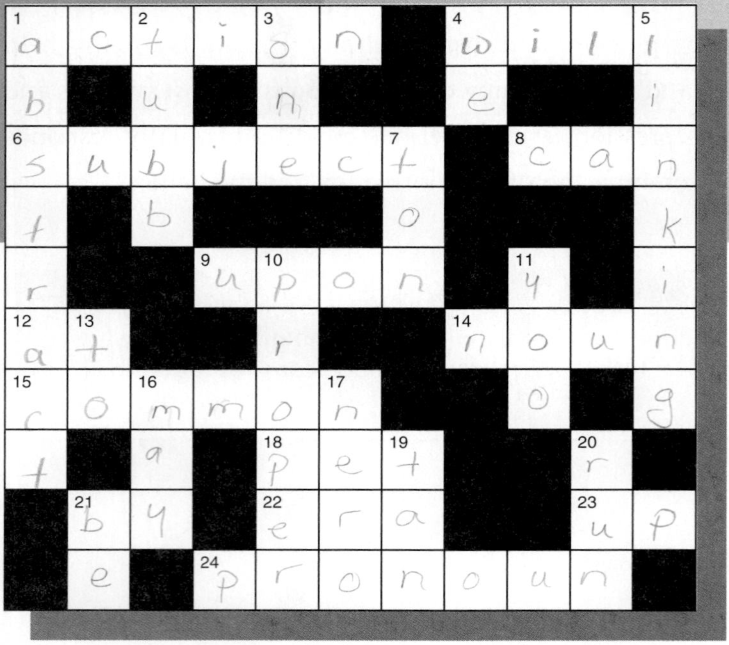

CROSSWORD PUZZLE: REVIEWING THE TERMS FOR SENTENCE PARTS

Review the names for sentence parts by doing this crossword puzzle. Feel free to work in pairs. If necessary, look back in the chapter for the answers.

ACROSS

1. Verbs like hop, sing, and play are called ______ verbs.
4. Which of the following is a helping verb?
   hear, when, will, only
6. Every sentence has a ______ and a verb.
8. A helping verb
9. Which of the following is a preposition?
   must, upon, they, open
12. A preposition
14. *Word, witch, wall,* and *willow* are examples of the part of speech called a ______.
15. Most nouns are ______ nouns. They are not capitalized.
18. In the following sentence, which word is used as an adjective?
    She has pet pigs for sale.
21. Which of the following is a preposition?
    he, be, by, if
22. In the following sentence, which word is an abstract noun?
    The era was not economically successful.
23. A preposition
24. A word that can take the place of a noun.

DOWN

1. *Joy, confidence, peace* are examples of this kind of noun; the opposite of a concrete noun.
2. Which word is the subject in the following sentence:
   Here is the tube of glue for Toby.
3. An indefinite pronoun
4. A plural pronoun
5. *Look, appear, feel,* and *seem* are examples of ______ verbs.
7. Which word is the object of the preposition?
   The car must weigh over a ton.
10. The opposite of a common noun.
11. A personal pronoun
13. A preposition
16. In the following sentence, which word is a helping verb?
    She may pay the fee for her son.
17. Which of the following is a proper noun?
    king, Nero, hero, teen
19. In the following sentence, which word is an adjective?
    Nan quickly ran toward the tan man.
20. Which word is the verb in the following sentence?
    Run down to the car for our bag.
21. A common linking verb.

Online Activity

For more word games and crossword puzzles to work together, visit http://www.thesaurus.com.

Chapter 4 Making Subjects and Verbs Agree

Preview

In Chapter 3, you learned that a sentence requires a subject and a verb. A related issue is that the verb of a sentence must also *agree* with its subject. The exercises in this chapter will give you practice in several problem areas of making verbs agree with their subjects. Even the most experienced writers are sometimes surprised to find they have made a mistake with subject-verb agreement.

Special Problems with Subject-Verb Agreement:

When the subject is a personal pronoun
When the verb is a form of *do* or *be*
When the subject is hard to find
When the subject is a collective noun
When the subject is an indefinite pronoun
When the subject is a compound subject
When the subject has an unusual singular or plural form

Key Terms

Number—in grammar, the singular or plural form

Rule

- A verb must agree with its subject in number.

Charts

List of personal pronouns
List of collective nouns
List of indefinite pronouns
List of nouns with unusual singular or plural forms

What Is Subject-Verb Agreement?

A verb must agree with its subject in *number* (singular or plural).

When the subject is a singular noun, the verb takes an *s* (or *es*) in the present tense.

The baby *sleeps.*

The baby *cries.*

When the subject is a plural noun, the verb does *not* take an *s* (or *es*) in the present tense.

The babies *sleep.*

The babies *cry.*

Notice that when you add *s* or *es* to an ordinary noun, you form the plural of that noun. However, when you add an *s* to a verb, and you want the verb to be in the present tense, you are writing a singular verb. This rule causes a lot of confusion for student writers, especially those whose first language is not English. It may also be confusing to students who already speak and write English, but whose local manner of speaking does not follow this rule. While there is no one way of speaking that is correct or incorrect, society does recognize a standard form that is agreed upon as acceptable in the worlds of school and business. Since we must all master this standard form, the material contained in this chapter is of the greatest importance to your success in college and beyond.

Pronouns Can Also Present Problems for Subject-Verb Agreement

The following chart shows personal pronouns used with the verb *sleep*. After you have studied the chart, what can you tell about the ending of a verb when the subject of that verb is a personal pronoun?

PERSONAL PRONOUNS

Singular	Plural
I *sleep*	we *sleep*
you *sleep*	you *sleep*
he, she, it *sleeps*	they *sleep*

Practice.......... Underline the correct verb in the following sentences.

1. The dog (bark, barks).

2. It (wake, wakes) up the neighborhood.

3. The neighbors (become, becomes) very angry.

4. These families (deserve, deserves) a quiet Sunday morning.

5. I (throws, throw) an old shoe at the dog.

Pay Special Attention to the Verbs *Do* and *Be*

Although you may have heard someone say, *It don't matter,* or *We was working,* these expressions are not considered standard English because the subjects do not agree with the verbs. Study the charts below to learn which forms of *to do* and *to be* are singular and plural.

THE VERB *TO DO*

Singular	Plural
I do	we, you, they } do
you do	
he, she, it } does	

(never use *he don't, she don't,* or *it don't*)

THE VERB *TO BE*

Present Tense		Past Tense	
Singular	*Plural*	*Singular*	*Plural*
I am	we, you, they } are	I was	we, you, they } were
you are		you were	
he, she, it } is		he, she, it } was	

(never use *we was, you was,* or *they was*)

Practice.......... Underline the verb that agrees with the subject.

1. He (doesn't, don't) study in the library anymore.

2. We (was, were) hoping to find him there.

3. The library (doesn't, don't) close until eleven o'clock.

4. (Was, Were) you late tonight?

5. Ann (doesn't, don't) care if you stay until closing time.

EXERCISE 1 Making the Subject and Verb Agree

In the blanks next to each sentence, write the subject of the sentence and the correct form of the verb.

	Subject	Verb
1. My brother (be, is, are) a comedian.	________	________
2. We (laughs, laugh) at everything he says.	________	________
3. He (expects, expect) us to attend his show tomorrow night.	________	________
4. He (doesn't, don't) like us to miss even one performance.	________	________
5. Every show (has, have) many comedians on the program.	________	________
6. My sister (hopes, hope) to bring her new friend.	________	________
7. She (says, say) we will all love him.	________	________
8. Yesterday, I (be, was, were) telling my friends to come too.	________	________
9. They (was, were) happy to accept.	________	________
10. It (promises, promise) to be a great evening.	________	________

EXERCISE 2 Making the Subject and Verb Agree

In the blanks next to each sentence, write the subject of the sentence and the correct form of the verb.

	Subject	Verb
1. Many companies today (wants, want) to test their workers for drugs.	________	________
2. To many people, it (appears, appear) to be an invasion of privacy.	________	________
3. Employers (worries, worry) that bus and train drivers are using drugs on the job.	________	________
4. They (doesn't, don't) want to risk the lives of passengers.	________	________
5. Even operators of rides in amusement parks (undergoes, undergo) tests.	________	________
6. Professional athletes on a team (has, have) special problems because of the publicity that surrounds them.	________	________
7. Some factories (installs, install) hidden video cameras to catch workers using drugs.	________	________
8. The General Motors Company (worries, worry) enough to hire undercover agents to pretend to be workers, in order to catch drug users.	________	________

9. In Kansas City, a newspaper wanted to use drug-sniffing dogs, but reporters from the newspaper (was, were) insulted. ________ ________

10. (Has, Have) you ever been asked to take a drug test? ________ ________

EXERCISE 3

Making the Subject and Verb Agree

In the blanks next to each sentence, write the subject of the sentence and the correct form of the verb.

	Subject	Verb
1. My father and mother (was, were) planning a celebration.	________	________
2. They (is, are) celebrating their twenty-fifth wedding anniversary.	________	________
3. My mother (doesn't, don't) approve of spending a lot of money.	________	________
4. It (doesn't, don't) do any good to argue with her.	________	________
5. My father (spends, spend) several days looking at brochures.	________	________
6. They (hasn't, haven't) been on a vacation in over fifteen years.	________	________
7. The travel agent (suggests, suggest) a cruise.	________	________
8. We (enjoys, enjoy) imagining their trip.	________	________
9. Hopefully she (doesn't, don't) change her mind at the last minute.	________	________
10. A cruise to the Caribbean (sounds, sound) good to me.	________	________

EXPLORING ONLINE FOR ESL STUDENTS

Subject-verb agreement can be a challenge if your first language is not English. Explore "Dave's ESL Cafe" for more help. http://www.eslcafe.com

Subject-Verb Agreement with Hard to Find Subjects

As we learned in Chapter 3, a verb does not always follow the subject immediately. Other words or groups of words called *phrases* (prepositional or appositive phrases, for example) can come between the subject and verb. Furthermore, subjects and verbs can be inverted when they are used in questions or in sentences beginning with the words *There* or *Here*.

When looking for subject-verb agreement in sentences where the subjects are more difficult to find, keep two points in mind:

- Subjects are *not* found in prepositional phrases or appositive phrases.
- Subjects can be found after the verb in sentences that are questions and in sentences that begin with the words *There* or *Here*.

EXERCISE 4 **Agreement with Hidden Subjects**

In each sentence below, cross out any prepositional or appositive phrases and the words *there* or *here*. Then underline the subject. Finally, circle the correct verb.

1. Here (is, are) a plan about time management.
2. Too much busywork in your day (prevents, prevent) efficiency.
3. A period of time without interruptions (is, are) crucial.
4. People usually (does, do) too many things at once.
5. Why (is, are) frequent breaks important?
6. Constant clutter on people's desks (causes, cause) frustration.
7. Why (does, do) perfectionists have so much difficulty?
8. The habit of procrastination (is, are) another area of time management.
9. There (is, are) also several distracting activities such as television viewing.
10. Children in a family (needs, need) to help with chores.

EXERCISE 5 **Agreement with Hidden Subjects**

In each sentence below, cross out any prepositional or appositive phrases and the words *there* and *here*. Then underline the subject. Finally, circle the correct verb in each sentence.

1. Here (is, are) some basic medical supplies needed for every home.
2. A thermometer in the medicine chest (is, are) crucial.
3. There (is, are) a box of bandages on hand for minor injuries.
4. A vaporizer in the bedroom at night (relieves, relieve) bronchial congestion.
5. Pads of sterile gauze often (tends, tend) to be forgotten.
6. A small bottle of Coca-Cola syrup (proves, prove) helpful for treating stomach upsets.
7. A useful tool, a pair of tweezers, (removes, remove) splinters.
8. In a home ready for emergencies, a list of emergency phone numbers (sits, sit) next to the telephone.
9. Why (has, have) cold compresses been useful in treating sprains?
10. Every person with the desire to be prepared (needs, need) a resource book on first aid at hand.

Special Problems with Subject-Verb Agreement

- **Subject-verb agreement with collective (or group) nouns**

Collective nouns name a group of people or things.

FREQUENTLY USED COLLECTIVE NOUNS			
audience	committee	group	public
assembly	council	herd	senate
board	crowd	jury	team
class	faculty	orchestra	tribe
club	family	panel	

- Usually, a collective noun takes a singular verb or requires a singular pronoun to refer to that noun. That is because the group acts as a single unit.

  The *class* **is** waiting for **its** turn to use the gym.

- Sometimes a collective noun takes a plural verb or requires a plural pronoun to refer to that noun. This applies when the members of a group are acting as individuals, with separate actions as a result.

  The *class* **are** putting on **their** coats.

EXERCISE 6 **Agreement with Collective Nouns**

Circle the correct verb in each sentence.

1. The Spanish club (is, are) planning refreshments for their next meeting. (acting as individuals)
2. The trio (performs, perform) mostly on weekends. (acting as a unit)
3. The group (needs, need) a sponsor for its organization. (acting as a unit)
4. The faculty (is, are) planning individual presentations for the conference. (acting as individuals)
5. The committee (is, are) undecided who should be invited. (acting as individuals)
6. A team (has, have) been selected to compete at the Spanish History Tournament. (acting as a unit)
7. A crowd usually (attends, attend) the competition. (acting as a unit)
8. The board of directors (disagrees, disagree) about the proposal. (acting as individuals)
9. The panel tonight (was, were) discussing the ancient culture of Castille in Spain. (acting as individuals)
10. The audience (was, were) very appreciative. (acting as a unit)

EXERCISE 7 Agreement with Collective Nouns

Circle the correct verb in each sentence.

1. The construction crew (seems, seem) responsible for the accident. (acting as a unit)
2. In this case, the union (accuses, accuse) the crew. (acting as a unit)
3. A few days later, the same group (files, file) charges. (acting as a unit)
4. The crew's legal team (is, are) uncertain about their strategy. (acting as individuals)
5. The public (attends, attend) the trial. (acting as a unit)
6. The crowd (grows, grow) impatient. (acting as individuals)
7. The audience (interrupts, interrupt) the proceedings. (acting as individuals)
8. The jury (hears, hear) the evidence. (acting as a unit)
9. The group (has, have) different opinions. (acting as individuals)
10. The crowd (waits, wait) to hear the verdict. (acting as a unit)

- **Subject-verb agreement with indefinite pronouns**

Care should be taken to learn which indefinite pronouns are singular and which are plural.

INDEFINITE PRONOUNS

Indefinite pronouns taking a singular verb:

everyone	someone	anyone	no one
everybody	somebody	anybody	nobody
everything	something	anything	nothing
each	another	either	neither

Everyone *is* expecting a miracle.

Indefinite pronouns taking a plural verb:

both	few	many	several

The talks between the two countries failed. Both *were* to blame.

Indefinite pronouns taking a singular or plural verb depending on the meaning in the sentence:

any	all	more	most
none	some		

The books are gone. All *were* very popular.

The sugar is gone. All of it *was* spilled.

EXERCISE 8 Agreement with Indefinite Pronouns

Circle the correct verb in each sentence.

1. Nobody (knows, know) how many drugs are contained in plants that grow in the rainforest.
2. Some (argues, argue) that wonderful drugs could be derived from many plants.
3. Most of the pharmaceutical experts (remains, remain) skeptical.
4. All of the research (is, are) expensive and often (proves, prove) fruitless.
5. Everybody (agrees, agree) the tropical forest is a source of medicine.
6. One of the dangers (is, are) that if we wait, the tropical forest may disappear.
7. One of the two U.S. companies in Costa Rica (is, are) Merck & Company.
8. Each of the companies (is, are) paying the country for the right to search the rainforest.
9. Among scientists, some (recommends, recommend) that governments subsidize drug research.
10. Vincristine and vinblastine are two medicines found in the rainforest; both (is, are) used for cancer treatment.

EXERCISE 9 Agreement with Indefinite Pronouns

Circle the correct verb in the sentences.

1. One of the classic Spanish colonial towns still existing today (is, are) St. Augustine, Florida.
2. Almost nobody (realizes, realize) the difference between the alligator of the Southern wetlands and the crocodile of southern Florida.
3. Most of the South's coast (is, are) lined with barrier islands.
4. Nobody (reaches, reach) Florida's Gulf Islands except by boat.
5. One of the special Southern treats (remains, remain) a bag of boiled peanuts.
6. Anyone visiting a Southern home (is, are) likely to be served iced tea, the "house wine" of the South.
7. (Doesn't, Don't) everybody love the music from Mississippi: rock 'n' roll, blues, and country western?
8. Some of the country's most colorful folk art (is, are) found by driving on the backroads.
9. Not all of the plantation houses in the Old South (looks, look) like Tara in *Gone with the Wind*.
10. Southern names can often be distinctive; many of them (uses, use) double names like Billie Jean, James Earl, or Peggy Sue.

- **Subject-verb agreement with compound subjects**
  - If the conjunction used to connect the compound subjects is *and,* the verb is usually plural.

    Mary and Steve *are* my good friends.

    The exception to this is if the two subjects are thought of as a single unit.

    Peanut butter and jelly *is* my favorite sandwich.

  - If the conjunction used to connect the compound subjects is *or, nor, either, either/or, neither, neither/nor, not only/but also,* you need to be particularly careful.
    The verb is singular if both subjects are singular.

    Mary or Steve *is* going to help me.

    The verb is plural if both subjects are plural.

    My friends or my two brothers *are* going to help me.

    The verb agrees with the subject closest to the verb if one subject is singular and one subject is plural.

    My friends or my brother *is* going to help me.

EXERCISE 10 **Subject-Verb Agreement with Compound Subjects**
Circle the correct verb in each sentence.

1. Macaroni and cheese (is, are) my son's favorite supper.
2. This meal and others like it (has, have) too much fat.
3. My mother and father, on the other hand, often (enjoys, enjoy) a fruit salad for their main meal.
4. Shopping or cooking habits (needs, need) to be changed.
5. Either a salad or another vegetable with a sprinkling of cheese (is, are) a better choice than macaroni and cheese.
6. Adults and children (does, do) need to watch their diets.
7. Too many pizzas and sodas (is, are) a disaster for people's health.
8. Either the lack of exercise or the eating of fatty foods (causes, cause) more problems than just overweight.
9. Neither potato chips nor buttered popcorn (is, are) a good snack choice.
10. An apple or grapes (makes, make) a better choice.

EXERCISE 11 **Subject-Verb Agreement with Compound Subjects**

Circle the correct verb in each sentence.

1. Students and a teacher (meets, meet) at the University of Indiana to do marriage research.
2. Either Robert Levenson or John Gollman (uses, use) the video to examine how couples interact during arguments.
3. Neither body language nor the spoken words (is, are) unimportant.
4. Criticism, whining, or withdrawal (reveals, reveal) potential trouble.
5. Sweating, blood flow, and heart rate (is, are) also monitored during arguments.
6. Positive moments or good memories (needs, need) to outnumber the negative moments.
7. A man or a woman who (marries, marry) someone with a different fighting style may be doomed to an unhappy marriage.
8. Courtrooms or a baseball field (provides, provide) structured times and places for people to fight.
9. A particular time and a particular place (needs, need) to be set aside for talking about marital problems.
10. A happy husband and wife (gives, give) each other support and friendship.

- **Subject-verb agreement with unusual nouns**

Don't assume that every noun ending in ***s*** is plural, or that all nouns that do not end in ***s*** are singular. There are some exceptions. Here are a few of the most common exceptions:

Some nouns are always singular in meaning, but end in *s*.

mathematics	diabetes	United States
economics	measles	Kansas

Mathematics *is* my major.

Some nouns are always plural in meaning.

clothes	scissors	fireworks
headquarters	tweezers	pants

My blue pants *are* ripped.

SOME NOUNS HAVE UNUSUAL PLURAL FORMS

	Singular	Plural
1. Some foreign words used in English use rules of their own languages to make words plural. For example, to the right are four Latin words that show the Latin rule (*-um* changes to *-a* to form the plural):	bacterium	bacteria
	datum	data
	medium	media
	stratum	strata
2. Some words change internally rather than add *-s* at the end:	foot	feet
	tooth	teeth
	child	children
	man	men
	woman	women
	mouse	mice
	ox	oxen
	goose	geese
3. Some words remain the same whether singular or plural:	deer	deer
	elk	elk
	fish	fish
	moose	moose

Mastery and Editing Tests

TEST 1

Making the Subject and Verb Agree

In the blanks next to each sentence, write the subject of the sentence and the correct form of the verb. An example follows.

	Subject	Verb
The price of airline tickets to England (has, have) remained fairly reasonable.	price	has
1. Included in the price of the trip (was, were) five nights in a lovely hotel and all meals.	________	________
2. Nobody in the family (knows, know) how to swim.	________	________
3. Jerry and Craig (works, work) well together.	________	________
4. The student senate (meets, meet) every Tuesday.	________	________
5. Where (is, are) the wrapping paper for these packages?	________	________
6. In the entire building there (is, are) only two windows.	________	________

7. Either the fruit pies or that chocolate cake (looks, look) like the best choice for your picnic. __________ __________

8. Public performances (makes, make) me nervous. __________ __________

9. One of my most favorite television shows (is, are) *The X-Files*. __________ __________

10. The book for the term paper (doesn't, don't) have to be from the reading list. __________ __________

TEST 2 Making the Subject and Verb Agree

Using your own words and ideas, complete each of the following sentences. Be sure that the verb you choose for each sentence is in the present tense and agrees with the subject of that sentence. An example follows:

The best *place* for wedding receptions *is* a restaurant with a view.

1. Our team ____________________
2. The box of chocolates ____________________
3. Both of my sisters ____________________
4. The effects of a pay cut on a family ____________________
____
5. Where is ____________________
6. Not only the teacher but also the students ____________________
____
7. The jury ____________________
8. Each of the contestants ____________________
9. Do you think there is ____________________
10. The table of contents in that book ____________________

TEST 3 Student Writing: Making the Subject and Verb Agree

The following paragraph contains five errors in subject-verb agreement. For each sentence, cross out any prepositional phrases, underline the subject, and circle the verb. On the lines following, list the subject and the correct form of the verb for each sentence.

[1]The course requirements for high school graduation has changed in the last few years. [2]Today's teachers and students are challenged by the new standards. [3]The typical student don't know where to turn for proper guidance. [4]Either a deficit in math or a deficit in English prevent many students from graduating. [5]The problems with the new standard are under discussion. [6]One of the most serious issues continue to be the illiteracy rate in the early grades. [7]There is several points of view on the matter. [8]Everyone agrees about the importance of literacy for any

democracy. [9]At a recent meeting of a major teachers' union, a list of recommendations was given. [10]A fifth year of high school for all students was at the top of the list.

Subject	Correct Form of the Verb
1. ________	________
2. ________	________
3. ________	________
4. ________	________
5. ________	________
6. ________	________
7. ________	________
8. ________	________
9. ________	________
10. ________	________

EXPLORING ONLINE

For more practice, work the two exercises provided by the Purdue Online Writing Lab (OWL). Answers are available:
http://owl.english.purdue.edu/handouts/esl/eslsubverb.html

WORKING TOGETHER

PRESERVING FAMILY HISTORY

Focused Freewriting: Preserving Family History

The photograph shows a family portrait taken early in the last century. What are some of the oldest photographs of family members that you have seen? Do you still have documents (such as birth certificates) that give you information about your relatives? What stories have you been told about them?

If you have no other information about these relatives except old photographs, what can you tell about the people by looking at their images? If you have not been left with any documents from the past, consider what you would like your descendents to possess so they will have some idea of your life and personality.

Use the next 20 minutes to do some focused freewriting on the topic of preserving family history. When you have finished, exchange papers with a classmate. As you read your classmate's paper,

continued on next page

make a check beside any idea or phrase that you think is interesting or any idea that could be further explored in a future writing project.

Portfolio Suggestion

Save the freewriting you have done on your family's history. This is a topic that you may want to return to again and again. Children will appreciate all the stories and memories you can gather about your relatives. This may be one of the greatest gifts you can give your family.

Online Activity

Explore genealogy tips for gathering family information and read family stories at http://www.rootsweb.com In groups, discuss the following question: What are the pros and cons of discovering one's roots?

The Internet is now a source of hundreds of free books that can be quickly downloaded onto your hard drive for you to read. One excellent offering is *Autobiography of a Female Slave* by Martha Griffith Browne, d. 1906. Visit http://www.ibiblio.org/docsouth/browne/menu.html to read her history. Discuss Browne's first chapter as a class. How could her style be described?

Chapter 5.

Understanding Fragments and Phrases

Preview

In order to correct the sentence fragments in your own writing, you need to understand more about sentence parts. Groups of words that go together may only be phrases or dependent clauses and not sentences. This chapter will make sure that you do not mistake a phrase for a sentence.

You will learn to recognize that a fragment lacks one of the following three elements:

Subject
Verb
Complete thought

You will learn to identify the six phrases:

Noun phrase
Prepositional phrase
Verb phrase
Infinitive phrase
Participial phrase
Gerund phrase

You will learn to practice three different uses of the present participle:

As part of a verb phrase
As an adjective
As a noun

Key Terms

Complete sentence
Fragment
Phrase
Participle
noun phrase
prepositional phrase
verb phrase
infinitive phrase
participial phrase
gerund phrase

Rule

- When a participle is used as a verb, there must be a helping verb with it.

Fragments in Everyday Conversations

The fragment is a major problem for many student writers. A thought may be clear in a writer's mind, but on paper this same idea may turn out to be incomplete because it does not include a subject, a verb, or express a complete thought. In this section, you will improve your ability to spot incomplete sentences or fragments, and you will learn how to correct them. This practice will help you avoid such fragments in your own writing. Here, for example, is a typical conversation between two people at lunchtime. It is composed entirely of fragments, but the two people who are speaking have no trouble understanding each other.

Ron: Had any lunch?

Jan: A sandwich.

Ron: What kind?

Jan: Ham and Swiss on rye.

If we use complete sentences to rewrite this brief conversation, the result might be the following:

Ron: Did you have any lunch yet?

Jan: Yes, I had a sandwich.

Ron: What kind of sandwich did you have?

Jan: I had ham and Swiss cheese on rye bread.

In the first conversation, misunderstanding is unlikely since the two speakers stand face to face, see each other's gestures, and hear the intonations of each other's voice in order to help each one grasp the other's meaning. These short phrases may be enough for communication since the speakers are using more than just words to convey their thoughts. They understand each other because each one has no difficulty completing the thoughts in the other person's mind.

In writing, however, readers cannot be present to observe the situation for themselves. They cannot be expected to read the writer's mind. Only words grouped into sentences and sentences grouped into paragraphs can provide the clues to the meaning. Since writing often involves thoughts that are abstract and even complex, fragments cause great difficulty and sometimes result in total confusion for the reader.

EXERCISE 1 **Putting a Conversation into Complete Sentences**

The following conversation could have taken place between two students at the start of their English class. Rewrite the conversation in complete thoughts or standard sentences. Remember the definition of a sentence:

> A **complete sentence** has a subject and a verb and expresses a complete thought.

John: Early again.

Elaine: Want to get a front row seat.

John: Your homework ready?

Elaine: Nearly.

John: Think he'll give a quiz today?

Elaine: Hope not.

John: Looks like rain today.
Elaine: Bad news.
John: Going to the game Saturday?
Elaine: Probably.
John: ______________________________
Elaine: ______________________________
John: ______________________________
Elaine: ______________________________
John: ______________________________
Elaine: ______________________________
John: ______________________________
Elaine: ______________________________
John: ______________________________
Elaine: ______________________________

Remember, when you write in complete sentences, the result may differ from the way you would express the same idea in everyday conversation with a friend.

Although you will occasionally spot incomplete sentences in professional writing, you may be sure the writer is using these fragments intentionally. In such cases, the fragment may be appropriate because it captures the way a person thinks or speaks, or creates a special effect. A student developing his or her writing skills should be careful to use only standard sentence form so that every thought will be communicated effectively. Nearly all the writing you will do in your life—letters to friends, business correspondence, papers in school, or reports in your job—will demand standard sentence form. Fragments will be looked upon as a sign of ignorance rather than evidence of a creative style!

What Is a Fragment?

A **fragment** is a piece of a sentence.

A group of words may look like a sentence but only make a fragment if one of the following is true:

a. The subject is missing:

Delivered the plans to my office.

b. The verb is missing:

The architect to my office.

c. Both the subject and verb are missing:

To my office.

d. The subject and verb are present but the words do not express a complete thought:

The architect delivered.

EXERCISE 2 **Understanding Fragments**

Each of the following ten examples is a fragment. In the blank to the right of each fragment, identify what part of the sentence is missing and what needs to be added to make the fragment into a complete sentence.

a. Add a subject.
b. Add a verb.
c. Add a subject and a verb.
d. The subject and verb are already present, but the sentence needs to express a complete thought.

An example follows:

Fragment	What Is Missing?
the red fox	b. verb
1. returned to the river	______
2. a bird on the oak branch	______
3. between the island and the mainland	______
4. the hawk in a soaring motion	______
5. the fishing boats on the lake	______
6. dropped like a stone into the water	______
7. the silence of the forest	______
8. carried the fish to the tree	______
9. the fisherman put	______
10. into the net	______

How Do You Correct a Fragment?

1. A fragment becomes a sentence when you add the missing part or parts.

Example: Fragment: across the lake
Add: subject and verb
Sentence: I swam across the lake.

Note: The prepositional phrase *across the lake* is a fragment because a prepositional phrase cannot function as the subject or the verb in a sentence. Furthermore, the words *across the lake* do not express a complete thought.

2. A fragment becomes a sentence when you join the fragment to the sentence that precedes it or to the sentence that follows it. This depends on where the information in the fragment belongs.

If a writer looks at the text where the fragment occurs, often the complete thought is already present. The writer did not recognize that the fragment belonged to the sentence that came earlier or to the sentence that followed. Study the example below:

Incorrect: In the middle of the night, I swam. Across the lake. The camp counselor was waiting at the other side.

Correct: In the middle of the night, I swam across the lake. The camp counselor was waiting at the other side.

There can be more than one reason for fragments to exist in a writer's work. A writer may become careless for a moment or may not fully understand how all the parts of a sentence work. Also, if the writer does not have a clear idea of what he or she is trying to say, fragments and other errors are more likely to occur. Sometimes further thought or another try at expressing the same idea may produce a better result.

In the following two exercises, practice correcting both kinds of fragments.

EXERCISE 3

Making Fragments into Sentences

Change the fragments of Exercise 2 into complete sentences by adding the missing part or parts that you have already identified.

1. returned to the river

____

2. a bird on the oak branch

____

3. between the island and the mainland

____

4. the hawk in a soaring motion

____

5. the fishing boats on the lake

____

6. dropped like a stone into the water

____

7. the silence of the forest

____

8. carried the fish to the tree

____

9. the fisherman put

____

10. into the net

____

EXERCISE 4 **Finding Fragments That Belong to Other Sentences**

Each of the following passages contains at least one fragment. First, read each passage carefully. Circle each fragment you find and draw an arrow to the sentence where it belongs. An example follows:

Adelle assisted the dancers. She stood backstage. (Between numbers.)
She helped the ballerinas change costumes.

Passage 1 Fishing is one of the oldest sports in the world. And can be one of the most relaxing. A person with a simple wooden pole and line can have as much fun as a sportsman. With expensive equipment. For busy executives, overworked teachers, and even presidents of nations. Fishing can be a good way to escape from the stress of demanding jobs.

Passage 2 The first electric car was built in 1887. It was sold commercially six years later. At the turn of the century, people had great faith in new technology. In fact, three hundred electric taxicabs were operating in New York City by 1900. However, electric cars soon lost their popularity. The new gasoline engine became more widely used. With our concern over pollution. Perhaps electric cars will become desirable once again.

Passage 3 Eskimos obtain most of their food from the sea. They eat seals and walruses. Whales, fish and sea birds in abundance. Eskimos boil some of their food. They eat other foods uncooked because of the scarcity of fuel. Eskimos get important vitamins and minerals. By eating every part of the animal they kill. The heart, the liver, and even the digestive tracts of the animals have great food value for the Eskimos.

What Is a Phrase?

A **phrase** is a group of words belonging together but lacking one or more of the three elements necessary for a sentence.

Fragments are usually made up of phrases. These phrases are often mistaken for sentences because they are words that go together as a group. However, they do not fit the definition of a sentence. *Do not confuse a phrase with a sentence.*

How Many Kinds of Phrases Are There?

The English language has six phrases (three of which you have already studied in Chapter 3). You should learn to recognize each of these phrases. Remember that a phrase is never a sentence.

1. **Noun phrase:** a noun plus its modifiers

    large square bricks

2. **Prepositional phrase:** a preposition plus its object and modifiers

    around our neighborhood

3. **Verb phrase:** the main verb plus its helping verbs

    is walking

    could have walked

    should have been walking

The three remaining phrases are formed from **verbs.** However, these phrases do not function as verbs in a sentence. Carefully study how to use them.

4. **Participial phrase:**
   How is the participial phrase formed?

   a. from the present form of a verb ending in *-ing* and any other words necessary to complete the phrase

      running home

      looking very unhappy

   b. from the past form of a verb ending in *-d* or *-ed* if it is a regular verb and any other words necessary to complete the phrase (Note: The past participles for irregular verbs must be memorized.)

      greatly *disappointed*

      told tearfully

How does the participial phrase function? Participial phrases function as **adjectives** in a sentence. By studying the following sentences, you can observe how the above phrases could be used in complete sentences. These phrases will function as adjectives for the noun or pronoun that follows.

Running home, the worker lost her wallet.

Looking very unhappy, she retraced her steps.

Greatly disappointed, she could not find it.

Told tearfully, her story saddened her friends.

A **participle** is formed from a verb but does not always function as a verb.

Present participle: **verb + *-ing***
Past participle: **verb + *-d* or *-ed* (for regular verbs)**

- When a participle is used as a verb, there must be a helping verb with it.

Present participle: **He *was crossing* the bridge.**
Past participle: **He *had crossed* the bridge.**

- Here the participles are used as adjectives modifying nouns.

Present participle: **The *crossing* guard was very observant.**
Past participle: **His *crossed* legs began to ache.**

- When the participle is used in a participial phrase, the entire phrase functions as an adjective.

Present participial phrase: ***Crossing the bridge,* the motorist drove slowly.**
Past participial phrase: ***Crossed out with black ink,* the answers could no longer be read.**

5. **Gerund phrase:** the present form of a verb ending in *-ing,* and any other words necessary to complete the phrase.
   The gerund phrase functions as a noun.

   a. subject of the sentence:

      Running in a marathon is strenuous exercise.

   b. direct object of the sentence:

      I like *running in a marathon.*

6. **Infinitive phrase:** *to* plus the base form of the verb and any other words necessary to complete the phrase

   to run the race

Note: The word *to* can also function as a preposition: I ran *to school.*

EXERCISE 5 Identifying Phrases

Identify each of the underlined phrases in the following sentences.

1. Visiting New York can be a nightmare or a thrill. ____________
2. Many people love to see the Broadway shows. ____________
3. Museums, restaurants, shopping, and the varied night life offer endless possibilities for the tourist. ____________
4. Riding the subways, tourists see another side of New York. ____________
5. My brother Don was pickpocketed on a hot and crowded subway last summer. ____________
6. Coming from the country, he thought the prices were outrageous and the noise and traffic unbearable. ____________
7. Finding a parking spot may have been his most frustrating experience. ____________
8. In addition to these problems, the question of physical safety concerns most tourists. ____________
9. The city has begun projects to clean up the Times Square area. ____________
10. New York's continual fascination is the rich mix of cultures and lifestyles from all over the world. ____________

EXERCISE 6 Identifying Phrases

The following six sentences come from a paragraph by John Steinbeck. Identify each of the underlined phrases.

1. At dawn Cannery Row seems — 1. ____________
   to hang suspended out of time — 2. ____________
   in a silvery light. — 3. ____________
2. The splashing of the waves — 4. ____________
   can be heard. — 5. ____________
3. Flapping their wings, the seagulls — 6. ____________
   come to sit on the roof peaks — 7. ____________
   shoulder to shoulder.
4. Cats drip over the fences and slither — 8. ____________
   like syrup over the ground to look
   for fishheads.
5. Silent early morning dogs parade — 9. ____________
   majestically.
6. No automobiles are running then. — 10. ____________

EXERCISE 7 **Identifying Phrases**

Identify each of the underlined phrases.

1. Exploring the farm, I could see the growing coffee plants. ____________
2. It is a very difficult job to supervise a farm. ____________
3. Growing any kind of crop is a time-consuming procedure. ____________
4. Tended constantly, crops will tend to do well. ____________
5. Appearing very tiny, the coffee plants needed more moisture. ____________
6. The plants should have been watered last week. ____________
7. I walked through different parts of the plantation to see what other problems I could identify. ____________
8. Around the edge of the farm I could see evidence of insect damage to the plants. ____________
9. Their discolored leaves showed signs of infestation. ____________
10. Organized properly, this farm could be a source of both profit and pride. ____________

Understanding the Uses of the Present Participle

The present participle causes a good deal of confusion for students working with the fragment. Because the participle can be used sometimes as a verb, sometimes as an adjective, and sometimes as a noun, you will want to be aware of which of these uses you intend.

EXERCISE 8 **Using the Participle in a Verb Phrase**

Below are five present participles. Use each of them as part of a verb phrase in a sentence you create. An example follows:

Present participle:	sitting
Verb phrase:	is sitting
Sentence:	The couple is sitting on the balcony.

1. building ____________
2. crying ____________
3. traveling ____________
4. writing ____________
5. lacking ____________

EXERCISE 9 Using the Participial Phrase as an Adjective

Each of the following phrases contains a present participle. Use each phrase to compose a sentence in which the phrase functions as an adjective. An example follows:

Present participle: sitting

Participial phrase: sitting on the balcony

Participial phrase used as an adjective phrase in the sentence: Sitting on the balcony, the couple enjoyed the moonlight.

1. Building a house

____

____

2. Crying over the broken vase

____

____

3. Traveling in Mexico

____

____

4. Hastily writing the letter

____

____

5. Lacking the courage to tell the truth

____

____

EXERCISE 10 Using the Participial Phrase as a Noun (Gerund)

Each of the following phrases contains a present participle. Use each phrase to compose a sentence in which the phrase functions as a noun. An example follows:

Present participle: sitting

Participial phrase: sitting on the balcony

Participial phrase used as a noun phrase in a sentence: Sitting on the balcony is relaxing.

1. Building a house

____

____

2. Crying over the broken vase

____

____

3. Traveling in Mexico

____

____

4. Hastily writing the letter

____

____

5. Lacking the courage to tell the truth

____

____

How Do You Make a Complete Sentence from a Fragment That Contains a Participle?

Fragment: he *talking* in his sleep

1. Add a helping verb to the participle:

He *is talking* in his sleep.

2. Change the participle to a different form of the verb:

He *talks* in his sleep.

3. Use the participle as an adjective, being sure to provide a subject and verb for the sentence:

Talking in his sleep, he muttered something about his credit card bills.

4. Use the participle as a noun:

Talking in his sleep revealed his innermost thoughts.

EXERCISE 11 **Correcting the Fragment That Contains a Participle**

Make four complete sentences from each of the following fragments. Use the following model as your guide.

Fragment: using the back stairway

a. He is using the back stairway. (verb phrase)

b. He uses the back stairway. (simple present tense)

c. Using the back stairway, he got away without being seen. (participial phrase used as an adjective)

d. Using the back stairway is not a good idea. (participial phrase used as a noun)

1. moving out of the house

a. ______________________________

b. ______________________________

c. ______________________________

d. ______________________________

2. talking on the telephone

a. ______________________________

b. ______________________________

c. ______________________________

d. ______________________________

3. driving the car down Highway 60

a. ______________________________

b. ______________________________

c. ______________________________

d. ______________________________

EXERCISE 12 **Correcting the Fragment That Contains a Participle**

The following passage is made up of fragments containing participles. Rewrite the passage, creating a complete sentence from each fragment. Use any of the four correction methods discussed above.

I walking through the deserted apartment building. Poking around in piles of junk. The brick walls crumbling. Two children playing in the dismal hallways. Waiting for someone to restore the house to its former glory.

____

____

____

____

____

EXERCISE 13 **Correcting the Fragment That Contains a Participle**

The following passage has four fragments containing participles. Circle the fragments. Then rewrite the passage using complete sentences. Use any of the four correction methods discussed previously.

At last taking the driving test. I felt very nervous. My mother was sitting in the back seat. All my papers sitting on the front seat. The inspector got into the car and sat on my insurance form. He looked rather sour and barely spoke to me. Trying not to hit the curb. I parallel parked surprisingly well. I managed to get through all the maneuvers. Now tensely waiting for the results.

EXERCISE 14 **Correcting Fragments**

Rewrite each fragment so that it is a complete sentence.

1. early morning a time of peace in my neighborhood

2. the gray mist covering up all but the faint outlines of nearby houses

3. the shapes of cars in the streets and driveways

4. to sit and look out the window

5. holding a steaming cup of coffee

6. the only sound the rumbling of a truck

7. passing on the highway a quarter-mile away

8. children all in their beds

9. no barks of dogs

10. in this soft, silent dreamworld

____

____

EXERCISE 15 Correcting Fragments

Each of the following groups of words is a phrase. First, name each phrase. Second, make each phrase into a complete sentence.

1. to earn a living

Name of phrase: ______________________________

Sentence: ______________________________

____

2. from another country

Name of phrase: ______________________________

Sentence: ______________________________

____

3. hanging dangerously

Name of phrase: ______________________________

Sentence: ______________________________

____

4. for children of any age

Name of phrase: ______________________________

Sentence: ______________________________

____

5. making candy

Name of phrase: ______________________________

Sentence: ______________________________

____

6. to sit outside

Name of phrase: ______________________________

Sentence: ______________________________

____

7. at the bottom of the hill

Name of phrase: ______________________________

Sentence: ______________________________

____

8. shaping the dough

Name of phrase: ______

Sentence: ______

______

9. the heavy oven door

Name of phrase: ______

Sentence: ______

______

10. walking slowly

Name of phrase: ______

Sentence: ______

______

EXERCISE 16 Correcting Fragments

Each of the following groups of words is a phrase. First, name each phrase. Second, make each phrase into a complete sentence.

1. two champion boxers

Name of phrase: ______

Sentence: ______

______

2. to watch

Name of phrase: ______

Sentence: ______

______

3. in the ring

Name of phrase: ______

Sentence: ______

______

______

4. hitting each other

Name of phrase: ______

Sentence: ______

______

5. at each sound of the bell

Name of phrase: ______

Sentence: ______

______

6. gratefully supported

Name of phrase: ______________________________

Sentence: ______________________________

____

7. to conduct the fight

Name of phrase: ______________________________

Sentence: ______________________________

____

8. the screaming fans

Name of phrase: ______________________________

Sentence: ______________________________

____

9. by the second round

Name of phrase: ______________________________

Sentence: ______________________________

____

10. knocked unconscious

Name of phrase: ______________________________

Sentence: ______________________________

____

Mastery and Editing Tests

TEST 1

Recognizing and Correcting the Fragment

The following description of people on a dance floor at the Peppermint Lounge appeared in *The New Yorker.* The description is made up entirely of fragments. Rewrite the description making each fragment into a sentence.

Place always jammed. Huge line outside. Portals closely guarded. Finally made it last night, after hour's wait. Exhilarating experience! Feel ten years younger. Hit Peppermint close to midnight, in blue mood. Inside, found pandemonium. Dance floor packed and popping. Was battered by wild swinging of hips and elbows. . . . Garb of twisters seems to run gamut. Some couples in evening dress, others in T shirts and blue jeans. Young. Old. Businessmen. Crew Cuts. Beatniks.

____

____

____

TEST 2

Recognizing and Correcting the Fragment

The following paragraph contains fragments. Read the paragraph and circle each fragment. Then rewrite the paragraph being careful to use only complete sentences.

HINT: 7 fragments

That afternoon the street was full of children. Taking a shower in the rain. Soaping themselves and rushing out into the storm. To wash off the suds. In a few minutes, it was all over. Including the rubdown. The younger children took their showers naked. Teetering on the tips of their toes and squealing to one another. The stately coconut palm in one corner of the patio. Thrashed its branches high over the dripping children bouncing on the cobblestones.

TEST 3 **Student Writing: Recognizing and Correcting the Fragment**

The following paragraph contains fragments. Read the paragraph and circle each fragment. Then rewrite the paragraph being careful to use only complete sentences.

HINT:
6 fragments

We called it our house. It was only one room. With about as much space as a tent. Painted in a pastel color with a red tiled roof. The front window reaching nearly from the sidewalk to the roof. We could look up and down the street. Sitting indoors on the window seat. Our kitchen was a small narrow area. With the brick stove and two benches to serve as shelves. Three steel bars and a short piece of lead pipe from a scrap heap to make a grate.

EXPLORING ONLINE

For more help with sentence fragments, go to the "Sentence Fragments" Section in "Guide to Grammar and Writing" at

http://webster.commnet.edu/grammar/index.htm

When you are ready, take the practice quiz at "Grammar Land,"

http://www.guilford.edu/ASC/grammarland/index.html

WORKING TOGETHER

EXAMINING AN ADVERTISEMENT FOR FRAGMENTS

1. Advertising companies devote a great deal of their time and attention to market research. This research helps the industry target its message to the most likely audience for their product or service. Who is the advertiser in this newspaper ad? Who is the intended audience? What is the product or service being advertised?

2. This Bankers Trust advertisement is similar to many advertisements we see in magazines and newspapers because it is made up of short, snappy constructions that are not always complete sentences. Advertisers write in this way because they want to attract our attention. However, when we write for school or for work, our compositions must be made up of only complete sentences. Review the above advertisement and identify all of the fragments you can find. Then use each fragment to create a complete sentence.

Portfolio Suggestion

Clip magazine or newspaper advertisements that you find appealing or provocative. Save them in your portfolio until you have gathered enough material to write an essay on how advertisers direct their messages to specific audiences.

Online Activity

Read five of the marketing tips on "Real Secrets of Coercive Persuasion" at http://www.maxxmktg.com/toc-index.html, and discuss the methods in small groups. Are the "secrets" ethical? Why or why not?

Chapter 6 Combining Sentences Using the Three Methods of Coordination

Preview

So far you have worked with the simple sentence. If you review some of these sentences (such as the practice sentences on page 60), you will see that writing only simple sentences results in a choppy style and also makes it difficult to express more complicated ideas. You will need to understand the possible ways of combining simple sentences. In this chapter, you will practice the skill of combining sentences using **coordination.**

Key Terms

Clause
Independent clause
Compound sentence
Coordination

Rules for Coordination

- First Method: Use a comma plus a coordinating conjunction.
- Second Method: Use a semicolon, an adverbial conjunction, and a comma.
- Third Method: Use only a semicolon.

Charts

List of coordinating conjunctions
List of adverbial conjunctions
Combining clauses (see also inside front cover)

What Is Coordination?

The following terms with their examples are needed for an understanding of coordination:

- A *clause* is a group of words that has a subject and a verb.

Examples: she spoke
when she spoke

Both of these groups of words have subjects and verbs. Therefore, they are both clauses.

- An *independent clause* is a clause that could stand alone as a simple sentence.

  Example: She spoke.

  Of the two clauses given above, only *she spoke* could be a sentence. *When she spoke* . . . could not stand alone as a sentence because it does not express a complete thought.

- A *compound sentence* results when two or more independent clauses are joined using coordination.

  Example: She spoke, and we listened.

Coordination is the combining of two or more independent clauses (you may think of them as simple sentences) that are related and contain ideas of equal importance. The result is a **compound sentence.**

First Method of Coordination: Use a Comma Plus a Coordinating Conjunction

FIRST METHOD OF COORDINATION

The most common way to form a compound sentence is to combine independent clauses using a comma plus a coordinating conjunction.

Independent Clause (IC)	*Comma and Coordinating Conjunction*	*Independent Clause (IC)*
He spoke forcefully	, and	I felt compelled to listen.

You will need to memorize the list of coordinating conjunctions given below. By doing this now, you will avoid confusion later on when you will be using a different set of conjunctions to combine clauses.

CONNECTORS: COORDINATING CONJUNCTIONS

and	*Used in Pairs:*
but	either . . . or
or, nor	neither . . . nor
for (meaning *because*)	not only . . . but also
yet	
so	

Practice.......... In each of the following compound sentences, draw a single line under the subject and draw two lines under the verb for each independent clause. Then circle both the coordinating conjunction and the comma. An example follows:

The speaker rose to his feet, and the room became quiet.

1. The audience was packed, for this was a man with an international reputation.
2. He could have told about all his successes, but instead he spoke about his disappointments.
3. His words were electric, so the crowd was attentive.
4. I should have brought a tape recorder, or at least I should have taken notes.

Did you find a subject and verb for both independent clauses in each sentence?

COORDINATING CONJUNCTIONS AND THEIR MEANINGS

Now that you understand the structure of a compound sentence, you need to think about the meanings of the different coordinating conjunctions and how they can be used to show the relationship between two ideas, when each idea is given equal importance.

and	to add an idea
nor	to add an idea when the first clause is in the negative
but, yet	to contrast two opposing ideas
for	to introduce a reason
or	to show a choice
so	to introduce a result

EXERCISE 1 **Combining Sentences Using Coordinating Conjunctions**

Each of the following examples contains two simple sentences that could be related by combining them with a coordinating conjunction. Decide what relationship the second sentence has to the first, and then choose the conjunction that makes sense. Then write the new compound sentence. Use the following model as your guide.

Two simple sentences: She broke her arm.

She couldn't play in the finals.

Relationship of second sentence to first: *result*

Conjunction that introduces this meaning: *so*

New compound sentence: She broke her arm, so she couldn't play in the finals.

1. Mr. Watson is kind and patient.
   His brother is sharp and nagging.

   Relationship of second sentence to first: ______________________

   Conjunction that introduces this meaning: ______________________

   New compound sentence: ______________________

   ____

2. The two adults are having great difficulty.
   They are trying to raise a teenager.

   Relationship of second sentence to first: ______________________

   Conjunction that introduces this meaning: ______________________

   New compound sentence: ______________________

   ____

3. Young Michael has no family of his own.
   He feels angry and alone.

   Relationship of second sentence to first: ______________________

   Conjunction that introduces this meaning: ______________________

   New compound sentence: ______________________

   ____

4. Michael hasn't been doing well in school.
   He isn't involved in any activities outside school.

   Relationship of second sentence to first: ______________________

   Conjunction that introduces this meaning: ______________________

   New compound sentence: ______________________

   ____

5. Mr. Watson encouraged Michael to do volunteer work at the hospital.
   This might give Michael the satisfaction of helping other people.

   Relationship of second sentence to first: ______________________

   Conjunction that introduces this meaning: ______________________

   New compound sentence: ______________________

   ____

6. Mr. Watson's brother wanted Michael to spend more time on his homework.
   He also wanted him to get a job to help with expenses.

   Relationship of second sentence to first: ______________________

   Conjunction that introduces this meaning: ______________________

   New compound sentence: ______________________

   ____

7. Michael liked going to the hospital.
He was doing something important.

Relationship of second sentence to first: ______________________

Conjunction that introduces this meaning: ______________________

New compound sentence: ______________________

____

8. He didn't earn any money.
He liked helping people.

Relationship of second sentence to first: ______________________

Conjunction that introduces this meaning: ______________________

New compound sentence: ______________________

____

9. Michael now wants to have a career working in a hospital.
He will have a reason to work harder in school.

Relationship of second sentence to first: ______________________

Conjunction that introduces this meaning: ______________________

New compound sentence: ______________________

____

10. Mr. Watson thinks the hospital work was a good idea.
His brother has to agree.

Relationship of second sentence to first: ______________________

Conjunction that introduces this meaning: ______________________

New compound sentence: ______________________

____

EXERCISE 2 **Combining Sentences Using Coordinating Conjunctions**

For each example, add a second independent clause using the given coordinating conjunction. Be certain that your new sentence makes sense.

1. Winona Ryder is my favorite actor, and ______________________

____

2. I loved the movie *Girl Interrupted,* but ______________________

____

3. Either I go to a movie on Friday night, or ______________________

____

4. I would like to have dinner in a fine restaurant, but ______________________

____

5. The weather this Friday night is supposed to be cold and wet, so ______

____

6. My friend Craig cannot go with me, for ______

7. I can't borrow my friend's car, nor ______

8. Not only are the beverages there too expensive, ______

9. It would be nice to own a video machine, for ______

10. Watching videos at home is cheap, yet ______

EXERCISE 3

Combining Sentences Using Coordinating Conjunctions

For each example, create a second independent clause using the given coordinating conjunction. Be certain that your new sentence makes sense.

1. (but) The two detectives carefully checked the scene for fingerprints ______

2. (and) The safe was open ______

3. (so) There was no sign of forced entry ______

4. (nor) The restaurant owner could not be found ______

5. (for) Suddenly they became interested in one of the tables ______

6. (so) The missing tablecloth could be significant ______

7. (and) One detective looked in the closets ______

8. (or) They might find another clue ______

9. (yet) There were no witnesses ______

10. (or) Either they get a break in the case ______

EXERCISE 4

Composing Compound Sentences

Compose ten of your own compound sentences using the coordinating conjunctions indicated.

1. and ______________________________

____

2. but ______________________________

____

3. or ______________________________

____

4. for (meaning *because*) ______________________________

____

5. yet ______________________________

____

6. so ______________________________

____

7. nor ______________________________

____

8. neither/nor ______________________________

____

9. not only/but also ______________________________

____

10. either/or ______________________________

____

Second Method of Coordination: Use a Semicolon, an Adverbial Conjunction, and a Comma

SECOND METHOD OF COORDINATION		
The second way to form a compound sentence is to combine independent clauses by using a semicolon, an adverbial conjunction, and a comma.		
Independent Clause (IC)	*Semicolon and Adverbial Conjunction and Comma*	*Independent Clause (IC)*
I had worked hard	; therefore,	I expected results.

The conjunctions used for this method are called **adverbial conjunctions** (or conjunctive adverbs). These conjunctions have meanings similar to the common coordinating conjunctions, but they sound more formal than the shorter conjunctions such as *and* or *but.* These connecting words give more emphasis to the clause than the use of coordinating conjunctions.

less emphasis: He was late, and he had the wrong documents.

more emphasis: He was late; furthermore, he had the wrong documents.

Just as you memorized the list of coordinating conjunctions on page 98, you should memorize the following list of adverbial conjunctions.

CONNECTORS: FREQUENTLY USED ADVERBIAL CONJUNCTIONS

Addition (and)	Contrast (but)	Likeness
in addition	however	likewise
also	nevertheless	similarly
besides	nonetheless	
furthermore		
moreover		
Alternative (or)	**Result (so)**	**Emphasis**
instead	accordingly	indeed
on the other hand	hence	in fact
otherwise	therefore	
	thus	
		To Show Time
		meanwhile

Practice.......... In each of the following compound sentences, draw a single line under the subject and draw two lines under the verb for both independent clauses. Then circle the semicolon, adverbial conjunction, and comma. An example follows:

The jet was the fastest way to get there; moreover, it was the most comfortable.

1. The restaurant is always too crowded on Saturdays; nevertheless, it serves the best food in town.
2. The land was not for sale; however, the house could be rented.
3. The lawsuit cost the company several million dollars; consequently, the company went out of business a short time later.
4. The doctor told him to lose weight; furthermore, she instructed him to stop smoking.

EXERCISE 5 **Combining Sentences Using Adverbial Conjunctions**

Combine each pair of sentences below to make a compound sentence. Use a semicolon, an adverbial conjunction, and a comma. Be sure the conjunction you choose makes sense in the sentence. An example follows:

Two simple sentences: Our family would like to purchase a computer.

We must wait until the price comes down.

Compound sentence: Our family would like to purchase a computer; however, we must wait until the price comes down.

1. Most people have preferred to write with a pen or pencil.
The computer is quickly becoming another favorite writing tool. (*Show contrast.*)

____

____

2. Computers provide a powerful way to create and store pieces of writing.
They will become even more important in the future. (*Show result.*)

____

____

3. Some people do not like the idea of using electronics to create words.
The modern typewriter is also an electronic tool. (*Show contrast.*)

____

____

4. Computers have already revolutionized today's offices.
No modern business can afford to be without them. (*Show emphasis.*)

____

____

5. Most schools are using computers in the classroom.
These same schools are helping students prepare for their working careers. (*Add an idea.*)

____

____

6. The prices of many computers are coming down these days.
Owning a computer is a real possibility. (*Show result.*)

____

____

7. Some children know more about computers than many adults.
Some children are teaching the adults. (*Show emphasis.*)

____

____

8. Professional writers have become enthusiastic about the use of computers.
Some writers still use paper and pencil. (*Show contrast.*)

____

____

9. The electronic revolution has just begun.
The nation faces a great challenge to keep up with such a fast-growing revolution. (*Show result.*)

____

____

10. We have many technological aids to writing.
The source for all our ideas is still the human brain. (*Show contrast.*)

____

____

EXERCISE 6 **Combining Sentences Using Adverbial Conjunctions**

Combine each pair of sentences below to make a compound sentence. Use a semicolon, an adverbial conjunction, and a comma. Be sure the conjunction you choose makes sense in the sentence.

1. She doesn't like her job anymore.
She cannot find another job that pays as well.

____

____

2. The office is clean and spacious.
Her coworkers are very kind.

____

____

3. The work is very repetitious and boring.
She finds herself looking at her watch twenty times a day.

____

____

4. Her best qualities are carefulness and industriousness.
Her problem is a need for excitement and challenge.

____

____

5. She long ago learned everything about the job.
She now has no sense of growth or personal satisfaction.

____

____

6. Even some business executives sometimes grow tired of their jobs.
They have invested too much time and energy to change careers.

____

____

7. One solution could be the establishment of regular refresher courses.
A person with years of experience in one field might leave it all behind for something new.

____

____

8. Society would lose the benefit of their expertise.
Individuals would lose the chance to be at the top of their fields.

____

____

9. Some large companies move employees around every few years.
Workers seem energized by new surroundings and people.

____

____

10. Perhaps every ten years we should all switch jobs.
We had better make the best of our present situations. *(Show time.)*

____

____

EXERCISE 7 **Combining Sentences Using Adverbial Conjunctions**

For each example, use the suggested adverbial conjunction and add another independent clause to create a compound sentence that will make sense. Remember to punctuate correctly.

1. (however) We were told not to leave the building ______________
____
2. (therefore) I hadn't done the homework very carefully ______________
____
3. (otherwise) She was happy to find a dress on sale ______________
____
4. (instead) Matthew doesn't like office work ______________
____
5. (in fact) The running shoes are expensive ______________
____
6. (furthermore) The windows were in poor condition ______________
____
7. (consequently) The hurricane struck last night ______________
____

8. (meanwhile) I worked feverishly for days on the report ______________________

____

9. (nevertheless) The young singer was nervous ______________________

____

10. (moreover) The car is the fastest way to get to work ______________________

____

Third Method of Coordination: Use a Semicolon

THIRD METHOD OF COORDINATION

The third and less commonly used way to form a compound sentence is to combine two independent clauses by using only a semicolon.

Independent Clause (IC)	*Semicolon*	*Independent Clause (IC)*
He arrived at ten	;	He left at midnight.

You choose the semicolon if the grammatical structure of each independent clause is similar or if the ideas of each independent clause are very closely related:

1. **The grammatical structure of each independent clause is similar.**

   Example: The women pitched the tents; the men cooked the dinner.

2. **The ideas of both independent clauses are closely related.**

   Example: The woman pitched the tents; they were happy to set up camp before dark.

EXERCISE 8 **Combining Sentences Using the Semicolon**

To create a compound sentence, add a semicolon and an independent clause to each of the following sentences. Both clauses in each compound sentence must have similar grammatical structures or have closely related ideas. Use the following example as your model.

Example:

Simple sentence: The assistant wrote the speech.

Compound sentence: The assistant wrote the speech; the manager delivered it at the national meeting.

1. The apartment was light and airy.

____

____

2. Shoppers were pushing grocery carts down the aisles.

____

____

3. I plan to learn two foreign languages.

____

____

4. I tried to explain.

____

____

5. Many teenagers spend hours listening to rock music.

____

____

EXERCISE 9 Combining Sentences Using the Semicolon

To create a compound sentence, add a semicolon and an independent clause to each of the following sentences. Both clauses in each compound sentence must have similar grammatical structures or have closely related ideas. Use the following example as your model.

Simple sentence: The guests are putting on their coats.

Compound sentence: The guests are putting on their coats; the cab is at the door.

1. The pickup truck was filled with old furniture.

____

____

2. Children played in the streets.

____

____

3. We expected them to understand.

____

____

4. The older men wore ties.

____

____

5. She hoped her friend would soon call.

Mastery and Editing Tests

TEST 1

Combining Sentences Using Coordination

Using each of the five following simple sentences as an independent clause, construct a compound sentence. Use each of the three possible methods at least once.

1. The beach was crowded. (*Add an idea.*)

2. The first apartment had no bedroom. (*Show a contrast.*)

3. January had been bitterly cold. (*Show a result.*)

4. The young model wore dark glasses. (*Introduce a reason.*)

5. The community waited for news. (*Show time.*)

TEST 2

Combining Sentences Using Coordination

Construct a compound sentence by adding another independent clause to each of the five simple sentences (or independent clauses) that follow. Use any one of the three methods of coordination. Do not use the same connector more than once.

1. Babysitters should stay awake.

2. A good babysitter will play with the children.

3. A parent should not expect a babysitter to do cleaning.

4. A list of emergency numbers should be left by the telephone.

____

____

5. A young babysitter should be escorted home.

____

____

TEST 3 **Student Writing: Combining Sentences Using Coordination**

After reading the paragraph, find three places where you could combine two simple sentences into a compound sentence using coordination. Use each of the three methods learned in this chapter.

My children were still in college. My old job with an accounting firm had ended. I needed to earn some money. The thought of a new job made me nervous. What would it be like? Then I saw an ad for openings with Old Navy. I decided to apply. They offered a salary plus a good discount for employees. At the interview, I was the only person over 25. They must have liked me. They hired me the next day! I was sent to their largest downtown location. The first day on the job was scary. I was assigned to a "buddy." The young woman could have been one of my daughters. She explained how to be in control of the stockroom. She showed me how to use a scanner to find out the current price of an item. She advised me on how to keep items on hold for customers. She gave me a feeling of confidence. I never thought I would feel that way. My spirit was willing. I learned a lot. My feet hurt by the end of the first day. I spent my first two months' salary on Old Navy clothes. I had wanted new clothes for a long time. Some of the clothes were for myself. Some of the clothes were for my daughters.

EXPLORING ONLINE FOR ESL STUDENTS

For help with clauses, *Eflweb: The Magazine for Teachers and Students of English (EFL/ESL)* at http://www.eflweb.com

WORKING TOGETHER

SUMMARIZING A CLASS DISCUSSION: WHAT IS A FAIR SALARY?

We often hear people expressing their outrage at the salaries some people earn. For instance, sports figures and entertainers enjoy multimillion-dollar salaries, while day-care employees or postal workers, who have serious responsibilities in their jobs, cannot earn a fraction of that money in their lifetimes.

Discuss this topic in class, making sure that each person has the opportunity to give an opinion. Choose one person to record the important points made during the class discussion. These points should be written on the board even though everyone is responsible to keep his or her own notes. While discussing this complicated topic, keep the following questions in mind:

1. How are salaries set in our society? Give specific examples, based on your own experience and what you have learned from the media.
2. Is today's minimum wage fair? Is it possible for a person to live on a salary based on today's minimum wage?
3. From time to time, there are discussions and disagreements among business and government leaders as to what the minimum wage should be—or even if there should be a minimum wage at all. What should be the minimum wage? In view of what entertainers and sports stars earn, should there be a *maximum* wage law?
4. How should society judge the value of some people's work over the work of others? In what kind of society could everyone receive the same salary, or is that not a desirable goal?

Following the class discussion, each student should use board notes and class notes to write a summary of the discussion. Remember, the summary must include all the important ideas that the discussion generated. If time permits, several students should read their summaries out loud. Did members of the class agree on the major points?

Portfolio Suggestion

Material such as the notes you have just taken from the class discussion can become the prewriting stage for an essay on this topic or a related topic. Save your notes and your summary in case you want to use any of the material for a future essay.

Online Activity

Research current "Labor and Employment" statistics from the Bureau of Labor Statistics at http://www.infoplease.com/ipa/A0854971.html In small groups, discuss the findings. What were the most surprising statistics you found?

Chapter 7 Combining Sentences Using Subordination

Preview

In Chapter 6, when you studied *coordination,* you saw that both clauses in a *compound sentence* carried ideas of equal weight. In this chapter you will study *subordination,* in which two clauses in a *complex sentence* do not carry ideas of equal weight; one idea will be dependent on (or subordinate to) the other. Just as in coordination, subordination uses special connecting words to indicate the relationship of one clause to the other. To use subordination with confidence in your writing, this chapter gives you practice in the following areas:

- Recognizing the difference between an **independent clause** and a **dependent clause**
- Understanding the two types of dependent clauses used in subordination:

  1. The dependent clause beginning with a **subordinating conjunction**
  2. The dependent clause beginning with a **relative pronoun**

Key Terms

Independent clause
Dependent clause
Complex sentence
Subordination

Rules

- Use a comma after an introductory dependent clause.
- Use comma(s) in sentences with relative clauses that are nonessential to the main idea.
- The relative pronoun and its clause must immediately follow the word to which it is related.

Charts

List of subordinating conjunctions
The functions of subordinating conjunctions
List of relative pronouns
Difference between restrictive and nonrestrictive clauses
Patterns of sentences with dependent clauses

What Is Subordination?

Subordination is the method of combining two clauses that contain ideas not equally important. The more important idea is in the **independent clause** and the less important idea is in the **dependent clause.** The result is a **complex sentence.**

In *coordination,* you combined ideas by using certain connecting words called *coordinating conjunctions* and *adverbial conjunctions.* In *subordination,* you combine ideas by using two different sets of connecting words called *subordinating conjunctions* and *relative pronouns.*

What Is the Difference Between an Independent Clause and a Dependent Clause?

An *independent clause* stands alone as a complete thought; it could be a simple sentence.

Independent clause: I drank the water.

A *dependent clause* begins with a connecting word, and even though the clause contains a subject and a verb, it does not stand alone as a complete thought. The idea is not complete.

Dependent clause: When I drank the water, . . .

Before you write your own complex sentences, practice the following exercises to be sure you understand the difference between an independent clause and a dependent clause.

EXERCISE 1 **Identifying Dependent and Independent Clauses**

In the blank to the side of each group of words, write the letters IC if the group of words is an independent clause (a complete thought) or DC if the group of words is a dependent clause (not a complete thought, even though it contains a subject and a verb).

_______________ **1.** before the show began

_______________ **2.** while Betty bought the tickets

_______________ **3.** I played some video games

_______________ **4.** the line at the concession stand was too long

_______________ **5.** seven movies were being shown at this Cineplex

_______________ **6.** unless we sat up close to the screen

_______________ **7.** we had to split up

_______________ **8.** I had time to get myself a box of popcorn

_______________ **9.** because the previews took fifteen minutes

_______________ **10.** when the main feature started

EXERCISE 2 Identifying Dependent and Independent Clauses

In the blank to the side of each group of words, write the letters IC if the group of words is an independent clause (a complete thought) or DC if the group of words is a dependent clause (not a complete thought, even though it contains a subject and a verb).

_______________ **1.** Harry Potter mania has been sweeping the country

_______________ **2.** hundreds of children and parents waited in line

_______________ **3.** because they wanted to purchase a copy of a book entitled *Harry Potter and the Goblet of Fire*

_______________ **4.** as they counted the minutes

_______________ **5.** while some brought cameras to record the event

_______________ **6.** at twelve midnight a guard opened the door

_______________ **7.** after J. K. Rowling enjoyed such extraordinary success with the three previous Harry Potter books

_______________ **8.** the first printing of 3.8 million copies is the largest printing ever

_______________ **9.** many are surprised at the book's length

_______________ **10.** since it is 752 pages

EXERCISE 3 Recognizing Dependent and Independent Clauses

In the blank to the side of each group of words, write the letters IC if the group of words is an independent clause (a complete thought) or DC if the group of words is a dependent clause (not a complete thought, even though it contains a subject and a verb).

_______________ **1.** William Faulkner was a regional writer

_______________ **2.** he was born near Oxford, Mississippi

_______________ **3.** where he lived and died

_______________ **4.** even if he used the dialect of the area

_______________ **5.** some of his books share the same characters and themes

_______________ **6.** because Faulkner devoted many pages to greed, violence, and meanness

_______________ **7.** until the year he died

_______________ **8.** he won the Nobel Prize in 1950

_______________ **9.** when he became one of America's greatest writers

_______________ **10.** although Faulkner departed from the traditional style of prose

Using Subordinating Conjunctions

Study the list of subordinating conjunctions given in the following chart. Notice that when one of these connecting words is used, it usually signals the beginning of a dependent clause. Since different groups of connecting words have different rules for punctuation, you must memorize these connectors in the same way you memorized the list of coordinate conjunctions and adverbial conjunctions in Chapter 6.

Note: Keep in mind that these words *usually* begin a dependent clause. Some of the words such as *after* or *before* could also be used as prepositions to begin a prepositional phrase.

1. ***After the game* is a prepositional phrase.**

   After the game, we all went out for pizza.

   After, in this case, is a preposition. It is not used as a subordinating conjunction to combine clauses. The result is a simple sentence.

2. ***After the game was over* is a dependent clause. (It has a subject and a verb.)**

   After the game was over, we all went out for pizza.

   After, in this case, is a subordinating conjunction. The result is a complex sentence.

CONNECTORS: FREQUENTLY USED SUBORDINATING CONJUNCTIONS

after	if, even if	unless
although	in order that	until
as, as if	provided that	when, whenever
as long as, as though	rather than	where, wherever
because	since	whether
before	so that	while
even though	though	

The following chart contains the subordinating conjunctions grouped according to their meanings. When you use one of these conjunctions, you must be sure that the connection made between the independent clause and the dependent clause is the meaning you intend.

THE FUNCTIONS OF SUBORDINATING CONJUNCTIONS

To introduce a *condition:* — if, even if, as long as, provided that, unless (after a negative independent clause)

I will go *as long as* you go with me.

I won't go *unless* you go with me.

To introduce a *contrast:* — although, even though, though

I will go *even though* you won't go with me.

To introduce a *cause:* — because, since

I will go *because* the meeting is very important.

To show *time:* — after, before, when, whenever, while, until (independent clause is negative)

I will go *whenever* you say.

I won't go *until* you say it is time.

To show *place:* — where, wherever

I will go *wherever* you send me.

To show *purpose:* — in order that, so that

I will go *so that* I can hear the candidate for myself.

When you write a complex sentence, you always have a choice. You can begin with the *independent clause,* or you can begin with the *dependent clause.* The following chart shows the same sentence written both ways.

First Method:	*Independent Clause (IC)*		*Dependent Clause (DC)*
Example:	We can finish our homework		if Barbara leaves.
Second Method:	*Dependent Clause (DC)*	*Comma*	*Independent Clause (IC)*
Example:	If Barbara leaves	,	we can finish our homework.

Notice that only the second version uses a comma; this is because the second version begins with the dependent clause. When a sentence begins with the independent clause, no comma is used. Your ear may help you with this punctuation. Read again the sentence above that begins with a dependent clause. Do you notice that there is a tendency to pause at the end of that dependent clause? Where you pause is the natural place to put a comma.

Practice.......... Use a subordinating conjunction to combine each of the following pairs of sentences. Remember, the independent clause will contain the more important of the two ideas in the sentence.

1. Use the subordinating conjunction *after:*

Joseph went out to celebrate.

He won the wrestling match.

a. Begin with the independent clause:

____

b. Begin with the dependent clause:

____

2. Use the subordinating conjunction *when:*

Carla returned from Venezuela this spring.

The family was excited.

a. Begin with the independent clause:

____

b. Begin with the dependent clause:

____

EXERCISE 4 **Combining Sentences Using Subordination**

Use each of the following subordinating conjunctions to compose a complex sentence. An example has been done for you.

Subordinating conjunction: *after*

Complex sentence: *After* the game was over, we all went out for pizza.

1. as if

____

____

2. before

____

____

3. until

____

____

4. although

____

____

5. because (Begin with the independent clause. Traditional English grammar frowns on beginning a sentence with *because*. Ask your instructor for his or her opinion.)

____

____

EXERCISE 5 Combining Sentences Using Subordination

Use subordination to combine each of the following pairs of sentences. Refer to the list of subordinating conjunctions if necessary.

1. He was eating breakfast.
   The results of the election came over the radio.

   ____

   ____

2. The town council voted against the plan.
   They believed the project was too expensive.

   ____

   ____

3. I will see Maya Angelou tonight.
   She is speaking at the university.

   ____

   ____

4. The worker hoped for a promotion.
   Not one person in the department had received a promotion last year.

   ____

   ____

5. The worker hoped for a promotion.
   He made sure all his work was done accurately and on time.

   ____

   ____

EXERCISE 6 Combining Sentences Using Subordination

On a separate piece of paper, rewrite the following paragraph using subordination to combine sentences wherever you feel it would be effective. Discuss your choices with your classmates. You might want to identify places in the paragraph where coordination might be effective.

At the present time, the United States recycles 10 percent of its trash. It burns another 10 percent. The remaining 80 percent is used as landfill. Over the next few years, many of our landfills will close. They are full. Some of them are leaking toxic wastes. Some parts of the Northeast already truck much of their trash to landfills in Pennsylvania, Ohio, Kentucky, and West Virginia. The garbage continues to pile up. The newspapers print stories about it every week. Trash is not a very glamorous subject. People in every town talk about the problem. One magazine, called *Garbage,* is printed on recycled paper. No town ever before gathered together information about garbage. The town of Lyndhurst, New Jersey, began what is the world's only garbage museum. One landfill now has a restaurant on its premises. Another landfill displays some of its unusual garbage. It displays these objects like trophies. We really want to solve the garbage problem. We must change our "buy more and throw everything old away" mentality.

Using a Relative Pronoun to Create a Complex Sentence

Sentences can often be combined with a relative pronoun.

RELATIVE PRONOUNS	
who whose whom	refer to people
which	refers to things
that	refers to people and/or things

Combining sentences with a relative pronoun:

Two simple sentences:

The researcher had a breakthrough.

He was studying diabetes.

These sentences sound short and choppy. To avoid this choppiness, a writer might want to join these two related ideas by using a relative pronoun.

Correctly combined:

The researcher *who* was studying diabetes had a breakthrough.

Incorrectly combined:

The researcher had a breakthrough *who* was studying diabetes.

Note: The relative pronoun *who* and its clause *who was studying diabetes* refers to *researcher.* The *who* clause must be placed immediately after the word *researcher.* Putting the clause in the wrong place will result in confusion for the reader.

The relative pronoun and its clause must immediately follow the word to which it is related.

A sentence could have more than one relative clause. Study the following sentence, which contains two relative clauses. Notice that each relative pronoun immediately follows the word to which it is related.

> The researcher *who* was studying diabetes had a breakthrough, *which* he reported to the press.

Practice..........

Combining Sentences Using Relative Pronouns

Combine each pair of sentences into one complex sentence by using a relative pronoun. Do not use commas. An example follows:

Simple sentence:	The florist created the flower arrangement.
Simple sentence:	She called us last weekend.
Complex sentence:	The florist *who* called us last weekend created the flower arrangement.

1. The chemistry lab is two hours long.
I attend that chemistry lab.

Combined: ______________________________

____

2. The student assistant is very knowledgeable.
The student assistant is standing by the door.

Combined: ______________________________

____

3. The equipment was purchased last year.
The equipment will make possible some important new research.

Combined: ______________________________

____

How Do You Punctuate Relative Clauses?

Both of the following two sentences have dependent clauses that begin with relative pronouns (*that* and *which*). Punctuating these sentences correctly depends on your understanding of the difference between the function of the two clauses.

> You should never eat fruit *that you haven't washed first.*
>
> Mother's fruit salad, *which she prepares every Sunday,* is delicious.

1. A relative clause is said to be a *restrictive clause* if it is essential to the meaning of the sentence. It does not require commas, and the pronoun *that* is often used.

Example: You should never eat fruit *that you haven't washed first.*

The basic meaning of the sentence is not that you should never eat fruit. The relative clause is necessary to restrict the meaning to only that fruit which is not washed. In this case, the relative clause is essential to the main idea of the sentence.

2. A relative clause is said to be a *nonrestrictive clause* if it is *not* essential to the meaning of the sentence. This clause does require commas to set it off, and the pronoun *which* is often used.

Example: Mother's fruit salad, *which she prepares every Sunday,* is delicious.

In this sentence, the relative clause is not essential to the main idea. In fact, if the clause were omitted, the main idea would not be changed. The commas are used to show that the information contained in the relative clause is not essential to the meaning of the main idea.

DIFFERENCE BETWEEN RESTRICTIVE AND NONRESTRICTIVE CLAUSES

Name of Relative Clause	*Are Commas Required?*	*Information*	*Pronoun Often Used*
Restrictive Clause	no commas	essential	that
Nonrestrictive Clause	commas	not essential	which

Practice.......... **Punctuating Relative Clauses**

Choose whether or not to insert commas in the following sentences. Use the following examples as your models.

The man *who is wearing the Hawaiian shirt* is the bridegroom.

In the sentence above, the bridegroom can only be identified by his Hawaiian shirt. Therefore, the relative clause *who is wearing the Hawaiian shirt* is essential to the meaning. No commas are necessary.

Al, *who was wearing a flannel shirt,* arrived late to the wedding.

In the sentence above, the main idea is that Al was late. What he was wearing is not essential to that main idea. Therefore, commas are needed to set off this nonessential information.

1. The poem that my classmate read in class was very powerful.
2. The teacher who guided our class today is my favorite college professor.
3. Her biology course which met four times a week for two hours each session was extremely demanding.

4. You seldom learn much in courses that are not demanding.
5. My own poetry which has improved over the semester has brought me much satisfaction.

Now you are ready to practice combining your own sentences by using relative pronouns. The following exercises ask you to insert a variety of relative clauses into simple sentences. Pay careful attention to the punctuation.

EXERCISE 7 Combining Sentences Using Relative Pronouns

Add a relative clause to each of the following ten sentences. Use each of the possibilities (*who, whose, whom, which, that*) at least once. Be sure to punctuate correctly. An example has been done for you.

Simple sentence: The leader was barely five feet tall.

Complex sentence: The leader, who was always self-conscious about his height, was barely five feet tall.

1. The president ____________________ asked his advisors for help.
2. His advisors ____________________ met with him in his office.
3. The situation ____________________ was at a critical point.
4. Even his vice president ____________________ appeared visibly alarmed.
5. Stacked on the table, the plans ____________________ looked impressive.
6. The meeting ____________________ began at two o'clock.
7. Every idea ____________________ was examined in great detail.
8. Several maps ____________________ showed the area in question.
9. One advisor ____________________ was vehemently opposed to the plan.
10. Finally the group agreed on a plan of action ____________________

EXERCISE 8 Combining Sentences Using Relative Pronouns

Combine each of the following pairs of sentences by using a relative pronoun.

1. Stress can do a great deal of harm.
   We experience stress every day.

   ____

   ____

2. People often use food to help them cope.
   Some people work long hours at demanding jobs.

   ____

   ____

3. The practice of eating to cope with stress is often automatic.
   The practice of eating to cope often goes back to childhood.

   ____

   ____

4. Foods can actually increase tension.
   People turn to foods in times of stress.

   ____

   ____

5. Sweet foods are actually not energy boosters.
   Sweet foods are popular with people who need a lift.

   ____

   ____

6. Another substance is caffeine.
   People use other substances to get an energy boost.

   ____

   ____

7. One of the biggest mistakes people make is to use alcohol as an aid to achieving calm.
   Alcohol is really a depressant.

   ____

   ____

8. People should eat three light meals a day and two small snacks.
   People want to feel a sense of calm.

   ____

   ____

9. Getting enough protein is also important in keeping an adequate energy level.
   An adequate energy level will get you through the day.

   ____

   ____

10. Most important is to eat regularly so you will avoid binges.
    Binges put on pounds and drain you of energy.

    ____

    ____

EXERCISE 9 Combining Sentences Using Relative Pronouns

Combine each of the following pairs of sentences by using a relative pronoun.

1. Murray, Kentucky, is a Norman Rockwell painting come to life.
   It is in the middle of America's heartland.

   ____

   ____

2. You will soon notice the blue, clean lakes.
   They are bustling with activity.

   ____

   ____

3. The town is surrounded by water.
   This water is perfect for sailing, water-skiing, fishing, and relaxing.

   ____

   ____

4. Scouting enthusiasts enjoy the National Scouting Museum.
   The museum has exhibits for hands-on experience.

   ____

   ____

5. The same museum has a large collection of paintings by Norman Rockwell.
   His work reflects the surrounding landscape.

   ____

   ____

6. Murray State University is an important part of local life.
   The university often has inexpensive concerts and other activities.

   ____

   ____

7. The Homestead is a working farm.
   It shows the way families lived a century ago.

   ____

   ____

8. The Homestead also puts on old-fashioned weddings.
   The wedding parties are made up of actors and actresses in beautiful antique attire.

   ____

   ____

9. People can see herds of buffalo.
People like to see rare sights.

____

____

10. At the end of the day, you can enjoy the local cooking.
Murray is famous for its local cooking.

____

____

PATTERNS OF SENTENCES WITH DEPENDENT CLAUSES

1. **Using Subordinating Conjunctions**
   - A. Introductory dependent clause, independent clause

     When night came, everyone headed for home.
   - B. Independent clause, dependent clause

     Everyone headed for home when night came.
2. **Using Relative Clauses with Pronouns**
   - A. Nonessential dependent clause

     My sister, who is registering, is a biology major.
   - B. Essential dependent clause

     Anyone who registers will be accepted.

Mastery and Editing Tests

TEST 1 **Combining Sentences with a Subordinating Conjunction or a Relative Pronoun**

Combine each of the following pairs of sentences by using either a subordinating conjunction or a relative pronoun.

1. I live alone with two dogs.
They sleep on the braided rug in my bedroom.

____

____

2. The police stood by the door.
They blocked our entrance.

3. She wore high heels.
They made marks in the wooden floor.

4. My aunt is a tyrant.
Her name is Isabel.

5. Her outfit was classy.
Her hair was dirty and unattractive.

6. The interviewer did not smile.
He discovered we had a friend in common.

7. I had a test the next day.
I stayed up to watch a Bette Davis movie.

8. The skater fell and broke his arm.
He was trying to skate backward.

9. For a moment her face glowed with pleasure.
Her face was usually serious.

10. I was thinking.
The toast burned.

TEST 2 Combining Sentences Using Coordination and Subordination

Now you are ready to have some fun! James Thurber, a famous American humorist, wrote a magazine article that included a portrait of a man named Doc Marlowe. Below are some simple sentences made from one of the paragraphs in that article. Review the sentences, and then rewrite the paragraph combining sentences wherever you think such combining would improve the meaning and style. Don't be afraid to change the wording slightly to accommodate the changes you want to make. Although your instructor can provide you with Thurber's original version, there is always more than one way to revise any paragraph.

> I met Doc Marlowe at old Mrs. Willoughby's rooming house. She had been a nurse in our family. I used to go and visit her over weekends sometimes. I was very fond of her. I was about eleven years old then. Doc Marlowe wore scarred leather leggings and a bright-colored bead vest. He said he got the vest from the Indians. He wore a ten-gallon hat with kitchen matches stuck in the band, all the way around. He was about six feet four inches tall, with big shoulders, and a long, drooping mustache. He let his hair grow long, like General Custer's. He had a wonderful collection of Indian relics and six-shooters. He used to tell me stories of his adventures in the Far West. His favorite expressions were "Hay, boy!" and "Hay, boy-gie!" He used these the way some people now use "Hot dog!" or "Doggone!" I thought he was the greatest man I had ever seen. He died. His son came in from New Jersey for the funeral. I found out something. He had never been in the Far West in his life. He had been born in Brooklyn.

Your Version:

____

____

____

____

____

____

____

____

____

____

____

____

____

____

____

TEST 3 Student Writing: Combining Sentences Using Coordination and Subordination

Below is a student paragraph composed of mostly simple sentences. Rewrite the paragraph, combining sentences wherever you think the combining would improve the meaning or style. Don't be afraid to change the wording slightly to accommodate the changes you want to make. Combine clauses using coordination and subordination.

> Every decade seems to have its own sports fad. The fad of the 80s was snowboarding. The fad of the 90s was in-line skating. In-line skates are a cross between ice skates and roller skates. The wheels are in a single row down the middle of the skate. They usually have only one brake. The brake is on the heel of the right foot. This skate was developed to help hockey players practice off the ice. This practice has blossomed into a multi-million dollar industry, sport, and pastime. Look around you. You can probably see in-line skaters. There are stunt teams, racing teams, and skating clubs. "Blading" is its commonly known name. It is a popular form of recreation and exercise. You should be careful when attempting in-line skating. You must wear the proper protection. Protective pads should be worn over the elbows, wrists, and knees in order to cover all joints. The head is particularly vulnerable. A helmet should be worn at all times. You can achieve speeds of 5 to 25 miles per hour or more. Be prepared. You can have a lot of fun using in-line skates.

Your Version:

EXPLORING ONLINE

More information on subordination and a quiz can be found in "Grammarland," http://www.guilford.edu/ASC/grammarland/index.html Also, see http://www.richmond.edu/~writing/wweb/subidea.html

WORKING TOGETHER

MY FIRST JOB

ANITA SANTIAGO

A Hard Lesson, Learned Door to Door

My first job seared me. I was 19 years old in Caracas, Venezuela, reading a local newspaper, when I saw a help-wanted ad for selling encyclopedias.

I loved books, so I thought the job would be perfect. I had all of these idealistic fantasies—picturing myself enlightening children, teaching them about flowering trees and Rome.

At first, I was absolutely lost. They just sent me out into the streets of Caracas to sell books. I planned to go to large apartment buildings. But people there wouldn't open their doors or talk to me. I felt humiliated, embarrassed.

We worked on commission. That was it. I did sell some, but I went through a lot.

I remember this huge gong in the center of the lobby at the office. Whenever you sold a set of books, the jolly little man in a black suit who hired us would hand you a hammer. The gong made a dull, hollow sound. You knew that when you heard the gong, somebody had just sold words.

Of course, I'm still selling words. And that first job taught me respect for how hard people have to work. It made me think analytically, to figure out who and what my target was. You have to walk through unpleasantness to get to success. No one is going to give you life direction; you have to create it for yourself.

The campaigns we create come quite easily to me, because I know this culture. Consider the "Got Milk?" campaign. If you translate the words literally into Spanish you get, "Are you lactating?" Instead, we focus our campaign on grandmothers, or abuelas, who are serving milk to their grandchildren.

I took all the lessons I learned in Caracas to heart. I didn't know it at the time, but I can trace my business success back to those six months.

I've always wanted be my own boss.

NARROWING THE TOPIC THROUGH GROUP DISCUSSION: A PERSON'S FIRST JOB

With a first job, you not only earn your first money, you also learn your earliest lessons about the world of work. In the newspaper article above, the Los Angeles advertising agency owner Anita Santiago tells about her first job in her native city of Caracas, Venezuela. Read the article and then, as a class, discuss the questions that follow. As you exchange ideas on issues raised by the article, you will discover where your own interests lie. Then you will be in a good position to write about an aspect of the topic that appeals to you the most.

Questions for Group Discussion:

1. At first, Anita Santiago thought the job of selling encyclopedias would be perfect because she loved books. What job experiences have members of the class had that turned out differently than expected?

2. When the writer tells us that her company in Caracas "just sent me out into the streets . . . to sell books" without any preparation, she is reporting a common experience people have who are hired for jobs but not given any training. What experiences have students in the class had with jobs that did not properly train the employees? What were the results?
3. Anita Santiago remembers that when someone sold a set of encyclopedias, a gong sounded in the company's office. In jobs that members of the class have had, how were accomplishments recognized or ignored? What were the results of this attention or neglect?
4. Anita Santiago concludes her essay by telling us that, although she did not know it at the time, her business success began with her first job in Caracas. When have you learned something important from experiences you have had, but you only realized it much later in life?
5. The writer admits that when she began her job, she was very idealistic, but at some point, she obviously became more realistic. When have you been idealistic about something in your life, but the circumstances forced you to modify your thinking?
6. Anita Santiago believes, "You have to walk through unpleasantness to get to success." Based on your experience, do you agree or disagree?
7. Who is the hardest-working person you have ever known? Describe what this person did that makes you admire him or her so much.
8. The writer tells us that her Spanish language advertising campaigns "come quite easily" to her because she knows the culture so well. When has something come easily to you because of your background or some other source of special knowledge or expertise?

Online Activity

With a partner, surf the Internet in search of biographies of famous people such as Albert Einstein, Bill Gates, and Princess Diana. Find the first jobs of three famous people; then share your findings with the class. What were the most surprising discoveries?

Chapter 8 Correcting Fragments and Run-Ons

Preview

For many students, revising their writing to eliminate fragments and run-ons is the most important editing skill they can learn in an entire semester. If you find that you have fragments or run-ons in your writing, this chapter will help you:

Identify three types of fragments

1. one or more phrases: A phrase is not a sentence.
2. one or more dependent clauses: A dependent clause is not a sentence.
3. combination of dependent clauses and phrases: A combination of dependent clauses and phrases is not a sentence.

Identify three types of run-ons

1. the *and* run-on: Joining two sentences with an *and* is not correct.
2. the fused run-on: Joining two sentences without any punctuation is not correct.
3. the comma splice: Joining two sentences with a comma is not correct.

Practice revising sentences and paragraphs to eliminate fragments and run-ons.

Key Terms

Fused run-on
Comma splice

Charts

Guide for Correcting Fragments
Guide for Correcting Run-ons

What Is a Fragment?

A **fragment** is a piece of a sentence.

How Many Kinds of Fragments Are There?

1. A fragment could be a phrase:

I sat down. *In the school bus.* Howard, the school bully, came and sat down beside me.

Note: The prepositional phrase *in the school bus* is not a sentence.

2. A fragment could be a dependent clause:

As I sat down. Howard, the school bully, came and sat down beside me.

Note: The dependent clause beginning with the conjunction *as* is not a sentence.

3. A fragment could be a combination of phrases and dependent clauses:

On a recent Friday afternoon, as I sat down in the school bus that was filled with screaming kids.

Note: *On a recent Friday afternoon* is a prepositional phrase; *as I sat down* is a dependent clause; *in the school bus* is a prepositional phrase; *that was filled* is a dependent clause *with screaming kids* is a prepositional phrase. A combination of phrases and dependent clauses is not a sentence.

How Do You Make a Complete Sentence from a Fragment?

GUIDE FOR CORRECTING FRAGMENTS

1. If the fragment is a phrase, revise it by using strategy a or b:

   Example containing a fragment: I sat down. *In the school bus.* Howard, the school bully, came and sat down beside me.

   Strategy a: Decide if the fragment belongs to the sentence before it or to the sentence that comes after it.

   Revision: I sat down in the school bus. Howard, the school bully, came and sat down beside me.

   Strategy b: Make the phrase into a sentence by adding an independent clause.

   Revision: I sat down. Forty screaming kids were *in the school bus.* Howard, the school bully, came and sat down beside me.

2. If the fragment has a combination of dependent clauses and phrases but has no independent clause, revise by using strategy a or b:

   Fragment: On a recent Friday afternoon, as I sat down in the school bus that was filled with forty screaming kids.

   Strategy a: Make one of the dependent clauses into an independent clause by removing the conjunction.

   Revision: On a recent Friday afternoon, I sat down in the school bus that was filled with forty screaming kids.

   Strategy b: Add an independent clause.

   Revision: On a recent Friday afternoon, as I sat down in the school bus that was filled with forty screaming kids, Howard, the school bully, came and sat down beside me.

EXERCISE 1 **Recognizing Fragments**

Identify each of the following examples as one of the following: a) sentence, b) fragment (phrase), c) fragment (dependent clause), d) fragment (combination of phrases and dependent clauses.)

______________ **1.** In the school parking lot.

______________ **2.** While the school bell was still ringing.

______________ **3.** Someone took my bookbag.

______________ **4.** Since so many students were watching.

_______________ **5.** Although someone must have seen the theft when they were waiting for the bus around three o'clock.

_______________ **6.** Even though I asked everyone.

_______________ **7.** Nobody seemed to have noticed.

_______________ **8.** After I reported the theft to the office since I knew I should because it's important to have a document of these kinds of incidents.

_______________ **9.** In case of a later police report.

_______________ **10.** When I got home and called my dad who was really mad at the situation.

EXERCISE 2 **Recognizing and Correcting Fragments**

Revise the ten examples from Exercise 1. Put your revised sentences into paragraph form, correcting all fragments.

____

____

____

____

____

____

____

____

____

____

____

EXERCISE 3 **Student Writing: Recognizing and Correcting Fragments**

Read the following paragraph carefully. Find the five fragments and underline them. Then rewrite the paragraph using the guide for correcting fragments on page 137.

Howard Crane the shortest kid in my entire seventh grade. He was always getting into fights, and he used terrible language. If you've ever known a bully. Howard was a prime example. One Friday afternoon as we sat in the school bus on our way home. Howard began taunting my younger brother. Since our parents had told us to ignore Howard, so my brother just looked straight ahead. Saying nothing. I was growing angrier and angrier. I had to do something.

What Is a Run-On?

In conversation, as we relate an event that involves a series of connected actions, we may string together our thoughts as if they were just one long thought. Here is what one person who was involved in a car accident reported to a police officer who arrived on the scene:

> I was driving along on Route 80 and my daughter asked my wife to change the radio station and my wife told my daughter to do it herself so she unhooked her seatbelt and reached over from the back seat to change the station but then her brother tickled her and she lost her balance and fell on the gear shift and that moved the gear into neutral so the car instantly lost power and that's when we were hit by the van behind us.

The man relating the accident ran each part of this entire event together without any separation. As a result, the account appears as a **run-on sentence.** In formal writing, a run-on sentence is considered a serious error.

> **Run-ons** are independent clauses that have been combined incorrectly.

How Many Kinds of Run-Ons Are There?

Run-on sentences occur when the writer is either unable to recognize where one complete idea has ended and another idea begins or is not sure of the standard ways of connecting the ideas. Certain marks of punctuation show where two clauses join. Other punctuation signifies the end of the thought. One of three mistakes is commonly made:

1. ***The "and" run-on:*** Two or more independent clauses are connected with a coordinating conjunction but there is no punctuation.

   incorrect: I met Charlyce and we soon became friends.

2. ***The fused run-on:*** Two or more independent clauses are run together without any punctuation.

   incorrect: I met Charlyce we soon became friends.

3. ***The comma splice:*** Two or more independent clauses are run together with only a comma.

   incorrect: I met Charlyce, we soon became friends.

How Do You Make a Complete Sentence from a Run-On?

GUIDE FOR CORRECTING RUN-ONS

1. Make two sentences with end punctuation.

   correct: I met Charlyce. We soon became friends.

2. Make a compound sentence using one of the three methods of coordination.

   correct: I met Charlyce, and we soon became friends.
   I met Charlyce; furthermore, we soon became friends.
   I met Charlyce; we soon became friends.

3. Make a complex sentence using subordination.

   correct: Soon after I met Charlyce, we became friends.
   Charlyce and I became friends soon after we met.

Note: See inside cover for quick review of coordination and subordination.

EXERCISE 4 **Recognizing and Correcting Run-Ons**

Here is the same run-on sentence that you read earlier in this chapter. Rewrite the report correctly. Put a period at the end of each complete thought. You may have to omit some of the words that loosely connect the ideas, or you may want to use coordination and subordination. Remember to make each new sentence begin with a capital letter.

> I was driving along on Route 80 and my daughter asked my wife to change the radio station and my wife told my daughter to do it herself so she unhooked her seatbelt and reached over from the back seat to change the station but then her brother tickled her and she lost her balance and fell on the gear shift and that moved the gear into neutral so the car instantly lost power and that's when we were hit by the van behind us.

EXERCISE 5 **Recognizing and Correcting Run-Ons**

The following story is written as one sentence. Rewrite the story correctly. Put a period at the end of each complete thought. You may have to omit some of the words that loosely connect the ideas, or you may want to use coordination and subordination. Remember to make each new sentence begin with a capital letter.

> My best friend is accident-prone if you knew her you'd know that she's always limping, having to write with her left hand or wearing a bandage on her head or ankle, like last week for example she was walking down the street minding her own business when a shingle from someone's roof hit her on the head and she had to go to the emergency room for stitches, then this week one of her fingers is purple because someone slammed the car door on her hand sometimes I think it might be better if I didn't spend too much time with her you know her bad luck might be catching!

EXERCISE 6 **Student Writing: Recognizing and Correcting Run-Ons**

The following story is written as one sentence. Rewrite the story correctly. Put a period at the end of each complete thought. You may have to omit some of the words that loosely connect the ideas, or you may want to use coordination and subordination. Remember to make each new sentence begin with a capital letter.

> One morning, not too early, I will rise and slip downstairs to brew the coffee and no baby will wake me up and no alarm clock will rattle my nerves and

the weather will be so warm that I will not have to put on my coat and hat to go out for the paper there will be no rush I will go to the refrigerator and take out eggs and sausage the bathroom will be free so I will be able to take a shower with no one knocking on the door and I will not have to run up and down the stairs first looking for someone's shoes and then for someone's car keys I will leisurely fix my hair and pick out a lovely suit to wear the phone might ring and it will be a friend who would like to have lunch and share the afternoon with me money will be no problem maybe we'll see a movie or drive to the nearby city to visit a museum and the countryside will be beautiful and unspoiled my life will seem fresh and promising.

____

____

____

____

____

____

____

____

____

____

____

____

Mastery and Editing Tests

TEST 1

Editing for Fragments and Run-ons

Identify each numbered group of words as S (sentence), F (fragment), or R (run-on). Then rewrite the paragraph correcting any fragments or run-ons.

[1]In laboratory experiments, scientists have discovered a diet. [2]Which extends the life of their animals up to 50 percent or more. [3]This diet prevents heart disease, diabetes, and kidney failure and it greatly retards all types of cancer. [4]Even slowing down the aging process of cataracts, gray hair, and feebleness. [5]Staying on this diet keeps the mind flexible and the body active to an almost biblical old age. [6]These rats, fish, and worms stay very slim, they are fed a diet of necessary vitamins and nutrients, but only 65 percent of the calories of the animal's normal diet. [7]Every creature fed this restricted diet has had a greatly extended life span. [8]The results of caloric restriction are spectacular. [9]Says Richard Weindruch, a gerontologist at the National Institute on Aging in Bethesda, Maryland. [10]Gerontologists have tried many things to extend life but this is the only experiment that works every time in the lab. [11]Animals who received enough protein, vitamins, and minerals to prevent malnutrition. [12]They survived to a grand old age and it does not seem to matter whether they eat a diet composed largely of fats or carbohydrates. [13]Researchers warn against people undertaking this diet too hastily, it is very easy to become malnourished. [14]Dr. Roy Walford is a pioneer in the field from the University of California he believes humans could live to an extraordinarily advanced age. [15]If they were to limit their caloric intake.

1. ____________	**5.** ____________	**9.** ____________	**13.** ____________
2. ____________	**6.** ____________	**10.** ____________	**14.** ____________
3. ____________	**7.** ____________	**11.** ____________	**15.** ____________
4. ____________	**8.** ____________	**12.** ____________	

Your Version:

____

____

____

____

____

____

____

____

____

____

____

____

____

____

____

TEST 2 Editing for Fragments and Run-ons

Identify each numbered group of words as S (sentence), F (fragment), or R (run-on). Then rewrite the paragraph correcting any fragments or run-ons.

[1]Last spring Geraldo Rivera presented a daytime show on laser peels and viewers watched a procedure that took less than two minutes. [2]In front of the television cameras and the live audience. [3]Rivera had the wrinkles zapped away from around his eyes. [4]These high-energy laser beams which are said to be quick, painless, safe, and without scarring. [5]Adding this new technology to face-lifts, dermabrasion, collagen injections, and chemical peels! [6]More than 30,000 laser peels have been performed since 1992. [7]Lasers were first used by dermatologists to remove port wine stains in the 1970s. [8]For many people, this means they can now look as young as they feel but the healing process can be painful and messy. [9]Most physicians believe this is a much more precise method of rejuvenating the skin. [10]Because it's so much more accurate, so much more predictable, and so much safer than other methods. [11]One note of caution. [12]Any physician can buy the equipment with little or no training therefore you should always check out the doctor's experience. [13]A practitioner without experience could zap too deeply and cause tissue damage. [14]Following a laser zap, you must scrupulously avoid the sun for several months, afterwards always wear a sunscreen. [15]One bad point. [16]Laser technology is expensive a full-face laser peel costs from $2,000 to $6,000. [17]Sorry, no long-term scientific studies to prove their safety.

1. ____________ 6. ____________ 11. ____________ 16. ____________

2. ____________ 7. ____________ 12. ____________ 17. ____________

3. ____________ 8. ____________ 13. ____________

4. ____________ 9. ____________ 14. ____________

5. ____________ 10. ____________ 15. ____________

Your Version:

____

____

____

____

____

____

____

____

____

____

____

____

____

____

____

____

TEST 3 Student Writing: Editing for Fragments and Run-ons

Identify each numbered group of words as S (sentence), F (fragment), or R (run-on). Then rewrite the paragraph correcting any fragments or run-ons.

[1]Many parents are worrying that their children are not reading enough others worry about what the children are reading. [2]In fact, most children are not reading anything at all, houses are filled with the sounds from CD players, television sets, and video games. [3]If children never see their parents reading or going to the library. [4]They will most likely not develop good reading habits. [5]Children who see their parents reading magazines, books, and newspapers. [6]These children will grow up thinking that reading is a natural part of daily life. [7]Parents can do many things to encourage reading. [8]Like accompanying them to the library and helping them pick out books. [9]Parents can encourage children to memorize poetry and they can show them how to read maps when they travel. [10]Since most kids like children's magazines with pictures and short texts on current topics. [11]Parents could subscribe to these magazines for their children. [12]Reading stories out loud as a family with everybody participating after a day when all the family members have been at work and school. [13]That is the best idea of all.

1. ____________________ **6.** ____________________ **11.** ____________________

2. ____________________ **7.** ____________________ **12.** ____________________

3. ____________________ **8.** ____________________ **13.** ____________________

4. ____________________ **9.** ____________________

5. ____________________ **10.** ____________________

Your Version:

____

____

____

____

____

____

____

____

____

____

____

____

____

EXPLORING ONLINE

Visit http://www.richmond.edu/~writing/wweb/runon.html for more help with run-ons.

WORKING TOGETHER

BRAINSTORMING IN GROUPS: MEETING THE RIGHT PERSON

How can a single person meet that "special someone?" Many single people want to establish friendships that could lead to something more serious, including possible marriage. However, these people are looking for dignified, appropriate ways to meet others. What do you think are the best approaches people should use in such a situation?

Brainstorming is usually an important first part of the writing process, a step that takes place before you actually begin to write. If you are fortunate enough to be able to brainstorm with a group of other people, you are very likely to find yourself inspired by several new and different ideas. Brainstorming with others is also very helpful because it stimulates each member of the group to evaluate his or her own ideas on a given topic. Use the brainstorming approach to develop ideas for the present topic.

Divide into groups to discuss the topic. Choose one person from each group to set down the most important points made. This listing is important for the students who will want to review those points later on, and also for the teacher who will want to evaluate each group's effort. After about 20 minutes of discussion, each member of the class should put his or her ideas in an arrangement that lists them in order of increasing importance. Each list will now become the plan each student will use to write about the topic.

At the end of class, stop what you are doing to come together and share reactions on the brainstorming experience. How well did each group develop a list of important points? How effective was each person's ordered list?

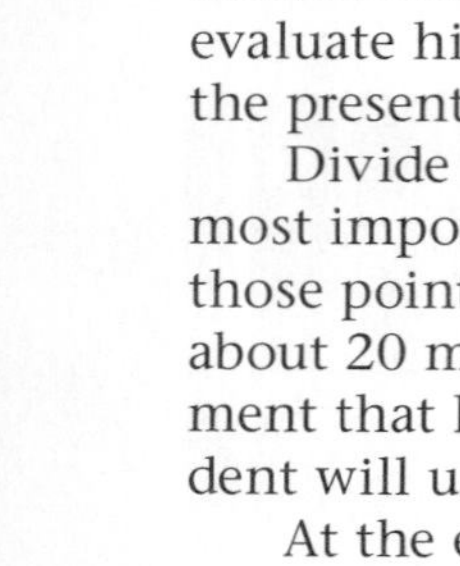

Online Activity

The Internet has become famous (as in the movie *You've Got Mail*), and in some cases infamous, for matchmaking. In small groups, brainstorm the advantages and disadvantages of net romance.

Chapter 9 Making Sentence Parts Work Together: Pronouns

Preview

Sentence parts work together to make meaning clear. In Chapter 4, you practiced making subjects and verbs agree (showing singular or plural). In this chapter, you will focus on the two major issues for using pronouns correctly:

- Pronouns and case
  Comparisons
  Compound structures
  Who/whom constructions
- Pronoun-antecedent agreement
  Agreement in number
  Agreement in person
  No missing, ambiguous, or repetitious antecedents

Key Terms

Case
Antecedent

Rules

- A pronoun must agree in *number* with any other word to which it refers.
- A pronoun must agree with its antecedent in *person*.
- The antecedent of a pronoun should not be *missing, ambiguous,* or *repetitious*.

Chart

Pronouns and case

Pronouns and Case

Most of us generally use the correct pronouns when we speak or write, but we must be careful how we use some special pronoun forms.

Case refers to the way some nouns or pronouns change their forms depending on how they are used in a sentence.

Notice in the following examples how the pronoun *I* changes form when it changes function:

Subject: *I* needed a car.

Object: Dad bought a used Honda for *me*.

Possessive: *My* commute to work will now be easier.

The title to the car is *mine*.

Reflexive: I've assumed all responsibility for the car *myself*.

The chart below is a helpful reference of pronoun forms.

PRONOUNS AND CASE

	Pronouns Used as Subjects	*Pronouns Used as Objects*	*Pronouns Used as Possessives*	*Pronouns Used as Reflexives*
Singular	I you he she it	me you him her it	my, mine you, yours his hers its	myself yourself himself herself itself
Plural	we you they	us you them	our, ours your, yours their, theirs	ourselves yourselves themselves
Singular or Plural	who	whom	whose	

Note: • There are no such forms as *hisself* or *theirselves*.
• Do not confuse *whose* with *who's* or *its* with *it's* (who's = who is; it's = it is).

Three types of construction involving pronouns require special attention:

Comparisons
Compound constructions
Use of who/whom

• Comparisons

In a comparison, picking the correct pronoun is easier if you complete the comparison.

That swimmer is much stronger than (he, him, his).

That swimmer is much stronger than (he, him, his) is.

The second sentence shows that *he* is the correct form because the pronoun is used as the subject for the clause *he is.*

Practice.......... Circle the correct pronoun in each of the sentences below.

1. My brother did not enjoy the vacation as much as (I, me, mine).

   Hint: Try completing the comparison:

   My brother did not enjoy the vacation as much as (I, me, mine) did.

2. The altitude in Quito affected my brother more than (I, me).

   Hint: Try completing the comparison:

   The altitude in Quito affected my brother more than it affected (I, me).

EXERCISE 1 **Choosing the Correct Pronoun in Comparisons**

Circle the correct pronoun in each of the sentences below.

1. I am as deeply involved in this report as (they, them).
2. Karen's research has been more extensive than (we, us, our, ours).
3. She studied the final report less than (I, me).
4. Unfortunately, the competing report was just as attractive as (we, us, our, ours).
5. Their company had acquired fewer clients than (we, us).
6. Our policies are much better than (them, theirs).
7. The contract was awarded to us rather than to (they, them).
8. The results will matter more to the client than to (she, her).
9. I will celebrate much longer tonight than (she, her).
10. An immediate vacation is more important for me than for (he, him).

• Compound Constructions

When you have a compound subject or a compound object, choosing the correct pronoun is easier if you read the sentence without one of the pronouns.

Today, you and (I, me) should buy the tickets.

Today, (I, me) should buy the tickets.

In the second sentence, it is easier to hear that *I* is correct since it is the subject of the verb phrase *should buy.*

Practice.......... Circle the correct pronoun in each of the sentences below.

1. Developers and (he, him) hope to renovate that building
   Hint: Try the sentence without *Developers.*

   (He, Him) hopes to renovate that building.

2. They spoke to the construction company and (I, me).
   Hint: Try the sentence without *construction company.*

   They spoke to (I, me).

EXERCISE 2 **Choosing the Correct Pronoun in Compound Constructions**

In each of the following sentences, circle the correct pronoun.

1. Sara called from Washington to speak with Leslie and (I, me).
2. Both Damon and (I, me) keep a daily journal.
3. Today we received the letters from you and (she, her).
4. Among Sasha, Jerry, and (I, me), Sasha is the best writer.
5. Karen and (she, her) are hoping for good grades this term.
6. Because Martin and (she, her) decided to go, the group could no longer fit into one car.
7. (He, Him) and (I, me) handed our journals in to the professor.
8. When we were sick, my aunt ran lots of errands for Kathleen and (I, me).
9. The dinner gave Mike and (he, him) the chance to be together.
10. The two men, (he, him) and Mike, were brothers.

• Who/Whom Constructions

The use of these two pronouns is at times confusing to most of us. When in doubt, you need to consider if the pronoun is used in a subject position or in an object position.

Subject position: *Who* is going with you to the performance?

Object position: *Whom* did the director choose for the solo?

To whom did the director give the solo?

If there is more than one clause in the sentence, you will find it helpful to cross out everything except the clause with the *who/whom.* Then you can focus on how *who/whom* functions in its own clause.

Practice..........

1. She is the friend (who, whom) I treasured.

   look at: (who, whom) I treasured

2. She is the friend (who, whom) I knew could be trusted.

   look at: (who, whom) could be trusted

3. I don't know (who, whom) should do the work.
4. That is the girl (who, whom) I hope will win.

EXERCISE 3 **Choosing the Correct Pronoun Using Who/Whom**
Circle the correct pronoun in each of the sentences below.

1. (Who, Whom) is singing at the choral concert tonight?
2. (Whoever, Whomever) sold us the tickets gave us the best seats in the house.
3. From (who, whom) can we obtain a program?
4. (Who, Whom) of these singers can you tell needs more practice?
5. The director gave the solo parts to (whoever, whomever) was qualified.
6. Our eyes were glued on (whoever, whomever) was singing the lead.
7. (Who's, Whose) solo did you think was performed with the most musicality?
8. (Whoever, Whomever) played the piano accompaniment did a wonderful job.
9. Just between the two of us, (who, whom) do you believe is the more musically inclined?
10. (Who's, Whose) music was left on the piano?

In order to avoid confusion, remember you can always cross out other clauses in the sentence so you can concentrate on the clause in question.

~~I don't know~~ (who, whom) ~~I think~~ should do the work.

~~That is the girl~~ (who, whom) ~~I believe~~ was dancing.

Practice all three constructions with pronouns and case in the next two exercises.

EXERCISE 4 **Choosing Correct Pronoun Forms**
Circle the correct pronoun in each of the sentences below.

1. Matthew and (she, her) presented the project today.
2. Between you and (I, me), I think it was outstanding.
3. Their visual materials will help (whoever, whomever) will study the project later.
4. He is usually a better speaker than (she, her).
5. (Whoever, Whomever) heard them agreed that it was an impressive presentation.
6. (Who, Whom) do you think made the best points?
7. I am not as deeply involved in my project as (they, them).
8. Their research was much more detailed than (us, our, ours).
9. The professor gave both Carolyn and (he, him) A's.
10. My partner and (I, me) will have to work harder to reach this standard.

EXERCISE 5 **Student Writing: Choosing Correct Pronoun Forms**

Circle each correct pronoun in the following paragraph.

When my mother and (I, me) decided to care for my very ill father at home, some of our friends objected. My sister and (they, them) said we would be exhausted and unable to handle the stress. To (who, whom) could we go for help in the middle of the night? My father, (who, whom) we believed would be happier at home, had been our first consideration. Of course, we would have benefited if my mother or (I, me) had been a nurse. However, we did have a visiting nurse available at times. We were more confident than (they, them) that we could handle the situation.

Pronoun-Antecedent Agreement

When you use a pronoun in your writing, that pronoun must refer to a word used previously in the text. This previously used word is called the ***antecedent.***

An **antecedent** is a word (or words) that is replaced by a pronoun later in a piece of writing.

The *pool* was crowded. *It* was a popular place on a hot summer day.

In this example, the pronoun *It* replaces the word *pool. Pool,* in this case, is referred to as the *antecedent* of the pronoun *it.*

The next three pronoun-related issues give writers a great deal of trouble. Study the discussion of each issue and carefully complete the related exercises.

- **A pronoun must agree in *number* (singular or plural) with any other word to which it refers.**

  The following sentence contains a pronoun-antecedent disagreement in **number.**

  Lacks agreement: *Everyone* worked on *their* final draft.

  The problem in this sentence is that *everyone* is a singular word, but *their* is a plural pronoun. Even though you may hear people use the plural pronoun *their* to refer to a singular subject, this usage is not correct in formal writing. Here are two other approaches writers often take:

  Sexist construction: *Everyone* worked on *his* final draft.

  Awkward construction: *Everyone* worked on *his or her* final draft.

  This last form is technically correct, but the continual use of the construction *his or her* will soon begin to sound awkward and repetitious. Often, the best solution to any of these three situations is to revise the construction so that the pronoun and the antecedent are plural:

Pronouns agree: *All* the students worked on *their* final drafts.

Another way around the problem is to change the pronoun to an article:

Avoids the pronoun: Everyone worked on *the* final drafts.

Another problem with pronoun-antecedent agreement in *number* occurs when a demonstrative pronoun *(this, that, these, those)* is used with a noun. In such a case, the pronoun must agree with the noun it modifies:

Singular: this kind, that type

Incorrect: *These kind* of shoes hurt my feet.

Correct: *This kind* of shoe hurts my feet.

Plural: these kinds, those types

Incorrect: *Those type* of cars always need oil.

Correct: *Those types* of cars always need oil.

Practice.......... Rewrite each of the following sentences so that the pronoun agrees with its antecedent in *number.*

1. Everyone should bring their suggestions to the meeting.

____

____

2. This sorts of clothes are popular now.

____

____

3. No one knew what they were doing.

____

____

4. If the bird watchers hope to see anything, one must get up early.

____

____

5. These type of book appeals to me.

____

____

- **Pronouns must also agree with their antecedents in *person*.** The following sentence contains a pronoun-antecedent disagreement in **person:**

Lacks agreement: When mountain climbing, *one* must maintain *your* concentration at all times.

When you construct a piece of writing, you choose a "person" as the voice in that piece of writing. Your instructor may advise you which personal pronoun to use for a particular writing assignment. Whatever guidelines you are given, the important point is to be consistent in using that person.

Below are some examples in which the pronouns agree:

When mountain climbing, *you* must maintain *your* concentration at all times.

When mountain climbing, *I* must maintain *my* concentration at all times.

When mountain climbing, *we* must maintain *our* concentration at all times.

Practice.......... Correct each of the following sentences so that the pronoun agrees with its *antecedent in person.*

1. I enjoy math exams because you can show what you know.
2. When I took geometry, we discovered that frequent review of past assignments helped make the course seem easy.
3. People always need to practice your skills in order not to forget them.
4. Math games can be fun for one if you have a spirit of curiosity.
5. When studying math, you must remember that we have to "use it or lose it."

- **The antecedent of a pronoun should not be *missing, ambiguous,* or *repetitious.***

a. **Missing antecedent:**

In Florida, *they* have many beautifully developed retirement areas.

Acceptable revision:

Florida has many beautifully developed retirement areas.

Explanation: In the first sentence, we do not know to whom *they* refers. If the text has not told us that *they* refers to the Florida government, real estate developers, or some other group, then we must say that the antecedent is *missing.* The sentence should be rewritten in order to avoid *they.*

b. **Ambiguous antecedent:**

Margaret told Lin that *she* needed to earn one thousand dollars during the summer.

Acceptable revision:

Margaret said that Lin needed to earn one thousand dollars during the summer.

Explanation: In the first example, *she* could refer to either Margaret or Lin. The sentence should be revised in a way that will avoid this confusion.

c. **Repetitious pronoun and antecedent:**

The newspaper article, *it* said that Earth Day, 1990, reestablished people's commitment to the earth.

Possible revision:

The newspaper article said that Earth Day, 1990, reestablished people's commitment to the earth.

Explanation: The subject should be either *article,* or if there is already an antecedent, *it.* Using both the noun and the pronoun results in needless repetition.

Practice..........

Rewrite the following sentences so that the antecedents are not *missing, ambiguous,* or *repetitious.*

1. The biologist asked the director to bring back his microscope.

____

____

2. In the report, it says that the number of science and engineering students seeking doctoral degrees has fallen 50 percent since the mid-sixties.

____

____

3. At the laboratory, they said the research had run into serious difficulties.

____

____

4. The testing equipment was accidentally dropped onto the aquarium, and it was badly damaged.

____

____

5. I don't watch the 10 o'clock news anymore because they have become too slick.

____

____

EXERCISE 6 Making Pronouns and Antecedents Agree

The following sentences contain errors with pronouns. Edit each sentence so that pronouns agree with their antecedents, and so that there are no missing, ambiguous, or repetitious antecedents in the sentence.

1. His father mailed him his high school yearbook.

2. No one wants their income reduced.

3. When a company fails to update its equipment, they often pay a price in the long run.

4. The woman today has many more options open to them than ever before.

5. Everybody knows their own strengths best.

6. Each of the workers anticipates their summer vacation.

7. If the campers want to eat quickly, each one should help themselves.

8. These sort of bathing suits look ridiculous on me.

9. On the application, it says you must pay a registration fee of 35 dollars.

10. The doctor said that those type of diseases are rare here.

EXERCISE 7 **Making Pronouns and Antecedents Agree**

Each of the following sentences may contain an error with pronouns. Edit each sentence so that pronouns agree with their antecedents, and so that there are no missing, ambiguous or repetitious antecedents in the sentence. If a sentence is correct, mark a C on the line provided.

1. The teacher suggested to the parent that he might have been too busy to have noticed the child's unhappiness.

____

____

2. The county submitted their proposal for the bridge repairs.

____

____

3. We all rushed to our cars because you had to wait for the thunderstorm to stop.

____

____

4. A young person does not receive enough advice on how they should choose their career.

____

____

5. These type of watches are very popular.

____

____

6. People were rescued from our homes.

____

____

7. No one brought their books today.

____

____

8. The college it is holding homecoming weekend on October 5.

____

____

9. They call it the "Hoosier" state.

____

____

10. Anyone who fails the final will be unlikely to get his or her diploma.

____

____

EXERCISE 8

Making Pronouns and Antecedents Agree

Each of the following sentences contains an error in pronoun-antecedent agreement. Edit each sentence so that pronouns agree with their antecedents, and so that there are no missing, ambiguous, or repetitious antecedents.

1. Everyone should go to a live concert once in their life.
2. Last month, Cynthia invited Vermell to a Tracy Chapman concert because she loved her music.
3. They said the tickets would be sold out quickly.
4. If you get up early enough, a person has a good chance to buy decent seats.
5. These types of events are very expensive.
6. The night of the concert, the arena it was jammed with young people.
7. The security guards told the fans that they must be careful about pushing and shoving.
8. People have been trampled in these sort of crowds.
9. Finally, you could hear the music begin; our long wait for tickets had been worth the trouble.
10. Her songs have positive lyrics; that's why I like it so much.

Mastery and Editing Tests

TEST 1

Using Pronouns Correctly

Each of the following sentences contains pronouns. Edit each sentence to correct any errors in pronoun case, any pronouns that do not agree with their antecedents, or any missing, ambiguous, or repetitious antecedents. If the sentence does not contain an error, mark it with a "C."

1. One should plant flowers if you like improving your front yard.

____

____

2. His friend sent him his favorite coffee.

____

____

3. In the book, it said that fish oil is good to take for arthritis.

____

____

4. My mom and me have a great day planned on Saturday.

____

____

5. Whom do you think is coming to our art show?

6. They ought to fix these potholes outside our school.

7. The customer and she agreed on a price.

8. That athlete is much faster than me.

9. These sorts of chairs tend to be uncomfortable.

10. He did all the work on the house hisself.

TEST 2 Using Pronouns Correctly

Each of the following sentences contains pronouns. Edit each sentence to correct any errors in pronoun case, any pronouns that lack agreement with their antecedents, or any missing, ambiguous, or repetitious antecedents. If the sentence does not contain an error, mark it with a "C."

1. In the ad it said you should send a resume.

2. To who do you think we should send these bulletins?

3. A pharmacist must triple check every order he fills.

4. Just between you and I, the firm is in financial trouble.

5. Those lessons helped Karen more than him.

6. We always buy these type of coats.

7. The bank warns people that you should always keep a careful balance of your checkbooks.

8. Janelle's sister brought her plan to the council.

9. The assignments they are going to require library research.

10. Everyone did his part.

TEST 3 Student Writing: Using Pronouns Correctly

Each of the following sentences contains an error with pronoun usage. Rewrite the paragraph in order to correct all the errors.

> Nobody wants their taxes increased. Last Tuesday, the tax assessor sent my father his statement. The letter reported a huge tax increase, so it was a shock. In the letter, they said the tax must be paid within five days. If one is not wealthy, you can have a hard time paying such a bill on time. My father, who is generally calm in these kind of situations, was furious. This hardworking man, he marched to the town hall. He gave him a piece of his mind. They had nothing to say. One of them shook their head sympathetically, but he still had to pay the bill.

EXPLORING ONLINE

For more help, go to the "Pronoun and Pronoun Antecedent" section of http://webster.commnet.edu/grammar/index.htm

WORKING TOGETHER

Princess Must Face Immigration Charges

SAN DIEGO, July 17 (AP)—A princess who fled Bahrain with fake documents to marry an American marine must face charges of illegally entering the United States, an immigration judge said today.

The judge, Ignacio Fernandez, refused to dismiss the charges, a ruling that prevents the princess, Meriam Al Khalifa, from applying for permanent residency without seeking political asylum.

Ms. Al Khalifa, who is 19, plans to apply for asylum on the ground that she faces extreme persecution for marrying a non-Muslim if she returns to Bahrain, her lawyer said. She has up to a year to apply for political asylum.

A spokesman for the Bahraini Embassy in Washington said that the princess' family was eager for her to return and that she would not face persecution.

The hearing was closed to the public, but her lawyer provided an account of the ruling.

Ms. Al Khalifa lives with her husband, Lance Cpl. Jason Johnson, on Camp Pendleton, a Marine base 40 miles north of San Diego. They met last year in the Bahraini capital of Manama, where the 25-year-old marine was assigned to a security unit.

Ms. Al Khalifa's father is a cousin of Bahrain's head of state, Emir Hamad bin Isa Al Khalifa.

WRITING A NEWS REPORT: LOVE OR DUTY

1. A good news report should answer the questions of who, what, when, where, why, and how:

Who was involved in the event?
What exactly happened?
When did the event take place?
Where did the event take place?
Why did the event take place?
How did the event take place?

The newspaper account above reports on an international incident involving two people from different cultures. Use a highlighter pen to mark the newspaper story. Mark those sentences that answer the standard journalistic questions. Then use this information to fill in each line below with the answers. Be sure to answer with complete sentences. These sentences will summarize the news event.

When: ____

Where: ______________________________

Who: ______________________________

What: ______________________________

How: ______________________________

Why: ______________________________

What additional information would you like to have known? ______________________________

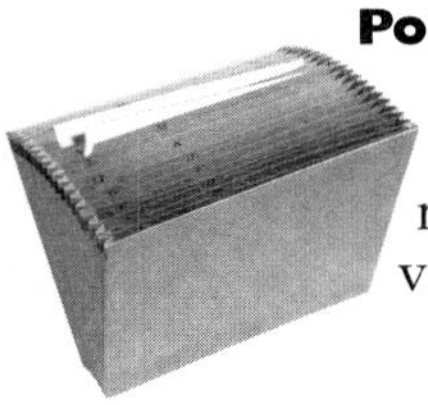

Portfolio Suggestion

You may want to clip newspaper and magazine articles on the subject of cross-cultural relationships and immigration problems. Essays on these subjects are of great interest to the many Americans who have had experience with these issues. Gathering news articles can provide interesting facts and examples you can use in your essays.

Online Activity

With a partner, surf the Internet until you find an online newspaper. Find an article in the editorial/opinion section of the Web site. Summarize the stance of one editorial or letter to the editor in three to five sentences.

Chapter 10 Making Sentence Parts Work Together: Parallel Structure and Modifiers

Preview

In addition to the work of Chapter 4 (Making verbs agree with their subjects) and the work of Chapter 9 (Making pronouns agree with their antecedents), two other topics concerned with sentence parts working together remain to be studied:

- Parallel structure
- Misplaced or dangling modifiers

Key Terms

Parallel structure
Modifiers
Misplaced modifier
Dangling modifier

Rules

- Words in a series should be the same parts of speech.
- Phrases in a series should be the same kinds of phrases.
- Clauses in a series should not be mixed with phrases or words.

Chart

List of modifiers often misplaced

Parallel Structure: Making a Series of Words, Phrases, or Clauses Balanced within the Sentence

Which one of the following sentences has a more balanced structure?

> His favorite hobbies are playing the trumpet, listening to jazz, and to go to concerts.
>
> His favorite hobbies are playing the trumpet, listening to jazz, and going to concerts.

If you selected the second sentence, you made the better choice. The second sentence uses parallel structure to balance the three phrases in the series (playing the trumpet, listening to jazz, going to concerts). By matching each of the items in the series with the same *-ing* structure, the sentence becomes easier to understand and more pleasant to read. Words, phrases, and even sentences in a series can be made parallel:

1. Words in a series should be the same parts of speech.

Not parallel: The town was small, quiet, and the atmosphere was peaceful.

The series is composed of two adjectives and one clause.

Parallel: The town was small, quiet, and peaceful.

The series is composed of three adjectives: *small, quiet,* and *peaceful.*

2. Phrases in a series should be the same kinds of phrases *(infinitive phrases, prepositional phrases, verb phrases, noun phrases, participial phrases).*

Not parallel: Her lost assignment is in her closet, on the floor, and a pile of clothes is hiding it.

The series is composed of two prepositional phrases and one clause.

Parallel: Her lost assignment is in her closet, on the floor, and under a pile of clothes.

The series is composed of three prepositional phrases beginning with *in, on,* and *under.*

3. Clauses in a series should not be mixed with phrases.

Not parallel: The street was narrow, the shops were charming, and crowds in the cafe.

The series is composed of two clauses and one phrase.

Parallel: The street was narrow, the shops were charming, and the cafe was crowded.

The series is composed of three clauses.

Practice

Each of the following sentences lacks parallel structure. In each sentence, revise the underlined section to make the series parallel.

1. My favorite armchair is lumpy, worn out, and <u>has dirt spots everywhere</u>.

____

____

2. She enjoys reading novels, studying the flute, and sews her own clothes.

____

____

3. He admires teachers who make the classroom an exciting place and willingly explaining material more than once.

____

____

EXERCISE 1 **Revising Sentences for Parallel Structure**

Each of the following sentences lacks parallel structure. Underline the word, phrase, or clause that is not parallel and revise it so that its structure will balance with the other items in the pair or series. An example has been done for you.

Not parallel: The best leather comes from Italy, from Spain, and is imported from Brazil.

Parallel: The best leather comes from Italy, Spain, and Brazil.

1. Winter in Chicago is very windy and has many bitterly cold days.

____

____

2. I would prefer to fix an old car to watching television.

____

____

3. George is a helpful neighbor, a loyal friend, and dedicated to his children.

____

____

4. The apartment is crowded and without light.

____

____

5. The dancer is slender and moves gracefully.

____

____

6. The nursery was cheerful and had a lot of sun.

____

____

7. My friend loves to play chess, to read science fiction, and working out at the gym.

____

____

8. For homework today I must read a chapter in history, do five exercises for Spanish class, and working on my term paper for political science.

____

____

9. The painting reveals the artist's talent and it is imaginative.

____

____

10. The cars race down the track, turn the corner at great speed, and then they are heading for the homestretch.

____

____

EXERCISE 2 Revising Sentences for Parallel Structure

Each of the following sentences lacks parallel structure. Underline the word, phrase, or clause that is not parallel and revise it so that its structure will balance with the other items in the pair or series.

1. The dog had to choose between jumping over the fence or he could have dug a hole underneath it.

____

____

2. She disliked going to the beach, hiking in the woods, and she didn't care for picnics, either.

____

____

3. As I looked down the city street, I could see the soft lights from restaurant windows, I could hear the mellow sounds of a nightclub band, and carefree moods of people walking by.

____

____

4. The singers have been on several road tours, have recorded for two record companies, and they would also like to make a movie someday.

____

____

5. They would rather order a pizza than eating their sister's cooking.

____

____

6. I explained to the teacher that my car had broken down, my books had been stolen, and I left my assignment pad home.

____

____

7. That night the prisoner was sick, discouraged, and she was filled with loneliness.

____

____

8. As the truck rumbled through the street, it suddenly lurched out of control, smashed into a parked car, and then the truck hit the storefront of my uncle's hardware store.

____

____

9. The teacher is patient, intelligent, and demands a lot.

____

____

10. He was determined to pass the math course, not only to get his three credits but also for a sense of achievement.

____

____

EXERCISE 3 Revising Sentences for Parallel Structure

Each of the following sentences lacks parallel structure. Underline the word, phrase, or clause that is not parallel and revise it so that its structure will balance with the other items in the pair or series.

1. The first-grade teacher told us that our child was unruly, mischievous, and talked too much.

____

____

2. The dog's size, its coloring, and whenever it barked reminded me of a wolf.

____

____

3. Carol is not only very talented, but she is also acting kindly to everyone.

____

____

4. He dried the dishes; putting them away was the job of his wife.

____

____

5. Jordan would rather travel and see the world than staying home and reading about other places.

____

____

6. For weeks he tried to decide if he should major in chemistry, continue with accounting, or to take a year off.

____

____

7. Her depression was a result of the loss of her job, the breakdown of her marriage, and a teenage daughter who was a problem.

____

____

8. She must either cut back on her expenses or selling her car.

____

____

9. His office is without windows, on the fourth floor, and you have to go down a dark hallway to get there.

____

____

10. He went through four years of college, one year of graduate school, and he has spent one year teaching seventh-grade science.

____

____

EXPLORING ONLINE

Visit the "Parallel Structures" section at

http://webster.commnet.edu/grammar/index.htm and
http://www.richmond.edu/~writing/wweb/parstruc.html

Misplaced and Dangling Modifiers

Discuss how the meaning of the sentences changes, depending on the placement of the modifier *only:*

Only Charlene telephoned my brother yesterday.

Charlene *only* telephoned my brother yesterday.

Charlene telephoned *only* my brother yesterday.

Charlene telephoned my *only* brother yesterday.

Charlene telephoned my brother *only* yesterday.

Modifiers are words or groups of words in a sentence that function as adjectives or adverbs.

my *only* brother

the marine *who is my brother*

just yesterday

A modifier must be placed close to the word, phrase, or clause that it modifies in order to be understood by the reader.

Misplaced Modifiers

Be especially careful in your own writing when you use the words from the following list. They are often misplaced.

MODIFIERS OFTEN MISPLACED				
almost	exactly	just	nearly	scarcely
even	hardly	merely	only	simply

A **misplaced modifier** is a modifier that has been placed in a wrong, awkward, or ambiguous position in a sentence.

Below are examples of some special problems that can happen when modifiers are not placed correctly. Study each sentence and how it has been revised, so you will be able to correct any similar misplaced or dangling modifiers that might occur in your own writing.

1. The modifier is in the wrong place.

Wrong placement: The salesperson sold the used car to the customer *that needed extensive body work.*

Who or what needed body work—the customer or the car?

Revised placement: The salesperson sold the customer the used car *that needed extensive body work.*

2. **The modifier is positioned awkwardly, interrupting the flow of the sentence, as in the following split infinitive.**

Awkward placement: Alex planned to exactly arrive on time.

The infinitive "to arrive" should not be split.

Revised sentence: Alex planned to arrive exactly on time.

3. **The modifier is in an ambiguous position; that is, the modifier could describe the word or words on either side of it. (This is sometimes called a *squinting modifier.*)**

Ambiguous placement: Ms. Douglass having arranged other parties secretly planned the surprise party for her friend.

Does the modifier *secretly* go with *arranging other parties* or *planned the surprise party?* From the wording, you cannot tell which is the correct interpretation.

Revised sentence: Having arranged other parties, Ms. Douglass secretly planned the surprise party for her friend.

Dangling Modifiers

A **dangling modifier** is a modifier without a word, phrase, or clause that the modifier can describe.

Sentence with a dangling modifier: Working on the car's engine, the dog barked all afternoon.

Who was working on the engine? Was it the dog? *Working on the car's engine* is a participial phrase that modifies the subject *dog.* As it stands, the sentence makes no sense.

Revised sentence: Working on the car's engine, I heard the dog barking all afternoon.

or

The dog barked all afternoon while I was working on the car's engine.

EXERCISE 4 Revising Misplaced or Dangling Modifiers

Revise each of the following sentences to avoid misplaced or dangling modifiers.

1. Victor fed the dog wearing his tuxedo.

____

____

2. Visiting Yellowstone National Park, Old Faithful entertained us by performing on schedule.

____

____

3. Hoping to see the news, the television set was turned on by seven o'clock.

____

____

4. A woodpecker was found in Cuba that had been considered extinct.

____

____

5. After running over the hill, the farm was visible in the valley below.

____

____

6. The truck caused a traffic jam, which was broken down on the highway, for miles.

____

____

7. Hanging from the ceiling in her bedroom, she saw three spiders.

____

____

8. After wiping my glasses, the redbird flew away.

____

____

9. Howling without a stop, I listened to the neighbor's dog all evening.

____

____

10. After painting my room all afternoon, my cat demanded her dinner.

____

____

EXERCISE 5 Revising Misplaced or Dangling Modifiers

Revise each of the following sentences to avoid misplaced or dangling modifiers.

1. Leaping upstream, we fished most of the day for salmon.

____

____

2. At the age of ten, my family took a trip to Washington, D.C.

____

____

3. Skimming every chapter, my biology textbook made more sense.

____

____

4. Running up the stairs, the train had already left for Philadelphia.

____

____

5. Working extra hours last week, my salary increased dramatically.

____

____

6. We watched a movie in the theater which we had paid five dollars to see.

____

____

7. Dressed in a Dracula costume, I thought my son looked perfect for Halloween.

____

____

8. Last week while shopping, my friend's purse was stolen.

____

____

9. While eating lunch outdoors, our picnic table collapsed.

____

____

10. Our car is in the parking lot with two bags of groceries unlocked.

____

____

EXPLORING ONLINE FOR ESL STUDENTS

Nonnative speakers of English encounter different grammatical difficulties than native speakers. For an active approach to English grammar, visit The LinguaCenter's Grammar Safari at

http://deil.lang.uiuc.edu/web.pages/grammarsafari.html

Mastery and Editing Tests

TEST 1 **Revising Sentences for Parallel Structure and Correct Use of Modifiers**

Each sentence has an error in parallel structure or in the use of a modifier. Revise each sentence so that it is correct.

1. He devoured the bone, tore up his new bed, and jumping up on the new sofa.

____

____

2. The student almost received enough money from his aunt to pay for his semester's tuition.

____

____

3. She returned from vacation rested, with a great deal of energy, and happy.

____

____

4. Josef managed to find time to coach the team with two other day jobs.

____

____

5. When acting on the stage, a good memory helps.

____

____

6. Discovered by accident, the football fan brought the diamond ring to the lost and found.

____

____

7. Books were piled on the reading tables, magazines were tossed, and scraps of paper everywhere.

____

____

8. Being nearly deaf, the whistle of the train did not warn him of the danger.

____

____

9. I would rather read a good mystery than to watch television.

____

____

10. The bus driving through the fog slowly came into view.

____

____

TEST 2 **Revising Sentences for Parallel Structure and Correct Use of Modifiers**

Each sentence has an error in parallel structure or in the use of a modifier. Revise each sentence so that it is correct.

1. The job demands computer skills, math ability, and with accounting background.

____

____

2. My sister is not only a talented musician, but she is also teaching with great success.

____

____

3. Raking the leaves this morning, over one hundred geese flew overhead.

____

____

4. Follow the directions for writing the essay carefully.

____

____

5. The astronomer completed the calculation at the observatory that he had been working on for nearly a decade.

____

____

6. We should bring a picnic lunch rather than to pay for an expensive restaurant lunch somewhere.

____

____

7. My older brother is guilty of lecturing me instead of a good example.

8. The new highway follows the river, bypasses the small towns, and you can save a lot of time.

9. He only ordered an appetizer.

10. She mowed the lawn, repaired the broken window, and a huge pile of newspapers to be recycled.

TEST 3 Revising Sentences for Parallel Structure and Correct Use of Modifiers

Each sentence has an error in parallel structure or in the use of a modifier. Revise each sentence so that it is correct.

1. After the move, he slumped into a chair, grabbed a bottle of soda, and with a wish for a good book.

2. My friend is generous, hard-working, and a talker.

3. The members of Congress would rather stonewall the proposal than to pass the new law.

4. When covered with thin ice, you should not skate on the lake.

5. Last year, the citizen just paid half of his taxes.

6. From the airport, I will either take the bus or the shuttle to the hotel.

7. For the holidays, we plan to do some cooking, see a few good movies, and listening to jazz.

____

____

8. Working late into the night, the page numbering on my report kept printing out wrong.

____

____

9. The crime not only involved the chief officer but also several of his assistants.

____

____

10. The witness told the whole story from the beginning of the incident to when the suspects were arrested.

____

____

WORKING TOGETHER

Gary Sommers
645 Franklin AVe.
Norman, Oklahoma
Home Telephone: 662-1919

Present Job Objective	A summer position as an assistant in *the* ~~teh~~ mayor's office
Education	High School Diploma, Kennedy High School, Norman, Oklahoma
	B.A., Business Administration, University of Oklahoma Expected date of graduation: june 2003
	Courses in Business and Computers: Principles of Accounting, Microeconomic Theory, Problem solving and Structured Programming, Computer Systems and Assembly
	WORK EXPERIENCE
9/96 to present	Tutor, Math Lab, University of Oklahoma
1993–1995	Summer Volunteer at Camp Sunshine, a day camp for disabled children
Special skills:	fluent in spanish

Computer Skills: familiar with Microsoft Word, EXCEL,

Interests: soccer, guitar

REFERENCES: Available on request

DEVELOPING A RÉSUMÉ

Above is a draft of a résumé written by a college student who is looking for a summer job. Study the résumé and then answer the following questions.

Questions for Résumé Editing

1. Can you find any typos, misspelled words, or errors in capitalization or punctuation?
2. Can you find anything inconsistent in the design or layout? (Look for places where parallel structures are needed.)
3. What do you think about Mr. Sommers correcting an error using pen rather than reprinting a corrected version? What conclusion might the potential employer have?
4. Is there any information that is missing?
5. Why has the person not included such facts as date of birth or marital status?
6. How does a person go about obtaining references? How many references does one need?
7. How could this person highlight his interest in the particular job for which he is applying?

Portfolio Suggestion: Write Your Own Résumé

Using the same general headings as contained in this sample résumé, write your own résumé. Copy it onto a disk of your own that you will keep. Remember to update the résumé regularly. You may have more than one version depending on what experiences or skills you want to emphasize.

Online Activity

With a partner, review the "Interviewing and Résumé Information" at http://www.msstate.edu/Dept/Coop/interview.html Together, make a list of new information. Then, with one of you role-playing the interviewer and the other playing the applicant, review the "Favorite Interviewing Questions." Switch roles and repeat.

Chapter 11 Practicing More with Verbs

Preview

You have already learned a great deal about verbs. In Chapter 3, you learned how to recognize the verb in a sentence. In Chapter 4, you learned that verbs must agree with their subjects. Chapter 5 showed you how to use verbs to form participles, gerunds, and infinitives. This chapter will continue your study of verbs, focusing on:

- Principal parts of irregular verbs
- Use of the present perfect and past perfect tenses
- Sequence of tenses
- Unnecessary shifts in verb tense
- The difference between the active voice and the passive voice
- The subjunctive mood
- Confusions using *should* and *would*

Key Terms

Present perfect tense
Past perfect tense
Sequence of tenses
Passive voice/Active voice
The Subjunctive

Charts

50 Irregular Verbs:
- **Eight verbs that do not change their forms**
- **Two verbs with the same simple form and past participle form**
- **Twenty verbs with the same past tense and past participle forms**
- **Twenty verbs with all three forms different**

The Six English Verb Tenses
Sequence of Tenses
Forming the Passive Voice

What Are the Principal Parts of the Irregular Verbs?

The English language has more than one hundred verbs that do not form the past tense or past participle with the usual *-ed* ending. Their forms are irregular. When you listen to children aged four or five, you often hear them use

-*ed* to form the past tense of every verb, as in "Yesterday, I *goed* to my aunt's house." Later on, they will hear that the verb "go" is unusual, and they will change to the irregular form, "Yesterday I *went* . . ." The best way to learn these verbs is to listen to how they sound. You will find an extensive list of these verbs in the appendix of this book. Pronounce them out loud over and over until you have learned them. If you find that you don't know the meaning of a particular verb, or you cannot pronounce a verb and its forms, ask your instructor for help. Most irregular verbs are very common words that you will be using often in your writing and speaking. You will want to know them well.

Practicing 50 Irregular Verbs

Learn the three principal parts of all irregular verbs.

EIGHT VERBS THAT DO NOT CHANGE THEIR FORMS (NOTICE THEY ALL END IN -T OR -D)

Simple Form (also called Dictionary Form, Infinitive Form, or Base Form)	*Past Tense*	*Past Participle (used with perfect tenses after "has," "have," "had," "will have" or with passive voice after the verb "to be.")*
bet	bet	bet
cost	cost	cost
cut	cut	cut
fit	fit	fit
hit	hit	hit
hurt	hurt	hurt
quit	quit	quit
spread	spread	spread

TWO VERBS WITH THE SAME SIMPLE FORM AND PAST PARTICIPLE FORM

Simple Form	*Past Tense*	*Past Participle*
come	came	come
become	became	become

Practice.......... Fill in the correct form of the verb in each of the following sentences.

(cost) **1.** Last year the tuition for my education __________ 7 percent more than the year before.

(quit) **2.** I have __________ trying to guess my expenses for next year.

(spread) **3.** The message has __________ that college costs continue to spiral.

(hit) **4.** Most parents have been __________ with large tax increases.

(become) **5.** Financing a child's higher education has __________ a difficult task.

TWENTY VERBS WITH THE SAME PAST TENSE AND PAST PARTICIPLE FORMS

Simple Form	*Past Tense*	*Past Participle*
bend	bent	bent
lend	lent	lent
send	sent	sent
spend	spent	spent
creep	crept	crept
keep	kept	kept
sleep	slept	slept
sweep	swept	swept
weep	wept	wept
teach	taught	taught
catch	caught	caught
bleed	bled	bled
feed	fed	fed
lead	led	led
speed	sped	sped
bring	brought	brought
buy	bought	bought
fight	fought	fought
think	thought	thought
seek	sought	sough

Practice.......... Fill in the correct form of the verb in each of the following sentences.

(buy) **1.** Last year the school district __________ new chemistry texts.

(spend) **2.** Some citizens felt the district had __________ too much money on these new books.

(bleed) **3.** They claimed the taxpayers were being __________ dry.

(keep) **4.** These citizens argued that the school should have __________ the old books.

(think) **5.** The teachers __________ the old books were worn out.

(seek) **6.** Parents, on the other hand, __________ to hire two new teachers.

(fight) **7.** They __________ for a smaller class size.

(teach) **8.** Most teachers __________ classes that were too large.

(lead) **9.** One father __________ a campaign to educate the community.

(send) **10.** He __________ every citizen a letter to explain the problem.

TWENTY VERBS WITH ALL THREE FORMS DIFFERENT

Simple Form	*Past Tense*	*Past Participle*
blow	blew	blown
fly	flew	flown
grow	grew	grown
know	knew	known
throw	threw	thrown
begin	began	begun
drink	drank	drunk
ring	rang	rung
shrink	shrank	shrunk
sink	sank	sunk
sing	sang	sung
spring	sprang	sprung
swim	swam	swum
bite	bit	bitten (or bit)
hide	hid	hidden (or hid)
drive	drove	driven
ride	rode	ridden
stride	strode	stridden
rise	rose	risen
write	wrote	written

Practice.......... Fill in the correct form of the verb in each of the following sentences.

(know) **1.** We have __________ many country and western singing stars over the years, but Patsy Cline remains a special figure.

(begin) **2.** She __________ her career near her small home town in Virginia.

(sing) **3.** She __________ wherever she could find people to listen.

(grow) **4.** People immediately recognized the exceptional quality of her voice, and her audiences __________.

(drive) **5.** At sixteen, Patsy Cline auditioned for a local radio station and __________ from town to town, singing in clubs and taverns.

(rise) **6.** During the early 1960s, her records __________ on popularity charts throughout the country.

(ride) **7.** After the worldwide success of "Walkin' after Midnight," Patsy Cline __________ her way to stardom.

(fly) **8.** In 1963, on her way back from Kansas City, the singer had __________ as far as Tennessee when her plane crashed and she was killed.

(spring) **9.** Other stars have __________ up in the last forty years, but Patsy Cline will remain one of the great legends of country music.

(write) **10.** Much has been __________ about Patsy Cline, and a feature-length film entitled *Sweet Dreams* has been made about her life.

EXERCISE 1 Knowing the Irregular Verb Forms

Supply the past form or the past participle for each verb in parentheses.

Ever since people __________ (begin) to write, they have __________ (write) about the great mysteries in nature. For instance, why did the dinosaurs disappear? In the past, no one __________ (know) why. Scientists now have __________ (bet) on one strong possibility. That possibility is that 65 million years ago, a six-mile-wide chunk of rock __________ (hit) the earth and __________ (throw) up a thick cloud of dust. The dust __________ (keep) the sunlight from the earth; therefore, certain life forms disappeared. Some scientists have __________ (think) that this could also have __________ (shrink) the earth's animal population by as much as 70 percent. Other scientists are not so sure that this is the answer. They believe time has __________ (hide) the real reason for the disappearance of the dinosaurs.

EXERCISE 2 Knowing the Irregular Verb Forms

Supply the past form or the past participle for each verb in parentheses.

Medical researchers have __________ (seek) a cure for the common cold, but so far they have __________ (fight) without success. The cold virus has __________ (spread) throughout the world and the number of cold victims has __________ (rise) every year. Past experience has __________ (teach) us that people who have __________ (drink) plenty of liquids and taken aspirin get over colds more quickly than those who have not, but this is not a good enough remedy. People once believed that if you __________ (feed) a fever, you starved a cold, but recent research has __________ (lead) to a disclaimer of this belief. It has __________ (cost) a lot of time and effort in the search for a vaccine, but so far the new knowledge has not __________ (bring) a cure.

EXERCISE 3

Knowing the Irregular Verb Forms

Rewrite the following paragraph in the past tense.

The jockey drives his pickup truck to the race track. He strides into the stalls where the horses are kept. His head swims with thoughts of the coming race. He springs into the saddle and rides to the starting gate. The bell rings and the horses fly out of the gate. They speed around the first turn. The crowd grows tense, and excitement spreads as the horses near the finish line.

____

____

____

____

____

Appendix B at the back of this book gives an alphabetical listing of nearly every irregular verb. Use that list to supply the correct form for each verb in the following exercises.

EXERCISE 4

Additional Irregular Verbs

Supply the past form or the past participle for each verb in parentheses.

1. The photographer __________ (to shoot) several rolls of film.
2. The contractor __________ (to build) two houses in the neighborhood.
3. The audience __________ (to flee) when the singer attempted the high notes.
4. The pipe __________ (to burst) yesterday; we are waiting for a plumber.
5. He __________ (to mistake) the dog for a wolf.
6. The firefighters __________ (to slide) down the ladder.
7. Life __________ (to deal) the family a cruel blow.
8. The artist had __________ (to draw) two portraits of his wife.
9. The pond was __________ (to freeze) enough for ice skating.
10. He had washed and __________ (to wring) out all his clothes in the bathtub.

EXERCISE 5

Additional Irregular Verbs

Read the following paragraph and find the ten irregular verbs that are written incorrectly. In the spaces provided, write the correct forms of the ten irregular verbs.

Mr. Weeks, an alumnus of our university, had gave a large sum of money to the school just before he died. A committee was choosen to study how the money should be used. Each member thunk about the possibilities for several weeks before the meeting. Finally, the meeting begun in late November. Each member brung his ideas. One gentleman fealt the school should improve the graduate program by hiring two new teachers. Another committee member layed down a proposal for remodeling the oldest dormitory on campus. Janice Spaulding had a writen plan for increasing the scholarships for deserving students. A citizen unexpectedly swang open the door and strode into the room. She pleaded with the school to provide more programs for the community. After everyone had spoke, the committee was asked to make a more thorough study of each project.

1. ______________________ 6. ______________________
2. ______________________ 7. ______________________
3. ______________________ 8. ______________________
4. ______________________ 9. ______________________
5. ______________________ 10. ______________________

EXERCISE 6 **Additional Irregular Verbs**

Supply the past form or the past participle for each verb in parentheses.

1. We __________ (to dig) in the sand for clams.
2. The director __________ (to fling) the script on the table.
3. The family had __________ (to forget) the child's birthday.
4. The clerk __________ (to wind) the clock before going home.
5. The door seemed to be __________ (to stick).
6. The dog __________ (to shake) itself as it came out of the water.
7. The youth __________ (to swear) he was telling the truth.
8. Yesterday, the food had __________ (to lie) on the table all day without being touched.
9. My friend __________ (to bear) her first child in a taxicab on the way to the hospital.
10. The hosts __________ (to forbid) their guests to drink in their home.

How Many Verb Tenses Are There in English?

Not all languages express time by using exactly the same verb tenses. Students for whom English is a second language know that one of their major tasks in learning English is to understand how to use each of these tenses. Since the next sections of this chapter concern common problems with tense, a chart of the English verb tenses is given in case you need to refer to this list from time to time. Along with the name of each verb tense, the chart gives a sentence using that particular tense.

THE SIX ENGLISH VERB TENSES

Three Simple Tenses	*Simple Continuous Forms*	*Three Perfect Tenses*	*Perfect Continuous Forms*
Present you walk	**Present continuous** you are walking	**Present perfect** you have walked	**Present perfect continuous** you have been walking
Past you walked	**Past continuous** you were walking	**Past perfect** you had walked	**Past perfect continuous** you had been walking
Future you will walk	**Future continuous** you will be walking	**Future perfect** you will have walked	**Future perfect continuous** you will have been walking

Note: The perfect tenses need special attention since they are generally not well understood or used consistently in the accepted way.

EXPLORING ONLINE FOR ESL STUDENTS

English verb tenses can be very confusing for nonnative speakers. For exercises and help with many confusing aspects of verbs, visit "Dave's ESL Cafe" at http://www.eslcafe.com

How Do You Use the Present Perfect and the Past Perfect Tenses?

Forming the Perfect Tenses

Present perfect tense: *has* or *have* + past participle of the main verb

has worked

have worked

Past perfect tense: *had* + past participle of the main verb

had worked

What Do These Tenses Mean?

The **present perfect tense** describes an action that started in the past and continues to the present time.

Jennifer *has worked* at the hospital for ten years.

This sentence indicates that Jennifer began to work at the hospital ten years ago and is still working there now.

Examine the following time line. What does it tell you about the present perfect tense?

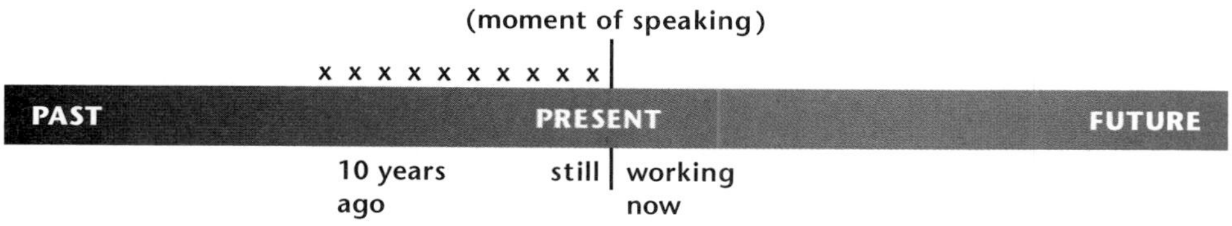

Other example sentences of the present perfect tense:

She *has studied* violin since 1980.

I *have* always *appreciated* his generosity.

The **present perfect tense** can also describe an action that has just taken place, or an action where the exact time in the past is indefinite.

Has Jennifer *found* a job yet?

Jennifer *has* (just) *found* a new job in Kansas City.

Have you ever *been* to San Diego?

Yes, I *have been* there three times.

If the time were definite, you would use the simple past:

Jennifer *found* a new job yesterday.

Yes, I *was* there last week.

The **past perfect tense** describes an action that occurred in the past before another activity or another point of time in the past.

Jennifer *had worked* at the hospital for ten years *before* she *moved* away.

In this sentence, there are two past actions: Jennifer *worked* and Jennifer *moved*. The action that took place first is in the past perfect *(had worked)*. The action that took place later, and was also completed in the past, is in the simple past *(moved)*.

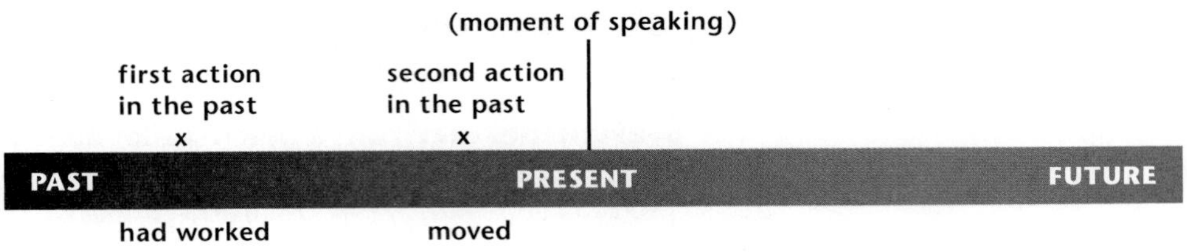

Other example sentences using the past perfect tense:

I *had* just *finished* when the bell *rang.*

He *said* that Randall *had told* the class about the experiment.

We *had provided* the information *long before* last week's meeting.

Practice.......... Complete each of the following sentences by filling in each blank with either the present perfect tense or past perfect tense of the verb given.

1. Yolanda told us that she __________ (live) in Fort Worth before she moved to Mexico City.

2. Mexico City __________ (fascinate) visitors for many years.

3. This city __________ (become) the third largest city in the world, and people __________ (watch) it grow larger every year.

4. The suburbs of the city __________ (replace) old villages that __________ (exist) peacefully since the days of the Aztecs.

5. Today, Mexico City __________ (build) a computer-controlled subway system to deal with its huge transportation problem.

What Do We Mean by the *Sequence of Tenses?*

The term **sequence of tenses** refers to the proper use of verb tenses in complex sentences (sentences that have an independent clause and a dependent clause).

The following guide shows the relationship between the verb in the independent clause (IC) and the verb in the dependent clause (DC).

SEQUENCE OF TENSES

Independent Clause	*Dependent Clause*	*Time of the DC in Relation to the IC*
If the tense of the independent clause is in the present (He *knows*), here are the possibilities for the dependent clause:		
He knows	that she *is* right.	**same time**
	that she *was* right.	**earlier**
	that she *will be* right.	**later**
If the tense of the independent clause is in the past (He *knew*), here are the possibilities for the dependent clause:		
He knew	that she *was* right.	**same time**
	that she *had been* right.	**earlier**
	that she *would be* right.	**later**
If the independent clause is in the future (He *will tell*), here are the possibilities for the dependent clause:		
He will tell us	if she *goes*.	**same time**
	if she *has gone*.	**earlier**
	if she *will go*.	**later**

Practice.......... In each of the following sentences, the verb in the independent clause has been underlined. Choose the correct verb tense for the verb in the dependent clause. Use the guide above if you need help.

1. The program will continue only after the coughing and fidgeting __________ (to stop).
2. Since he was poor and unappreciated by the music world when he died in 1791, Mozart did not realize the importance that his music __________ (to have) in the twentieth century.
3. Dad will tell us tonight if he __________ (to buy) a new car next month.
4. Albert Einstein failed the entrance exam at the Swiss Federal Institute of Technology because he __________ (to be) + never a very disciplined student.
5. Einstein only studied subjects that he __________ (to like).
6. Cancer researchers think it's likely that a cure for most cancers __________ (to be) + soon found.

7. We know that science __________ (to be) now close to finding a cure for leukemia.

8. The interviewer felt that the young woman __________ (to know) more than she was telling him.

9. The doctor went into the operating room. She hoped that the operation __________ (to turn) out all right.

10. The doctor came out of the operating room. She said that the operation __________ (to go) well.

Avoid Unnecessary Shifts in Verb Tense

Unless there is some reason to change tenses, inconsistent shifting from one tense to another should be avoided. Study the following examples:

Shifted tenses: The customer *asked* (past tense) to see the manager. He *was* (past tense) angry because every jacket he *tries* on (Why present tense?) *has* (Why present tense?) something wrong with it. A button *was* (past tense) missing on the first, the lining *did* not *fit* (past tense) right on the second, and the collar *had* (past tense) a stain on the third.

Revised: The customer *asked* (past tense) to see the manager. He *was* (past tense) angry because every jacket he *tried* on (past tense) *had* (past tense) something wrong with it. A button *was* (past tense) missing on the first, the lining *did* not *fit* (past tense) right on the second, and the collar *had* (past tense) a stain on the third.

Note: When the subject is a created work, such as a book, play, poem, or piece of music, be especially careful about the verb tense. Although the work was created in the past, it is still enjoyed in the present. In this case, the present tense is used.

Shakespeare's *Hamlet* is a great play. It was written four centuries ago.

EXERCISE 7 **Correcting Unnecessary Shifts in Verb Tense**

Each sentence has an unnecessary shift in verb tense. Revise each sentence so that the tenses remain consistent.

1. After I complete that writing course, I took the required history course.

____

____

2. In the beginning of the movie, the action was slow; by the end, I am sitting on the edge of my seat.

3. The textbook gives the rules for writing a bibliography, but it didn't explain how to do footnotes.

4. While working on her report in the library, my best friend lost her note cards and comes to me for help.

5. The encyclopedia gave several pages of information about astronomy, but it doesn't give any information about "black holes."

6. The invitation requested that Juan be at the ceremony and that he will attend the banquet as well.

7. This is an exciting book, but it had too many characters.

8. The senator was doing just fine until along comes a younger and more energetic politician with firm support from the middle class.

9. At the end of *Gulliver's Travels,* the main character rejects the company of people; he preferred the company of horses.

10. My sister arrives, late as usual, and complained that her dinner was cold.

EXERCISE 8

Correcting Unnecessary Shifts in Verb Tense

The following paragraph contains unnecessary shifts in verb tense. Change each incorrect verb to its proper form.

Charles Dickens was a nineteenth-century author whose work is well known today. One of the reasons Dickens remained so popular is that so many of his stories are available not only as books but also as movies, plays, and television productions. We all knew from our childhood the famous story of Uncle Scrooge and Tiny Tim. Often we saw a television version of *A Christmas Carol* at holiday time. If we have never read the story of Oliver Twist in book form, we might see the musical *Oliver!* Also, there was a movie version of *Great Expectations*. Many students still studied *A Tale of Two Cities* in high school. No matter how many adaptations of Dickens's books we see, people seem to agree that there was no substitute for the books themselves. At first, the vocabulary seemed hard to understand, but if we concentrate on the story and read a chapter or two every day, we will find ourselves not only comprehending these wonderful stories but loving the richness of Dickens's use of language.

EXERCISE 9

Student Writing: Correcting Unnecessary Shifts in Verb Tense

The following paragraph was part of an essay written for a college admissions application. It contains unnecessary shifts in verb tense. Revise the paragraph so that verb tenses are consistent.

I remember last year when I was trying to choose the right school and worrying about it a lot. One day a friend says that instead of talking about it all the time, I should visit a few places and actually see them. One afternoon I decide to do just that. I take the bus, get off in the center of town, and from there I walked to the campus. It's very clean, with no graffiti on any of the walls. The visitor's desk had two people there, with lots of brochures and information on programs and majors. The student union looks nice, so I went in to get a soda and check it out. I sit down and started listening to the students at the other tables. It was really good to hear everyone talk so kindly to each other. I could hardly believe it. I did not hear one sarcastic remark and no one is rude to anyone else. I went to the library and had the same experience. Everyone seems so helpful and friendly. I knew this was the kind of atmosphere I was looking for. On my way out, I pick up an application from the visitor's desk. Both of the students behind the desk are still smiling at me as I leave.

What Is the Difference between the Passive Voice and the Active Voice?

PASSIVE AND ACTIVE VOICE

In the ***active voice,*** the subject does the acting:

The committee made the decision.

Choose the active voice generally in order to achieve direct, economical and forceful writing. Most writing, therefore, should be in the active voice.

In the ***passive voice,*** the subject is acted upon:

The decision was made by the committee.

or

The decision was made.

Notice in these passive sentences, the actor is not only deemphasized by moving out of the subject place but may be omitted entirely from the sentence.

Choose the passive voice to deemphasize the actor or to avoid naming the actor altogether.

Study the three sentences that follow. All three state the fact of President Kennedy's assassination. Discuss with your classmates and instructor what would cause a writer to choose each of the following sentences to express the same basic fact.

1. Lee Harvey Oswald shot President John F. Kennedy in 1963.
2. President John F. Kennedy was shot by Lee Harvey Oswald in 1963.
3. President John F. Kennedy was shot in 1963.

How Do You Form the Passive Voice?

FORMING THE PASSIVE VOICE

Subject Acted Upon	*+ Verb "To Be"*	*+ Past Participle*	*+ "by" Phrase (Optional)*
The race	was	won	(by the runner)
The fish	was	cooked	(by the chef)
The books	are	illustrated	(by the artists)

EXERCISE 10 Active Voice and Passive Voice

Fill in the following chart by showing how the sentences in the active voice could be put into passive voice and how the sentences in the passive voice could be put into the active voice. Then discuss with your classmates and instructor the circumstances under which you would choose active or passive voice to express these ideas.

Active Voice	Passive Voice
1. ____________________	1. The wrong number was dialed by the child.
2. ____________________	2. The sweater was crocheted very carefully by my grandmother.
3. The tornado struck Cherry Creek last spring.	3. ____________________
4. The wind blew the leaves across the yard.	4. ____________________
5. ____________________	5. In the sixties, platform shoes were worn by many fashionable young men and women.

EXERCISE 11 Active Voice and Passive Voice

Fill in the following chart by showing how the sentences in the active voice could be put into passive voice and how the sentences in the passive voice could be put into the active voice. Then discuss with your classmates and instructor the circumstances under which you would choose active or passive voice to express these ideas.

Active Voice	Passive Voice
1. The jury announced the verdict after five hours of deliberation.	1. ____________________
2. ____________________	2. Modern pop music was created by Elvis Presley.
3. The sleet turned the old municipal building into an ice castle.	3. ____________________
4. ____________________	4. The priceless vase was smuggled (by someone) out of the country.
5. ____________________	5. More concern was shown by television viewers over the Super Bowl than over the outbreak of an international conflict.

What Is the Subjunctive Mood?

Verbs in the English language have three possible moods:

1. ***The indicative mood:*** **expresses statements of fact**

   He *drives* home every Sunday.

   Most sentences call for the indicative mood.

2. ***The imperative mood:*** **expresses commands**

   Drive home on Sunday!

3. ***The subjunctive mood:*** **expresses conditions contrary to fact, or follows certain verbs of demand or urgency**

   If I were you, I would drive home on Sunday.

   I insist that he drive home on Sunday.

Of the three moods possible for verbs in English, the subjunctive mood has the most limited use.

> **The subjunctive mood,** the most limited of the three moods for English verbs, uses special verb forms to express certain statements contrary to fact, or to express demand or urgency after certain verbs.

Recognize the three instances that call for the subjunctive:

1. **Unreal conditions using *if* or *wish***

   If he were my teacher, I would be pleased.

   I wish he were my teacher.

2. **Clauses starting with *that* after verbs such as *ask, request, demand, suggest, order, insist,* or *command***

   I demand that she work harder.

   Sullivan insisted that Jones report on Tuesday.

3. **Clauses starting with *that* after adjectives expressing urgency, as in *it is necessary, it is imperative, it is urgent, it is important,* and *it is essential***

   It is necessary that she wear a net covering her hair.

   It is essential that Robert understand the concept.

In each of these three instances, notice that the -s is not added in the third person singular present tense.

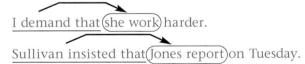

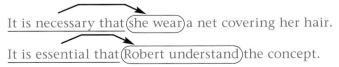

Practice.......... In the following sentences, underline the word or phrase that determines the subjunctive and circle the subjunctive. An example has been done for you.

Truman suggested that the country adopt the Marshall plan in 1947.

1. When President Roosevelt died in 1945, the law required that Vice President Truman take over immediately.
2. It was essential that President Truman act quickly and decisively.
3. Truman must have wished that he were able to avoid using the atomic bomb to bring an end to World War II.
4. He felt it was necessary that the United States help Europe recover from the destruction of World War II.
5. President Truman always insisted that other countries be economically strong.

Confusions with *Should* and *Would*

Do not use more than one modal auxiliary (*can, may, might, must, should, ought*) with the main verb.

Incorrect: Matt *shouldn't ought* to sell his car.

Correct: Matt *ought not* sell his car.

or

Matt *shouldn't* sell his car.

Do not use *should of, would of,* or *could of* to mean *should have, would have,* or *could have.*

Incorrect: Elana *would of* helped you if she *could of.*

Correct: Elana *would have* helped you if she *could have.*

Mastery and Editing Tests

TEST 1 **Solving Problems with Verbs**

Revise each of the following sentences to avoid problems with verbs.

1. He hadn't ought to drive so fast.

____

2. The officer said that the motorist drove through a red light.

____

3. I wish I was a senior.

____

4. She sung for a huge crowd Saturday night.

____

5. I was shook up by the accident.

____

6. The map was studied by the motorist. (use active voice)

____

7. My father ask me last night to help him build a deck.

____

8. I should of kept the promise I made.

____

9. I insist she keeps her clothes on her side of the room.

____

10. The ship sunk off the coast of Florida.

____

TEST 2 Student Writing: Solving Problems with Verbs

Find all twelve incorrect forms of verbs in the following paragraph and correct each one.

When the day arrived, my mother was jubilant. We drive to the synagogue. My aunt Sophie and her daughters comes with us. Once in the temple, the women were not allowed to sit with the men. They had to go upstairs to their assigned places. I was ask to keep my hat on and was given a shawl to wear which I seen before. I was suppose to watch for the rabbi to call me. My turn finally come. I was brung to a table in the front. There I read from the Bible in Hebrew. I knew I could of read louder, but I was nervous. My mother had said that if I was good, she would be especially proud of me, so I done my best. Afterward, I was lead by my mother and other relatives to a fine kosher restaurant where we celebrated. I receive a fine gold watch.

TEST 3 Student Writing: Solving Problems with Verbs

Find all thirteen forms of verbs in the following paragraph and correct each one.

I knowed I was in big trouble in chemistry when I took a look at the midterm exam. My semester should of been a lot better. The first week I had my new textbook, I lend it to a friend who lost it. Then I catched a cold and miss two classes. When I finally start off for class, I missed the bus and walked into the classroom half an hour late. The teacher scowls at me and ask to speak to me after class. I always use to sit in the front row so I could see the board and hear the lectures, but since I am late, I will have to take a seat in the last row. I wish I was able to start this class over again the right way. No one had ought to have such an unlucky start in any class.

WORKING TOGETHER

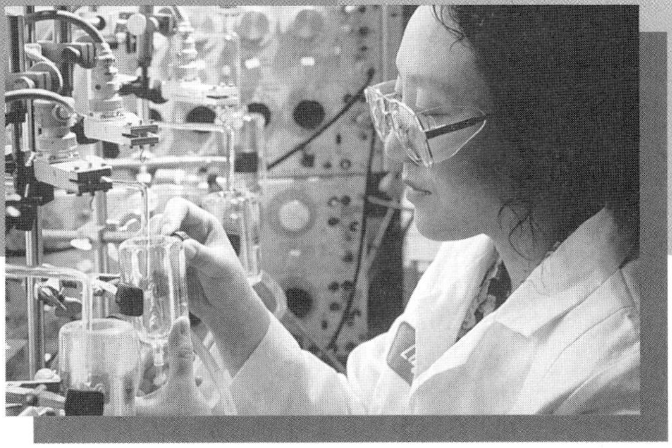

USING FACTS AND FIGURES: FACTORS IN CHOOSING A CAREER

Choosing a career is an important milestone in a person's life. How can someone decide which career is best? One of the factors that may be important is whether or not there will be a demand for a certain job in the foreseeable future. Below is a chart from a government agency listing the most promising occupations.

Divide into groups to discuss the information given in the chart. What probable training is needed for these jobs? What is the likely salary range? What are the specific advantages or disadvantages that go with some of these jobs? Next, discuss the other factors that go into a career decision. Develop a list of these factors.

Finally, each person should develop his or her own paragraph or essay on the subject of *factors in choosing a career*. Since one factor mentioned will be that of job demand, support this factor by using one or two facts from the chart. Be sure to cite the source of the information in your paragraph or essay.

Fastest-Growing Occupations

The Bureau of Labor Statistics projects that U.S. businesses will add nearly 25 million new jobs before 2005. In general, the highest rates of job growth—that is, the percentage increases—will occur in occupations that require higher levels of education and training. A substantial number of those jobs will be in health-services industries. Many slower-growing occupations are expected to add significant numbers of new jobs, primarily because of their large employment bases.

Occupation	Employment 1990	Employment 2005	Numerical change	% change
	(numbers in thousands)			
Home health aides	287	550	263	91.7
Paralegals	90	167	77	85.2
Systems analysts and computer scientists	463	829	366	78.9
Personal and home-care aides	103	183	79	76.7
Physical therapists	88	155	67	76.0
Medical assistants	165	287	122	73.9
Operations-research analysts	57	100	42	73.2
Human-services workers	145	249	103	71.2
Radiologic technologists and technicians	149	252	103	69.5
Medical secretaries	232	390	158	68.3
Physical and corrective therapy assistants and aides	45	74	29	64.0

continued on next page

Occupation	Employment 1990	Employment 2005	Numerical change	% change
	(numbers in thousands)			
Psychologists	125	204	79	63.6
Travel agents	132	214	82	62.3
Correction officers	230	372	142	61.4
Data-processing equipment repairers	84	134	50	60.0
Flight attendants	101	159	59	58.5
Computer programmers	565	882	317	56.1
Occupational therapists	36	56	20	55.2
Surgical technologists	38	59	21	55.2
Medical-records technicians	52	80	28	54.3
Management analysts	151	230	79	52.3
Respiratory therapists	60	91	31	52.1
Child-care workers	725	1,078	353	48.8

Online Activity

Write down your employment expectations for the next five years. Next, read the "Economic Outlook Through 2008" provided by the Bureau of Labor Statistics at http://www.infoplease.com/ipa/A0300371.html In small groups, discuss how each member will achieve his or her goals in the future.

Chapter 12 Using Correct Capitalization and Punctuation

Preview

In college and at work, you will have to be in control of capitalization and punctuation. Basically, this means learning the fundamental rules and applying them. Study the examples that are given under each rule. Notice that an example is often given to show you what *not* to do. Doing the practices and exercises in this chapter will help you master the following material:

- Ten basic rules for capitalization
- Eight basic uses of the comma
- Three uses for the apostrophe
- Four uses for quotation marks
- Italics or underlining
- Three uses for the semicolon
- Four uses for the colon
- Use of the dash
- Use of parentheses

EXPLORING ONLINE

How well do you use capitalization and punctuation? Take the online quiz at http://www.grammarbook.com/tests/punctuation/punTest.html Answers are provided at the bottom of the page.

Ten Basic Rules for Capitalization

Many people are often confused or careless about the use of capital letters. Sometimes writers capitalize words without thinking, or they capitalize "important" words without really understanding what makes them important enough to deserve a capital letter. The question of when to capitalize words becomes easier to answer when you study the following rules and carefully apply them to your own writing.

1. Capitalize the first word of every sentence.

Every building was old. Our house was the oldest.

2. Capitalize the names of specific things and places.

Specific buildings:

I went to the Jamestown Post Office.

but

I went to the post office.

Specific streets, cities, states, countries:

She lives on Elam Avenue.

but

She lives on the same street as my mom and dad.

Specific organizations:

He collected money for the March of Dimes.

but

Janice contributed to more than one charity at the office.

Specific institutions:

The loan is from the First National Bank.

but

The loan is from one of the banks in town.

Specific bodies of water:

My uncle fishes every summer on Lake Michigan.

but

My uncle spends every summer at the lake.

3. Capitalize days of the week, months of the year, and holidays. Do not capitalize the names of seasons.

The last Thursday in November is Thanksgiving Day.

but

I cannot wait until spring.

4. Capitalize the names of all languages, nationalities, races, religions, deities, and sacred terms.

My friend who is Ethiopian speaks very little English.

The Koran is the sacred book of Islam.

5. **Capitalize the first word and every important word in a title. Do not capitalize articles, prepositions, or short connecting words in a title.**

    For Whom the Bell Tolls is a famous novel by Ernest Hemingway.

    Her favorite short story is "A Rose for Emily."

6. **Capitalize the first word of a direct quotation.**

    The teacher said, "You have been chosen for the part."

    but

    "You have been chosen," she said, "for the part."

Note: *for* is not capitalized because it is the continuation of the sentence in quotation marks.

7. **Capitalize historical events, periods, and documents.**

    The American Revolution

    The Colonial Period

    The Bill of Rights

8. **Capitalize the words *north, south, east,* and *west* when they are used as places rather than as directions.**

    He comes from the Midwest.

    but

    The farm is about twenty miles west of Omaha.

9. **Capitalize people's names.**

    Proper names:

    George Hendrickson

    Professional titles when they are used with the person's proper name:

    Judge Samuelson but the judge

    Professor Shapiro but the professor

    Terms for relatives (mother, sister, nephew, uncle) when they are used in the place of proper names:

    I told Grandfather I would meet him later.

Note: Terms for relatives are not capitalized if a pronoun, article, or adjective is used with the name.

I told my grandfather I would meet him later.

10. Capitalize brand names.

Lipton's Noodle Soup	but	noodle soup
Velveeta Cheese	but	cheese

EXERCISE 1 **Capitalization**

Capitalize wherever necessary.

1. The italian student got a job in the school cafeteria.
2. Our train ride through the canadian rockies was fabulous.
3. The author often made references in his writing to names from the bible.
4. A student at the university of delaware was chosen for the national award.
5. My uncle's children always have a party on halloween.
6. I met the president of american telephone and telegraph company last friday at a convention in portland, oregon.
7. In 1863 president Lincoln wrote his famous emancipation proclamation.
8. My niece said, "why don't you consider moving farther south if you hate the winter so much?"
9. The united auto workers voted not to go on strike over the new contract.
10. A very popular radio program in the east is called a prairie home companion.

EXERCISE 2 **Capitalization**

Capitalize wherever necessary.

1. Every tuesday the general visits the hospital.
2. On one level, the book *the lord of the rings* can be read as a fairy tale; on another level, the book can be read as a christian allegory.
3. The golden gate bridge in san francisco may be the most beautiful bridge in the world.
4. She is the sister of my french teacher.
5. I've always wanted to take a trip to the far east in spring.
6. The kremlin, located in moscow, once housed the soviet government.
7. I needed to see dr. Madison, but the nurse told me the doctor would not be in until next week.
8. He shouted angrily, "why don't you ever arrive at your history class on time?"
9. The scholastic aptitude test will be given on january 18.
10. While yet a teenager growing up in harlem, james Baldwin became a baptist preacher.

EXERCISE 3 **Capitalization**
Capitalize wherever necessary.

1. The lawyer's office is located on south pleasant street.
2. My uncle lives farther south than grandmother.
3. I'd like to move to the south if I could find a job there.
4. The well-known anthropologist Margaret Mead was for many years director of the museum of natural history in new york city.
5. The constitution of the united states was signed in constitution hall on september 17, 1787.
6. Sculptor John Wilson was commissioned to create a bust of rev. Martin Luther King, jr.
7. The money will be funded partly from the national endowment for the arts.
8. I read the magazine article in *newsweek* while I was waiting in the dentist's office yesterday.
9. The tour took the retired teachers above the arctic circle.
10. Many gerber baby foods no longer have sugar and salt.

Eight Basic Uses of the Comma

You may feel uncertain about when to use the comma. The starting point is to concentrate on a few basic rules. These rules will cover most of your needs.

The tendency now in English is to use fewer commas than in the past. There is no one complete set of rules on which everyone agrees. However, if you learn these eight basic uses, your common sense will help you figure out what to do in other cases. Remember that a comma usually signifies a pause in a sentence. As you read a sentence out loud, listen to where you pause within the sentence. Where you pause is often your clue that a comma is needed. Notice that in each of the examples for the following eight uses, you can pause where the comma is placed.

- **Use a comma to separate items in a series (more than two items).**

  I was angry, fretful, and impatient.

  I was dreaming of running in the race, finishing among the top ten, and collapsing happily on the ground.

  Note: It is also considered acceptable to omit the comma before the *and* that introduces the last item.

  I was angry, fretful and impatient.

  - When an address or date occurs in a sentence, each part is considered an item in a series. A comma is put after each item, including the last:

    I lived at 428 North Monroe Street, Madison, Wisconsin, for many years.

    I was born on August 18, 1965, in the middle of a hurricane.

- If a number of adjectives modify a noun, but those adjectives do not go together to give us a single meaning, they are thought of as items in a series. In such a case, they are separated by commas.

  I carried my *favorite, old, green* coat.

- If two or more adjectives in front of a noun are thought of as going together to give a single meaning, they are not separated by commas:

  I carried my *dark green* coat.

- The words *dark* and *green* belong together to give the meaning of a single color; *dark* modifies the color *green* and the two words together describe the color of the coat.

Practice.......... In each of the following sentences, insert commas wherever they are needed.

1. Problems with the water supply of the United States Europe Canada and other parts of the world are growing.
2. Water is colorless tasteless odorless and free of calories.
3. You will use on an average day twenty-four gallons of water for flushing thirty-two gallons for bathing and washing clothes and twenty-five gallons for other uses.
4. It took 120 gallons of water to create the eggs you ate for breakfast 3,500 gallons for the steak you might eat for dinner and over 60,000 gallons to produce the steel used to make your car.
5. On November 14 1977 officials discovered a major body of polluted water in Oswego New York.

- **Use a comma along with a coordinating conjunction to combine two simple sentences (also called independent clauses) into a single compound sentence. (See Chapter 6 on coordination.)**

  The house was on fire, but I was determined not to leave my place of safety.

  Be careful that you use the comma with the conjunction only when you are combining sentences. If you are combining words or phrases, no comma is used.

  I was safe but not happy.

  My mother and father were searching for me.

  She was neither in class nor at work.

Practice.......... In each of the following sentences, insert commas wherever they are needed.

1. The most overused bodies of water are our rivers but they continue to serve us daily.
2. American cities often developed next to rivers and industries followed soon after in the same locations.

3. The people of the industrial age can try to clean the water they use or they can watch pollution take over.

4. The Great Lakes are showing signs of renewal yet the struggle against pollution there must continue.

5. Many people have not yet been educated about the dangers to our water supply nor are all our legislators fully aware of the problem.

- **Use a comma to follow introductory words, expressions, phrases, or clauses.**

A. Introductory words (such as *yes, no, oh, well*)

Oh, I never thought he would do it.

B. Introductory expressions (transitions such as *as a matter of fact, finally, secondly, furthermore, consequently*)

Therefore, I will give you a second chance.

C. Introductory phrases

Long prepositional phrase:	In the beginning of the course, I thought I would never be able to do the work.
Participial phrase:	Walking on tiptoe, the young mother quietly peeked into the nursery.
Infinitive phrase:	To be quite honest, I don't believe he's feeling well.

D. Introductory dependent clauses beginning with a subordinating conjunction (See Chapter 7.)

When the food arrived, we all grabbed for it.

Practice.......... In each of the following sentences, insert commas wherever they are needed.

1. To many people from the East the plans to supply more water to the western states seem unnecessary.

2. However people in the West know that they have no future without a good water supply.

3. When they entered Salt Lake Valley in 1847 the Mormons found dry soil that needed water before crops could be grown.

4. Confidently the new settlers dug ditches that brought the needed water.

5. Learning from the past modern farmers are trying to cooperate with nature.

- **Use commas surrounding a word, phrase, or clause when the word or group of words interrupts the main idea.**

A. Interrupting word

We will, however, take an X-ray.

B. Interrupting phrase

Prepositional phrase: I wanted, of course, to stay.

Appositive phrase: Ann, the girl with the braids, has a wicked sense of humor.

C. Interrupting clause

He won't, I think, try that again.

Ann, who wears braids, has a wicked sense of humor.

- Sometimes the same word, phrase, or clause can be used in more than one way. Often this changes the rule for punctuation. For example, consider the word *however:*

Use commas if the word interrupts in the middle of a clause.

We will, *however,* take an X-ray.

Use a semicolon and a comma if the word connects two independent clauses.

We will take an X-ray; *however,* the doctor cannot read it today.

Now consider the example of the relative clause *who wears braids:*

Use commas if the clause interrupts and is not essential to the main idea.

My sister, *who wears braids,* has a wicked sense of humor.

Do not use commas if the clause is part of the identity, necessary to the main idea.

The girl *who wears braids* is my sister.

Note: The clause *who wears braids* is necessary for identifying which girl is the sister.

Practice.......... In each of the following sentences, insert commas wherever they are needed.

1. Some parts of our country I believe do not have ample supplies of water.

2. The rocky soil of Virginia for example cannot absorb much rainwater.

3. Johnstown, Pennsylvania an industrial city of 48,000 is situated in one of the most flood-prone valleys of America.

4. It is not therefore a very safe place to live.
5. The Colorado which is one of our longest rivers gives up most of its water to farmers and cities before it can reach the sea.

- **Use a comma around nouns in direct address. (A noun in direct address is the name or title used in speaking to someone.)**

  I thought, Maria, that I saw your picture in the paper.

Practice.......... In each of the following sentences, insert commas wherever they are needed.

1. Dear your tea is ready now.
2. I wonder Jason if the game has been canceled.
3. Dad could I borrow five dollars?
4. I insist sir on speaking with the manager.
5. Margaret is that you?

- **Use a comma in numbers of one thousand or larger.**

  1,999

  1,999,999,999

Practice.......... In each of the following numbers, insert commas wherever they are needed.

1. 4876454
2. 87602
3. 156439600
4. 187000
5. 10000000000000

- **Use a comma to set off exact words spoken in dialogue.**

  "Let them," she said, "eat cake."

Note: Commas as well as periods are always placed inside the quotation marks.

Practice.......... In each of the following sentences, insert commas wherever they are necessary.

1. "I won't" he insisted "be a part of your scheme."
2. He mumbled "I plead the Fifth Amendment."
3. "I was told" the defendant explained "to answer every question."
4. "This court case" the judge announced "will be televised."
5. "The jury" said Al Tarvin of the press "was hand-picked."

- **Use a comma where it is necessary to prevent a misunderstanding.**

  Before eating, the cat prowled through the barn.

Practice.......... In each of the following sentences, insert commas wherever they are needed.

1. Kicking the child was carried off to bed.
2. To John Russell Baker is the best columnist.
3. When you can come and visit us.
4. Whoever that is is going to be surprised.
5. Some types of skin cancer can kill doctors say.

EXERCISE 4 **Using the Comma Correctly**
In each of the following sentences, insert commas wherever they are needed.

1. In Weaverville California the local high school administrators made an interesting discovery.
2. At a cost of $400 a year per student a private company was offering college-level advanced placement courses on the Web.
3. Since some students need these courses to get into more competitive colleges everyone thought this would be a perfect way to take advantage of the new technology.
4. The problems however soon became apparent when two students signed up for a government course.
5. Brian Jones a senior who wants to be a record producer and Jeremy Forbes a classmate who dreams of being a cartoonist found these problems very frustrating.
6. Among the worst problems they encountered were long delays getting online many technical glitches and the absence of a teacher to encourage persistence.
7. Out of 600 students in 28 states who enrolled in one of the company's online advanced placement courses in the last school year two-thirds did not complete enough course work to take the final exam.
8. Government officials have praised the use of this electronic support for schools but others say online courses are a poor replacement for the 180000 new teachers the country really needs.
9. Others are critical that much of the instruction in cyberspace is made up of only supplemental kinds of instruction such as SAT training college counseling and virtual field trips.
10. Francisco J. Hernandez an educator at the University of California at Santa Cruz says "Our intent is not to be an alternative to a high quality teacher and classroom but to be an alternative to nothing because that's what students are getting right now."

EXERCISE 5 **Using the Comma Correctly**
In each of the following sentences, insert commas wherever they are needed.

1. Abraham Lincoln was born on February 12 1809 in Kentucky.
2. In December 1816 after selling most of their possessions the Lincoln family moved to Indiana.

3. During their first weeks in Indiana the family hunted for food drank melted snow and huddled together for warmth.

4. After a little formal education Lincoln worked on a ferryboat on the Ohio River.

5. The first large city that Lincoln visited was New Orleans an important center of trade in 1828.

6. Among the 40000 people Lincoln found himself with on that first visit there were people from all the states and several foreign countries.

7. New Orleans also showed Lincoln such city luxuries as fancy clothes gleaming silverware expensive furniture and imported china and glassware.

8. As a result of this visit Lincoln must have compared the log cabin of his childhood with the wealthy houses of this big city.

9. A few years later Lincoln became a merchant but his failure in business left him in debt for over ten years.

10. We should be grateful that Lincoln who started off in a business career turned his attention to politics.

EXERCISE 6 Using the Comma Correctly

In each of the following examples, insert commas wherever they are needed.

1. The Hope Diamond is one of the most famous if not *the* most famous gems in the world.

2. Mined in India the diamond reached Europe in 1668 along with the story that there was a curse on the stone.

3. The curse or so the legend goes is that bad fortune followed the diamond because it had been stolen from a temple in India.

4. Nearly all of its owners including Marie Antoinette of France a French actress who was shot to death and an American woman whose children were killed in accidents have met with tragedy.

5. Well if we cannot share in the history of the Hope Diamond we can see it in the Smithsonian Institution in our nation's capital.

6. Other gems not as famous have served people throughout history as payments for ransom as bribes and as lavish wedding presents.

7. One of the most famous mines in South America is in Colombia where an emerald mine started in 1537 is still being worked today.

8. Some gems are difficult to find but as the earth's crust changes rough stones may find their way into streams rivers and other bodies of water.

9. The greatest number of diamonds emeralds amethyst topaz and other precious and semiprecious stones are to be found in Africa and South America.

10. We could travel to these places if we had the time the money and the interest.

Three Uses for the Apostrophe

1. Use 's to form the possessive:

A. Add an *'s* to any singular noun:

the pen of the teacher = the teacher*'s* pen

the strategy of the boss = the boss*'s* strategy

the wheel of the car = the car*'s* wheel

Be careful to choose the right noun when you form the possessive. Always ask yourself *who* or *what* possesses something. In the previous examples, the teacher possesses the pen, the boss possesses the strategy, and the car possesses the wheel.

Note these unusual possessives:

Hyphenated words:	mother-in-law*'s* advice
Joint possession:	Lucy and Desi*'s* children
Individual possession:	John*'s* and Steve*'s* ideas

B. Add an *'s* to any irregular plural noun that does not end in *-s.*

the hats of the children = the children*'s* hats

the harness for the oxen = the oxen*'s* harness

C. Add an *'s* to any indefinite pronouns:

everyone*'s* responsibility

somebody*'s* wallet

INDEFINITE PRONOUNS

anyone	everyone	no one	someone
anybody	everybody	nobody	somebody
anything	everything	nothing	something

Note: A **possessive pronoun** *(his, hers, its, ours, yours, theirs, whose)* never uses an apostrophe.

Whose key is this?

The key is *his.*

The car is *theirs.*

D. Add only an apostrophe (without any *-s*) to a regular plural noun that ends in *-s*.

the coats of the ladies = the ladies' coats

the store of the brothers = the brothers' store

- A few singular nouns ending in the *s* or *z* sound are awkward-sounding if another *s* sound is added. You may drop the final *s*. Let your ear help you make the decision.

Jesus' robe *not* Jesus'*s* robe
Moses' law *not* Moses'*s* law

2. Use '*s* to form certain plurals in order to prevent confusion.

A. Numbers:

The teller gave the customer the money in 100'*s*.

B. Letters:

All his a'*s* look like o'*s*.

C. Years:

He was born in the 1800'*s*. He was born in the 1800s.

Note: Both are considered correct.

D. Abbreviations:

My sisters both have Ph.D.'*s* from Berkeley.

E. Words referred to in a text:

He uses too many *and's* in his writing.

Note: Be sure never to use the apostrophe to form a plural in any other case.

3. Use an apostrophe to show where one or more letters have been omitted in a contraction.

cannot = can't

should not = shouldn't

will not = won't (the only contraction that changes its spelling)

I am = I'm

she will = she'll

EXERCISE 7 Using the Apostrophe

Fill in each of the blanks below using the rules you have just studied for uses of the apostrophe.

1. rays of the sun	the ________ rays
2. sleeve of the dress	the ________ sleeve
3. length of the room	the ________ length
4. the house of Antony and Maria (joint possession)	________ house
5. the idea of nobody	________ idea
6. The book belongs to him.	The book is ________.
7. in the century of 1700	in the ________
8. That is her opinion. (contraction)	________ her opinion.
9. shirts for boys	________ shirts
10. the cover of the book	the ________ cover

EXERCISE 8 Using the Apostrophe

Fill in each of the blanks below using the rules you have just studied for uses of the apostrophe.

1. clarity of the diamond	the ________ clarity
2. the flight of the geese	the ________ flight
3. the work of Ann and Chris (individual possession)	________ work
4. the plan of someone	________ plan
5. The drums belong to her.	The drums are ________.
6. the terrible year of two	the terrible ________
7. We cannot leave yet. (contraction)	We ________ leave yet.
8. the leaves of the tree	the ________ leaves
9. the cheese of the farmers	the ________ cheese
10. the life-style of my brother-in-law	my ________ life-style

EXERCISE 9 Using the Apostrophe

Fill in each of the blanks below using the rules you have just studied for uses of the apostrophe.

1. the engine of the train	the ________ engine
2. the spirit of the class	the ________ spirit
3. the center for women	the ________ center
4. the wish of everybody	________ wish
5. The toys belong to them.	The toys are ________.
6. The child mixes up *b* and *d*.	The child mixes up ________.
7. I will not leave this house. (contraction)	I ________ leave this house.

8. the grain of the wood — the ________ grain

9. the verdict of the jurors — the ________ verdict

10. the policies of Ridge School and Orchard School (individual possession) — ____________________ ________ policies

Other Marks of Punctuation

Four Uses for Quotation Marks

1. Use quotation marks for a direct quotation:

"Please," I begged, "go away."

Note: Do not use quotation marks for an indirect quotation.

I begged her to go away.

2. Use quotation marks for material copied word for word from a source:

According to *The New York Times,* "The average adult body contains 40 to 50 quarts of water. Blood is 83 percent water; muscles are 75 percent water; the brain is 74 percent water; and even bone is 22 percent water."

3. Use quotation marks for titles of shorter works such as short stories, one-act plays, poems, articles in magazines and newspapers, songs, essays, and chapters of books:

"A Modest Proposal," an essay by Jonathan Swift, is a masterpiece of satire.

"The Lottery," a short story by Shirley Jackson, created a sensation when it first appeared in *The New Yorker.*

4. Use quotation marks for words used in a special way:

"Duckie" is a term of affection used by the British, the way we would use the word "honey."

A Note about Italics and Underlining

The title of a full-length work (such as a book, a play of several acts, a magazine, or a newspaper) is italicized in print and underlined when handwritten.

In print: Many famous short stories have first appeared in *The New Yorker.*

Handwritten form: *Many famous short stories have first appeared in* <u>*The New Yorker*</u>*.*

Practice.......... In each of the following sentences, insert quotation marks wherever they are needed.

1. The Gift of the Magi is one of the short stories contained in O. Henry's book *The Four Million.*
2. Franklin Delano Roosevelt said, We have nothing to fear but fear itself.
3. The president told his cabinet that they would have to settle the problem in the next few days.
4. Punk is a particular form of rock music.
5. She read the article Trouble in Silicon Valley in a recent issue of *Newsweek.*

If these five sentences had been handwritten, which words would have been underlined?

Three Uses for the Semicolon

1. **Use a semicolon to join two independent clauses whose ideas and sentence structures are related:**

   He decided to consult the map; she decided to ask a pedestrian.

2. **Use a semicolon to combine two sentences using an adverbial conjunction:**

   He decided to consult the map; however, she decided to ask a pedestrian.

3. **Use a semicolon to separate items in a series when the items themselves contain commas:**

   I had lunch with Linda, my best friend; Mrs. Armstrong, my English teacher; and Jan, my sister-in-law.

Note: If the writer had used only commas to separate items in this example, the reader might think five or six people had gone to lunch.

Practice.......... In each of the following sentences, insert a semicolon wherever needed.

1. One of the best ways to remember a vacation is to take numerous photos one of the best ways to recall the contents of a book is to take notes.
2. The problem of street crime must be solved otherwise, the number of vigilantes will increase.
3. The committee was made up of Kevin Corey, a writer Anita Poindexter, a professor and Jorge Rodriguez, a politician.
4. The bank president was very cordial however, he would not approve the loan.
5. Robots are being used in the factories of Japan eventually they will be common in this country as well.

Four Uses for the Colon

1. **Use a colon after an independent clause when the material that follows is a list, an illustration, or an explanation:**

   A. A list:

   > Please order the following items: five dozen pencils, twenty rulers, and five rolls of tape.

   Notice that in the sentence below, no colon is used because there is not a complete sentence before the list.

   > The courses I am taking this semester are Freshman Composition, Introduction to Psychology, Art Appreciation, and Survey of American Literature.

   B. An explanation or illustration:

   > She was an exceptional child: at seven she was performing on the concert stage.

2. **Use a colon for the salutation of a business letter:**

   > To whom it may concern:
   >
   > Dear Madam President:

3. **Use a colon when telling time:**

   > We will eat at 5:15.

4. **Use a colon between the title and subtitle of a book:**

   > *Plain English Please: A Rhetoric*

Practice.......... In each of the following sentences, insert colons where they are needed.

1. Three pianists played in New York on the same weekend André Watts, Claudio Arrau, and Jorge Bolet.
2. The official has one major flaw in his personality greed.
3. The restaurant has lovely homemade desserts such as German chocolate layer cake and baked Alaska.
4. The college offers four courses in English literature Romantic Poetry, Shakespeare's Plays, The British Short Story, and The Modern Novel.
5. Arriving at 615 in the morning, Marlene brought me a sausage and cheese pizza, soda, and a gallon of ice cream.

The Dash and Parentheses

The comma, dash, and parentheses can all be used to show an interruption of the main idea. The particular form of punctuation you choose depends on the degree of interruption.

1. **Use the dash for a less formal and more emphatic interruption of the main idea. Dashes are seldom used in formal writing.**

   He came—I thought—by car.

   She arrived—and I know this for a fact—in a pink Cadillac.

2. **Use parentheses to insert extra information that some of your readers might want to know but that is not at all essential for the main idea. Such information is not emphasized.**

   Johann Sebastian Bach (1685–1750) composed the "Six Brandenburg Concertos."

   Plea bargaining (see Section 4.3) was developed to speed court verdicts.

Practice.......... Insert dashes or parentheses wherever needed.

1. Herbert Simon is and I don't think this is an exaggeration a genius.
2. George Eliot her real name was Mary Ann Evans wrote *Silas Marner.*
3. You should in fact I insist see a doctor.
4. Unemployment brings with it a number of other problems see the study by Brody, 1982.
5. Mass media television, radio, movies, magazines, and newspapers are able to transmit information over a wide range and to a large number of people.

EXERCISE 10 Other Marks of Punctuation

In each of the following sentences, insert marks of punctuation wherever they are needed.

1. To measure crime, sociologists have used three different techniques official statistics, victimization surveys, and self-report studies.
2. The Bells is one of the best-loved poems of Edgar Allan Poe.
3. The lake this summer has one major disadvantage for swimmers seaweed.
4. E. B. White wrote numerous essays for adults however, he also wrote some very popular books for children.
5. Tuberculosis also known as consumption has once again become a serious health issue.
6. The Victorian Period 1837–1901 saw a rapid expansion in industry.
7. He promised me I know he promised that he would come to my graduation.
8. Do you know what the French expression déjà vu means?
9. She wanted to go to the movies he decided to stay home and see an old film on his new videocassette recorder.
10. She has the qualifications needed for the job a teaching degree, a pleasant personality, two years' experience, and a love of children.

EXERCISE 11

Other Marks of Punctuation

In each of the following sentences, insert marks of punctuation wherever they are needed.

1. Many young people have two feelings about science and technology awe and fear.
2. The three people who helped work out the real estate transaction were Mr. Doyle, the realtor Mrs. White, the bank officer and Scott Castle, the lawyer.
3. The book was entitled *English Literature The Victorian Age.*
4. I decided to walk to school, she said, because the bus fare has been raised again.
5. She brought the following items to the beach a bathing suit, towel, sunglasses, and several books.
6. The conference I believe it is scheduled for sometime in January will focus on the development of a new curriculum.
7. The song Memories comes from the Broadway show *Cats.*
8. The complex lab experiment has these two major problems too many difficult calculations and too many variables.
9. The mutt that is to say my dog is smarter than he looks.
10. Violent crime cannot be reduced unless the society supports efforts such as strengthening the family structure, educating the young, and recruiting top-notch police.

EXERCISE 12

Other Marks of Punctuation

In each of the following sentences, supply marks of punctuation wherever they are needed.

1. Star Wars is the popular term for the development of atomic weapons for use in space.
2. Remember, the doctor told the patient, the next time I see you I want to see an improvement in your condition.
3. The student's short story Ten Steps to Nowhere appeared in a collection entitled *The Best of Student Writing.*
4. The report stated specifically that the company must if it wanted to grow sell off at least 10 percent of its property.
5. The foreign countries she visited were Mexico, Israel, and Morocco.
6. My father enjoyed spending money my mother was frugal.
7. These students made the high honor roll David Hyatt, Julie Carlson, and Erica Lane.
8. The scientist showed the class a glass of H_2O water and asked them to identify the liquid.
9. He said that he would give us an extension on our term papers.
10. The work was tedious nevertheless, the goal of finding the solution kept him motivated.

Mastery and Editing Tests

TEST 1 Editing for Correct Capitalization and Punctuation

Read the following paragraph and insert the correct capitalization and marks of punctuation wherever they are needed.

will rogers 1879–1935 is often remembered as the cowboy philosopher. He was born on november 4 1879 on a ranch near oologah oklahoma. After two years in a military academy he left school and became a cowboy in the texas panhandle. Then he drifted off to argentina later he turned up in south africa as a member of texas jacks wild west circus. He was one of the best ropers of all times but his real talent was his ability as a writer. He became famous for his homespun humor and his shrewd timely comments on current events. his comments on the news appeared in 350 daily newspapers. He always began a performance by saying all I know is what I read in the papers. This saying became a byword in the 1920s. Rogers married betty blake an arkansas school teacher in 1908 and together they had four children. Although he started his motion picture career in 1918 it was not until 1934 that he made his first appearance in a stage play *ah, wilderness!* by Eugene O'Neill. Unfortunately Rogers was killed the following year in a plane crash near Point Barrow Alaska on his way to the orient.

TEST 2 Editing for Correct Capitalization and Punctuation

Read the following paragraph and insert the correct capitalization and marks of punctuation wherever they are needed.

The expression your name is mud has its origin in a person from history. Samuel Mudd was a doctor in Maryland during the civil war. About 4 a.m. on april 15 1865 at his home in charles county Maryland dr. Mudd was awakened by men who needed medical attention. One was john wilkes booth who had just killed president Abraham Lincoln at ford's theatre in Washington, d.c. Mudd set and bandaged booths broken leg before the assassin went on his way. A few days later the doctor was arrested and charged with being part of the conspiracy to kill the president. He was convicted by a military court and sentenced to life in prison but in 1869 president Andrew Johnson commuted his sentence. Since that time dr. Mudds descendants have tried unsuccessfully to have that original conviction overturned but without success. One politician united states representative Steny Hoyer introduced a bill the Samuel Mudd relief act that would have cleared the doctors name but it failed to pass. Last march after another setback Richard Mudd the grandson of Samuel Mudd said to reporters as long as the United States lasts the story of my 31-year-old grandfather being put in prison for life for setting a broken leg is never going to end.

TEST 3 **Editing for Correct Capitalization and Punctuation**

Read the following paragraph and insert the correct capitalization and marks of punctuation wherever they are needed.

valentines day is celebrated on february 14 as a festival of romance and affection. People send their sweethearts greeting cards that ask won't you be my valentine? Children like to make their own valentines from paper doilies red construction paper bright foils and wallpaper samples. These customs probably came from the ancient roman festival of lupercalia which took place every february 15. The festival honored juno the roman goddess of women and marriage and pan the god of nature. Young men and women chose partners for the festival by drawing names by chance from a box. After exchanging gifts they often continued to enjoy each others company long after the festival and many were eventually married. In the year 496 the church changed the lupercalia festival of february 15 to saint valentines day on February 14 but the sentimental meaning of the old festival has remained to the present time. According to the book *popular antiquities* which was written in 1877 people were observing this holiday in england as early as 1446. One account tells of young men wearing the names of their ladies on their sleeves for several days. The expression he wears his heart on his sleeve probably came from this custom. In the united states valentines day became popular in the 1800s at the time of the civil war. Many of the valentines of that period were hand painted and today their beautiful decorative qualities make them collectors items.

WORKING TOGETHER

WRITING A RESTAURANT REVIEW

What is your idea of the perfect job? Some people might think that eating out all the time and then writing reviews of the restaurants visited would be the perfect occupation.

Read this typical newspaper review of a neighborhood restaurant. The review contains certain important information that a reader would want to know, such as location, days and hours of operation, menu, atmosphere, price, and unique features.

Divide into groups. Together compose a restaurant review. (It would be nice if your group could actually go to the eatery you choose to write about.) First, decide what factors should be considered for the review. Each person should have fifteen minutes to compose his or her part of the review. Allow half an hour at the end to put the parts together and to decide on an introduction and a conclusion to the review.

Portfolio Suggestion

Keep this review in your portfolio. Whenever you eat out, go to a musical event, or see a movie, keep in mind that these are all places where reviewers go and write down their reactions. You can too!

Online Activity

Go to the "Diner Reviews" section at "Diner City: Your Online Guide to Classic Diners of the American Roadside" at http://www.dinercity.com Using one of the reviews as a departure point, rewrite the review while supplying details to make the writing more vivid.

EATING OUT

If you appreciate authentic Chinese food, you should go for lunch or dinner to the Golden Fortune Restaurant, located at 99 Elm Avenue in Ellington. It is just above the South Side Plaza, walking distance from the center of town. The Golden Fortune Restaurant is the kind of restaurant you will want to visit more than once. The food is expertly prepared, the prices are very moderate, and the service is always friendly. We particularly liked the warm and relaxed atmosphere, partly the result of soft classical music playing in the background.

Many of the lunch and dinner selections at the Golden Fortune are traditional, with a few surprises. All of the vegetables used are fresh, and there is a choice of white or brown rice. The appetizers are large enough to serve two people. On our first visit, we were delighted with the combination platter. It is the most popular appetizer on the menu because it allows diners to sample a half dozen of the house specialties.

One unique touch at this restaurant is the choice of 24 different teas. Instead of the ordinary pot of green tea that is placed in front of you in most Chinese restaurants, at the Golden Fortune you can choose from a wide variety. These include green tea with passion fruit, peach tea, or even milk tea with oatmeal. Customers enjoy trying new combinations each time they visit. Our favorite is the black tea with plum. If you like, you may bring your own wine or beer, and the waiters will be happy to serve it.

Some of the most popular main courses are beef with garlic sauce, crispy honey chicken on a bed of rice and vegetables, and a variety of delicious stir-fry dishes. If you choose a stir-fry at the Golden Fortune, you may select a favorite sauce and type of noodle along with a meat or fish, and the kitchen will make up the dish you want.

The Golden Fortune is open for lunch from noon to 4 P.M. and for dinner from 5 P.M. until 11 P.M. every day of the week. No reservations are needed. For take-out orders, call 548-4407 after 11 A.M.

PART III UNDERSTANDING THE POWER OF WORDS

Some writers approach their work by first brainstorming or clustering their ideas; other writers feel more comfortable doing freewriting to produce their first drafts. No matter what approach is taken, an important part of any finished piece of writing is the choice of words a writer makes. When the writer and social activist Malcolm X was educating himself in prison, he obtained a dictionary and copied it word for word—certainly a systematic approach to studying words! You too should concentrate on individual words. This unit focuses on that part of the writing process that pays attention to words: word choice, word meanings, wordiness, appropriate words, words often confused, and finally the editing of words.

The work of this unit leads up to the editing of student drafts. Using commonly accepted editing symbols, you will work with student paragraphs and essays, finding and correcting word and sentence level errors. By doing this kind of editing, you will be taking a word-by-word approach. You will use all the analytical language skills that you have been developing so far to make effective changes to your own writing and the work of others.

Chapter 13 Choosing Words that Work

Preview

Many people find the subtle meanings of words fascinating. If you have learned a second language, you understand how significant a single word can be, depending if it is used correctly or incorrectly. In this chapter you will explore several issues that need to be addressed in all formal writing.

- Words rich in meaning
- Denotation/connotation
- Wordiness
  - Redundant expressions
  - Wordy phrases
  - Overuse of the verb *to be*
  - Unnecessary repetition of the same word
  - Unnecessary use of *there is* or *there are*
  - Flowery or pretentious language
  - Apologetic, tentative expressions
- Inappropriate language for formal writing
  - slang
  - clipped language
  - sexist language
  - trite expressions (clichés)

Key Terms

Denotation
Connotation

Using Words Rich in Meaning

Writing is a constant search to find the right words to express thoughts and feelings as accurately as possible. When a writer wants to be precise or wants to give a flavor to a piece of writing, the creative possibilities are almost endless for word choice and sentence construction. The creative writer looks for words that have rich and appropriate meanings and associations.

For instance, if you were describing a young person under five years of age, you might choose one of these words:

imp	brat	preschooler
toddler	tot	youngster
child		

Some words have no associations beyond their strict dictionary meaning. These words are said to be neutral. Which word in the list is the most neutral, with the least negative or positive emotional associations?* The person who is writing a brochure for a nursery school would probably choose the word *preschooler* because it identifies the age of the child. A person talking about a child who has just learned to walk would possibly use the word *toddler* because it carries the association of a small child who is toddling along a bit unsteadily. What informal and unkind word might an angry older sibling shout when a younger brother or sister has just colored all over a favorite book?†

EXERCISE 1 Using Words Rich in Meaning

The five words in Column A all have the basic meaning of *thin*. For each word, however, an additional meaning makes the word richer and more specific. Match each word in Column A with the letter of the definition from Column B that best fits the meaning of the word.

Column A		Column B
__________	**1.** slender	a. unattractively thin
__________	**2.** emaciated	b. thin and bony with a haggard appearance
__________	**3.** lean	c. gracefully long and slim
__________	**4.** skinny	d. containing little fat, in shape, fit
__________	**5.** gaunt	e. extremely thin, undernourished, and sickly

Most languages are rich with words that describe eating. Column A contains a few English words about eating. Match each word in Column A with the letter of the definition from Column B that best fits the meaning of the word.

Column A		Column B
__________	**1.** taste	a. to eat with small quick bites
__________	**2.** devour	b. to bite or chew on something persistently
__________	**3.** nibble	c. to eat between meals
__________	**4.** gorge	d. to test the flavor of a food
__________	**5.** gnaw	e. to stuff oneself with food
__________	**6.** snack	f. to eat up greedily

EXERCISE 2 Using Words Rich in Meaning

The words *eat, drink, hit,* or *walk* are neutral words (having no positive or negative associations). Underneath each neutral term are four words, each one having its own more precise meaning. In each case, give a definition for the word.

---

* Your answer should be *child*.

† Your answer to the second question should be *brat*.

Example: crunch—to eat with a noisy crackling sound

to eat

1. gobble ______________________

2. savor ______________________

3. munch ______________________

4. chomp ______________________

to drink

1. sip ______________________

2. gulp ______________________

3. slurp ______________________

4. lap ______________________

to hit

1. swat ______________________

2. slap ______________________

3. paddle ______________________

4. flog ______________________

to walk

1. lumber ______________________

2. amble ______________________

3. stride ______________________

4. roam ______________________

EXPLORING ONLINE

Access online thesaurus and dictionary entries at http://www.xrefer.com

Understanding Loaded Words: Denotation/Connotation

The careful writer must consider more than the dictionary meaning of a word. Some words have different meanings for different people.

The **denotation** of a word is its strict dictionary meaning.

The **connotation** of a word is the meaning (apart from the dictionary meaning) that a person attaches to a word because of the person's personal experience with the word.

word: liberal

denotation (political): to favor nonrevolutionary progress or reform

possible connotations: socially active, free thinking, too generous, far left, favoring many costly government programs

Politicians are usually experts in understanding the connotations of a word. They know, for instance, that if they want to get votes in a conservative area, they should not refer to their own views as liberal. The strict dictionary meaning of *liberal* is "to favor nonrevolutionary progress or reform," certainly an idea that most people would support. However, when most people hear the words *liberal* or *conservative,* they bring to the words many political biases and experiences from their past: their parents' attitudes, the political and social history of the area in which they live, and many other factors that may correctly or incorrectly influence their understanding of a word.

Choosing words that are not neutral but that have more exact or appropriate meanings is a powerful skill for your writing, one that will help your reader better understand the ideas you want to communicate. As your vocabulary grows, your writing will become richer and deeper. Your work will reflect your understanding of all the shades of meanings that words can possibly have.

EXERCISE 3 Denotation/Connotation

In this exercise you have the opportunity to think of words that are richer in associations than the neutral words that are underlined in the sentences below. Write your own word choice in the space to the right of each sentence. Discuss with others in your class the associations you make with the words you have chosen.

1. I live in a house at the edge of town. ____________
2. I walk home from work every night. ____________
3. Usually the same person is always walking behind me. ____________
4. She is always carrying a lot of stuff. ____________
5. She looks as if she is old. ____________
6. She has marks all over her face. ____________
7. Sometimes I try to talk with her. ____________
8. She has such an unusual look in her eyes. ____________
9. Sometimes I can hear her talking to herself. ____________

10. At night when I am sitting in my favorite armchair, I often think of her and wish she could tell me the story of her life. ______________

EXERCISE 4

Denotation/Connotation

The following sentences contain words that may have positive or negative associations for you. Read each sentence and study the underlined word or phrase. Below each sentence, write the emotional meaning the underlined word or phrase has for you. Discuss your answers with your classmates. An example follows.

Her *brother* went with her, so she would not have to drive alone.

Explanation: The word *brother* has a positive connotation. We expect a *brother* to be someone who is helpful and protective.

1. The dog stood at the door; his size was quite astounding.

____

____

2. The foreigner approached the ranch slowly.

____

____

3. His pick-up truck was parked in front.

____

____

4. A woman and child were peering out from behind the fence.

____

____

5. The stranger carried a long object of some kind.

____

____

EXERCISE 5

Denotation/Connotation

When you write, you create a tone by the words you choose. Review the sentences you have worked with in Exercise 4. For each sentence, create a more positive tone either by changing each underlined word or phrase to a different word or phrase, or by adding adjectives to modify the underlined word or phrase.

1. ______________________________

____

2. ______________________________

____

3. ______________________________

____

4. ______________________________

____

5. ______________________________

____

Wordiness: In Writing, Less Can Be More!

In his book *The Elements of Style,* the famous writer E. B. White quotes his old teacher William Strunk, Jr., who said that a sentence "should contain no unnecessary words" and a paragraph "no unnecessary sentences." Strunk's philosophy of writing also includes the commandment he gave many times in his class at Cornell University: "Omit needless words!" It was a lesson that E. B. White took to heart, with the wonderful results that we see in his own writing.

Below is a summary of some important ways you can cut the actual number of your words in order to strengthen the power of your ideas. As you read each example of wordiness, notice how the revision has eliminated unnecessary words.

1. Redundant expressions	**Revisions**
circle around	circle
blue in color	blue
past history	history
connect together	connect
true fact	fact

2. Wordy phrases	**Revisions**
in the event that	if
due to the fact that	because
for the stated reason that	because
in this day and age	today
at this point in time	now
in the neighborhood of	about

3. Overuse of the verb *to be*	**Revision**
The man is in need of help.	The man needs help.

4. Unnecessary repetition of the same word	**Revision**
The book is on the table. The book is my favorite. I have read the book five times	The book on the table is my favorite. I have read it five times.

5. Unnecessary use of *there is* or *there are*	**Revision**
There are two major disadvantages to the new proposal.	The new proposal has two major disadvantages.

6. **Flowery or pretentious language**	**Revision**
It is delightful to contemplate the culinary experience we will enjoy after the termination of this cinematic event.	I can't wait until we have pizza after the movie.

7. **Apologetic, tentative expressions**	**Revisions**
In my opinion, the grading policy for this course should be changed.	The grading policy for this course should be changed.
Right now, it seems to me that finding a job in my field is very difficult.	Right now, finding a job in my field is very difficult.
In this paper, I will try to explain my views on censorship of the campus newspaper.	Censoring the campus newspaper is a mistake.

EXERCISE 6 Revising Wordy Sentences

For each of the following sentences, underline the part that is unnecessarily wordy, and on the line below revise the sentence.

1. The date for the final completion of your project is May 18.

   ____

   ____

2. The thought of the exam is causing her to be in a constant state of tension.

   ____

   ____

3. There is no better place to study than in our library.

   ____

   ____

4. Some people have the belief that astrology is a science.

   ____

   ____

5. We are all in need of better organizational skills.

   ____

   ____

6. As far as mechanical ability is concerned, Mike is very handy.

   ____

   ____

7. She is in the process of cooking dinner.

8. Due to the fact of the rain, the game will be cancelled.

9. In my opinion, it would seem to me that the reasons for unemployment are complex.

10. The box had an oblong shape.

EXERCISE 7 **Revising Wordy Sentences**

For each of the following sentences, underline the part that is unnecessarily wordy, and on the line below revise the sentence.

1. The gentleman is of a kindly nature.

2. I was told he is a male actor.

3. The price was in the neighborhood of fifty dollars.

4. In regard to the letter, it was sent to the wrong address.

5. It is everyone's duty to be in attendance at the meeting today.

6. My best friend is above me in height.

7. I tiptoed down the stairs on my toes in order to surprise everyone.

8. They made the discovery that I was not upstairs.

____

____

9. A member of the teaching staff at this institution of higher learning failed to submit in a timely fashion the fruits of my endeavors for the course during this entire period from September to December.

____

____

10. Even though I am not an expert, I think that more neighborhood health clinics are needed.

____

____

Recognizing Appropriate Language for Formal Writing

In speaking or writing to our family and friends, an informal style is always appropriate because it is relaxed and conversational. On the other hand, writing and speaking in school or at work requires a more formal style, one that is less personal and more detached in tone. In formal writing situations, slang is not appropriate. Furthermore, any use of language that is seen as sexist or disrespectful to any individual, or groups of individuals, is not at all acceptable.

Slang is a term that refers to a special word or expression that a particular group of people use, often with the intention of keeping the meaning to themselves. A characteristic of a slang word or expression is that it is often used only for a limited period of time and then is forgotten. For example:

The party was *swell.* (1940s)

The party was *groovy.* (1960s)

The party was *awesome.* (1990s)

Slang or informal words	Acceptable
bucks	dollars
kids	children
cops	police
a bummer	a bad experience
off the wall	crazy
yummy	delicious
chow	food

Clipped language is the use of shortened words to make communication more relaxed and informal. Clipped language is not appropriate usage in more formal writing, which requires standard English.

Clipped language	**Acceptable**
doc	doctor
fridge	refrigerator
pro	professional
t.v.	television

Sexist language is the use of single gender nouns or pronouns to refer to both men and women. This was standard usage in the past, but writers and publishers today avoid such language.

Sexist: Everyone must bring *his* project on Tuesday.

Three options for revising a sentence with sexist language:

1. Revise the sentence using plural pronouns and plural antecedents.

All students must bring *their* projects on Tuesday.

2. Change the pronoun to an article.

Everyone must bring *the* project on Tuesday.

3. Change the sentence into the passive voice.

All projects must be brought to class on Tuesday.

Sexist language	**Acceptable**
fireman	firefighter
mailman	mail carrier
stewardess	flight attendant
common man	average person
actress	actor
mankind	humanity
The teacher is an important man. He can influence the lives of many children in the community.	Teachers are important people. They can influence the lives of many children in a community.

Trite expressions (or clichés) are those expressions which may have been fresh at one time but now have become stale from overuse.

Trite expressions	Acceptable
cool as a cucumber	calm
mad as a hornet	angry
a golden opportunity	an exceptional opportunity
blind as a bat	blind
busy as a bee	busy
dead as a doornail	dead
slowly but surely	gradually
without rhyme or reason	senseless

EXERCISE 8 Recognizing Inappropriate Language for Formal Writing

The following sentences contain words that are informal, slang, or sexist. Circle the word in each sentence that is inappropriate for formal writing, and on the line to the right of each sentence, provide a more formal word or expression to replace the inappropriate word.

1. Melanie brought her boom box along to the party for some music. ________________
2. She told her friends to chill out. ________________
3. The entire evening turned out to be a bummer. ________________
4. The businessmen in the community support the science project. ________________
5. The time has come to level with the director. ________________
6. The first experiment turned out to be a downer. ________________
7. The scientist has guts to continue the research. ________________
8. The entire lab is a dump. ________________
9. The guys often spend the night there. ________________
10. They work until two or three in the morning and then crash. ________________

EXERCISE 9 Recognizing Inappropriate Language for Formal Writing

The following sentences contain words that are informal, slang, or sexist. Circle the word in each sentence that is inappropriate for formal writing, and on the line to the right of each sentence, provide a more formal word or expression to replace the inappropriate word.

1. Don't bug me about studying. ________________
2. I aced the last French test. ________________
3. Bring me some grub tonight. ________________
4. He's my buddy. ________________
5. What's the lousy weather like outside? ________________

6. That idea doesn't grab me just right. ____________

7. I still have a crush on that intern. ____________

8. The medical doctor is a well-respected person in most communities; he is considered a role model for our children. ____________

9. I think it's gonna be nice tomorrow. ____________

10. I ain't seen the new neighbors yet. ____________

Studying a Student Essay for Word Choices

ACTIVITY 1 **Making Better Word Choices**

When Sandra Russell wrote an essay on the experience of living through a tornado, she composed more than one draft. Below are six sentences that the student could have written when she worked on the first draft of her essay.

Rewrite each of the sentences. Your revisions could include different word choices or added words, phrases, and clauses that make the sentences more descriptive and interesting.

1. All afternoon clouds were getting dark.

____

____

2. I could see lightning and hear thunder.

____

____

3. She took my hand and took me to the storm cellar.

____

____

4. We sat in the cellar.

____

____

5. Stuff lay around our yard.

____

____

6. The storm came through my neighborhood destroying lots of property.

____

____

ACTIVITY 2 **Sharing Sentence Revisions**

Share your revised sentences with other members of your class. For each of the six sentences, write three revised examples on the board for the class to review.

ACTIVITY 3 **Working with a Student Essay**

Read the complete student essay out loud. Following the reading, search through the essay to discover how Sandra Russell expressed these six ideas that you have revised in Activity 2. Underline each of the six sentences as you find them. Discuss with class members how these ideas were successfully expressed by the student writer.

Bad Weather

I was born in Booneville, Arkansas, and grew up on a small farm about five miles south of Paris. Naturally, I grew up in an area where tornados are feared each spring. I didn't really understand this until one humid, still night in April of 1985.

All afternoon, dark threatening clouds had been building up in the west, blocking out the sun. I could see the lightning dance about the sky, as the thunder responded by shaking the ground beneath my feet. The wind softly stirred the tree tops but then quickly died as it got darker and darker.

I walked outside and listened to the silence ringing in my ears. In the distance I could hear a rumble, soft at first but slowly and steadily intensifying. My mom came outside and stood at my side and listened to the rumbling noise. Everything was still, nothing dared to move. Even my dog Moose lay quietly, as if punished, in his doghouse. It was almost as if he knew what was about to happen.

"Mama, what's that noise?" I asked her, but she didn't answer. She grabbed my hand and dragged me to the storm cellar. I didn't have time to argue with her before I heard the rumble nearly upon us. We huddled in the musty smelling cellar. The roar was so loud it hurt my ears. I could hear the whistling of the wind above us. I cried and screamed for the awful noise of the whistle to stop, but no one could hear me above the ferocious noise. The rumble barreled on us and it seemed as if it would never end. The air was still in the dark cellar, but I could hear it as it moved violently above our heads. I didn't think the thundering noise would ever end.

I hadn't realized that I had quit breathing until it finally stopped. I drew a quick breath and thanked God it was over and my mother and I were safe. We crawled out of the cellar and took the first real look at our home. Trees were uprooted. Glass and boards and even a stop sign lay scattered around our yard. The roof on our house was damaged and a few windows were broken out, but that was all. Even most of our animals we had survived that day, including Moose.

That night I'll never forget. A moderately sized tornado (about an F3 on the Fujita scale) ripped through my neighborhood, destroying ten houses and damaging fifty others. No tornado warnings were issued for that area until ten minutes after it was already over, but still no one was seriously injured. The local television station didn't even bother to comment on their mistake. Until that night I never realized that something could happen that could change the way you feel about something for the rest of your life. I look at the television and see the tornado, hurricane, and even flood victims with new eyes. They are real, just like me.

by Sandra Russell

Mastery and Editing Tests

TEST 1 **Student Writing: Editing for Wordiness**

Below is an introductory paragraph of six sentences, taken from a student essay. Revise the paragraph so that wordiness is eliminated from each sentence.

In the paragraph that follows, I am going to make an attempt to name at least some of the earliest Spanish explorations in the New World. To take just the first example, it was in 1513 that an extraordinary event of considerable magnitude took place in what is now Florida when the Spanish explorer Ponce de Leon landed there. It was in the same area, and little more than a quarter of a century later, that the explorer Hernando de Soto, who later discovered the Mississippi River, also landed in Florida in 1539. Among Historians and among those who are interested in cultural history, Florida has reached noteworthy status for another reason. In 1565 Pedro Menendez de Aviles landed in Florida and began building the city of St. Augustine, the oldest permanent settlement in the United States. We all know that explorers in every age and in every part of the world have to be of a courageous nature and personality, but in those days Spanish explorers were especially brave because they were among the very first to set foot in what was then known as the New World.

____

____

____

____

____

____

____

____

____

TEST 2 **Student Writing: Editing for Inappropriate Language**

Each sentence in the following paragraph contains an example of inappropriate language. Rewrite the paragraph revising all language to be acceptable as formal writing.

> When my sis was hired by a major electronics company last summer, we were a little worried about her. She had flunked math in school, so we wondered if she had chosen the right kind of company. The person who had the job before her was let go because he had an attitude. Imagine our surprise when she soon announced that she had been selected chairman of an important committee at work. She said that she really didn't want to be in a leadership position, but we all knew she was nuts about it.

TEST 3 Editing for Wordiness and Inappropriate Language

The following paragraph contains examples of wordiness as well as inappropriate language (slang, clipped words and sexist terms). Underline the problems as you come to them and then revise the paragraph. (Hint: Find and revise at least 10 words or phrases.)

One of the most outstanding scientists in the U.S. today came from China in 1936. She is Chien-Hsiung Wu, and her story is the story of the development of physics in our century. When Miss Wu came to America in 1936, she intended to do grad work and hightail it back to China. However, World War II broke out and she remained instead to teach at Smith College, where she enjoyed working with the Smithies. Very soon after that, she was employed by Princeton U. At that time, she was the only girl physicist hired by a top research university. Later, she became an important worker on Columbia University's Manhattan Project, the project that developed the A bomb. She hunkered down at Columbia for more than thirty years, her many scientific discoveries bringing her world recognition. In 1990, Wu became the first living scientist to have an asteroid named in her honor. This celestial object whirling in the darkest corners of outer space is now carrying her name.

WORKING TOGETHER

BEING TACTFUL IN THE WORKPLACE

Words are charged with meanings that can be encouraging and supportive or hurtful and wounding. Although workers in government buildings and other public places are there to help the public, they often are so overwhelmed or overworked that they do not always respond in a positive way. Below are seven comments that might be heard in an office where a person has gone to get help. In each case, revise the language so that the comment is more encouraging.

a. I don't have any idea what you're talking about.

____

____

b. Why don't you learn to write so people can read it?

____

____

c. We don't accept sloppy applications.

____

____

d. How old are you anyway?

____

____

e. Can't you read directions?

____

____

continued on next page

f. What's the matter with you? Why can't you understand this simple procedure?

____

____

g. I don't have time today for people like you!

____

____

Share some of these revisions with each other. Then, as a class, discuss some of your individual experiences involving incidents where the use of language made you or someone you know feel hurt or upset. You may remember incidents from a campus office, a local bank, or a local shop. How could a change of language have made the situation better?

Portfolio Suggestion

Using the Working Together activity and using class discussion, write on one of the following:

- The importance of using polite language in the workplace. (You can use the examples given during classroom discussion.)
- Advice to employers on training their employees how to speak to people on the job.
- The difficulty workers have because many customers or clients are rude. (If you have had a job, you may have examples of some of these experiences. How did you deal with the situation?)

Online Activity

Observing etiquette on the Internet can be just as important to your professional and academic life as at your workplace and college. Read "The Core Rules of Netiquette" at http://www.albion.com/netiquette/corerules.html In small groups, review what you have learned and list the new information your group encountered.

Chapter 14 Paying Attention to Look-Alikes and Sound-Alikes

Preview

Many words are confusing because they either sound alike or look alike, but they are spelled differently and have different meanings. In this chapter, words that are often confused have been placed into six manageable groups so that you can study one group at a sitting.

- Group I   10 sets of words that sound alike
- Group II   10 sets of words that sound alike
- Group III   5 contractions that sound like other words
- Group IV   10 sets of words that sound or look *almost* alike
- Group V   10 sets of words that sound or look *almost* alike
- Group VI   3 verb sets most often confused

Every writing student must be sure to watch out for the troublesome word confusions that follow. ESL students will find this chapter especially helpful. Master the word sets of each group before proceeding to the next. In each group, the first column lists the sets of words, the second column defines the words, and the third column uses the words in sentences.

EXPLORING ONLINE

Read the brief explanation as to the reason spell checkers are not always the answer: "Garbage In, Garbage Out: Errors Caused by Over-Reliance on Spelling Checkers" at http://www.wsu.edu/~brians/errors/spellcheck.html

Group I: Words that Sound Alike

Words often confused	Word meanings	Sentence examples
1. aural/oral		
aural	related to hearing	The child has *aural* nerve damage.
oral	related to the mouth	The student gave an *oral* report.

Words often confused	**Word meanings**	**Sentence examples**
2. buy/by		
buy (verb)	to purchase	He hopes to *buy* a car.
by (prep.)	near; past; not later than	Let's meet *by* the clock. They drive *by* my house every morning. Please arrive *by* six o'clock.
3. capital/capitol		
capital (adj.)	major; fatal	He made a *capital* improvement on his home. The governor opposes *capital* punishment.
capital (noun)	leading city; money	The *capital* (city) of Wyoming is Cheyenne. The retailer has *capital* to invest.
capitol	a legislative building	The dome of the state *capitol* (building) is gold.
4. close/clothes		
close	to shut	*Close* the door.
clothes	garments	The *clothes* were from the GAP.

Note: *Cloth* is a piece of fabric, not to be confused with *clothes*, which is always plural.

5. coarse/course		
coarse (adj.)	rough; common or of inferior quality	He told a *coarse* joke. The coat was made from a *coarse* fabric.
course (noun)	direction; part of a meal; a unit of study	What is the *course* of the spaceship? The main *course* of the meal was served. This is a required *course*.
6. complement/compliment		
complement (noun)	something that completes	The library has a full *complement* of books.
(verb)	to complete	Her shoes *complement* the outfit.
compliment (noun)	an expression of praise	The chef received a *compliment*.
(verb)	to praise	He *complimented* the chef.

Words often confused	Word meanings	Sentence examples
7. forward/foreword		
forward	to send on to another address; moving toward the front or the future; bold	Please *forward* my mail. He took one step *forward*. She is very *forward* when she speaks.
foreword	introduction to a book	Read the *foreword* first.
8. passed/past		
passed (verb)	moved ahead	She *passed* the library.
past (noun)	time before the present	Don't live in the *past*.
past (prep.)	beyond	He walked *past* the house.
past (adj.)	no longer current	Her *past* failures have been forgotten.
9. plain/plane		
plain (adj.)	ordinary; clear	His *plain* clothing was of good quality. We appreciated the *plain* directions.
plain (noun)	flat land without trees	They crossed the *plain* by covered wagon.
plane	an aircraft; a flat, level surface; a carpenter's tool for leveling wood; a level of development	159 passengers were on the *plane*. The *planes* of the crystal shone. A carpenter's *plane* and saw are needed. They think on a different *plane*.
10. presence/presents		
presence (noun)	the state of being present; a person's manner	His *presence* is needed. She has a wonderful *presence*.
presents (noun)	gifts	The child's birthday *presents* were many.
(verb)	to introduce, to offer	The senator *presents* the award.

EXERCISE 1 **Group I Words**

Fill in the blanks in each of the following sentences by choosing the correct word to complete that sentence.

1. When I telephoned the doctor, he warned me that the ______________ (aural, oral) medicine was to be used only in my child's ear; this medicine was not an ______________ (aural, oral) medicine.

2. ________ the time I arrived at the store, the sale was over and I could
(Buy, By)
not ________ what I needed.
(buy, by)

3. The senators met in Athens, the ________ of Greece, to discuss the
(capital, capitol)
question of ________ punishment.
(capital, capitol)

4. I hurried to bring several yards of wool ________ to the tailor,
(close, clothes, cloth)
who will make some new winter ________ for my family; I knew
(close, clothes, cloth)
he would ________ at five o'clock.
(close, clothes, cloth)

5. I would have enjoyed the ________, but some of the students told
(coarse, course)
________ jokes during every class.
(coarse, course)

6. She always wears clothes that ________ each other, but she
(complement, compliment)
never expects a ________.
(complement, compliment)

7. I looked ________ to reading the new book so much that I read
(forward, foreword)
the ________ the very first day.
(forward, foreword)

8. I have spent the ________ few days wondering if I ________
(passed, past) (passed, past)
the exam.

9. The storm had been raging over the ________ for hours when
(plain, plane)
the ________ suddenly went down.
(plain, plane)

10. Each year the mayor always ________ an award as well as several
(presence, presents)
lovely ________ to outstanding members of the community.
(presence, presents)

EXERCISE 2 **Group I Words**

Edit the following paragraph for word confusions. Circle the errors and write the correct words on the lines below the paragraph.

Wolfgang Mozart was a child star of the eighteenth century. At three years old, he could pick out chords and tunes on the piano. Buy age four, he was composing at the piano. As a musical genius, Mozart had an extremely well-developed oral sense. When Mozart was only six, he and his sister played before the emperor in Vienna, the capitol of Austria. The emperor paid Mozart a complement by having his portrait painted. Among the other presence was an embroidered suit of cloths. In the coarse of his life, Mozart wrote church music, sonatas, operas, and chamber music. Like many great artists of the passed, he was ahead of his time and created on such a different plain that his own era never fully appreciated him. Today, Mozart is recognized as one of music's greatest composers. You might be interested in reading a book of Mozart's letters which has been published in English. Be sure to read the forward.

____________________ ____________________

____________________ ____________________

____________________ ____________________

____________________ ____________________

____________________ ____________________

Group II: Words that Sound Alike

Words often confused	Word meanings	Sentence examples
1. principal/principle		
principal (adj.)	most important; main	The *principal* dancer was superb. What is the *principal* reason for your decision?
principal (noun)	the head of a school; a sum of money	The *principal* of the school arrived late. The *principal* and interest on the loan were due.
principle (noun)	a rule or standard	He is a man of *principle*.
2. rain/reign/rein		
rain	water falling to earth in drops	I'm singing in the *rain*.
reign	a period of rule for a king or queen	When was the *reign* of Henry the Eighth?
rein	a strap attached to a bridle, used to control a horse	I grabbed the pony's frayed *rein*.
3. sight/site/cite		
sight	the ability to see; a view	His *sight* was limited. The Grand Canyon is an awesome *sight*.
site	the plot of land where something is located; the place for an event	Here is the *site* for the new courthouse.
cite	to quote as an authority or example	Please *cite* the correct law.

Words often confused	Word meanings	Sentence examples
4. stationary/stationery		
stationary (adj.)	standing still	He hit a *stationary* object.
stationery (noun)	writing paper and envelopes	She wrote the letter on her *stationery*.
5. to/too/two		
to (prep.)	in a direction toward	We walked *to* the movies.
too (adv.)	also; very	We walked home *too*. The tickets were *too* expensive.
two	number	She has *two* children.
6. vain/vane/vein		
vain	conceited; unsuccessful	He was attractive but *vain*. We made a *vain* attempt.
vane	an ornament that turns in the wind (often in the shape of a rooster and seen on tops of barns)	The weather *vane* pointed southwest.
vein	a blood vessel; the branching framework of a leaf; an area in the earth where a mineral like gold or silver is found; a passing attitude	The *veins* carry blood to the heart. The miner found a *vein* of silver. She spoke in a humorous *vein*.
7. waist/waste		
waist	The middle portion of a body or garment	His *waist* was 36 inches around.
waste (verb)	to use carelessly	He *wasted* too much time watching television.
waste (noun)	discarded objects	The *waste* was put in the garbage.
8. weather/whether		
weather (noun)	atmospheric conditions	The *weather* in Hawaii is gorgeous.
whether (conj.)	if it is the case that	I'll go *whether* or not I'm finished.
9. whole/hole		
whole	complete	He ate the *whole* apple.
hole	an opening	I found a *hole* in the sock.
10. write/right/rite		
write	to form letters and words; to compose	I will *write* a poem for your birthday.

Words often confused	Word meanings	Sentence examples
right	correct	What is the *right* answer?
	to conform to justice, law, or morality	Trial by jury is a *right* under the law.
	toward a conservative point of view	The senator's position is to the *right*.
rite	a traditional, often religious ceremony	A birthday is a *rite* of passage.

EXERCISE 3 **Group II Words**

Fill in the blanks in each of the following sentences by choosing the correct word to complete that sentence.

1. The ________ (principal, principle) was respected because he would not compromise his one fundamental ________ (principal, principle).

2. The museum had on display a horse's ________ (rain, reign, rein) that dated from the ________ (rain, reign, rein) of Henry the Eighth.

3. You do not have to ________ (sight, site, cite) statistics to convince me of the importance of caring for my ________ (sight, site, cite).

4. He bought the ________ (stationary, stationery) from a clerk who said nothing and remained ________ (stationary, stationery) all the time behind the counter.

5. I want ________ (to, too, two) go ________ (to, too, two) the movies, and I hope you do ________ (to, too, two).

6. I could tell the actress was ________ (vain, vane, vein) when she kept hiding a long blue ________ (vain, vane, vein) on her leg.

7. It is a ________ (waist, waste) of time to try and get him to admit the size of his ________ (waist, waste).

8. We always listen to the ________ (weather, whether) report ________ (weather, whether) it's right or wrong.

9. I am telling you the ________ (whole, hole) story about the ________ (whole, hole) in our new carpet.

10. Every American has the ________ (right, write, rite) to participate in any religious ________ (right, write, rite) of his or her own choosing.

EXERCISE 4 **Group II Words**

Edit the following paragraph for word confusions. Circle the errors and write the correct words on the lines below the paragraph.

The dance performance I attended last weekend at our local community college was a spectacular site. The hole piece tells the story of a queen who is so vein that she brings about her own downfall with her selfishness. The principle dancer who plays the queen dances the part with remarkable sensitivity and grace. At first the queen is such an unlikable character: not only is she manipulative and greedy, but she feels it is her rite to put her own needs above all others. Yet by the end, one doesn't know weather to hate her or pity her. Her subjects denounce the queen and storm the castle, to. The queen looks out at the chaos and realizes her rain is coming to an end. As she stands stationery in her room looking out of her window, she hears the many cries of her subjects who are determined to destroy her, and she realizes for the first time that it was her own vanity and selfishness that led to these sad events. The last moments of the piece show the queen dancing alone in her room. She wraps a black scarf around her waste as the curtain comes down.

______________________ ______________________

______________________ ______________________

______________________ ______________________

______________________ ______________________

______________________ ______________________

Group III: Words that Sound Alike

Words often confused	Word meanings	Sentence examples
1. it's/its		
it's	contraction of *it is*	*It's* early.
its	possessive pronoun	*Its* tail is short.
2. they're/their/there		
they're	contraction of *they are*	*They're* happy.
their	possessive pronoun	*Their* children are beautiful.
there	at that place	Look over *there.*

Words often confused	Word meanings	Sentence examples
3. we're/were/where		
we're	contraction of *we are*	*We're* happy.
were	past tense of *are*	They *were* happy.
where	at or in what place	*Where* are we?
4. who's/whose		
who's	contraction of *who is*	*Who's* the author of this book?
whose	possessive pronoun	*Whose* clothes are these?
5. you're/your		
you're	contraction of *you are*	*You're* the boss.
your	possessive pronoun	*Your* team has won.

EXERCISE 5

Group III Words

Fill in the blanks in each of the following sentences by choosing the correct word to complete that sentence.

1. __________ (It's, Its) obvious that the car has lost __________ (it's, its) muffler.

2. The dog has no license, so __________ (it's, its) possible __________ (it's, its) owner doesn't care about the dog very much.

3. When __________ (they're, their, there) in school, __________ (they're, their, there) parents work in the restaurant __________ (they're, their, there) on the corner.

4. Now that __________ (they're, their, there) living in the country, __________ (they're, their, there) expenses are not so great, so they might stay __________ (they're, their, there).

5. __________ (We're, Were, Where) hoping our friends __________ (we're, were, where) not hurt at the place __________ (we're, were, where) the accident occurred.

6. __________ (We're, Were, Where) did the coupons go that __________ (we're, were, where) saving?

7. __________ (Who's, Whose) car is double-parked outside, and __________ (who's, whose) going to move it?

8. __________ (Who's, Whose) the pitcher at the game today, and __________ (who's, whose) glove will he use?

9. When __________ (you're, your) a father, __________ (you're, your) free time is never guaranteed.

10. Please give me __________ (you're, your) paper when __________ (you're, your) finished writing.

EXERCISE 6 **Group III Words**

Edit the following paragraph for word confusions. Circle the ten errors in the paragraph and on the lines provided write the correct words.

Psychologists tell us that laughter is found only among human beings. Of all creatures, were the only ones who laugh. Psychologists are interested in what makes people laugh, but so far there best explanations are only theories. From a physical point of view, your healthier if you laugh often. Its good for you're lungs and its an outlet for extra energy. Among it's other effects are the release of anxieties and anger. The comedian, who's job depends on figuring out what makes people laugh, often pokes fun at the behavior of other people. However, a joke about a local town might not be funny in front of an audience of people who like living their. We're all familiar with jokes that are in bad taste. Its a good idea to recognize who your audience is.

____________________ ____________________

____________________ ____________________

____________________ ____________________

____________________ ____________________

____________________ ____________________

Group IV: Words that Sound or Look Almost Alike

Words often confused	Word meanings	Sentence examples
1. accept/except		
accept (verb)	to receive; to admit; to regard as true or right	I *accept* with pleasure. I *accept* responsibility. I *accept* your apology.
except (prep.)	other than, but	Everyone *except* me was ready.
2. advice/advise		
advice (noun)	opinion as to what should be done about a problem	I need good *advice.*
advise (verb)	to suggest; to counsel	He *advised* me to take a different course.

Words often confused	Word meanings	Sentence examples
3. affect/effect		
affect (verb)	to influence; to change	Smoking will *affect* your health.
effect (noun)	result	The *effect* of the hurricane was evident.
(verb)	to bring about a result	The hurricane *effected* a devastating change in the community.
4. breath/breathe		
breath (noun)	air that is inhaled or exhaled	You seem out of *breath.*
breathe (verb)	to inhale or exhale	Don't *breathe* in these fumes.
5. choose/chose		
choose (present tense)	select	Today I *choose* the purple shirt.
chose (past tense)	selected	Yesterday I *chose* the red one.
6. conscience/conscious/conscientious		
conscience	recognition of right and wrong	His *conscience* bothered him.
conscious	awake; aware of one's own existence	The patient was *conscious.*
conscientious	careful; thorough	The student was *conscientious* about doing her homework.
7. costume/custom		
costume	a special style of dress for a particular occasion	The child wore a clown *costume* for Halloween.
custom	a common tradition	One *custom* at Thanksgiving is to serve turkey.
8. council/counsel/consul		
council (noun)	a group that governs	The student *council* meets every Tuesday.
counsel (verb)	to give advice	Please *counsel* the arguing couple.
counsel (noun)	advice; a lawyer	The couple needs *counsel.* The prisoner has requested *counsel.*
consul	a government official in the foreign service	He was appointed a *consul* by the president.

Words often confused	Word meanings	Sentence examples
9. desert/dessert		
desert (verb)	to abandon	Don't *desert* me now.
desert (noun)	barren land	The cactus flowers on the *desert* are beautiful.
dessert	last part of a meal, often sweet	We had apple pie for *dessert.*
10. diner/dinner		
diner	a person eating dinner; a restaurant with a long counter and booths	The *diner* waited for her check. I prefer a booth at the *diner.*
dinner	main meal of the day	What is for *dinner?*

EXERCISE 7 Group IV Words

Fill in the blanks in each of the following sentences by choosing the correct word to complete that sentence.

1. The judge refused to ____________ (accept, except) most of the evidence ____________ (accept, except) for the testimony from one witness.

2. I need some good ____________ (advice, advise); is there anyone here who could ____________ (advice, advise) me?

3. How does the allergy medicine ____________ (affect, effect) you? Some medicine may have an adverse side ____________ (affect, effect).

4. The injured skier was told to ____________ (breath, breathe) deeply and exhale slowly; the doctor could see her ____________ (breath, breathe) in the chilly winter air.

5. Today we ____________ (choose, chose) fruit for a snack; in the past we usually ____________ (choose, chose) junk food.

6. The thief, when he became ____________ (conscience, conscientious, conscious), gave himself up to the police because his ____________ (conscience, conscientious, conscious) was bothering him.

7. Before you visit a foreign country, you should read about its ____________ (costumes, customs) so that you will not unknowingly offend someone.

8. The town ____________ (council, counsel, consul) met to discuss a new ordinance.

9. We made a chocolate layer cake for ____________ (desert, dessert); don't ____________ (desert, dessert) me until we eat it all.

10. All I want for ____________ (diner, dinner) is a salad; do you think I can get a good one at this ____________ (diner, dinner)?

EXERCISE 8 **Group IV Words**

Edit the following paragraph for word confusions. Circle the errors and write the correct words on the lines below the paragraph.

For thousands of years, it has been a costume to enjoy wine. Today, some people chose to drink wine with diner, while others wait until desert. There are wine clubs where people look for advise as to what they should drink; these people are very conscience that they should do the correct thing. Others look for council in magazines which tell them how to chose the correct wine for the right food. They except the words of the experts, but the prices of some wines would take your breathe away.

____________________ ____________________

____________________ ____________________

____________________ ____________________

____________________ ____________________

____________________ ____________________

Group V: Words that Sound or Look Almost Alike

Words often confused	Word meanings	Sentence examples
1. emigrate/immigrate; emigrant/immigrant		
emigrate (verb)	to leave a country	They *emigrated* from Europe.
immigrate (verb)	to come into a country	Many people have *immigrated* to the United States.
emigrant (noun)	a person who leaves one country to settle in another	Each *emigrant* left with memories.
immigrant (noun)	a person who comes into a country to settle there	Nearly every *immigrant* landed first at Ellis Island.
2. farther/further		
farther	greater distance (physically)	They had to walk *farther* down the road.
further	greater distance (mentally); to help advance a person or a cause	The speaker made a *further* point. The tutor will *further* my chances on the exam.

Words often confused	Word meanings	Sentence examples
3. loose/lose		
loose	not tightly fitted	The dog's collar is *loose.*
lose	unable to keep or find; to fail to win	Don't *lose* your keys. Don't *lose* the game.
4. personal/personnel		
personal	relating to an individual; private	He asked for his *personal* mail.
personnel	people employed by an organization	All *personnel* in the company were interviewed.
5. quiet/quit/quite		
quiet	free from noise; calm	They loved the *quiet* village.
quit	to give up; to stop	He *quit* smoking.
quite	completely; rather	She is not *quite done.* She is coming *quite* soon.
6. receipt/recipe		
receipt	a bill marked paid	No exchanges can be made without a *receipt.*
recipe	a formula to prepare a mixture, especially in cooking	I found my *recipe* for caramel flan.
7. special/especially		
special (adj.)	not ordinary	We're planning a *special* weekend.
especially (adv.)	particularly	She is *especially* talented in art.
8. than/then		
than (conj. or prep.)	used to make a comparison	This cake is sweeter *than* that one.
then (adv.)	at that time; next	I was at work *then.* First he was late; *then* he blamed me.
9. thorough/though/thought/through/threw		
thorough (adj.)	accurate and complete	She always does a *thorough* job.
though (adv. conj.)	however, despite the fact	I worked even *though* I was exhausted.

Words often confused	Word meanings	Sentence examples
thought (verb)	past tense of *to think*	I *thought* about my goals.
through (prep.)	to enter one side and exit from the other side	We drove *through* the tunnel.

Note: *Thru* is not considered standard spelling.

threw (verb)	past tense of *to throw*	He *threw* the ball to me.
10. use/used to		
use	to bring or put into service, to make use of	Present: I usually *use* a bike to get to school. Past: Yesterday, I *used* my father's car.
used to	an expression that indicates an activity that is no longer done in the present	I *used to* take the bus to school, but now I ride my bike.
	accustomed to or familiar with	I am *used to* walking to school.

EXERCISE 9 **Group V Words**

Fill in the blank in each of the following sentences by choosing the correct word to complete that sentence.

1. My parents ________________ from Greece.
   (emigrated, immigrated)
2. Let's not travel any ______________ tonight.
   (farther, further)
3. Your belt is too __________.
   (loose, lose)
4. Most of the ______________ at this company are well trained.
   (personal, personnel)
5. Please be ______________ while she is performing.
   (quiet, quit, quite)
6. Keep this ____________ for tax purposes.
   (receipt, recipe)
7. He made a ___________________ trip to visit his daughter.
   (special, especial, especially)
8. I would rather read a good book __________ listen to television.
   (than, then)
9. When she walked _______________________ the door, he didn't
   (thorough, though, through, threw)
   recognize her even _______________________ he had known her
   (thorough, though, through, threw)
   all his life.
10. I am not _________ to staying up so late.
    (use, used)

EXERCISE 10 **Group V Words**

Edit the following paragraph for word confusions. Circle the ten errors and write the correct words on the lines below the paragraph.

Advertising is very old: some advertisements on paper go back farther than three thousand years. In ancient Greece, it was quiet common to see signs advertising different kinds of services, but it was not until printing was invented that modern advertising was born. In Europe, in the seventeenth century, they use to place ads in newspapers; some of these ads were personnel messages, but most were for business. When many emigrants came to the United States, they used advertisements to get jobs; we can imagine them going thorough each newspaper very carefully. Today, advertising is all around us, special on television. If we are not careful, we can loose our focus when we watch some programs. For example, when a commercial interrupts a chef who is giving us a receipt for a complicated new dish, we are likely to remember the flashy commercial better then the chef's directions.

__________	__________
__________	__________
__________	__________
__________	__________
__________	__________

Group VI: Lie/Lay; Rise/Raise; Sit/Set

These six verbs are perhaps the most troublesome verbs in the English language. Not only must you learn their principal parts, which are irregular and easily confused with each other, but in addition, one set is reflexive and cannot take an object while the other set must always take a direct object.

First, learn the principal parts of the three reflexive verbs whose action is accomplished by the subject only.

Reflexive Verbs: Lie—Rise—Sit

When these reflexive verbs are used, the subject is doing the action without any help. No other person or object is needed to accomplish the action. *Reflexive verbs never take an object.*

I *lie* down.

I *rise* up.

I *sit* down.

PRINCIPAL PARTS OF REFLECTIVE VERBS LIE—RISE—SIT				
Verb Meaning	**Present**	**Present Participle**	**Past**	**Past Participle**
to *lie* = to recline	lie	lying	lay	has or have lain
to *rise* = to stand up or move upward	rise	rising	rose	has or have risen
to *sit* = to take a sitting position	sit	sitting	sat	has or have sat

Here are some additional examples of reflexive verbs:

The cat is lying on the rug.

The sun rose in the East.

The woman sat on the sofa.

Practice.......... Fill in each blank below with the correct form of one of the reflexive verbs.

1. The sun is __________ at about 6 A.M. this week.
2. Last week he __________ at 7 o'clock every morning.
3. He is __________ at the breakfast table by 7:30.
4. He will not __________ down again until after midnight.
5. His cat is always __________ on the rug.
6. Yesterday he __________ there for seven hours without moving.

Verbs Requiring a Direct Object: Lay—Raise—Set

These three verbs *always* require a direct object.

I lay the book down.

I raise the flag.

I set the table.

PRINCIPAL PARTS OF THE VERBS LAY—RAISE—SET				
Verb Meaning	**Present**	**Present Participle**	**Past**	**Past Participle**
to *lay* = to put something	lay	laying	laid	has or have laid
to *raise* = to move something up	raise	raising	raised	has or have raised
to *set* = to place something	set	setting	set	has or have set

Here are some additional examples of these verbs:

The cat *laid her ball* on the rug.

The sunshine *raised our spirits*.

The woman *set her hat* on the sofa.

Practice.......... Fill in each blank with the correct form of the verb and its direct object.

1. The postal worker __________ the __________ on the back porch.

2. The father __________ his __________ to be a sensitive individual.

3. We __________ the __________ on the counter.

EXERCISE 11 **Group VI Words**

Fill in each blank with the correct form of the verb.

1. I have __________ the suitcases in your room.

2. I am __________ in my favorite rocking chair.

3. She likes me to __________ by her bed and read to her in the evening.

4. Last spring the manufacturers __________ the prices.

5. Yesterday the price of the magazine __________ by a dime.

6. When I entered the room, the woman __________ to greet me.

7. The woman __________ her head when I entered the room.

8. I usually __________ down in the afternoon.

9. The auto mechanic is __________ under the car.

10. I can't remember where I __________ my keys.

EXERCISE 12 **Group VI Words**

Fill in each blank with the correct form of the verb.

1. The cat has __________ (lie, lay) in the sun all day.

2. If you feel sick, __________ (lie, lay) down on that bed.

3. The elevator always __________ (rise, raise) quickly to the tenth floor.

4. The boss __________ (rise, raise) her salary twice this year.

5. The parents __________ (lie, lay) down the law when their son came home late.

6. The carpenters __________ (rise, raise) the roof when they remodeled the house.

7. The dog __________ (sit, set) up every night and begs for food.

8. Last week I __________ (sit, set) in front of my television set nearly every night.

9. I always watch the waiter __________ (sit, set) on a stool after his shift is done.

10. We have ________ (sit, set) a plate of cookies and milk out for Santa Claus every year since the children were born.

Mastery and Editing Tests

TEST 1 **Choosing Correct Words**

Fill in each blank with the correct word.

One of the ________ (principal, principle) ways to identify people is the use of fingerprints. Each set of fingers has ________ (it's, its) unique pattern of ridges and designs. In the ________ (passed, past), this knowledge was not recognized as useful, but one hundred years ago, during the ________ (rain, reign, rein) of Queen Victoria, an Englishman named Sir Edward Henry devised a ________ (hole, whole) system of identifying ________ (who's, whose) prints belong to whom. During the ________ (coarse, course) of his investigation, he discovered that we really have two layers of skin, and where ________ (they're, their, there) joined, the upper layer of skin forms a number of ridges. These ridges are divided by type, into loops, double loops, arches, whorls, and accidentals. ________ (Buy, By) studying these different patterns, we are able to match people with ________ (they're, their, there) prints.

TEST 2 **Choosing Correct Words**

Fill in each blank with the correct word.

Coffee has a long history and an interesting one. Long before it was brewed, coffee was enjoyed ________ (plain, plane) or mixed with vegetables and eaten as food. The ________ (sight, site, cite) of the first cultivated coffee was most likely Kaffa, a part of Ethiopia not far from the ________ (capital, capitol) of that country. That is ________ (we're, were, where) coffee most likely got ________ (it's, its) name. ________ (Than, Then), in the fourteenth century, merchants came across the ________ (desert, dessert) from Arabia to Kaffa, obtained coffee seeds, and began to grow coffee in their own countries. The people of Arabia were

__________ (quite, quit, quiet) happy to enjoy coffee, __________ (special, especially) because it took the place of alcohol, which they were not allowed to drink. The first __________ (lose, loose) coffee beans came to Europe in 1615, and the drink has remained popular ever since.

TEST 3 Choosing Correct Words

Fill in each blank with the correct word.

People have pierced their ears __________ (thorough, though, thought, through, threw) every period of recorded history. Ancient Egyptians, Persians, Hebrews, and others would __________ (sit, set) pieces of gold and silver with jewels, pearls, and other precious stones. Some earrings would hang from the ear, while others would __________ (lie, lay) against the earlobe itself. They even __________ (use, used) to hang earrings from the statues of their gods and goddesses. When the Egyptians put mummies in their tombs, they would place earrings in the coffin as a decoration for the person to wear in the afterlife. Centuries ago, both men and women wore earrings, and one Roman emperor thought his people were becoming __________ (to, too, two) __________ (vain, vane, vein). He spoke out against the use of earrings and __________ (farther, further) stated that men could not wear them. We do not know how people reacted to that announcement, but there would be an uproar today because everyone sees wearing their jewelry as a __________ (right, write, rite). Can you imagine police officers trying to enforce a law that forbids such a popular __________ (costume, custom)? Hardly anyone would __________ (accept, except) such a regulation today.

EXPLORING ONLINE

For an excellent list of common "confusables," go to

http://www.wsu.edu/~brians/errors/errors.html

WORKING TOGETHER

EXAMINING THE ISSUE OF PLAGIARISM

Plagiarism is the unethical use of someone else's ideas or words as if they were your own. When your writing contains material from the work of another writer, you must give credit to the person who produced that material, or you will be accused of plagiarism. All writers are expected to be responsible and acknowledge the sources for their work. College students should be especially careful about plagiarism because students are often under stress to get assignments in on time, and it is tempting to take the easy way out and copy from someone else's work. This lack of honesty in submitting someone else's work as your own is usually severely punished.

One professional writer who should have been aware of the seriousness of plagiarism is the American writer Alexander Theroux. When Theroux, who has taught at Harvard and Yale, published a collection of essays entitled *The Primary Colors,* a woman happened to be reading Theroux's book along with another work, *Song of the Sky* by Guy Murchie. The Guy Murchie book, published in 1954, was little known and had been out of print for some time. The reader noticed some remarkable similarities between certain passages from both books. Review two passages from these books given below:

Song of the Sky, Page 29:

"Blue water is salty, warm, and deep and speaks of the tropics where evaporation is great and dilution small—the Sulu Sea, the Indian Ocean, the Gulf Stream. Green water is cool, pale with particles, thin with river and rain, often shallow."

The Primary Colors, Page 16:

"Incidentally, blue water is invariably salty, warm, and deep and speaks of the tropics, where evaporation is great and dilution minimal—the Sulu Sea, the Indian Ocean, the Gulf Stream. Green water, on the other hand, is cool, pale with particles, thin with river and rain, often shallow."

continued on next page

Questions for Small Group Discussion:

1. Review the two passages and discuss the extent to which they differ.
2. When asked about the striking similarities between his book and *Song of the Sky,* Alexander Theroux stated: "I just thought it was my own work. I can't always remember the source of where I found something." Discuss the writer's explanation. Is it satisfactory? Do you think there is a more likely explanation?
3. When this example of plagiarism was discovered, the publisher of the Theroux book announced that future editions would either leave out the embarrassing passages or give direct credit to *Song of the Sky.* Was this a good solution? In your opinion, is there anything else the publisher should do in such a case?
4. If a college student is found guilty of plagiarism, what should the penalty be?
5. It has been said that when students plagiarize material in school, those students really cheat themselves because any benefit from learning is lost. Discuss.
6. What is the policy on plagiarism in the catalogue of the educational institution you attend?

Related Writing Topics: cheating on tests
buying papers on the Internet
the underlying reasons why some people cheat

Online Activity

The Internet has tempted many students to plagiarize: from buying papers to pasting paragraphs and whole articles into their work. However, did you know that a plagiarized essay can now be chased down with ease by typing a suspicious-looking sentence into the Search Box on any Internet search engine and pressing "Go." Many professors also subscribe to a service that searches the entire Internet known as Plagiarism.Com. You may test the truth of the first example by working in pairs. One student should find an article on the Internet and type one sentence from the article and another sentence of his or her own into a word processor. The second student will type both sentences (or copy and paste) into the Search Box. The search engine should reveal from which article the sentence was plagiarized.

Chapter 15 Review: Editing Student Writing

Preview

This chapter asks you to use all the skills you have learned in the first three parts of this text. First, you will study the chart of editing symbols and a few other editing suggestions. Then, you will work with these editing symbols to correct student paragraphs. Finally, you will read several student essays and work to edit and revise them. This will be good practice for editing your own papers when they are returned to you by your instructor throughout the semester. The chapter is divided into three sections:

- Understanding editing symbols
- Correcting student paragraphs with the help of editing symbols
- Editing student essays

Understanding Editing Symbols

The list on page 268 contains most of the symbols and abbreviations used by instructors to mark student drafts.

GUIDE TO EDITING SYMBOLS

Editing symbols for word errors:

Symbol	*Meaning*
abbr	do not abbreviate
apos	an apostrophe is needed or used incorrectly
cap	capitalization is needed
dic	faulty diction: do not use slang, sexist language, or nonstandard English
lc	use lower case
pl	correct plural needed
sp	spelling error
vb	verb error (wrong tense, form, or shift)
wrd. ch.	make a different word choice
wrdy	too many words, repetitious
wrd. fm.	word form is incorrect
/	slash: eliminate the letter, word, or punctuation mark
∧	indicates where letters or words are missing or needed
∼	transpose or reverse the letters or words
ℓ	delete
⁀‿	join to make one word

Editing symbols for sentence level errors:

Symbol	*Meaning*
agr	faulty agreement: subject with verb or pronoun with antecedent
dm, mm	dangling modifier, misplaced modifier
frag	fragment
punc	incorrect or missing punctuation
ro	run-on sentence ("and" run-on, comma splice, fused sentence)
subord/coord	passage needs sentence combining/improved sentence combining
//	faulty parallelism

Editing symbols for paragraph and essay development:

Symbol	*Meaning*
awk	expression or idea is awkwardly stated: needs revision
coh	coherence: the parts are not related in a clear and logical way
dev	ideas are not developed sufficiently
log	muddy thinking, not logical
sup	insufficient supporting details
trans	a transition is needed
U	lacks unity
var	needs more sentence variety
¶, no ¶	begin a new paragraph; do not begin a new paragraph
?	meaning unclear
✓	interesting point; point well made

EXPLORING ONLINE

Review the editing checklist at http://www.richmond.edu/~writing/wweb/finaled.htm

Other Editing Suggestions

1. Usually, if a number can be written in one or two words, then the number is written out (except for dates, of course).
2. Avoid contractions.
3. Avoid sentences that begin with *There is* or *There are.*
4. Whenever possible, choose active verbs rather than the verb *to be.*
5. Avoid ending sentences with prepositions.
6. Avoid apologizing.
7. Avoid beginning a sentence with *and* or *because.*

EXPLORING ONLINE

Review the basics of grammar and usage at "11 Rules of Writing" at http://www.junketstudies.com/rulesofw/frules.html An in-depth treatment can be found in William Strunk Jr.'s online reference work *The Elements of Style* at http://www.bartleby.com/141/index.html

Practice..........

Working with Editing Symbols

The following paragraph was a student's first draft. Begin by reading the paragraph as it was first written. Next, read the same paragraph with the addition of the instructor's markings (editing symbols) in the margins. Finally, rewrite the paragraph making all the necessary changes.

First Draft

```
    My aunt Edith use to live on Winsor street one of the
streets steepest in Jamestown. In Winter a person some-
times had to slide from one tree on one side of the
street to a tree slightly father down the street on the
other side of the street in order to get to the bottom of
the street without falling down. Our family went their
for every holiday. Aunt Edith entertained in great style,
she must of owned 5 or 6 different sets of dishes. Any
dinner she served included at least three kind of meats
and several homemade deserts. It was worth sliding from
tree to tree to get to her house for diner.
```

First Draft with Editing Symbols Added

cap; vb; cap; punc	My aunt Edith use to live on Winsor street^one of the
lc	streets steepest in Jamestown. In Winter a person some-
	times had to slide from one tree on one side of the
sp-typo	street to a tree slightly father down the street on the
wrdy	other side of the street in order to get to the bottom of
wd fm	the street without falling down. Our family went their
ro	for every holiday. Aunt Edith entertained in great style
wd ch	she must of owned 5 or 6 different sets of dishes. Any
ag	dinner she served included at least three kind of meats
wd ch	and several homemade deserts. It was worth sliding from
wd ch	tree to tree to get to her house for diner.

Corrected Student Paragraph

Correcting Student Paragraphs with the Help of Editing Symbols

The following paragraphs are taken from actual student papers. Editing symbols have been added in the margins to mark words or sentences needing correction. Using the list of editing symbols on page 268, rewrite the following paragraphs correctly. Your instructor may encourage you to work with a partner.

Paragraph 1 From a Student Essay Describing the Family Room of His Home

punc; wrdy	On the south wall of the family room^ there is a
sp-typo	bricked hearth the runs all the way up to the ceiling. In
punc; numeral	the middle of this hearth^ sits a six hundred and eighty
sp-typo	pound wood stove. Our house id all electric, and even in
ro	the year 2000, we still have power outages, this stove
dic	sure comes in handy. It keeps our large house really
wrdy	warm. There is a large couch that occupies one end of the
ro	family room, that is where we usually end up after being
	out in the cold for a long spell. This family room also
wrdy; jsp	is connected to our kitchen. There is a built in bar that
apos	surrounds my mothers stove. Under the bar are cabinets
awk	that she stores her canned goods in. In front of the bar
	is a bench made out of pine that my late grandfather made
//	for us. We use the bar for a lot of things, like for
ro	doing homework and we usually eat there in the mornings
//	for breakfast. My mother likes to sit at the bar and roll
punc	out her buttermilk biscuits, or to mix up a good tasting
	apple cake.

Paragraph 2 From a Student Narrative Essay

vb; ro	The four-wheeler send me crashing through a window and
?	my friend whose leg got caught underneath the four-wheel
punc	as slid into a pole. As I got up off the window I
	noticed my leg had a very huge cut around my calf. I
punc	lifted my leg off the window and wrapped it up, and
	quickly went to the aid of my friend. He lay there with
	the four-wheeler on top of him and his head bleeding from
awk	the pole. I managed somehow to lift the four-wheeler off
	of him. After we aided each other, we began to hobble to
wrd ch	my house. My house ended up to be to far to reach, so we
vb; apos; punc	stop at my neighbors house. Now you have to understand I
sp	had a cut all around my leg, and Thomas had a concusion
vb; awk	and a broken leg. We ended up walk an estimated 1/2 a mile
apos; punc	to my neighbors house. Well my neighbors saw the us and
	immediately called an ambulance. Thomas and I were rushed
vb; word ch; punc	to the hospital and cure of our wounds. Then after three
punc	days, thirty-seven staples, and a cast I was released
	from the hospital.

Paragraph 3 From a Student Essay Entitled "Who Needs Movie Critics?"

agr	Unless <u>they</u> get scared easily, <u>everyone</u> enjoys watch-
	ing a good scary movie every now and then. I enjoy watch-
apologetic	ing at least one every month. <u>I couldn't think of</u>
	<u>anything to write about, in which I had more knowledge</u>
	<u>about than movies</u>. Everyone has his or her favorite
pl	<u>movie, actors, and actresses</u>. I've spent a large amount
punc	of time building up my collection of movies. I feel very
avoid contractions	confident that I <u>don't</u> need a movie critic telling me
	<u>what's</u> good or bad. I would have missed watching a lot of
	great movies if I had listened to movie critics. Movie
	critics <u>aren't</u> always right, for they give a lot of good
wrdy	movies bad ratings. I think when it comes to movies <u>that</u>
agr	people should be <u>their own critic</u>.

Paragraph 4 From a Student Essay Entitled "A White House Summer"

avoid overuse of verb "to be" | before what? | use subord | punc | awk | sp-typo | awk | punc | sp

My mother was in Conway that summer. She was an elementary school teacher. She taught my brother and me in first grade. We took her to Conway the week before. It was a Sunday. Our car was a four door. A '63 or '64 model, it was blue. It had blue vinyl bucket seats, with a stick shift on the floor. When I opened the doors it reminded me of a tack shop, the smell that is. I would put my nose deep in the sear and take a deep breath. I loved that smell. I remember racing to the door that would allow me to sit behind my mother. I was eight when we left my mom in Conway. My brother was six. I can still see my mom standing at the bottom of those school building stairs. As I got older, I looked back and thought those stairs looked like those to the Capitol. Tears in my eyes, a lump in my throat, we drove away. I remember getting on my knees with my arms resting on the back seat, watching her as long as I could until she was visible no more. As we pulled up into the driveway of our white house on the hill, little did I know how we would grow that summer, not in inches but in self reliance.

Paragraph 5 From a Student Essay Describing the Ideal Place to Study

wrdy; wrd ch	You start to precede up the stairs made of aged
wrdy	cedar. Your hand holds onto the rail made of hickory. In
DM	the rail, you see the ax marks and grooves. Looking back
sp-typo	tot he wall, it portrays black and white portraits of
sp	ancestors and their decedents. Nearing the top of the
punc	stairs^ you look to your right and see an open window.
wrd ch; sp	Scanning down tot he wooden floor, you see antique lace
pl	curtain blowing^ the fragrant breeze. You walk toward it.
log; wrd ch	Seeing yourself standing in the doorway, you look about
pl; wrd ch	the ominous view of book, videos, and tapes concealed
	within the room. As you take a few steps forward, you
awk	notice that your feet placed you on an oriental rug.
frag	Woven in and out with intricate colors that enliven the
	splendor of it all. Shelves of books line the log wall. A
frag/log	projector in one corner, a television/VCR in the other,
awk	and a black cherry desk sits in between. Envelopes and
awk	papers line the sides of the desk while a stamp dispenser
awk;	sits close by. The computer and keyboard belong where
agr; wrdy	they should. Antique hardware adorn the desk. There is a
lc; wrdy	miniature water fall next to the Encyclopedias that let
	off a musty smell.

Editing Student Essays

Each of the following essays is to be read first of all for enjoyment. After you have done a relaxed first reading, read each essay again and underline any word or phrase that seems wrong or confusing to you. Identify the mistakes wherever you are able to do so by adding editing symbols in the margins. Finally, work in groups to discuss the corrections and revisions needed for the writer's next draft.

Essay #1

In the following short essay, a student recalls a moment from her childhood when she came to a terrible realization about her life. The subject is a painful one, but the piece is a pleasure to read because of its honest tone and the degree of unity and coherence that is remarkable for any student writer. You should, however, look for several places where punctuation is incorrect or missing. See if you can find other errors, including two omitted words and two misspellings.

Grandma's Front Porch

Sharon Gibson

One bright summer morning, I woke up early and outside to the front porch of my grandparents house. From the edge of this porch I could see for miles above the town. I watched and waited forever and finally a car started up the long driveway. I rushed into the house and quickly threw on that perfect outfit I had spent so long picking out last night. Then I frantically combed my hair and brushed my teeth. As the doorbell rang I could hardly contain my excitement. Finally from down stairs I hard my grandmother say those words that would forever ring in my heart "Your Dad's here." At the sound of these words, for some reason, I forgot all the broken promises and missed holidays. He was here now and just to see me, that was all that mattered. A giant smile ran across my face, I ran down stairs as fast as I could, and jumped into my dad's arms with such force that he almost fell. At last I would get to spend the day with my dad.

We got in the car and headed for the mall. On the way I told him everything that had been happening in my little life. I told him everything from my grade in school, to how annoying my little brother was. I went on and on about how I missed him and wished he could be around more. My conversation seemed to spill into the car overtaking everything even the radio. Before I knew it, we were at the mall. I wanted so much for every second of this day to be perfect. I would skip along holding his hand as we went store to store, pretending we had this blissful father daughter relationship. Four stores and a piece of pizza later he was ready to leave.

On the way home the once vibrant conversation had died to a few yes or no questions. As we pulled up the drive he gave me two dollars for ice cream later. He walked me up the sidewalk to the front and stopped. He told me he wasn't going to come in because he had to get up early for work, so he kissed my check and left. I looked at my watch and it was only 1:30. It was only hour ago I stood on that same front porch with butterflies in my stomach. That once wonderful view now somehow seemed kind of sad. I watched his car leave and tears welled up in my eyes as I realized the truth. Work was not the reason why my dad left. An hour away from his habit was all he could handle. My dad wanted to drink his beer more than spend the day with me. In one single instant my world was changed forever. From this point on I knew I could never depend on him. And although this would not be the last great change in my life, it is one that will always be remembered.

Essay #2

One of the most controversial topics in recent years has been what most people refer to as the English only *question. Some people think that, since English has been so widely used from the beginnings of our country, it should be declared the official language of the United States. Other people feel strongly that the widespread use of other languages in the United States means that we should not place any one language ahead of any other, and, in fact, we should go out of our way to accommodate people from other cultures by providing bilingual educational programs, making translations of government documents, and using more than one language when people vote, take driving tests, and participate in other public activities. This student essay deals with the issue of making the United States a one-language country. The writer disagrees with a statement made by President Theodore Roosevelt nearly a century ago. Look for errors that may be the result of speaking and writing English as a second language. Also look for problems with the lack of concise expression and coherence. Does she make a strong case for her position?*

Say No to English Only

Ana Ferreira

Many people have argued that English should be the official language of the United States. Theodore Roosevelt once quoted, "We have room for but one language here and that is the English language . . ." I strongly disagree with what Theodore said. Perhaps he thought such a regulation would help unify the people, but he was not realizing how unfortunate such a law would be. Today, this question is being raised again, probably because so many people are speaking Spanish. I see no reason to have an official language, not now or ever.

Since the first moment that America was discover it was never a country of one language or one culture. There were rich Indian languages, fur trappers speaking French, settlers from Holland speaking Dutch. Later there were immigrants speaking languages such as German, Italian, Polish or Swede. There were also Africans who were forced to come. They had their own African languages. Once here, people wanted a better life and slowly adapted to their new culture and the dominant language which was English. Younger people would pick up English more easily than the elderly who might stay mostly in there own neighborhoods and hold on to their custumes and first languages.

Those Americans who spoke only English, the people Roosevelt considered the true Americans were not more American because of that. If those same Americans learned other languages and enjoyed learning about other cultures, that would not mean they were being unloyal to America. They would simply be trying to go beyond what's already known and discover their horizons. It does not hurt anyone to learn about another culture including it's language. In fact, it benefits us because we become more knowledgeable.

How could Roosevelt ever have said something like that when he knew himself that if it wasn't for other cultures there would have never been the America as he knew it. Nevertheless, if people come to America from other countries it does not mean that they will not be loyal to the American people. According, to what Roosevelt said, ". . . we have room for but one loyalty and that is a loyalty to the American people," he beleived that you have to cut all ties with your ethnic roots if you are to be loyal to the United States. But loyalty to one's country is not the willingness to speak only English. Being loyal to a country is respecting their laws and not commiting crimes.

Of course, immigrants today do need to learn English, not because it is a law, but because it is our most important public language, the one we use when we deal with the government and do business. English should be taught to all school children and older people should also try to speak it. A language professor, Barbara Mujica, recently wrote an article for the New York Times. She told the story of her niece who lived in Miami and was able to study all her subjects at school in Spanish. When she was ready to go to college, she was at a big disadvantage. In this case, I believe she should have studied only in English at school but not for any reason forget about her first language. She should speak that language at home and with her family and friends.

The United States of America should be proud of having so many cultures and languages being adapted here. We can learn from each other. English will neve need to be the official language. We have I think a public language and we also have many private languages. These we can use in our homes and with ourselves. For example, I know several families where they speak their own language at home and English outside. In my family, we always speak Portuguese at home and whenever we sit down to eat together, only Portuguese is allowed at the table so nobody will ever forget our roots.

The United States is a country where people from all over the world decide to come and live here because it offers many opportunities. This is why we are great. Since I myself am from another country, speak another language, it is not because of that, that I am not loyal to the America. In fact, I find that I am more American than Portuguese because I have lived my whole life here. However, I would never want to stop learning other cultures and their languages because for me it's a way of understanding others. Don't people say the more you know the merrier?

Essay #3

This essay is a good example of a student's first draft. The piece is filled with promise. The writer is clearly very knowledgeable about the subject and has an enthusiasm that is contagious. However, too many word level errors, problems with clarity of expression, and too conversational a tone prevent the reader from fully appreciating the piece as it now stands. The writer is probably very comfortable in conversation, but he will need some direction in order to revise this first draft. Find as many errors as you can and correct them. You may want to work in groups to recast some sentences, so that the meaning will become more clear and concise.

Running: A Complex Process

Shane P. Brown

Running is a complex exercise that take years of experience to really understand the concept. Many people practiced all their lives and still never achieve what is truly the understanding of which my nine years of track has left with me. As easy as you think running might be, I've yet to find someone to just go out on a track and run around it like they were like Micheal Johnson or another top Olympican in track sports today. Well, in beginning to learn how to run you might want to buy or find a comfortable pair of running shoes. Also you will need a accurated watch or some sort of timer to be able to keep track of your pace.

Your first step should be these few questions. When, where, and how long so I run? In deciding this, you probaly need to consult a physician on this if you overweight. For those who don't have the time to consult their physician I would advise running one lap around a track. If this is to tiresome, you might want to start at a slow pace, short distance, and increase from there. Now heres a simple question in running, where do I run? Anywhere really, somewhere like a track, running around you block, running in a park, but remember depending on where you run the surface can affect your running. A harder surface will end up later hurting you body. In my opinion running around a track would be in your best place to run, because of the surface of most tracks or made of rubber. This provides very good for you legs and you back, which will soften any hardships of concert or any other surfaces.

Altering the way you improve is really easily done when changing you routine of running try to keep the same running style you began with to prevent any loss of improvement. Pacing is a very great way of improving. Also pacing is a great step, and by doing this you can improve a lot faster then normal. Especially endurance wise, pacing is very crucial. Though pacing isn't the only way of improving endurance though running. Speed work, which you run at a fast speed for awhile, then slow down for a while, and speed up again is widely used today also. This also help you improve, though speed work is mostly for athleles looking to increase their speed. Now when should you speed up, if your not an awesome athlete, but just learning how to run. You look at how easily you completing you running, if you know that you cannot improve in any direction you might want to advance to the next step by picking up the pace or increasing the amount of hills and obstacles that you have to run though. Remember improving and truing to keep the same running style by not altering your running is what you should think of most of the time you running.

After the third week or so you probably will come to a question where you will make a decision about is running really for you. This decision is totally up to the runner, most of the time confidence builds up and keeps you in the running spirit, and some never encounter this question. Making decisions right depends on you, which only you can find the answers to these questions. One thing you will have to face is some people are meant to run, so spent all their life running to gain what they are not naturally born with (talent in running), and other quit before they get to deep into what they cannot do. Really running only for those who are determine and confident in theirself, which I'm not going to lie to you, because these things could be gained in time.

Now you know how to begin running. Running can be complexed, but still can be learned or taught to the ones who are determined and confident in theirselves. Many people think they can just get out their running shoes, go outside and begin running. Truly those few haven't or never understood the concept of running. Then again some people have natural talent that even surpasses the best of all the runners. Running though very complexed are only for the ones willing to learn, and the ones that believe in themselves.

WORKING TOGETHER

USING THE INTERNET: FACTORS OF ACADEMIC SUCCESS

The first year of college presents many challenges to students, regardless of age or background. Many colleges have instituted orientation classes to help freshmen successfully overcome the transition to college. With a partner, visit the list of "Sites to Promote Academic Success" at http://www.uni.edu/walsh/linda7.html Choose five topics and review the material together. Write a list of changes you both will make in your study habits, time management, test-taking strategies, and so on. Keep track of the methods that work for you.

Topic 1 ______________________________

____

____

Topic 2 ______________________________

____

____

Topic 3 ______________________________

____

Topic 4 ______________________________

____

____

Topic 5 ______________________________

____

____

PART IV CREATING EFFECTIVE PARAGRAPHS

In many ways, Part IV is the heart of your work in this course. After you have carefully focused on the importance of the topic sentence, you will study the different methods used to develop ideas, with particular emphasis on achieving coherence. You will then have several opportunities to write paragraphs of your own, using more than one approach: following a step-by-step process, learning from the work of professional writers, and working directly from a list of topics intended to evoke your reactions to interests and experience.

Chapter 16 Working with Paragraphs: Topic Sentences and Controlling Ideas

Preview

The well developed paragraph requires a topic sentence. In this chapter you will make several discoveries about paragraphs and their topic sentences. These discoveries include the following:

- Knowing the characteristics of an acceptable paragraph
- Finding the topic sentence in a paragraph
- Understanding the difference between a topic sentence and a title
- Finding the topic in a topic sentence
- Finding the controlling idea in a topic sentence
- Choosing controlling ideas for topic sentences
- Writing your own topic sentences

Key Terms

Paragraph
Topic sentence
Controlling idea

What Is a Paragraph?

A **paragraph** is a group of sentences that develops one main idea. A paragraph may stand by itself as a complete piece of writing, or it may be a section of a longer piece of writing, such as an essay.

No single rule will tell you how long a paragraph should be, but if a paragraph is too short, the reader will feel that basic information is missing. If the paragraph is too long, the reader will be bored or confused. An effective paragraph is always long enough to develop the main idea that is being presented. An adequate paragraph usually consists of at least six sentences and no more than ten or twelve sentences. You have undoubtedly read paragraphs in newspapers that are only one sentence long, but in fully developed writing one sentence is usually not an acceptable paragraph.

What Does a Paragraph Look Like?

Some students come to college unaccustomed to using margins, indentation, and complete sentences, all of which are essential parts of paragraph form. Study the following paragraph to observe the standard form.

First word indented. Consistent margin of at least one inch on each side. Blank space after the final word.

> I got the job. I worked in a bank's city collection department. For weeks I was like a mouse in a maze: my feet scurried. Every seventh day I received thirteen dollar bills. It wasn't much. But, standing beside the pneumatic tube, unloading the bundles of mail that pelted down and distributing them according to their texture, size, and color to my superiors at their desks, I felt humble and useful.

EXERCISE 1 **Standard Paragraph Form**

Rewrite the following six sentences in standard paragraph form. As you write, use margins, indentation, and complete sentences. Each sentence must begin with a capital letter and end with a period, question mark, or exclamation point. Your instructor may prefer the paragraph to be typed on a computer.

1. In the large basement of the school, thirty families huddled in little groups of four or five.
2. Volunteer workers were busy carrying in boxes of clothing and blankets.
3. Two Red Cross women stood at a long table sorting through boxes to find sweaters and blankets for the shivering flood victims.
4. One heavyset man in a red woolen hunting jacket stirred a huge pot of soup.
5. Men and women with tired faces sipped their steaming coffee and wondered if they would ever see their homes again.
6. Outside the downpour continued.

____

EXERCISE 2 **Standard Paragraph Form**

Rewrite the following seven sentences in standard paragraph form. As you write, use margins, indentation, and complete sentences. Each sentence must begin with a capital letter and end with a period, question mark, or exclamation point. Your instructor may prefer the paragraph to be typed on a computer.

1. Friday afternoon I was desperate to get my English homework finished before I left the campus.
2. The assignment was due on Monday, but I really wanted my weekend free.
3. As I sat at the table in the library, I could see dictionaries and other reference books on the nearby shelves.
4. I felt in a good mood because I knew that if I had to find information for my assignment, it would be available to me.
5. The only worry I had was whether or not I would be interrupted by my friends who might stop by, wanting to chat.
6. Luckily, I worked along with no interruptions and was able to finish my work by five o'clock.
7. My weekend was saved!

What Is a Topic Sentence?

A **topic sentence** states the main idea of a paragraph. It is the most general sentence of the paragraph. All the other sentences serve to explain, describe, extend, or support this main-idea sentence.

Most paragraphs you read will begin with the topic sentence. However, some topic sentences come in the middle of the paragraph; others come at the end. Some paragraphs have no stated topic sentence at all; in those cases, the main idea is implied. Students are usually advised to use topic sentences in all their work in order to be certain that the writing has a focus and develops a single idea at a time. Whether you are taking an essay exam in a history course, doing a research paper for a sociology course, or writing an essay in a composition course, thoughtful use of the topic sentence will always bring better results. Good topic sentences help both the writer and the reader to think clearly about the main points.

Below are two paragraphs. Each paragraph makes a separate point, which is stated in its topic sentence. In both of these paragraphs, the topic sentence happens to be first. Read the paragraphs and notice how the topic sentence is the most general sentence; it is the main idea of each paragraph. The other sentences explain, describe, extend, or support the topic sentence.

MODEL PARAGRAPH 1

I went through a difficult period after my father died. I was moody and sullen at home. I spent most of the time in my bedroom listening to music on the radio, which made me feel even worse. I stopped playing soccer after school with my friends. My grades in school went down. I lost my appetite and seemed to get into arguments with everybody. My mom began to look worried, but I couldn't bring myself to participate in an activity with any spirit. It seemed life had lost its joy for me.

MODEL PARAGRAPH 2

Fortunately, something happened that spring that brought me out of my depression. My uncle, who had been crippled in the Vietnam War, came to live with us. I learned many years later that my mother had asked him to come and live with us in the hope that he could bring me out of myself. I, on the other hand, was told that it was my responsibility to help my uncle feel at home. My mother's plan worked. My uncle and I were both lonely people. A friendship began that was to change both our lives for the better.

EXERCISE 3 **Finding the Topic Sentence of a Paragraph**

Each of the following five paragraphs contains a topic sentence that states the main idea of the paragraph. Find which sentence best states the main idea and underline it. The topic sentence will not always be the first sentence of the paragraph.

1. Mountains of disposable diapers are thrown into garbage cans every day. Tons of yogurt containers, soda cans, and other plastic items are discarded without so much as a stomp to flatten them out. If the old Chevy is not worth fixing, tow it off to sit with thousands of others on acres of fenced-in junkyards. Radios, televisions, and toasters get the same treatment because it is easier and often less expensive to buy a new product than to fix the old one. Who wants a comfortable old sweater if a new one can be bought on sale? No thought is given that the new one will soon look like the old one after two or three washings. We are the great "Let's junk it" society!

2. Anyone who has been in the hospital with a serious illness can tell you that the sight of a good nurse is the most beautiful sight in the world. Today, the hospital nurse has one of the hardest jobs of all. Although a doctor may direct the care and treatment of a patient, it is the nurse who must see to it that this care and treatment is carried out. A nurse must pay attention to everything, from the condition of the hospital bed to the scheduling of medication throughout the day and night. In addition to following a doctor's orders for the day, the nurse must respond to whatever the patient might need at any given moment. A sudden emergency requires the nurse to make an immediate judgment: can the situation be handled with or without the doctor being called in? More recently, nurses have become increasingly burdened by paperwork and other administrative duties. Many people worry that the increasing demands on nurses will take them away from what they do best, namely, taking care of people on a one-to-one basis.

3. Anything can happen at a county agricultural fair. It is the perfect human occasion, the harvest of the fields and of the emotions. To the fair come the man and his cow, the boy and his girl, the wife and her green tomato pickle, each anticipating victory and the excitement of being separated from his money by familiar devices. It is at a fair that a man can be drunk forever on liquor, love, or fights; at a fair that your front pocket can be picked by a trotting horse looking for sugar, and your hind pocket by a thief looking for his fortune.

4. This was one of the worst situations I had ever been in. There was a tube in my nose that went all the way to the pit of my stomach. I was being fed intravenously, and there was a drain in my side. Everybody came to visit me, mainly out of curiosity. The girls were all anxious to know where I had gotten shot. They had heard all kinds of tales about where the bullet struck. The bolder ones wouldn't even bother to ask: they just snatched the cover off me and looked for themselves. In a few days, the word got around that I was in one piece.

5. On hot summer days, the only room of the house that was cool was the sunporch. My mother brought out all her books and papers and stacked them up on the card table. There she would sit for hours at a stretch with one hand on her forehead trying to concentrate. Baby Kathleen would often sit in her playpen, throwing all her toys out of the pen or screeching with such a piercing high pitch that someone would have to come and rescue mom by giving the baby a cracker. Father would frequently bring in cups of tea for everyone and make mother laugh with his Irish sense of humor. It was there I would love to curl up on the wicker sofa (which was too short for my long legs even at twelve) and read one of the forty or fifty books I had bought for ten cents each at a local book fair. The sounds of neighborhood activities—muted voices, a back door slamming, a dog barking—all these were a background that was friendly yet distant. During those summer days, the sunporch was the center of our lives.

EXERCISE 4 Finding the Topic Sentence of a Paragraph

Each of the following five paragraphs contains a topic sentence that states the main idea of the paragraph. Find the sentence that best states the main idea and underline it. The topic sentence will not always be the first sentence of the paragraph.

1. Last evening at a party, a complete stranger asked me, "Are you a Libra?" Astrology is enjoying increasing popularity all across the United States. My wife hurries every morning to read her horoscope in the paper. At the local stores, cards, books, T-shirts, and other useless astrological products bring fat profits to those who have manufactured them. Even some public officials, like the British royal family, are known to consider the "science" of astrology before scheduling an important event.

2. Travelers to the United States have usually heard about the wonders of Niagara Falls and the Grand Canyon. These same tourists are not always so aware that an impressive variety of other sights awaits them in this country. The spectacular beauty of the Rocky Mountains and the wide majesty of the Mississippi River are sure to please the tourist. The green hills and valleys of the East are a contrast to the purple plains and dramatic skies of the West. The sandy beaches of the southern states are becoming increasingly popular. Even the area of the Great Lakes becomes a center of activity for boating, fishing, and swimming throughout the summer months.

3. When you remember something, your brain uses more than one method to store the information. You have short-term memory, which helps you recall recent events; you have long-term memory, which brings back items that are further in the past; and you have deep retrieval, which gives you access to long-buried information that is sometimes difficult to recall. Whether these processes are chemical or electrical, we do not yet know, and much research remains to be done before we can say with any certainty. The brain is one of the most remarkable organs, a part of the body that we have only begun to investigate. It will be years before we even begin to understand all its complex processes.

4. Some of the homes were small with whitewashed walls and thatched roofs. We were eager to see how they were furnished. The living rooms were simple, often with only a plain wooden table and some chairs. The tiny bedrooms usually had room for only a single bed and a small table. Occasionally, a bedroom would be large enough to have a stove made of richly decorated tiles. Visiting these houses was an experience that would always stay in our memory. All of the windows held boxes for flowers so that even in the dark of winter there was the promise of a blaze of colors in the spring.

5. Advertisements that claim you can lose five pounds overnight are not to be trusted. Nor are claims that your luck will change if you send money to a certain post office box in a distant state. You should also avoid chain letters you receive in the mail that promise you large amounts of money if you will cooperate and keep the chain going. Many people are suspicious of the well-publicized million-dollar giveaway promotions that seem to offer enormous cash prizes, even if you do not try the company's product. We should always be suspicious of offers that promise us something for little or no effort or money.

EXERCISE 5 **Finding the Topic Sentence of a Paragraph**

The topic sentence is missing in each of the following four paragraphs. Read each paragraph carefully and circle the letter of the best topic sentence for that paragraph.

Ninety-five percent of the population in China had been illiterate. He knew that American public schools would take care of our English, but he had to be the watchdog to nurture our Chinese knowledge. Only the Cantonese tongue was ever spoken by him or my mother. When the two oldest girls arrived from China, the schools of Chinatown received only boys. My father tutored his daughters each morning before breakfast. In the midst of a foreign environment, he clung to a combination of the familiar old standards and what was permissible in the newly learned Christian ideals.

a. Education was always a priority in our family.
b. My father made sure that his sons received a proper education.
c. Learning Cantonese was an essential part of my education.
d. My father believed that the girls deserved educational opportunities just as much as the boys in the family.

How to hold a pair of chopsticks (palm up, not down); how to hold a bowl of rice (one thumb on top, not resting in an open palm); how to pass something to elders (with both hands, never one); how to pour tea into the tiny, handleless porcelain cups (seven-eighths full so that the top edge would be cool enough to hold); how to eat from a center serving dish (only the piece in front of your place; never pick around); not to talk at table; not to show up outside of one's room without being fully dressed; not to be late, ever; not to be too playful—in a hundred and one ways, we were molded to be trouble-free, unobtrusive, quiescent, cooperative.

a. From a very young age, I was taught proper table manners.
b. Very early in my life, I was taught the manners of a Chinese lady.
c. Many Chinese customs differ from American customs.
d. Learning manners in a Chinese American household.

I was never hungry. Though we had no milk, there was all the rice we wanted. We had hot and cold running water—a rarity in Chinatown, as well as our own bathtub. Others in the community used the YWCA or YMCA facilities, where for twenty-five cents, a family could draw six baths. Our sheets were pieced from dishtowels, but we had sheets. I was never neglected, for my mother and father were always at home. During school vacation periods, I was taught to operate many types of machines—tacking (for pockets), overlocking (for the raw edges of seams), buttonhole, double seaming; and I learned all the stages in producing a pair of jeans to its final inspection, folding, and tying in bundles of a dozen pairs by size, ready for pickup. Denim jeans are heavy—my shoulders ached often. My father set up a modest nickel-and-dime piecework reward for me, which he recorded in my own notebook, and he paid me regularly.

a. Learning the family trade.
b. Life in Chinatown for most people was very hard.
c. Learning how to sew was an important part of my upbringing.
d. Life was often hard, but there was little reason for unhappiness.

Mother would clean our living quarters very thoroughly, decorate the sitting room with flowering branches, fresh oranges, and arrange candied fruits or salty melon seeds for callers. All of us would be dressed in bright new clothes, and relatives or close friends, who came to call, would give each of us a red paper packet containing a good luck coin—usually a quarter. I remember how my classmates would gleefully talk of *their* receipts. But my mother made us give our money to her, for she said that she needed it to reciprocate to others.

a. I always enjoyed dressing up for Chinese holidays.
b. Each holiday was unique and had its own special blend of traditions and festivities.
c. The Chinese New Year, which would fall sometime in late January or early February, was the most special time of the year.
d. There was much work to be done during times of celebration.

How Can You Tell a Topic Sentence from a Title?

The topic sentence works like a title by announcing to the reader what the paragraph is about. However, keep in mind that the title of an essay or book is usually a single word or short phrase, whereas the topic sentence of a paragraph must *always* be a complete sentence.

Title: Backpacking in the mountains
Topic sentence: Backpacking in the mountains last year was an exciting experience.

Title: The stress of college registration
Topic sentence: College registration can be stressful.

EXERCISE 6

Distinguishing a Topic Sentence from a Title

Each of the following ten examples could be a title (T) or a topic sentence (TS). In each of the spaces provided, identify the example by writing T or TS.

_______________ **1.** The benefits of a college education
_______________ **2.** The outstanding achievements of aviator Charles Lindbergh
_______________ **3.** The president's cabinet faced two major problems
_______________ **4.** The basis of the Arab–Israeli Conflict
_______________ **5.** The Japanese diet is perhaps the healthiest diet in the world
_______________ **6.** The astounding beauty of the Rocky Mountains at dusk
_______________ **7.** The finest sports car on the market
_______________ **8.** Fast-food restaurants are popular with families having small children
_______________ **9.** The expense of maintaining a car
_______________ **10.** Maintaining a car is expensive

EXERCISE 7

Distinguishing a Topic Sentence from a Title

Each of the following ten examples could be a title (T) or a topic sentence (TS). In each of the spaces provided, identify the example by writing T or TS.

________ **1.** Dreams can be frightening

________ **2.** The advantages of getting a job after high school

________ **3.** *Grumpy Old Men* was an unusual movie because it portrayed the unpopular subject of growing old

________ **4.** The home of my dreams

________ **5.** Walking on the beach at sunset calms me down after a stressful day at work

________ **6.** Making your own clothes requires great patience as well as skill

________ **7.** Selecting the right camera for an amateur

________ **8.** Finding the right place to study was my most difficult problem at college

________ **9.** The worst bargain of my life

________ **10.** The old car I bought from my friend's father turned out to be a real bargain

EXERCISE 8

Distinguishing a Topic Sentence from a Title

Each of the following ten examples could be a title (T) or a topic sentence (TS). In each of the spaces provided, identify the example by writing T or TS.

________ **1.** How to make friends at college and still have time to study

________ **2.** With the widespread use of computers, word processing skills are needed for many jobs

________ **3.** The disadvantages of living alone

________ **4.** The fight to keep our neighborhood park

________ **5.** The peacefulness of a solitary weekend at the beach

________ **6.** Our investigation into the mysterious death of Walter D.

________ **7.** The flea market looked promising

________ **8.** The two main reasons why divorce is common

________ **9.** The single life did not turn out to be as glamorous as I had hoped

________ **10.** The increasing popularity of board games

How Do You Find the Topic in a Topic Sentence?

To find the topic in a topic sentence, ask yourself what subject the writer is going to discuss. In the first sentence that follows, the topic is underlined for you. Underline the topic in the second example.

Backpacking in the mountains last year was an exciting experience.

College registration can be stressful.

EXERCISE 9 **Finding the Topic in the Topic Sentence**

Find the topic in each of the following topic sentences. For each example, ask yourself this question: What topic is the writer going to discuss? Then underline the topic.

1. Remodeling an old house can be frustrating.
2. College work demands more independence than high school work.
3. A well-made suit has three easily identified characteristics.
4. Growing up near a museum had a profound influence on my life.
5. My favorite room in the house would seem ugly to most people.
6. A student who goes to school full-time and also works part-time has to make careful use of every hour.
7. One of the disadvantages of skiing is the expense.
8. Spanking is the least successful way to discipline a child.
9. An attractive wardrobe does not have to be expensive.
10. Of all the years in college, the freshman year is usually the most demanding.

EXERCISE 10 **Finding the Topic in the Topic Sentence**

Find the topic in each of the following topic sentences. For each example, ask yourself this question: What topic is the writer going to discuss? Then underline the topic.

1. Taking care of a house can easily be a full-time job.
2. Many television news programs are more interested in providing entertainment than newsworthy information.
3. One of the undisputed goals in teaching is to be able to offer individualized instruction.
4. Whether it's a car, a house, or a college, bigger isn't always better.
5. Violence on television is disturbing to most child psychologists.
6. In today's economy, carrying at least one credit card is probably advisable.
7. Much highway advertising is not only ugly but also distracting for the driver.
8. Figuring out a semester course schedule can be a complicated process.
9. In recent years, we have seen a dramatic revival of interest in quilting.
10. The grading system of the state university is quite different from that of the small liberal arts college in my hometown.

EXERCISE 11 **Finding the Topic in the Topic Sentence**

Find the topic in each of the following topic sentences. For each example, ask yourself this question: What topic is the writer going to discuss? Then underline the topic.

1. To my surprise, the basement had now been converted into a small studio apartment.
2. Of all the presidents, Abraham Lincoln probably enjoys the greatest popularity.
3. Scientists cannot yet explain how an identical twin often has an uncanny knowledge of what the other twin is doing or feeling.
4. If you don't have a car in the United States, you have undoubtedly discovered that public transportation is in a state of decay.
5. When we met for dinner that night, I was shocked at the change that had come over my friend.
6. According to the report, current tax laws greatly benefit those who own real estate.
7. Marian Anderson, the famous singer, began her career in a church choir.
8. As we rode into town, the streets seemed unusually empty.
9. The United Parcel Service offers its employees many long-term benefits.
10. Many people claim that clipping coupons can save them as much as 30 percent of their food bill.

What Is a Controlling Idea?

A topic sentence should contain not only the topic but also a controlling idea.

The **controlling idea** of a topic sentence is the attitude or point of view that the writer takes toward the topic.

Backpacking trips are *exhausting*.

A particular topic could have any number of possible controlling ideas, depending on the writer's attitude. On the same topic of *backpacking,* three writers might have different points of view:

A family backpacking trip can be much more *satisfying* than a trip to an amusement park.

or

Our recent backpacking trip was a *disaster*.

or

A backpacking trip *should be a part of every teenager's experience*.

How Do You Find the Controlling Idea of a Topic Sentence?

When you look for the controlling idea of a topic sentence, ask yourself this question: What is the writer's attitude toward the topic?

In each of the following examples, underline the topic and circle the controlling idea.

Sealfon's Department Store is my favorite store in town.

Sealfon's Department Store is too expensive for my budget.

EXERCISE 12 **Finding the Controlling Idea**

Below are ten topic sentences. For each sentence, underline the topic and circle the controlling idea.

1. Vigorous exercise is a good way to reduce the effects of stress on the body.
2. Buffalo and Toronto differ in four major ways.
3. Television violence causes aggressive behavior in children.
4. Athletic scholarships available to women are increasing.
5. Caffeine has several adverse effects on the body.
6. Marion Jones, the dominant female track star in the world, has a grueling training schedule.
7. Training a parakeet to talk takes great patience.
8. Babysitting for a family with four preschool children was the most difficult job I've ever had.
9. The hours between five and seven in the morning are my most productive.
10. The foggy night was spooky.

EXERCISE 13 **Finding the Controlling Idea**

Below are ten topic sentences. For each sentence, underline the topic and circle the controlling idea.

1. Piano lessons turned out to be an unexpected delight.
2. The training of Japanese policemen is quite different from American police training.
3. An Olympic champion has five distinctive characteristics.
4. The candidate's unethical financial dealings will have a negative impact on this campaign.
5. A bicycle ride along the coast is a breathtaking trip.
6. The grocery store is another place where people waste a significant amount of money every week.
7. Being an only child is not as bad as people think.
8. Rewarding children with candy or desserts is an unfortunate habit of many parents.

9. A childhood hobby often develops into a promising career.
10. The writing of a dictionary is an incredibly detailed process.

EXERCISE 14 **Finding the Controlling Idea**

Below are ten topic sentences. For each sentence, underline the topic and circle the controlling idea.

1. Learning to type takes more practice than talent.
2. Shakespeare's plays are difficult for today's students because English has undergone many changes since the sixteenth century.
3. Atlanta, Georgia, is one of the cities in the Sunbelt that is experiencing significant population growth.
4. Half a dozen new health magazines are enjoying popularity.
5. The importance of good preschool programs for children has been sadly underestimated.
6. The disposal of toxic wastes has caused problems for many manufacturers.
7. Censorship of school textbooks is a controversial issue in most towns.
8. Finding an inexpensive method to make salt water drinkable has been a difficult problem for decades.
9. Developing color film is more complicated than developing black and white.
10. The cloudberry is one of the rare berries of the world.

Choosing Your Own Controlling Idea

Teachers often assign one general topic on which all students must write. Likewise, when writing contests are announced, the topic is generally the same for all contestants. Since very few people have exactly the same view or attitude toward a topic, it is likely that no two papers would have the same controlling idea. There could be as many controlling ideas as there are people to write them. The secret of a successful topic sentence is to find the controlling idea that is right for you.

EXERCISE 15 **Choosing Controlling Ideas to Write Topic Sentences**

Below are two topics. For each topic, think of three possible controlling ideas, and then write a topic sentence for each of these controlling ideas. An example is done for you.

Topic: My mother

Three possible controlling ideas:

1. Unusual childhood
2. Silent woman
3. Definite ideas about alcohol

Three different topic sentences:

1. My mother had a most unusual childhood.
2. My mother is a very silent woman.
3. My mother has definite ideas about alcohol.

1. Topic: My grandmother

First controlling idea: ______________________________

First topic sentence: ______________________________

____

Second controlling idea: ______________________________

Second topic sentence: ______________________________

____

Third controlling idea: ______________________________

Third topic sentence: ______________________________

____

2. Topic: California

First controlling idea: ______________________________

First topic sentence: ______________________________

____

Second controlling idea: ______________________________

Second topic sentence: ______________________________

____

Third controlling idea: ______________________________

Third topic sentence: ______________________________

____

EXERCISE 16 Choosing Controlling Ideas to Write Topic Sentences

Below are two topics. For each topic, think of three possible controlling ideas, and then write a topic sentence for each of these controlling ideas. An example is done for you.

Topic: The movie *Apollo 13*

Three possible controlling ideas:

1. Filled with suspense
2. Reveals the bravery of the astronauts
3. Explores the importance of teamwork

Three different topic sentences:

1. *Apollo 13* is a movie filled with suspense.
2. *Apollo 13* is a movie that reveals the bravery of the astronauts when faced with life and death situations.
3. *Apollo 13* is a movie that explores the importance of teamwork.

1. Topic: Thanksgiving

First controlling idea: ______________________________

First topic sentence: ______________________________

____

Second controlling idea: ______________________________

Second topic sentence: ______________________________

____

Third controlling idea: ______________________________

Third topic sentence: ______________________________

____

2. Topic: Working in a nursing home

First controlling idea: ______________________________

First topic sentence: ______________________________

____

Second controlling idea: ______________________________

Second topic sentence: ______________________________

____

Third controlling idea: ______________________________

Third topic sentence: ______________________________

____

EXERCISE 17 Choosing Controlling Ideas to Write Topic Sentences

Below are two topics. For each topic, think of three possible controlling ideas, and then write a topic sentence for each of these controlling ideas. An example is done for you.

Topic: Fitness and health

Three possible controlling ideas:

1. The growth of new lines of products
2. Increased popularity of health clubs
3. Use of exercise videos and equipment at home

Three different topic sentences:

1. Recent years have seen the creation of entire lines of products devoted to fitness and health.
2. The high level of interest in physical fitness and health has resulted in a widespread growth of health clubs across the country.
3. A person can improve his or her health by exercising at home with a professional video or working out on one of the many pieces of equipment available for private use.

1. Topic: Rap music

First controlling idea: ______________________________

First topic sentence: ______________________________

____

Second controlling idea: ______________________________

Second topic sentence: ______________________________

____

Third controlling idea: ______________________________

Third topic sentence: ______________________________

____

2. Topic: Junk food

First controlling idea: ______________________________

First topic sentence: ______________________________

____

Second controlling idea: ______________________________

Second topic sentence: ______________________________

____

Third controlling idea: ______________________________

Third topic sentence: ______________________________

____

Mastery and Editing Tests

TEST 1

Further Practice Writing the Topic Sentence

Develop each of the following topics into a topic sentence. In each case, the controlling idea is missing. First, decide on an attitude you might take toward the topic. Then include that attitude as part of your topic sentence. When you are finished, underline your topic and circle your controlling idea. Be sure your topic sentence is a complete sentence and not a fragment. An example has been done for you.

Topic: My brother's car accident

Controlling idea: Tragic results

Topic sentence: My brother's car accident had (tragic results) for the entire family.

1. **Topic:** Teaching a child good manners

   Controlling idea: ______________________________

   Topic sentence: ______________________________

   ____

2. **Topic:** Two years in the military

   Controlling idea: ______________________________

   Topic sentence: ______________________________

   ____

3. **Topic:** Living with your in-laws

   Controlling idea: ______________________________

   Topic sentence: ______________________________

   ____

4. **Topic:** Moving to a new location

   Controlling idea: ______________________________

   Topic sentence: ______________________________

   ____

5. **Topic:** Going on a diet

   Controlling idea: ______________________________

   Topic sentence: ______________________________

   ____

TEST 2 Further Practice Writing the Topic Sentence

Develop each of the following topics into a topic sentence. In each case, the controlling idea is missing. First, decide on an attitude you might take toward the topic. Then include that attitude as part of your topic sentence. When you are finished, underline your topic and circle your controlling idea. Be sure your topic sentence is a complete sentence and not a fragment.

1. **Topic:** Camping

   Controlling idea: ______________________________

   Topic sentence: ______________________________

   ____

2. Topic: Vegetarians

Controlling idea: ______________________________

Topic sentence: ______________________________

____

3. Topic: Noisy neighbors

Controlling idea: ______________________________

Topic sentence: ______________________________

____

4. Topic: Driving lessons

Controlling idea: ______________________________

Topic sentence: ______________________________

____

5. Topic: Subways

Controlling idea: ______________________________

Topic sentence: ______________________________

____

TEST 3 **Further Practice Writing the Topic Sentence**

Develop each of the following topics into a topic sentence. In each case, the controlling idea is missing. First, decide on an attitude you might take toward the topic. Then include that attitude as part of your topic sentence. When you are finished, underline your topic and circle your controlling idea. Be sure your topic sentence is a complete sentence and not a fragment.

1. Topic: Computer programming

Controlling idea: ______________________________

Topic sentence: ______________________________

____

2. Topic: Body piercing

Controlling idea: ______________________________

Topic sentence: ______________________________

____

3. Topic: Allergies

Controlling idea: ______________________________

Topic sentence: ______________________________

____

4. Topic: Motorcycles

Controlling idea: ______________________________

Topic sentence: ______________________________

____

5. Topic: Eating out

Controlling idea: ______________________________

Topic sentence: ______________________________

____

EXPLORING ONLINE

For more about topic sentences see

http://www.as.ttu.edu/uwc/topicsen.html

WORKING TOGETHER

EXPLORING CONTROLLING IDEAS

Topic: Marriage

To develop an essay on any given topic, a writer has an almost endless number of possible controlling ideas from which to choose. Student writers often express amazement when they discover how another writer has approached a given topic. "I never thought of doing that," they say. Let's explore some of these possible approaches to a topic as we brainstorm for different controlling ideas on the topic of *marriage*.

What follows is an example of just one controlling idea on marriage that uses comparison or contrast as a method of development.

My parents' marriage was *a completely different arrangement from my own.*

Begin by dividing into groups. Each person in each group should provide at least two controlling ideas for possible use in a piece of writing on marriage. One person in the group should bring all the controlling ideas together and make up a single list that will be shared with the entire class. Finally, all the groups should come together and share their lists. How many different controlling ideas have come out of the work of all the groups? Do these controlling ideas cover all the different methods for developing ideas discussed in this textbook?

Portfolio Suggestion

Each student in the class should copy the list of controlling ideas developed by the class. Organize the ideas into groups according to each group's most obvious method of development: description, example, narration, process, classification, cause and effect, definition, comparison and contrast, or argument. Save this list in your portfolio as a reminder of the ways you could develop your own thinking on a given topic.

Choose the controlling idea that is most interesting to you, and then write a piece on this aspect of marriage.

Chapter 17 Working with Paragraphs: Supporting Details

Preview

To develop a paragraph, you must support the main idea with details. In this chapter, you will learn several points about supporting details:

- The choice of paragraph development determines the type of supporting details. Writers choose from descriptive images, anecdotes, examples, steps, reasons, definitions, causes, effects, comparison/contrast, or classification.
- Supporting details are different from restatements of the main idea.
- Making supporting details more specific will improve a paragraph.

Key Term

Supporting detail

Chart

Methods of Paragraph Development

What Is a Supporting Detail?

Once you have constructed a topic sentence made up of the topic and its controlling idea, you are ready to support your statement with details. The quality and number of these details will largely determine the effectiveness of your writing. You can hold your readers spellbound with your choice of details, or you can lose your readers' interest because your details are not compelling.

A **supporting detail** is a piece of evidence used by the writer to make the controlling idea of the topic sentence convincing and interesting to the reader. A piece of evidence might include a descriptive image, an example taken from history or personal experience, a reason, a fact (such as a statistic), a quotation from an expert, or an anecdote to illustrate a point.

Poor supporting details: Many people died of the flu in the 1960s.

Effective supporting details: In 1968, 70,000 people died of the Hong Kong flu in the United States.

For a paragraph to be developed, the main idea of the paragraph must be supported with several details. As we work through the chapters in this section, you will have opportunities to use many types of supporting details. In the chart below, you can see the different methods of paragraph development. A writer chooses his supporting details according to what best fits the method of development. For instance, if the writer is describing someone's appearance, the details would be sensory images.

METHODS OF PARAGRAPH DEVELOPMENT	
Narration:	telling a story in a sequence of events
Description:	using sensory images to create a picture with words
Process:	using steps to explain how to do something or to explain how something works
Example:	giving instances or illustrations of the main idea
Comparison/contrast:	showing similarities or differences
Cause and effect:	examining the reasons why or examining the outcomes for an event
Extended definition:	analyzing the meaning of a word or concept
Classification:	dividing the subject up into groups or parts

As you choose your supporting details, keep in mind that the readers do not necessarily have to agree with your point of view. However, your supporting details must be good enough so that your readers will at least respect your attitude. Your goal should be to educate your readers. Try to give them some understanding about your subject. Don't assume they know about your topic or are interested in it. If you provide enough specific details, your readers will feel they have learned something new about the subject, and this alone is a satisfying experience for most people.

Supporting details will encourage readers to keep on reading, will make your points more memorable, and will give pleasure to those who are learning new material or trying to picture the images you have created.

Read the following paragraph and observe how it provides effective details that support the point of the topic sentence.

> Everyone has heard of sure-fire formulas to prevent getting a cold. Popular home methods include a cold shower, regular exercise, and a hot rum toddy. Some people swear by cod-liver oil, tea with honey, citrus fruit juices, or keeping one's feet dry. Americans spent billions last year for cold and cough remedies. Advertisers have claimed preventive and curative virtues for vitamins, alkalizers, lemon drinks, antihistamines, decongestants, timed-release capsules, anti biotics, antiseptic gargles, bioflavonoids, nose drops and sprays, and a variety of other products. There are at least 3 over-the-counter products, most of which are a combination of ingredients sold for the treatment of symptoms of the common cold. Many of these drugs neither benefit nor harm the cold victim, but there is no doubt that they benefit the drug manufacturers! Now—just as fifty years ago—Americans on average will suffer two to three colds a year, with the infectious stages lasting about a week, regardless of any physical measure, diet, or drug used. U.S. Public Health Service studies show that, during the winter

quarter of the year, 50 percent of the population experiences a common cold; during the summer quarter, the figure drops to 20 percent. The increased incidence of colds in winter reflects the fact that people spend more time indoors, thereby allowing the viruses to travel from person to person. In fact, one is less likely to catch a cold after exposure to the elements than after mixing with a convivial group of sniffers and sneezers at a fireside gathering.

Practice.......... Using the lines provided, copy the topic sentence from the previous paragraph. Then answer the questions about the details that support the topic sentence.

Topic sentence: ______________________________

____

What are some examples of home remedies?

____

____

What are some examples of over-the-counter remedies?

____

____

What fact is given?

____

____

What expert is named? What is the statistic given by that source?

____

____

EXERCISE 1 **Finding the Topic Sentence and Supporting Details**

In each paragraph below, find the topic sentence and identify the sentences of supporting details.

1. Saturday afternoon was a blessed time on the farm. First of all, there would now be no mail in till Monday afternoon, so that no distressing business letters could reach us till then, and this fact in itself seemed to close the whole place in. Secondly, everybody was looking forward to the day of Sunday, when they would rest or play all the day, and the Squatters could work on their own land. The thought of the oxen on Saturday pleased me more than all other things. I used to walk down to their paddock at six o'clock, when they were coming in after the day's work and a few hours' grazing. Tomorrow, I thought, they would do nothing but graze all day.

From Isak Dinesen,
Out of Africa

Topic sentence: ______________________________

First reason: ______________________________

____

____

Second reason: ______________________________

____

Third reason: ______________________________

2. More people watched the Superbowl than watched Neil Armstrong's walk on the moon. Fifteen percent of all television programs produced are sports programs. Professional football games have a yearly attendance of over ten million spectators and both baseball leagues together draw over three million spectators every year. In one year, North American spectators spent over $3 million for tickets to sports events. There probably is not a person in the United States who does not recognize a picture of Muhammad Ali, and who cannot identify a picture of the soccer star Pele? The popularity of sports is enormous.

Adapted from Ronald W. Smith and Andrea Fontana, *Social Problems*

Topic sentence: ______________________________

First statistical fact: ______________________________

____

Second statistical fact: ______________________________

____

____

Examples of recognizable sports stars: ______________________________

____

EXERCISE 2 **Finding the Topic Sentence and Supporting Details**

In each paragraph below, find the topic sentence and identify the sentences of supporting details.

1. Hilda takes an enormous amount of space, though so little time, in my adolescence. Even today, her memory stirs me; I long to see her again. She was three years older than I, and for a short while all I wanted was to look like, sound like, and dress like her. She was the only girl I knew who told me I wrote excellent letters. She made a plaster cast of my face. She had opinions on everything. She took a picture of me, at sixteen, which I have still. She and I were nearly killed, falling off a hillside road in her small car. Hilda was so full of life, I cannot believe her dead.

From Han Suyin, *A Mortal Flower*

Topic sentence: ______________________________

____

First example: ______________________________

____

Second example: ______________________________

Third example: ______________________________

Fourth example: ______________________________

Fifth example: ______________________________

Sixth example: ______________________________

2. A steadily accumulating body of evidence supports the view that cancers are caused by things that we eat, drink, breathe, or are otherwise exposed to. That evidence is of three kinds. First, the incidence of many types of cancers differs greatly from one geographic region of the world to another. Second, when groups of people permanently move from one country to another, the incidence of some types of cancer changes in their offspring. For example, when Japanese move to this country, the relatively high rate of occurrence of stomach cancer they experience in Japan falls so that their children experience such cancer only a fifth as frequently, the same incidence as other Americans. Asians have low incidence of breast cancer, but when they come to the United States, it increases sixfold. Third, we are becoming aware of an increasing number of chemical pollutants in air and water and food that have proven to be cancer-producing.

FROM MAHLON B. HOAGLAND,
The Roots of Life

Topic sentence: ______________________________

____

First piece of evidence: ______________________________

____

Second piece of evidence (and example): ______________________________

____

____

Third piece of evidence: ______________________________

____

EXERCISE 3 **Finding the Topic Sentence and Supporting Details**

In each paragraph below, find the topic sentence and identify the sentences of supporting details.

1. Transportation was simple then. Two good horses and a sturdy wagon met most needs of a villager. Only five or six individuals possessed an automobile in the Pueblo of 300. A flatbed truck fixed with wooden rails and a canvas top made a regular Saturday trip to Sante Fe. It was always loaded beyond capacity with Cochitis taking their wares to town for a few staples. With an escort of a dozen barking dogs, the straining truck made a noisy exit, northbound from the village.

FROM JOSEPH H. SUINA,
And Then I Went to School

Topic sentence: ______________________________

____

First example: ______________________________

Second example: ______________________________

____

Third example: ______________________________

____

Fourth example: ______________________________

____

____

____

2. Fairness is the ability to see more than one side in a situation, and sometimes it even means having the ability to decide against your own interests. For example, in San Antonio, Texas, a woman was locked in a bitter custody dispute that involved her thirteen-year-old son. The mother loved her son and wanted custody of him, even though she had a major health problem. She listened patiently while her ex-husband argued for full custody of the child. The woman felt that she had presented a good case before the judge, but when the boy was asked for his feelings in the matter, the mother found herself faced with a difficult situation: her son wanted to live with his father. Fairness to the child led the mother to give up her fight. Fairness, she discovered, is often painful because it means recognizing what is right instead of insisting on your own personal bias.

Topic sentence: ______________________________

____

Anecdote: ______________________________

____

____

____

____

____

____

EXPLORING ONLINE

Read about the paragraph as a miniature essay at:

http://www.wuacc.edu/services/zzcwwctr/paragraphs.txt
http://www.indiana.edu/~wts/wts.paragraphs.html
http://www.cohums.ohio-state.edu/english/programs/writing_center/elmnts1c.htm
http://bsuvc.bsu.edu/~wctutor19/paragraph.html
http://www.dartmouth.edu/~compose/student/ac-paper/write.html#constructing

Avoid Restating the Topic Sentence

You should be able to recognize the difference between a genuine supporting detail and a simple restatement of the topic sentence. The following is a poor paragraph because all its sentences merely restate the topic sentence.

> The wedding day was the highest point in a girl's life—a day to which she looked forward all her unmarried days and to which she looked back for the rest of her life. All the events of the day were unlike any other day in her life before or after. Everyone would remember this day. Each event was unforgettable. The memories would last a lifetime. A wedding was the beginning of living "happily ever after."

By contrast, this paragraph, "From Popping the Question to Popping the Pill" by Margaret Mead, has excellent supporting details:

> The wedding day was the highest point in a girl's life—a day to which she looked forward all her unmarried days and to which she looked back for the rest of her life. The splendor of her wedding, the elegance of dress and veil, the cutting of the cake, the departure amid a shower of rice and confetti, gave her an accolade of which no subsequent event could completely rob her. Today people over fifty years of age still treat their daughter's wedding this way, prominently displaying the photographs of the occasion. Until very recently, all brides' books prescribed exactly the same ritual they had prescribed fifty years before. The etiquette governing wedding presents—gifts that were or were not appropriate, the bride's maiden initials on her linen—was also specified. For the bridegroom the wedding represented the end of his free, bachelor days, and the bachelor dinner the night before the wedding symbolized this loss of freedom. A woman who did not marry—even if she had the alibi of a fiancé who had been killed in war or had abilities and charm and money of her own—was always at a social disadvantage while an eligible bachelor was sought after by hostess after hostess.

EXERCISE 4 **Distinguishing a Supporting Detail from a Restatement of the Main Idea**

Each of the following topic sentences is followed by four additional sentences. Three of these additional sentences contain acceptable supporting details, but one of the sentences is simply a restatement of the topic sentence. In the space provided, identify each sentence as SD for supporting detail or R for restatement.

1. I am surprised when I think how neat I used to be before school started.

_________ a. In my closet, I had my clothes arranged in matching outfits with shoes, hats, and even jewelry to go with them.

_________ b. I always used to take great pride in having all my things in order.

_______ c. If I opened my desk drawer, compartments of paper clips, erasers, staples, pens, pencils, stamps, and rulers greeted me without one lost penny or safety pin out of place.

_______ d. On top of my chest of drawers sat a comb and brush, two oval frames with pictures of my best friends, and that was all.

2. Iceland has a very barren landscape.

_______ a. One-tenth of the island is covered by ice.

_______ b. There is not a single forest on the entire island.

_______ c. Nearly everywhere you look in Iceland, you see vast desolate areas.

_______ d. Three-fourths of the island is uninhabitable.

3. Until recently, books have been the most important method of preserving knowledge.

_______ a. Without books, much of the knowledge of past centuries would have been lost.

_______ b. Leonardo da Vinci kept notebooks of his amazing inventions and discoveries.

_______ c. During the Middle Ages, monks spent their entire lives copying books by hand.

_______ d. The Library of Congress in Washington, D.C., is given a copy of every book published in the United States.

4. Most people no longer wonder whether cigarette smoking is bad for their health.

_______ a. Following the evidence from over 30,000 studies, a federal law requires that cigarette manufacturers place a health warning to all smokers on their packages.

_______ b. Studies have shown that smoking presently causes nearly 80 percent of lung cancer deaths in this country.

_______ c. Few authorities today have any doubts about the connection between cigarette smoking and poor health.

_______ d. We know that 30 percent of the deaths from coronary heart disease can be attributed to smoking.

5. When the Mexican earthquake struck in 1985, scientists and city planners learned a great deal about the kinds of buildings that can survive an earthquake.

_______ a. Buildings that had foundations resting on giant rollers suffered very little damage.

_______ b. Buildings that were made only of adobe material simply fell apart when the earthquake struck.

__________ c. Many of the modern buildings were designed to vibrate when earthquakes occur, so these received the least amount of shock.

__________ d. After the earthquake was over, officials realized why some buildings were destroyed while others suffered hardly any damage at all.

EXERCISE 5 Recognizing a Supporting Detail from a Restatement of the Main Idea

Each of the following topic sentences is followed by four additional sentences. Three of these additional sentences contain acceptable supporting details, but one of the sentences is simply a restatement of the topic sentence. In the space provided, identify each sentence as SD for supporting detail or R for restatement.

1. In the last thirty years, the number of people living alone in the United States has increased by 400 percent.

__________ a. People are living alone because the number of divorces has dramatically increased.

__________ b. Many young people are putting off marriage until they are financially more secure or emotionally ready.

__________ c. More and more Americans are finding themselves living alone.

__________ d. An increasing percentage of our population is the age group over sixty-five, among whom are many widows and widowers.

2. Today, people are realizing the disadvantages of using credit cards too often.

__________ a. People should think twice before using their cards.

__________ b. Interest rates on credit cards can reach alarming rates.

__________ c. Credit cards encourage buying on impulse, rather than planning a budget carefully.

__________ d. Many credit card companies charge an annual fee for the privilege of using cards.

3. In medicine, prevention is just as important as treatment.

__________ a. A good way for a person to keep in touch with his or her health is to have an annual physical.

__________ b. In order to stay healthy, people must watch their weight carefully.

__________ c. Some researchers claim an aspirin every day will thin the blood and thereby prevent clotting.

__________ d. We know now that learning how to prevent disease is equal in importance to getting proper treatment once one has a disease.

4. Since World War II, the status of women in Japan has changed.

__________ a. In 1947, women won the right to vote.

__________ b. The women's position in Japanese society has altered over the past forty-five years.

__________ c. Many Japanese women now go on to get a higher education.

__________ d. Women can now own property in their own name and seek divorce.

5. Certain factors which cannot be changed have been shown to contribute to heart attacks and stroke.

__________ a. Three out of four heart attacks and six out of seven strokes occur after the age of sixty-five, so age is definitely a factor.

__________ b. Heart attacks and strokes have many causes, some of which we can do nothing about.

__________ c. African Americans have nearly a 45 percent greater risk of having high blood pressure, a major cause of heart attacks and strokes.

__________ d. Men are at greater risk than women in their chance of suffering from cardiovascular disease.

How Do You Make Supporting Details Specific?

Students often write paragraphs that are made up of only general statements. When you read such paragraphs, you doubt the author's knowledge and you suspect that the point being made may have no basis in fact. Here is one such paragraph that never gets off the ground.

> Doctors are terrible. They cause more problems than they solve. I don't believe most of their treatments are necessary. History is full of the mistakes doctors have made. We don't need all those operations. We should never ingest all those drugs doctors prescribe. We shouldn't allow them to give us all those unnecessary tests. I've heard plenty of stories that prove my point. Doctors' ideas can kill you.

Here is another paragraph on the same topic. This topic is much more interesting and convincing because the writer has made use of supporting details rather than rely on general statements.

> Evidence shows that "medical progress" has been the cause of tragic consequences and even death for thousands of people. X-ray therapy was thought to help patients with tonsillitis. Now many of these people are found to have developed cancer from these X-rays. Not so long ago, women were kept in bed for several weeks following childbirth. Unfortunately, this cost many women their lives since they developed fatal blood clots from being kept in bed day after day. One recent poll estimates that 30,000 people each year die from the side effects of drugs that were prescribed by doctors. Recently, the Center for Disease

Control reported that 25 percent of the tests done by clinical laboratories were done poorly. All this is not to belittle the good done by the medical profession, but to impress on readers that it would be foolish to rely totally on the medical profession to solve all our health problems.

This paragraph is much more likely to be of real interest. Even if you would like to disprove the author's point, it would be very hard to dismiss these supporting details, which are based on facts and information that can be researched. Because the author sounds reasonable, you have respect for the presentation of specific facts, even if you have a different position on the topic.

In writing effectively, the ability to go beyond the general statement and get to the accurate pieces of information is what counts. A writer tries to make his or her reader an expert on the subject. Readers should go away excited to share with the next person they meet the surprising information they have just learned. A writer who has a statistic, a quotation, an anecdote, a historical example, or a descriptive detail has the advantage over all other writers, no matter how impressive these writers' styles may be.

Good writing, therefore, is filled with supporting details that are specific, correct, and appropriate for the subject. Poor writing is filled with generalizations, stereotypes, vagueness, untruths, and even sarcasm and insults.

EXPLORING ONLINE

See more about supporting details:

http://www.powa.org/thesfrms.htm

EXERCISE 6 **Creating Supporting Details**

Below are five topic sentences. Supply three supporting details for each one. Be sure each detail is specific and not general or vague.

1. The first semester in college can be overwhelming.

a. ______________________________

b. ______________________________

c. ______________________________

2. Designer clothing is a bad investment.

a. ______________________________

b. ______________________________

c. ______________________________

3. Dr. Kline is a dedicated teacher.

a. ______________________________

b. ______________________________

c. ______________________________

4. It is difficult to stop snacking between meals.

a. ______________________________

b. ______________________________

c. ______________________________

5. My sister is the sloppiest person I know.

a. ______________________________

b. ______________________________

c. ______________________________

EXERCISE 7 Creating Supporting Details

Below are five topic sentences. Supply three supporting details for each one. Be sure each detail is specific and not general or vague.

1. December has become a frantic time at our house.

a. ______________________________

b. ______________________________

c. ______________________________

2. My best friend can often be very immature.

a. ______________________________

b. ______________________________

c. ______________________________

3. Each sport has its own peculiar injuries associated with it.

a. ______________________________

b. ______________________________

c. ______________________________

4. My car is on its "last wheel."

a. ______________________________

b. ______________________________

c. ______________________________

5. Watching too much television has serious effects on family life.

a. ______________________________

b. ______________________________

c. ______________________________

EXERCISE 8

Creating Supporting Details

Below are five topic sentences. Supply three supporting details for each one. Be sure each detail is specific and not general or vague.

1. Maintaining a car is a continual drain on one's budget.

a. ______________________________

b. ______________________________

c. ______________________________

2. Climate can affect a person's mood.

a. ______________________________

b. ______________________________

c. ______________________________

3. Last year I redecorated my bedroom.

a. ______________________________

b. ______________________________

c. ______________________________

4. Washington, D.C., is the best city for a family vacation.

a. ______________________________

b. ______________________________

c. ______________________________

5. The amateur photographer needs to consider several points when selecting a camera.

a. ______________________________

b. ______________________________

c. ______________________________

EXPLORING ONLINE

Take a paragraph development quiz:

http://www.uottawa.ca/academic/arts/writcent/hypergrammar/rvpardev.html

WORKING TOGETHER

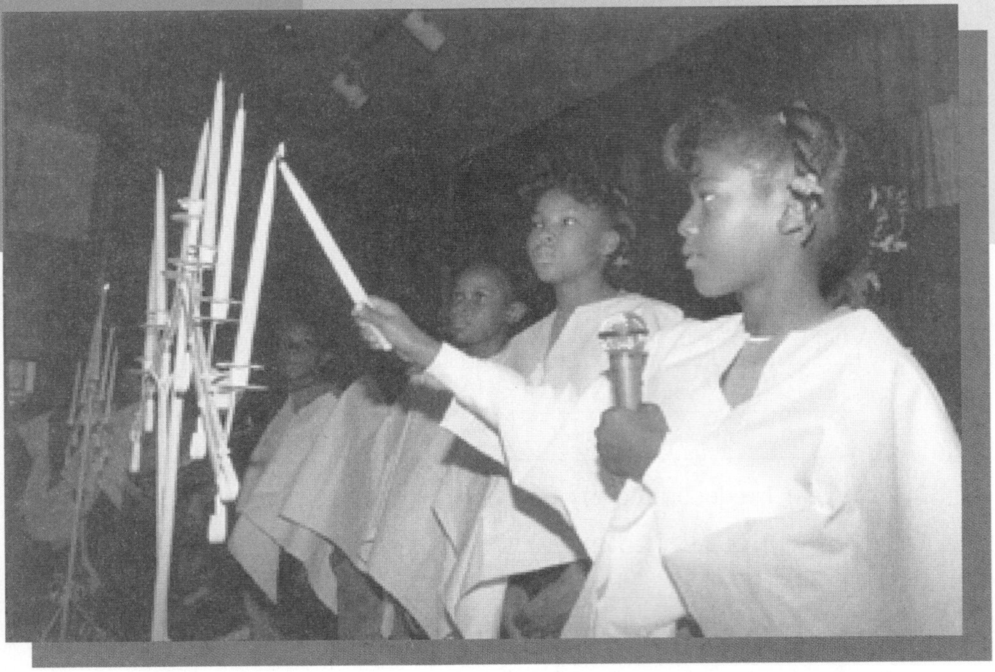

RECORDING FAMILY TRADITIONS

Celebrations are important milestones in the living traditions of individuals, groups, and even entire nations. Traditional celebrations give affirmation to people's lives and help them feel connected to each other. Celebrations also support a country's need to preserve a sense of its own history. The photograph above shows children at the Martin Luther King, Jr. School in Phoenix, Arizona, as they celebrate the birthday of their school's namesake.

Divide into groups. Make a list of celebrations (such as birthdays or Thanksgiving) celebrated by the members of each group. Next, consider what makes each celebration special. If you were to write about each holiday, what supporting details would you use? In the case of Thanksgiving, for example, the details would probably center around the meal that would be served. For how many other celebrations named by your group would this be true?

Each person should then write a paragraph describing a chosen celebration. Be sure to have a topic sentence and at least eight more sentences that support the topic sentence. Be sure that these eight sentences provide details that will help the reader construct a picture of the event.

Exchange papers. After you have read the paper you have been given, mark it in the following ways:

1. Underline the topic sentence.
2. Make a "✔" in front of the sentence you believe contains the most effective supporting detail.
3. Make an "**X**" in front of the sentence you believe has the weakest supporting detail.
4. Using the editing symbols from the inside back cover of your book, mark any errors that you find.
5. In the upper right-hand corner, rate the paper according to the following guide:

Rating 1 The details are very specific.

Mamma always ordered her fresh Thanksgiving turkey three weeks in advance from Ike at Goldfinger's Meat Market on Fourth Street.

Rating 2 The details are often specific.

Mamma ordered our Thanksgiving turkey from the local meat market.

Rating 3 The details are often too general.

Mamma fixed a turkey every Thanksgiving.

Rating 4 The details are almost always too general.

Thanksgiving dinner was always great.

6. Select a sentence you believe is too general. Rewrite it with more specific details that you think would make the sentence more interesting. Write your new version at the bottom of the student's paper.

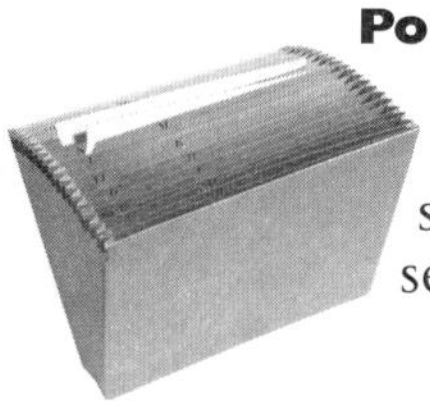

Portfolio Suggestion

When your paragraph has been returned to you, mark it as your first draft. Write a second version in which you make your details more specific. Label this your second draft. Be sure to show both versions to someone who can comment on your changes. Are you happier with the second version? Save both versions in your portfolio.

Online Activity

Find out the origins and customs of world holidays:

http://candlegrove.com/home.html

Go to "Holiday Links."

Chapter 18 Developing Paragraphs: Illustration

Preview

In order to make an abstract idea or general idea clear, every writer needs to use *illustration* or *example.* This method of development is the focus for this chapter. The following topics are presented:

- Three ways to illustrate a point
- Knowing where to find examples
- Transitions for introducing examples
- Analyzing paragraphs with examples
- Practicing your own example paragraphs
  - Using a step-by-step approach
  - Using model paragraphs with suggested topics

Key Term

Illustration

Charts

List of transitions for illustration
Steps for writing a paragraph using illustration

What Is Illustration?

In Chapter 17, we learned that details are needed to support the main idea. The *illustration* (or *example*) is usually the detail most writers think of first.

Illustration (often called **example**) is a method of developing an idea by providing one or more instances of that idea. Such an illustration or example serves to clarify the idea, make the idea more convincing, or make an abstract idea more concrete.

One example of American craftsmanship is the Tiffany lamp.

Three Ways Writers Use Illustration

1. Brief examples given without any particular grouping:

Example: As a child I had pen pals from all over the world. These included my Cousin Britt-Marie from Sweden, Ying from Hong Kong, Simone from France, Etsuko from Japan, and several children from Kenya.

2. Brief examples arranged into groups:

Example: As a child I had pen pals from all over the world. From Europe was my Swedish cousin Britt-Marie, and from the south of France was a pretty girl named Simone. From the Pacific came the beautiful monthly letters of Etsuko and an occasional postcard from Ying in Hong Kong. Finally, from Africa came a number of charming letters from several schoolchildren in Kenya.

3. A longer and more developed example, called an *extended example* (possibly consisting of an *anecdote* using the principles of narration):

Example: As a child I had pen pals from all over the world. How it all first started was a letter of a few sentences that came unexpectedly from my cousin Britt-Marie in Sweden. It was a hot August morning . . .

Then the story of that first letter would follow, written as a paragraph or two. Always remember that the anecdote must support the larger point contained in the topic sentence, namely, the writer had pen pals from all over the world.

Working with Illustration: Where Does the Writer Find Examples?

Personal Experiences and One's Own Knowledge of the World

Writers find supporting examples for their work everywhere, beginning with their own experience. What you have observed and what has happened to you are two excellent sources of examples for your own writing. All of us have gained a great deal of knowledge either formally or informally, and you can call upon that knowledge when you look for examples to illustrate your points.

Interviews and Surveys

Another source for examples is to interview other people or take an informal survey. Gathering this kind of material can enrich your writing by presenting very specific information and facts about your main idea. We see and hear interviews on television and radio every day, as people from all walks of life tell their stories on every topic imaginable. We are accustomed to seeing professional interviewers asking questions, but you can also gain examples in this way by talking to your friends and classmates and learning from them.

Outside Research from Books and Magazines

A third method of finding specific examples for your work is to do outside research. This usually involves going to a library and finding information from books and magazines as well as consulting the World Wide Web. This kind of research is necessary for term papers and many other kinds of college work, and it always requires a careful listing of the sources that are used.

Using Your Imagination to Create Hypothetical Examples

A final way to obtain examples is a method that does not require any outside sources. This is your own imagination. Writers often find it very useful to create imaginary examples or situations that can provide the specific details for them when they need examples in their writing. Humorous writers do this all the time when they tell jokes. You, too, can use your imagination to generate examples when your writing does not require strictly factual information. The hypothetical example is also useful to illustrate a point. This example often begins with a phrase such as "Imagine the following situation . . ." or "Put the case that . . ." or "What if this were to happen . . ."

EXERCISE 1

The Sources for Illustrations

Each of the following three paragraphs develops an idea by using illustration. Read each paragraph and decide what the source was for the illustration. Choose from the following list:

Example from personal experience or knowledge

Made up or hypothetical example

Information from an interview or survey you conduct yourself

Outside research (using material found in books or articles)

PARAGRAPH 1

Most students today believe they must learn how to use the computer if they are to be competitive in the job market. A case in point is my freshman writing class. Out of the 23 students surveyed, all but two felt they must be computer literate before they leave college or they might not be able to get the jobs they want. Three of the students currently own their own computers and claim they are able to get their college work done more easily. Two of these three students actually have part-time jobs, one in the library and one in the history department where they both enter data on computers. This seems to show that these students already are at an advantage over the rest of the students who are still learning to use the computer.

Type of example: ______________________________

PARAGRAPH 2

Most students today believe they must learn how to use the computer if they are to be competitive in the job market. Just to illustrate, if a person wants a career in auto mechanics and thinks he has no need to learn how to use a computer, the person is likely to be surprised. What if the auto mechanic needs to operate a sophisticated computer to determine certain malfunctions in the cars he is repairing? What if the office staff expects the mechanic to understand how to enter data on their computer and also expects the person to know how to read the computer printout of information? What if he must go to school periodically to learn the newest technology, and everyone sits in a room filled with computers for the class instead of underneath an actual car?

Type of example: ______________________________

PARAGRAPH 3

Most students today realize they must learn how to use computers in order to be competitive in the job market. Last semester, I took my first computer course. To my great pleasure, I found that my new skills helped me not only write compositions but also practice my math. I discovered that I could go online and talk all over the world with people who have similar interests to my own. In addition, I was able to use the computer to access information from the school library. Since I plan to be a teacher, I will be able to use my computer skills making tests and worksheets, researching information for class and helping students make discoveries for themselves.

Type of example: ______________________________

EXERCISE 2 **The Sources for Illustrations**

Below is a topic sentence. Write a paragraph in which you support the idea with one or more illustrations. Label the source of your illustration from one of the following:

Example from first-hand experience or knowledge

Made up or hypothetical example

Information from an interview or survey you conduct yourself

Outside research (using material found in books or articles)

Topic sentence: *Many advertising claims are deceptive.*
Your paragraph:

____

____

____

____

____

____

____

____

____

____

Type of example used: ______________________________

EXERCISE 3 **The Sources for Illustrations**

Below is a topic sentence. Write a paragraph in which you support the idea with one or more illustrations. Label the source of your illustration from one of the following:

Example from first-hand experience or knowledge

Made up or hypothetical example

Information from an interview or survey you conduct yourself

Outside research (using material found in books or articles)

Topic sentence: *Taste in music is very personal.* (Consider doing a survey of your class members.)
Your paragraph:

____

____

____

____

____

____

____

____

____

____

Type of example used: ______________________________

Working for Coherence: Deciding on Order and Using Transitions

Order for Illustration

1. If the illustration is a *story* or *anecdote,* the author usually uses *time order.*
2. If the illustration is made up of *several descriptive examples,* the author might use *spatial order* (top to bottom, right to left, etc.).
3. If the illustrations call for a certain *logical order,* this logic will determine the sequence.
4. If there seems to be no special order necessary, authors often place their *strongest or most important example last,* since this is what the reader is likely to remember best.

TRANSITIONS COMMONLY USED IN ILLUSTRATION

Writers often signal the beginning of an illustration by using a key phrase. Below is a list of phrases commonly used to signal the beginning of an illustration.

Let me give you an example.
For example, . . .
Another example is . . .
To illustrate, . . .
An illustration of this idea is . . .
A case in point is . . .
Take the case of . . .
For instance, . . .
A personal anecdote will illustrate my point.

EXERCISE 4 **Analyzing Paragraphs Using Examples**

Read the following paragraph and answer the questions about the paragraph.

Being a connoisseur of junk has wonderfully mucked up my entire life. You know the song about favorite things like raindrops on roses and whiskers on kittens? Well, I've got my own list of favorite things: I like the insides of filthy bus stations, unsavory characters, a Dr. Pepper can floating on the sun-flecked water, Jujubes, the greasy tug and tang of beef jerky wrapped in cellophane, the kitchen drawer beside the phone, the Sunday clutter around the house, the noble whiff of manure, the sweaty odor of a person you love, the smoke-filled room in which I get to inhale the equivalent of eleven cigarettes without breaking my promise to quit, the pigeon droppings in the square, the grease under the finger nails of a gas station attendant (if you can still find one), the rusty Brillo on the sink, the bathroom glass placidly growing bacteria for the whole family, *People* magazine, a dog-eared paperback, a cold pork chop eaten at the refrigerator door.

Questions

1. State the main idea in your own words.

____

2. How many examples are given in the paragraph? ______________

3. Underline the examples in the paragraph.

4. Does the author use any words or phrases to signal any of the examples? If so, circle each one.

5. If there is more than one example, can you suggest any order for them?

____

EXERCISE 5 Analyzing Paragraphs Using Examples

Read the following paragraph and answer the questions about the paragraph.

Dr. George Gallup and his American Institute of Public Opinion conducted surveys for two years on the reading habits of Americans in all walks of life and different sections of the land; one of the striking facts "that is scored and underscored in these studies is the tremendous influence of Hollywood on reading tastes." Gallup points out that Hollywood boosts the classics of literature into new and extraordinary popularity. When the movie *David Copperfield* was being publicized, the Cleveland Public Library ordered over 125 extra copies of the book to meet the probable rise in demand; and although the library had over five hundred copies of the book, the shelves were bare of *David Copperfield* and other Dickens novels for weeks. The film *Wuthering Heights* served as a remarkable boomerang to the book's popularity. Four publishing houses sold out all their editions of the work in a short time, and bookstores and public libraries could not cope with the rediscovery of the Brontë masterpiece.

Questions

1. State the main idea in your own words.

____

2. How many examples are given in the paragraph? ______________

3. Underline the examples in the paragraph.

4. Does the author use any words or phrases to signal any of the examples? If so, circle each one.

5. If there is more than one example, can you suggest any order for the examples?

____

EXERCISE 6 Analyzing Paragraphs Using Examples

Read the following paragraph and answer the questions about the paragraph.

One of the most wonderful aspects of Sabatini's teaching was his desire to give encouragement. Even if the student did not have a great voice or did not show true promise, Sabatini would find something to praise, some little ray of hope that might help the student continue in the right direction. Let me relate an anecdote that will demonstrate this man's positive approach. One day, I was called in to Sabatini's studio to play the piano for a new pupil. This young man had come many miles in order to study with Sabatini and I could see at once that he was very nervous. The fact that he knew just a few words of Italian only made him more apprehensive. I started to play the music for the test aria. As usual, Sabatini sat in his chair with his eyes closed, listening. The young man's voice floated through the room, small and shaky at first, but growing a little more confident as he went on. Finally, after it was over, we all waited for the great man's judgment. Sabatini looked up and spoke through me. "I cannot do much for this young man," he said slowly, "because God has already done so much for him." When I translated this for the student, his face gained a new color and he smiled for the first time. That day started his period of study with Sabatini and three years later he made his first appearance in the opera house. I have always known that his great career really began with those first words of encouragement from his teacher.

Questions

1. State the main idea in your own words.

____

2. How many examples are given in the paragraph? ____________

3. Underline the examples in the paragraph.

4. Does the author use any words or phrases to signal the use of an illustration? If so, circle each one.

5. If there is more than one example, can you suggest any order for the examples?

____

Writing the Paragraph Using Illustration Step-by-Step

To learn a skill, such as writing, that makes so many demands, one approach is to work step-by-step, focusing on one issue at a time. In this way, anxiety is often reduced, and the writer will not miss a crucial point or misunderstand a part of the whole process. There certainly are other ways to go about writing an effective paragraph, but here is one logical method you can use to achieve good results.

STEPS FOR WRITING A PARAGRAPH USING ILLUSTRATION

1. Compose your topic sentence, being sure to consider carefully what you want for your controlling idea.
2. When using examples, consider the options: personal experience, hypothetical examples, surveys, interviews, library research. What type of examples will fit your idea best? At this stage brainstorming with a group of classmates is usually very helpful.
3. Decide how many examples you will provide in your paragraph: one extended example with several sentences or several brief examples of one sentence each.
4. If you have more than one example, decide on the order to present them. Many writers put their examples in order by starting with the least important and ending with the most important.
5. Write down each example using complete sentences. Does each example support your main idea? If not, your paragraph will lack unity and the example should be deleted.
6. Write a final sentence that concludes what you want to say about this idea.
7. Finally, copy your sentences into standard paragraph form. Indent five spaces to begin the paragraph and double-space.
8. Always make a final check for spelling errors and other mistakes, such as omitted words. When you use a computer spellcheck feature, keep in mind that this feature will only alert you to spellings that do not match words in its dictionary. If you type *there* when you mean *their,* the spellchecker will see an acceptable word. When it comes to a final editing, there is no substitute for your own careful reading.

EXERCISE 7 **Writing the Paragraph Using Illustration Step-by-Step**

This exercise will guide you through the construction of a paragraph using illustration. Start with the topic suggested below. Use the eight steps to help you work through each stage of the writing process.

Topic: Childhood memories

You know from experience that your family and friends talk a great deal about events from their childhoods. These events, for better or worse, have shaped their lives in important ways. So many of the essays and articles found in books and magazines contain the stories and lessons learned from childhood. Using this general subject of childhood memories, choose a controlling idea that will allow you to use one or more rich examples from your childhood that the readers in your class might find interesting, informative, or amusing.

1. Topic sentence: ______________________________

____

2. Which type of example (or types of examples) would you like to use?

____

____

3. How many examples will you give? ____________________

4. List the order of your examples. (One good example may be enough. Probably no more than three or four brief examples would fit in one paragraph.)

1. ____________________
2. ____________________
3. ____________________
4. ____________________

5. Write down each example.

____

6. Write the sentence that will conclude your paragraph.

____

7. On a separate piece of paper, copy your sentences into standard paragraph form.

8. Do a final reading to check for errors and omissions.

EXERCISE 8 **Writing the Paragraph Using Illustration Step-by-Step**

This exercise will guide you through the construction of a paragraph using illustration. Start with the topic suggested below. Use the eight steps to help you work through each stage of the writing process.

Topic: How to convince a family member to change a bad habit

Few of us live in the perfect family situation where every family member is helpful, productive, and happy. We struggle to encourage our loved ones to better themselves and thus make everyone's life in the family happier. What examples can you offer that would help a family member change a bad habit?

1. Topic sentence: ______________________________

____

2. Which type of example (or types of examples) would you like to use?

____

____

3. How many examples will you give? ______________________________

4. List the order of your examples. (One good example may be enough. Probably no more than three or four brief examples would fit in one paragraph.)

1. ______________________________
2. ______________________________
3. ______________________________
4. ______________________________

5. Write down each example.

____

____

____

____

____

____

____

____

____

____

____

____

6. Write the sentence that will conclude your paragraph.

____

____

7. On a separate piece of paper, copy your sentences into standard paragraph form.

8. Do a final reading to check for errors and omissions.

EXERCISE 9 **Writing the Paragraph Using Illustration Step-by-Step**

This exercise will guide you through the construction of a paragraph using illustration. Start with the topic suggested below. Use the eight steps to help you work through each stage of the writing process.

Topic: Art

What good is art? How does art affect our lives? What contact do you have with art in your everyday life? Do we have to go to an art gallery to appreciate fine art? Is a Hallmark card a work of art? Is your living room a work of art? Are there art works on display on your campus that you have opinions about? Talk about these questions with your classmates and then think of what you might want to say about art.

1. Topic sentence: ______________________________

____

2. Which type of example (or types of examples) would you like to use?

____

____

3. How many examples will you give? ______________________________

4. List the order of your examples. (One good example may be enough. Probably no more than three or four brief examples would fit in one paragraph.)

1. ______________________________
2. ______________________________
3. ______________________________
4. ______________________________

5. Write down each example.

____

____

____

____

____

____

____

____

____

____

____

____

____

____

6. Write the sentence that will conclude your paragraph.

____

____

7. On a separate piece of paper, copy your sentences into standard paragraph form.
8. Do a final reading to check for errors and omissions.

On Your Own: Writing Paragraphs Using Illustration from Model Paragraphs

Things Are Not Always What They Seem

Assignment 1

Write a paragraph on something that, at first glance, appears positive and appealing, but on second look gives a very different feeling. The following paragraph is taken from *Grand Canyon,* a book by the naturalist and essayist Joseph Wood Krutch.

MODEL PARAGRAPH: APPEARANCES CAN BE DECEIVING

Quite frequently it is the "cute" animals who create problems under even the slightly unnatural conditions of a park. Take, for instance, the chipmunks and the ground squirrels. No creature is more endearing, and the fact that some species eat the flower stalks of the agave, a spectacularly beautiful flowering plant, is not serious so long as the ground squirrel population is kept down by foxes. But once the fox has been exterminated, the agave also is threatened with extinction. Even the trays of seed put out to attract birds for the benefit of visitors mean that the chipmunks who come uninvited multiply so alarmingly that they, like the beggar deer, have to be periodically transported to remoter areas where artificial overpopulation is not a problem.

Ten suggested topics

Things that may not be what they seem:

1. Politicians
2. Jobs
3. Babies
4. Expensive clothing
5. Teachers
6. Houses
7. Games
8. Cars
9. Marriage
10. Drugs

Shopping

Assignment 2 Most people have very strong feelings about having to do certain shopping tasks. Write a paragraph that gives one or more examples of your worst shopping task(s) or your favorite shopping task(s). The following paragraph is taken from Phyllis Rose's essay "Shopping and Other Spiritual Adventures in America Today."

MODEL PARAGRAPH: SHOPPING FOR BLUE JEANS

Try to think of a kind of shopping in which the object is all-important and the pleasure of shopping is at a minimum. For example, consider the purchase of blue jeans. I buy new blue jeans as seldom as possible because the experience is so humiliating. For every pair that looks good on me, fifteen look grotesque. But even shopping for blue jeans at Bob's Surplus on Main Street—no frills, bare-bones shopping—is an event in the life of the spirit. Once again I have to come to terms with the fact that I will never look good in Levi's. Much as I want to be mainstream, I never will be.

Ten suggested topics Shopping:

1. For weekly groceries
2. For a bathing suit
3. For a hat that fits
4. For a very fussy relative
5. By catalogue
6. On the home shopping network
7. For the person who never says thank you
8. When you haven't got enough money to get what you really want
9. For a gift for your in-laws
10. For holiday gifts

What People Have a Right to Expect from Others

Assignment 3 We enter into relationships believing that people will behave in a certain expected way. Oftentimes we are sadly disappointed. Write a paragraph in which you give one or more examples of how you expect people to act when they are in certain relationships. The paragraph on page 335 is from a piece of advice written by the famous columnist Ann Landers.

MODEL PARAGRAPH: ADVICE TO PARENTS

Parents have the right to expect their children to pick up after themselves and perform simple household chores. For example, every member of the family over six years of age should clean the bathtub and the sink so they will be in respectable condition for the next person. He or she should also run errands and help in the kitchen if asked—in other words, carry a share of the load without feeling persecuted. The days of "hired help" are, for the most part, gone. And this is good. Boys as well as girls should be taught to cook and clean, do laundry, and sew on buttons. This is not "sissy stuff." It makes for independence and self-reliance.

Ten suggested topics

Expectations of:

1. Husbands and wives
2. Engaged couples
3. Teachers
4. Students
5. Waiters
6. Customers
7. Patients
8. Employers
9. Co-workers
10. Friends

Remedies to Cure What Ails Us

Assignment 4

Health food stores are enjoying great popularity, partly because so many people believe that natural products can alleviate a wide range of complaints. Write a paragraph in which you give examples of popular trends for solving an everyday problem. In the paragraph on page 336, the author provides several examples of currently available remedies that people are using in place of traditional prescriptions.

MODEL PARAGRAPH: THE POPULARITY OF NATURAL REMEDIES

Many stores today are selling newly accepted natural remedies for all types of human ailments. For instance, an herb called *astragalus* is being used by people with AIDS as a natural way to boost their immune systems. Other people concerned about their immune systems but only worried about colds or flu use a plant extract called *ichinacea* to help them resist sickness. People who want to lose weight also are seeking out help from natural remedies. One of the most popular examples of remedies for overweight people is the Chinese herb *ma huang*. This is a powerful substance and can be dangerous for some since it may cause heart attacks or strokes, especially if it is used with caffeine. One of the cures most sought after is the cure for cancer, and again there are natural substances that hold out some promise of relief. For example, shark cartilage is believed by many to stop the growth of cancerous tumors or even eliminate them altogether. Many users of herbs and other natural healing substances take these supplements to improve their general health. For instance, *ginseng* is used throughout the world as a revitalizing tonic, and garlic has been said to combat infections, prevent blood clots and lower blood pressure. There are many claims for different natural remedies, but we do not always have proof that they work as well as some people say they do.

Ten suggested topics

Remedies for:

1. Relaxation
2. The common cold
3. The "blues"
4. The hiccoughs
5. Thumbsucking
6. Kicking the smoking habit
7. Shyness
8. Writer's block
9. Insomnia
10. Wanderlust

EXPLORING ONLINE

For more information about developing paragraphs by illustration, see

http://www.uottawa.ca/academic/arts/writcent/hypergrammar/parunif.html

WORKING TOGETHER

CLASS DISCUSSION: EXCHANGING EXAMPLES OF FRIENDSHIP

Life would be very lonely without special people to share our good times (and not so good times); every friend is a treasure.

Divide into groups for a brief discussion on the topic, "What is a friend?" Students should take notes on each other's ideas. Then each student should think back over his or her own life and select three people who were friends. Write three paragraphs, one for each of these three friends. Include your analysis of the qualities that made each person a friend. Did all of these friendships last? If not, why not? These paragraphs could later form the basis for an essay on friendship.

Online Activity

- Read and compare quotations and proverbs about friendship:

  http://www.friendship.com.au/quotes/quofri.html
  http://www.friendship.com.au/quotes/quopro.html

- Send free e-cards to your friends:

  http://www.greetingcards.msn.com
  http://www.bluemountain.com

Chapter 19 Developing Paragraphs: Narration

Preview

If you are a good storyteller, or if you just like to have a good story told to you, you will probably enjoy this chapter on narration. You will improve your writing skills by focusing on these narrative elements:

- Narration should make a point.
- Coherence in narration is usually achieved by ordering details according to time sequence.
- Transitions used in narration show a shift in time.
- Practice your own narrative paragraphs.
  - Using a step-by-step approach
  - Using model paragraphs with suggested topics

Key Terms

narration
time sequence
transitions

Charts

List of transitions used in narration
Steps for writing the narrative paragraph

What Is Narration?

Narration is the oldest and best-known form of verbal communication. It is, quite simply, the telling of a story.

Every culture in the world, past and present, has used narration to provide entertainment as well as information for the people of that culture. Since everyone likes a good story, the many forms of narration, such as novels, short stories, soap operas, and full-length movies, are always popular.

The following narrative paragraph, taken from Helen Keller's autobiography, tells the story of her realization that every object has a name. The paragraph shows the enormous difficulties faced by a seven-year-old girl who was unable to see, hear, or speak.

The morning after my teacher came, she led me into her room and gave me a doll. The little blind children at the Perkins Institution had sent it and Laura Bridgman had dressed it; but I did not know this until afterward. When I had played with it a little while, Miss Sullivan slowly spelled into my hand the word "d-o-l-l." I was at once interested in this finger play and tried to imitate it. When I finally succeeded in making the letters correctly, I was flushed with childish pleasure and pride. Running downstairs to my mother I held up my hand and made the letters for doll. I did not know that I was spelling a word or even that words existed; I was simply making my fingers go in monkey-like imitation. In the days that followed I learned to spell in this uncomprehending way a great many words, among them *pin, hat, cup* and a few verbs like *sit, stand,* and *walk.* But my teacher had been with me several weeks before I understood that everything has a name.

Working with Narration: Using Narration to Make a Point

At one time or another you have probably met a person who loves to talk on and on without making any real point. This person is likely to tell you everything that happened in one day, including every sight and every sound. Your reaction to the unnecessary and seemingly endless supply of details is probably one of fatigue and the hope for a quick getaway. This is not narration at its best! A good story is almost always told to make a point: It can make us laugh, it can make us understand, or it can change our attitudes.

When Helen Keller tells the story of her early experiences with her teacher, she is careful to use only those details that are relevant to her story. For example, the doll her teacher gave her is an important part of the story. Not only does this doll reveal something about Helen Keller's teacher, but it also reveals the astounding fact that Helen began to understand that objects have names. With this story, we see the beginning of Helen's long struggle to communicate with other people.

EXERCISE 1 **Using Narration to Make a Point**

Each of the following examples is the beginning of a topic sentence for a narrative paragraph. Complete each sentence by providing a controlling idea that could serve as the point for the story.

1. Since my family is so large (or small), I have had to learn to ____________

____

2. When I couldn't get a job, I realized ______________________________

____

3. After going to the movies every Saturday for many years, I discovered

____

____

4. When I arrived at the room where my business class was to meet, I found ______________________________

____

5. When my best friend got married, I began to see that ____________

____

EXERCISE 2 Using Narration to Make a Point

Each of the following examples is the beginning of a topic sentence for a narrative paragraph. Complete each sentence by providing a controlling idea that could serve as the point for the story.

1. When I looked more closely at the man, I realized that ____________

____

2. When the president finished his speech, I concluded that ____________

____

3. By the end of the movie, I decided that ____________

____

4. After I changed the course as well as the teacher, I felt ____________

____

5. When I could not get past the office secretary, I realized that ____________

____

EXERCISE 3 Using Narration to Make a Point

Each of the following examples is the beginning of a topic sentence for a narrative paragraph. Complete each sentence by providing a controlling idea that could serve as the point for the story.

1. When the art teacher tore up my sketches in front of the class, I decided ____________

____

2. When there were no responses to my ad, I concluded ____________

____

3. After two days of trying to sell magazine subscriptions, I knew ____________

____

4. After I had actually performed my first experiment in the lab, I understood ____________

____

5. The first time I tried to cook a dinner for a group of people, I found out

____

____

Working for Coherence: Placing Details in Order of Time Sequence

When you write a narrative paragraph, the details given usually follow a certain order according to time sequence. That is, you tell what happened first, then what happened next, and next, until finally you get to the end of the story. In your narrative, you could be describing events that took place in a matter of minutes or over a period of many years.

In the following paragraph, the story takes place in a single day. The six events that made the day a disaster are given in the order in which they happened. Although some stories flash back to the past or forward to the future, most use the natural chronological order of the events.

> My day was a disaster. First, it had snowed during the night, which meant I had to shovel before I could leave for work. I was mad that I hadn't gotten up earlier. Then I had trouble starting my car, and to make matters worse, my daughter wasn't feeling well and said she didn't think she should go to school. When I eventually did arrive at work, I was twenty minutes late. Soon I found out my assistant had forgotten to make copies of a report I needed at nine o'clock. I quickly had to make another plan. By five o'clock, I was looking forward to getting my paycheck. Foolish woman! When I went to pick it up, the office assistant told me that something had gone wrong with the computers. I would not be able to get my check until Tuesday. Disappointed, I walked down the hill to the parking lot. There I met my final defeat. In my hurry to park the car in the morning, I had left my parking lights on. Now my battery was dead. Even an optimist like me had the right to be discouraged!

EXERCISE 4 **Working for Coherence: Using Details in Order of Time Sequence**

Each of the topics below is followed by supporting details. These supporting details are not given in any order. Put the events in order according to time sequence by placing the appropriate number in the space provided.

1. A fight in my apartment building

_______ Some of the neighbors became so frightened that they called the police.

_______ The man and the woman began to fight around six o'clock.

_______ When the police came, they found the couple struggling in the kitchen.

_______ The neighbors heard the man's voice shouting angrily.

_______ There were no arrests, but the police warned both individuals not to disturb the peace again.

2. The cloverleaf

_______ A decade later the design had sprouted so widely that architecture critic Lewis Mumford ironically nominated the concrete cloverleaf as the national flower.

_______ By the late 1950s, however, the cloverleaf had fallen out of favor because it took up too much land and caused too many accidents.

_______ Next time your car is caught in a messy cloverleaf interchange, blame Arthur Hill.

_______ The first cloverleaf in the United States was constructed in Woodbridge, New Jersey.

_______ This designer patented the idea of the cloverleaf in 1916.

EXERCISE 5 **Working for Coherence: Using Details in Order of Time Sequence**

Each of the topics below is followed by supporting details. These supporting details are not given in any order. Put the events in order according to time sequence by placing the appropriate number in the space provided.

1. From the life of Amelia Earhart, pioneer aviator and writer

_______ Amelia Earhart was born in Atchison, Kansas, in 1897.

_______ Before 1920, she worked as a nurse's aide.

_______ When she was sixteen, her family moved to St. Paul, Minnesota.

_______ Four years after her history-making flight across the Atlantic, she made her solo flight across that same ocean.

_______ After learning to fly in the early 1920s, she became, in 1928, the first woman to cross the Atlantic, although on that trip she was a passenger and not a pilot.

_______ Three years after her solo Atlantic flight, she became the first person to fly from Hawaii to California.

_______ On her last flight, in 1937, she was lost at sea; no trace of her was ever found.

2. From the life of Sojourner Truth, crusader, preacher, and the first African American woman to speak out against slavery

_______ She was received by Abraham Lincoln in the White House the year before that president was assassinated at the end of the Civil War.

_______ She was forty-six when she took the name of Sojourner Truth.

_______ Sojourner Truth began life as a slave when she was born in 1797, but she was set free in 1827.

_______ She spent her final years giving lectures throughout the North.

_______ In 1850 she traveled to the West, where her speeches against slavery and for women's rights drew large crowds.

_______ At the beginning of the Civil War she was active in gathering supplies for the black regiments that were fighting in the war.

_______ Not long after her first trip west, she settled in Battle Creek, Michigan.

EXERCISE 6 **Working for Coherence: Using Details in Order of Time Sequence**

Each of the topics below is followed by supporting details. These supporting details are not given in any order. Put the events in order according to time sequence by placing the appropriate number in the space provided.

1. The novel *Gone with the Wind* by Margaret Mitchell

__________ A widow for the second time, Scarlett marries Rhett Butler, but the marriage is not a happy one.

__________ Scarlett O'Hara, the daughter of Gerald O'Hara, the owner of Tara Plantation, is in love with Ashley Wilkes as the Civil War begins.

__________ When Ashley Wilkes marries Melanie Hamilton, Scarlett marries Melanie's brother Charles, who is soon killed in the war. At the same time, Scarlett is interested in the blockade runner Rhett Butler.

__________ By the time Scarlett discovers that she truly loves Rhett Butler after all, Rhett announces that it is too late and that he is leaving her forever.

__________ Scarlett marries a store owner, Frank Kennedy, who pays the back taxes on Tara. Kennedy is killed by Union Troops.

2. The novel *Great Expectations* by Charles Dickens

__________ Pip realizes Miss Havisham has had nothing to do with his inheritance.

__________ Pip, an orphan, is born and raised in a small English village by a blacksmith, Joe Gargery, and his sister.

__________ After his adventure with the convict, Pip works in a mansion near his home for a Miss Havisham, a crazed old woman who still wears the wedding dress she wore on the day her bridegroom failed to show up for the wedding.

__________ One day, Pip sees a stranger in the marshes near his home. The man asks Pip to bring him food and a filing iron—he is an escaped convict.

__________ Pip is contacted by a lawyer, who tells him that he must leave Miss Havisham and go to London, all expenses paid, to begin life as a gentleman.

__________ On his twenty-first birthday, Pip receives a visitor; it is the convict, Abel Magwitch, whom he had helped years before—it is he who has given Pip the money.

Working for Coherence: Using Transitions that Show a Shift in Time

Transitions are words and phrases that help a reader move smoothly from one idea to another and make the proper connection between those ideas.

Although transitions must not be overused, they are important tools for every writer. Here is the Helen Keller paragraph you studied earlier, but this time printed with each of the transitional words and phrases in boldface.

> **The morning after** my teacher came, she led me into her room and gave me a doll. The little blind children at the Perkins Institution had sent it and Laura Bridgman had dressed it; but I did not know this **until afterward.** When I had played with it **a little while,** Miss Sullivan slowly spelled into my hand the word "d-o-l-l." I was **at once** interested in this finger play and tried to imitate it. When I **finally** succeeded in making the letters correctly, I was flushed with childish pleasure and pride. Running downstairs to my mother I held up my hand and made the letters for doll. I did not know that I was spelling a word or even that words existed; I was simply making my fingers go in monkey-like imitation. **In the days that followed** I learned to spell in this uncomprehending way a great many words, among them *pin, hat, cup* and a few verbs like *sit, stand,* and *walk.* But my teacher had been with me **several weeks** before I understood that everything has a name.

Notice how the time transitions used in this paragraph make the order of events clear. "*The morning after* my teacher came" gives the reader the sense that the action of the story is being told day by day. In the second sentence Helen Keller gives information she learned later—*afterward.* The writer then tells us that when she played with the doll *a little while,* she suddenly—*at once*—became interested in the connection between an object and the word for that object. This realization was one of the central lessons in young Helen Keller's education, and it became the starting point for all of her later learning. She uses two more transitional phrases to tell us about the beginning of this education: *In the days that followed,* we learn, she mastered a great many words, although it took her *several weeks* before she learned the even more important concept that everything had a name. Much of the meaning of this paragraph would not have been clear without the careful use of these time transitions.

As you write your own narrative paragraphs, you will find yourself using your own transitional words and expressions. However, as a reminder and a guide, the following chart will serve as a helpful reference.

TRANSITIONS COMMONLY USED FOR NARRATION TO SHOW A SHIFT IN TIME

recently	now, by now	soon, soon afterward	finally
previously	at once	later, later on	eventually
earlier	suddenly	after a little while	in the end
in the past	immediately	then	
a few days ago	meanwhile	next, the next day	
a hundred years ago	at the same time	several weeks later	
	within a few minutes	the following month	

EXERCISE 7

Working with Transitions

Fill in each of the blanks in the following student paragraph with an appropriate transition.

I arrived at Aunt Lorinda's in the middle of a heat wave. It was 105 in the shade and very humid. As usual, Aunt Lorinda greeted me with the list of activities she had scheduled for the day. __________ we went to the attic to gather old clothes for the Salvation Army. I nearly passed out up in the attic. Sweat poured down my face. Aunt Lorinda, in her crisp cotton sundress, looked cool and was obviously enjoying herself. "If you see something you want, take it," she said graciously. "It's so nice of you to give me a hand today. You're young and strong and have so much more energy than I." __________ her plans included the yard work. I took off my shirt and mowed the lawn while my eighty-year-old aunt trimmed hedges and weeded the flower beds. __________ it was time to drive into the dusty town and do errands. Luckily, Auntie stayed behind to fix lunch and I was able to duck into an air-conditioned coffee shop for ten minutes' rest before I dropped off the old clothes at the Salvation Army. I wasn't anxious to find out what help I could be to my aunt in the afternoon. I hoped it wouldn't be something like last year when I had to put a new roof on the old shed in the backyard. I could already feel the beginning of a painful sunburn.

EXERCISE 8

Working with Transitions

Below is a narrative paragraph. On the lines provided, list all the transitions of time that give order to the paragraph.

By now, Jason was skating along feeling in the best of moods. He was aware every moment that he was wearing his new pair of roller blades, and several times he even visibly smiled from so much inner pleasure. He hardly noticed when suddenly he found himself skating down his own street. Immediately, neighborhood children spotted him and ran up to him calling to him by name, "Jason, Jason, where did you get those skates?" In a short time, Jason found himself surrounded by nine or ten children who were running alongside of him. Finally, with a flair, he turned, stopped dead and blurted out happily, "It's my birthday today!"

__________________ __________________

__________________ __________________

__________________ __________________

__________________ __________________

EXERCISE 9

Working with Transitions

Below is a narrative paragraph from a story by the Russian writer Ivan Turgenev. Note all the transitions of time that give order to the paragraph and copy them on the lines below.

I went to the right through the bushes. Meantime the night had crept close and grown up like a storm cloud; it seemed as though, with the mists of evening, darkness was rising up on all sides and flowing down from overhead. I had come upon some sort of little, untrodden, overgrown path; I walked along it, gazing intently before me. Soon all was blackness and silence around—only the quail's cry was heard from time to time. Some small nightbird, flitting noiselessly near the ground on its soft wings, almost flapped against me and scurried away in alarm. I came out on the further side of the bushes, and made my way along a field by the hedge. By now I could hardly make out distant objects; the field showed dimly white around; beyond it rose up a sullen darkness, which seemed moving up closer in huge masses every instant. My steps gave a muffled sound in the air that grew colder and colder. The pale sky began again to grow blue—but it was the blue of night. The tiny stars glimmered and twinkled in it.

________________ ________________

________________ ________________

________________ ________________

________________ ________________

Writing the Narrative Paragraph Step-by-Step

To learn a skill that has so many different demands, the best approach is to work step-by-step so that one aspect can be worked on at a time. This will ensure that you are not missing a crucial point or misunderstanding a part of the whole. There certainly are other ways to go about writing an effective paragraph, but here is one logical method you can use to achieve results.

STEPS FOR WRITING THE DESCRIPTIVE PARAGRAPH

1. Study the given topic, and then plan your topic sentence, especially the dominant impression.
2. List at least ten details that come to your mind when you think about the description you have chosen.
3. Then choose the five or six most important details from your list. Be sure these details support the dominant impression.
4. Put your list in order.
5. Write at least one complete sentence for each of the details you have chosen from your list.
6. Write a concluding statement that offers some reason for describing this topic.
7. Finally, copy your sentences into standard paragraph form.
8. Always make a final check for spelling errors and other mistakes, such as omitted words. When you use a computer spellcheck feature, keep in mind that this feature will only alert you to spellings that do not match words in its dictionary. If you type *there* when you mean *their,* the spellchecker will see an acceptable word. When it comes to a final editing, there is no substitute for your own careful reading.

EXERCISE 10 Writing the Narrative Paragraph Step-by-Step

This exercise will guide you through the construction of a complete narrative paragraph. Start with the suggested topic. Use the eight steps on page 347 to help you work through each stage of the writing process.

Topic: Nearly every family has a favorite story they like to tell about one of their members, often a humorous incident that happened to one of them. There are also crises and tragic moments in the life of every family. Choose a story, funny or tragic, from the life of a family you know.

1. Topic sentence: ______________________________

____

2. Make a list of the events that took place.

a. ______________________________

b. ______________________________

c. ______________________________

d. ______________________________

e. ______________________________

f. ______________________________

g. ______________________________

h. ______________________________

i. ______________________________

j. ______________________________

3. Circle the five or six events you believe are the most important for the point of the story.

4. Put your final choices in order by numbering each of them.

5. Using your final list, write at least one sentence for each event you have chosen.

a. ______________________________

____

b. ______________________________

____

c. ______________________________

____

d. ______________________________

____

e. ______________________________

____

f. ______________________________

____

g. ______________________________

____

6. Write a concluding statement. ______________________________

____

____

7. On a separate piece of paper or on the computer, copy your sentences into standard paragraph form.

8. Do a final reading to check for errors and omissions.

EXERCISE 11 **Writing the Narrative Paragraph Step-by-Step**

This exercise will guide you through the construction of a complete narrative paragraph. Start with the suggested topic. Use the eight steps on page 347 to help you work through each stage of the writing process.

Topic: Tell the story of an incident you witnessed, one that revealed an unfortunate lack of sensitivity (or even cruelty) on someone's part. What did you observe the person doing? How did other people react? What did you do or wish that you had done in response to this incident?

1. Topic sentence: ______________________________

____

2. Make a list of the events that took place.

a. ______________________________

b. ______________________________

c. ______________________________

d. ______________________________

e. ______________________________

f. ______________________________

g. ______________________________

h. ______________________________

i. ______________________________

j. ______________________________

3. Circle the five or six events you believe are the most important for the point of the story.

4. Put your final choices in order by numbering each of them.

5. Using your final list, write at least one sentence for each event you have chosen.

a. ______________________________

____

b. ______________________________

____

c. ______________________________

____

d. ______________________________

____

e. ______________________________

____

f. ______________________________

____

g. ______________________________

____

6. Write a concluding statement. ______________________________

____

____

7. On a separate piece of paper or on the computer, copy your sentences into standard paragraph form.

8. Do a final reading to check for errors and omissions.

On Your Own: Writing Narrative Paragraphs from Model Paragraphs

The Story of How You Faced a New Challenge

Assignment 1

Write a paragraph telling the story of a day when you faced an important challenge of some kind. It could have been a challenge in school, at home, or on the job. The following paragraph by the journalist Betty Rollin is an example of such an experience.

MODEL PARAGRAPH: DEADLINE

When I awoke that morning I hit the floor running. I washed my face, brushed my teeth, got a pot of coffee going, tightened the sash on my bathrobe, snapped my typewriter out of its case, placed it on the kitchen table, retrieved my notes from the floor where they were stacked in manila folders, unwrapped a pack of bond paper, put the top sheet in the typewriter, looked at it, put my head on the keys, wrapped my arms around its base and cried.

Ten suggested topics

1. The day I started a new job
2. My first day in history class
3. The day I began my first term paper
4. The day I tried to wallpaper my bedroom
5. The morning of my big job interview
6. Facing a large debt
7. Trying to reestablish a friendship gone sour
8. The day I started driving lessons
9. Coping with a death in the family
10. The day I faced a deadline

The Story of a Fight or Argument

Assignment 2

Write a paragraph in which you tell the story of a fight or confrontation you were involved in or witnessed. What are the important details of the incident that remain most clearly in your mind? The following paragraph, from Albert Halper's short story "Prelude," tells the story of a street fight.

MODEL PARAGRAPH: THE FIGHT

But the people just stood there afraid to do a thing. Then while a few guys held me, Gooley and about four others went for the stand, turning it over and mussing and stamping on all the newspapers they could find. Syl started to scratch them, so they hit her. Then I broke away to help her, and then they started socking me too. My father tried to reach me, but three guys kept him away. Four guys got me down and started kicking me and all the time my father was begging them to let me up and Syl was screaming at the people to help. And while I was down, my face was squeezed against some papers on the sidewalk telling about Austria and I guess I went nuts while they kept hitting me, and I kept seeing the headlines against my nose.

Ten suggested topics

A confrontation between:

1. A police officer and a guilty motorist
2. A teacher and a student
3. An angry customer and a store clerk
4. A frustrated parent and a child
5. A manager and an unhappy employee
6. A judge and an unwilling witness
7. A museum guard and a careless tourist
8. A politician and an angry citizen
9. A mugger and a frightened victim
10. An engaged couple about to break up

The Beginning of a Special Relationship

Assignment 3

Write a paragraph that tells the story of how you became close to another person. Select one particular moment when the relationship changed from casual friendliness to something deeper and more lasting. Perhaps you shared an experience that brought you together. The following paragraph, taken from Morley Callaghan's short story "One Spring Night," tells of a young man who is falling in love.

MODEL PARAGRAPH: FALLING IN LOVE

Bob had taken her out a few times when he had felt like having some girl to talk to who knew him and liked him. And tonight he was leaning back good-humoredly, telling her one thing and then another with the wise self-assurance he usually had when with her; but gradually, as he watched her, he found himself talking more slowly, his voice grew serious and much softer, and then finally he leaned across the table toward her as though he had just discovered that her neck was full and soft with her spring coat thrown open, and that her face under her little black straw hat tilted back on her head had a new, eager beauty. Her warm, smiling softness was so close to him that he smiled a bit shyly.

Ten suggested topics

1. My relationship with a teacher
2. My relationship with a fellow student
3. A moment when I understood my clergyman in a new way
4. When I learned something new about a neighborhood merchant
5. When I shared an experience with a fellow worker
6. When I made friends with someone older or younger than myself
7. When my relationship with my brother or sister changed
8. The moment when my attitude about a grandparent changed
9. When a stranger became a friend
10. When a relationship deepened

You Won't Believe What Happened to Me Today!

Assignment 4

Tell the story of a day you found yourself facing a difficult or frustrating situation. The example on page 353 from Berton Roueche's short story "Phone Call," describes a day in the life of a young man, a day when nothing seems to go right.

MODEL PARAGRAPH: THE TRUCK BREAKS DOWN

I got out of the truck and got down on my knees and twisted my neck and looked underneath. Everything looked O.K. There wasn't anything hanging down or anything. I got up and opened the hood and looked at the engine. I don't know too much about engines—only what I picked up working around Lindy's Service Station the summer before last. But the engine looked O.K., too. I slammed down the hood and lighted a cigarette. It really had me beat. A school bus from that convent over in Sag Harbor came piling around the bend, and all the girls leaned out the windows and yelled. I just waved. They didn't mean anything by it—just a bunch of kids going home. The bus went on up the road and into the woods and out of sight. I got back in the truck and started it up again. It sounded fine. I put it in gear and let out the clutch and gave it the gas, and nothing happened. The bastard just sat there. So it was probably the transmission. I shut it off and got out. There was nothing to do but call the store. I still had three or four deliveries that had to be made and it was getting kind of late. I knew what Mr. Lester would say, but this was one time when he couldn't blame me. It wasn't my fault. It was him himself that told me to take this truck.

Ten suggested topics

1. When I ran out of money
2. When I ran out of gas
3. When I was accused of something I didn't do
4. When I was stopped by the police (or by some other authority)
5. When I was guilty of . . .
6. When something terrible happened just as everything seemed to be going so well
7. When the weather didn't cooperate
8. When I locked myself out of the house
9. When I couldn't reach my family by phone
10. When my entire report was deleted by mistake

A Memorable Experience from Childhood

Assignment 5 Write a paragraph in which you remember a special moment from your childhood. The following childhood memory is from George Orwell's novel *Coming Up for Air.*

MODEL PARAGRAPH: THE FORGOTTEN POOL

It was an enormous fish. I don't exaggerate when I say it was enormous. It was almost the length of my arm. It glided across the pool, deep under water, and then became a shadow and disappeared into the darker water on the other side. I felt as if a sword had gone through me. It was by far the biggest fish I'd ever seen, dead or alive. I stood there without breathing, and in a moment another huge thick shape glided through the water, and then another and then two more close together. The pool was full of them. They were carp, I suppose. Just possibly they were bream or tench, but more probably carp. Bream or tench wouldn't grow so huge. I knew what had happened. At some time this pool had been connected with the other, and then the stream had dried up and the woods had closed round the small pool and it had just been forgotten. It's a thing that happens occasionally. A pool gets forgotten somehow, nobody fishes in it for years and decades and the fish grow to monstrous sizes. The brutes that I was watching might be a hundred years old. And not a soul in the world knew about them except me. Very likely it was twenty years since anyone had so much as looked at the pool, and probably even old Hodges and Mr. Farrel's **bailiff** had forgotten its existence.

bailiff: *in England, a person who looks after a large estate*

Ten suggested topics

1. The first time I went swimming
2. My first time on a roller coaster (or on another ride)
3. A frightening experience when I was home alone
4. My most memorable Halloween (or other holiday)
5. The best birthday party I ever had
6. My first bicycle (or car)
7. The greatest present I ever received
8. A memorable visit to a favorite relative
9. My first time traveling alone
10. The first time I went camping

EXPLORING ONLINE

Read further about the principles of narration:

http://www.wuacc.edu/services/zzcwwctr/org-narration.wm.txt
http://www.clearcf.uvic.ca/writersguide/Pages/ParOrderNarr.html

WORKING TOGETHER

TELLING STORIES THAT MAKE A POINT

Aesop is believed to have been a Greek slave who lived about 2,500 years ago. He created over 200 fables, many of which have become part of our international literary heritage. The following example of his work is a classic fable, one that has a timeless moral.

> A farmer realized he was dying. He did not want to leave this world without being sure that all of his sons knew how to be good farmers. He called them to his bedside and said, "My sons, I am about to depart from this world. Before I go, however, I want you to search for what I have hidden in the vineyard. When you find it, you will possess all that I am able to leave you."
>
> The young men were convinced their father had buried some great treasure on the property. After he died, they all took their shovels and dug up every part of the vineyard. They found no treasure at all, but their digging helped the grapevines so much that the next year's harvest saw the best crop of grapes in many years.
>
> **Moral:** *Our greatest treasure is what comes from our own hard work.*

Group Discussion

Wouldn't all of us like to get something for nothing? Share with your classmates a current story of someone you know or have heard about, who, like the sons of the farmer in the fable above, wanted to get something for nothing. (Do you know people who gamble? Do you know people who expect their relatives to keep supporting them? Do you know anyone who has inherited money?)

Then, share with your classmates a story about someone you know or have heard about who achieved something by working very hard. Do you think Aesop's moral is true, namely, that what we achieve by our own hard work is the greatest treasure?

Portfolio Suggestion

Write a true story or a fictional tale of one of the following:

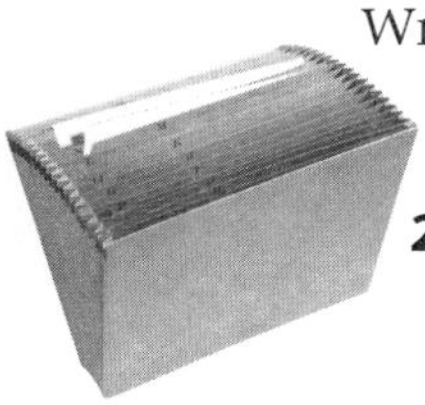

1. What happened to someone who wanted to get something for nothing?
2. What happened to someone who, by his or her own hard work, achieved something significant?

continued on next page

Give your story the same one-sentence moral that Aesop gave to his fable, or using the same one-sentence model, make up your own moral.

Online Activity

Read and listen to more fables by Aesop:

http://www.pacificnet.net/~johnr/aesop/
http://www.umass.edu/aesop/

Chapter 20 Developing Paragraphs: Description

Preview

Writing descriptive paragraphs largely involves using your senses. This chapter focuses on several issues important to descriptive writing:

- How to create a topic sentence containing a *dominant impression*
- How to avoid *vague* dominant impressions
- How to support the topic sentence with details that use *sensory images,* allowing the reader to imagine what is being described
- How to put the details in a logical order, which in descriptive writing is usually a *spatial order* of some kind
- Practicing your own descriptive paragraphs
    - Using a step-by-step approach
    - Using model paragraphs and suggested topics

Key Terms

Description
Dominant impression
Sensory images
Spatial order

Charts

Sample lists of dominant impressions
List of vague and overused words
Steps for writing descriptive paragraphs

What Is Description?

One method of developing a paragraph is to use descriptive details. In almost any novel you might pick up, for example, the story is likely to begin with one or more paragraphs of description because the author needs to set the stage for the story to come.

Description uses sensory images to create a picture with words.

The following example comes from a personal essay written by Joseph H. Suina. In this paragraph, he describes his childhood home. As you study this description, look for the details that make this paragraph effective.

> During those years, Grandmother and I lived beside the plaza in a one-room house. It consisted of a traditional fireplace, a makeshift cabinet for our few tin cups and dishes, and a wooden crate that held our two buckets of all-purpose water. At the far end of the room were two rolls of bedding we used as comfortable sitting "couches." Consisting of thick quilts, sheepskin, and assorted blankets, these bed rolls were undone each night. A wooden pole the length of one side of the room was suspended about 10 inches from the ceiling beams. A modest collection of colorful shawls, blankets, and sashes draped over the pole making this part of the room most interesting. In one corner was a bulky metal trunk for our ceremonial wear and few valuables. A dresser, which was traded for some of my grandmother's well-known pottery, held the few articles of clothing we owned and the "goody bag." Grandmother always had a flour sack filled with candy, store bought cookies, and Fig Newtons. These were saturated with a sharp odor of moth balls. Nevertheless, they made a fine snack with coffee before we turned in for the night. Tucked securely in my blankets, I listened to one of her stories or accounts of how it was when she was a little girl. These accounts seemed so old fashioned compared to the way we lived. Sometimes she softly sang a song from a ceremony. In this way I fell asleep each night.

When you write using descriptive details, your choices of sensory images will make an enormous difference whether or not your reader will be able to imagine what you are describing. Answer the following questions about the descriptive paragraph on Suina's childhood home.

1. What do you see? ______________________________

2. What do you hear? ______________________________

3. What suggests how something would feel to the touch? ______________

4. What can you smell? ______________________________

5. What can you taste? ______________________________

Working with Description: Selecting the Dominant Impression

It is not enough to give random pieces of information about any particular person, object, or place you are describing. The overall effect of a piece of descriptive writing should be to create a *dominant impression*. Each individual sentence that you write should be part of a picture that becomes clear when the reader finishes the paragraph.

The **dominant impression** is the overall impression created by a descriptive piece of writing. This impression is often summed up by one word or phrase in the topic sentence.

Topic sentence: My childhood home was unpretentious.

When you write a descriptive paragraph, you should know what impression you are trying to achieve with your supporting details. For example, when you describe a place, the dominant impression you might want to create could be one of *comfort,* or it could be one of *elegance.* When you write a description of a person, you might want to present the impression of an outgoing gregarious person or perhaps the very opposite, that of a shy, withdrawing sort of person. Often it is useful to incorporate the dominant impression into the topic sentence. This will help you focus as you write and will leave no doubt in the reader's mind as to the direction of your thinking. All the other sentences should support this impression you are working to create.

Here is a short list of possible dominant impressions for you to use as a guide while you work through this chapter.

DOMINANT IMPRESSIONS FOR DESCRIPTIONS OF PLACE				
crowded	cozy	inviting	cheerful	dazzling
romantic	restful	dreary	drab	uncomfortable
cluttered	ugly	tasteless	unfriendly	gaudy
stuffy	eerie	depressing	spacious	sunny

DOMINANT IMPRESSIONS FOR DESCRIPTIONS OF PEOPLE				
creative	angry	independent	proud	dependable
tense	shy	aggressive	generous	sullen
silent	witty	pessimistic	responsible	efficient
snobbish	placid	bumbling	bitter	easygoing

EXERCISE 1 **Selecting the Dominant Impression**

Each of the following places could be the topic for a descriptive paragraph. Fill in each blank to the right of the topic with an appropriate dominant impression. Use the guide above if you need help. Remember, there is no single right answer.

Topic	Dominant impression
1. A high school gym on prom night	______________
2. Your barber or hairdresser's shop	______________
3. The room where you are now sitting	______________

4. The grocery store nearest you ____________
5. A hardware store ____________
6. The post office on Saturday morning ____________
7. An overcrowded waiting room ____________
8. San Francisco in the spring ____________
9. The home of your best friend ____________
10. The kitchen in the morning ____________

EXERCISE 2 **Selecting the Dominant Impression**

Each of the following persons could be the topic for a descriptive paragraph. Fill in each blank to the right of the topic with an appropriate dominant impression. Use the guide at the top of the page if you need help. Remember, there is no single right answer.

Topic	Dominant impression
1. An actor being interviewed on television	____________
2. An old woman in a nursing home	____________
3. A librarian	____________
4. A bank clerk on a busy day	____________
5. A farmer	____________
6. A politician running for office	____________
7. A cab driver	____________
8. A shoe salesperson	____________
9. A bride	____________
10. A soldier just discharged from the service	____________

Revising Vague Dominant Impressions

Certain words in the English language have become so overused that they no longer have any specific meaning for a reader. Careful writers avoid these words because they are almost useless in descriptive writing. Here is a list of the most commonly overused words:

VAGUE AND OVERUSED WORDS

good	normal
bad	typical
nice	interesting
fine	beautiful
okay	

The paragraph on page 361 is an example of the kind of writing that results from the continued use of vague words:

I had a typical day. The weather was nice and my job was interesting. The food for lunch was okay; supper was really good. After supper I saw my girlfriend, who is really beautiful. That's when my day really became fun.

Notice that all of the details in the paragraph are vague. The writer has told us what happened, but we cannot really see any of the details that are mentioned. This is because the writer has made the mistake of using words that have lost much of their meaning.

Practice.......... On a separate piece of paper rewrite this vague paragraph you have just read. Replace the vague words with details that are more specific.

The next group of exercises will give you practice in recognizing and eliminating overused words.

EXERCISE 3 **Revising Vague Dominant Impressions**

In each of the spaces provided, change the underlined word to a more specific dominant impression. An example has been done for you. You might want to work in groups to think of words that are more specific.

Vague: The tablecloth was <u>beautiful</u>.

Revised: The tablecloth was of <u>white linen with delicate blue embroidery</u>.

1. The sky looked <u>beautiful</u>. ______________________
2. The water felt <u>nice</u>. ______________________
3. Walking along the beach was <u>fun</u>. ______________________
4. The storm was <u>bad</u>. ______________________
5. The parking lot was <u>typical</u>. ______________________
6. The main street is <u>interesting</u>. ______________________
7. The dessert tasted <u>good</u>. ______________________
8. My brother seems <u>normal</u>. ______________________
9. Our house is <u>fine</u>. ______________________
10. My job is <u>okay</u>. ______________________

EXERCISE 4 **Revising Vague Dominant Impressions**

In each of the spaces provided, change the underlined word to a more specific dominant impression. Working in groups may be helpful.

1. It turned out to be a really <u>nice</u> date. ______________________
2. The window display was <u>beautiful</u>. ______________________
3. The boat ride was <u>fine</u>. ______________________
4. The circus was <u>fun</u>. ______________________

5. The lemonade tasted awful. ____________________

6. The play was bad. ____________________

7. His new suit looked okay. ____________________

8. The dance class was fine. ____________________

9. Her new watch was nice. ____________________

10. It was a good lecture. ____________________

Working with Description: Sensory Images

One of the basic ways all good writers communicate experiences to their readers is by using sense impressions. We respond to writing that makes us see an object, hear a sound, touch a surface, smell an odor, or taste a flavor. When a writer uses one or more of these sensory images in a piece of writing, we tend to pay more attention to what the writer is saying, and we tend to remember the details of what we have read.

For example, if you come across the word *door* in a sentence, you might or might not pay attention to it. However, if the writer tells you it was a *heavy wooden door, rough to the touch and creaking loudly when it opened,* you would not be likely to forget it. The door would stay in your mind because the writer used sensory images to make you more aware of it.

Sensory images are those details that relate to our senses: sight, smell, touch, taste, or hearing.

> **The floors were of black and white tile, the walls cream-colored with huge casement windows that opened onto a long veranda where the strains of violin music, soft voices, and the clink of glasses could be heard.**

Practice.......... The following sentences are taken from a description of a delicatessen. Notice how in each sentence the writer uses at least one sensory image to make the details of that sentence remain in your mind. As you read each of the sentences, identify the physical sense the writer appeals to when a sensory image is used.

1. A large refrigerator case against one wall was always humming loudly from the effort of keeping milk, cream, and several cases of soda and beer cool at all times.

   Physical senses: ____________________

   ____

2. Stacked on top of the counter were baskets of fresh rolls and breads which gave off an aroma that contained a mixture of onion, caraway seed, and pumpernickel.

   Physical senses: ____________________

   ____

3. He was always ready with a sample piece of cheese or smoked meat as a friendly gesture.

Physical senses: ____________________

____

When you use sensory images, you will stimulate the readers' interest, and these images will stay in their minds.

EXERCISE 5 **Recognizing Sensory Images**

The following paragraph contains examples of sensory images. Find the images and list them in the spaces provided.

> I knew how a newspaper office should look and sound and smell—I worked in one for thirteen years. The paper was the *New York Herald Tribune,* and its city room, wide as a city block, was dirty and disheveled. Reporters wrote on ancient typewriters that filled the air with clatter; copy editors labored on coffee-stained desks over what the reporters had written. Crumpled balls of paper littered the floor and filled the wastebaskets—failed efforts to write a good lead or a decent sentence. The walls were grimy—every few years they were painted over in a less restful shade of eye-rest green—and the atmosphere was hazy with the smoke of cigarettes and cigars. At the very center the city editor, a giant named L. L. Engelking, bellowed his displeasure with the day's work, his voice a rumbling volcano in our lives. I thought it was the most beautiful place in the world.

FROM WILLIAM ZINSSER,
Writing with a Word Processor

Sensory images

Sight: ____________________

____

Sound: ____________________

____

Smell: ____________________

____

EXERCISE 6 **Recognizing Sensory Images**

The following paragraph contains examples of sensory images. Find the images and list them in the spaces provided.

> The lake ice split with a sound like the crack of a rifle. Thick slabs of ice broke apart, moving ponderously, edge grinding against edge, upthrusting in jagged peaks, the green-gray water swirling over half-submerged floes. In an agony of rebirth, the splitting and booming of the ice reverberated across the thawing land. Streams raced toward the lake, their swift currents carrying fallen branches and undermining overhanging banks of earth and softened snow. Roads became mires of muck and slush, and the meadows of dried, matted grass oozed mud.

FROM NAN SALERNO,
Shaman's Daughter

Sensory images

Sight: ______________________________

____

Sound: ______________________________

____

Touch: ______________________________

____

EXERCISE 7

Recognizing Sensory Images

The following paragraph contains examples of sensory images. Find the images and list them in the spaces provided.

> In the waiting room there were several kerosene stoves, placed about to warm the shivering crowd. The stoves were small black chimneys with nickel handles. We stood around them rubbing hands and watching our clothes steam. An American lady, in a slicker, like the men, and rubber boots up to her knees kept bringing bowls of soup and shiny tin cups with hot coffee. Whatever she said to us and whatever we said to her neither understood, but she was talking the language of hot soup and coffee and kindness and there was perfect communication.

FROM ERNESTO GALARZA, *Barrio Boy*

Sensory images

Sight: ______________________________

____

Sound: ______________________________

____

Touch: ______________________________

____

Taste: ______________________________

____

Smell: ______________________________

EXERCISE 8

Creating Sensory Images

Each of the following topic sentences contains an underlined word that identifies a physical sense. For each topic sentence, write three sentences that give examples of sensory images. For example, in the first sentence the sensory image of sound in the vicinity of a hospital could be explained by writing sentences that describe ambulance sirens, doctors being called over loudspeaker systems, and the voices of people in the waiting room.

1. I knew I was walking past the hospital emergency room from the sounds I could hear.

Three sentences with sensory images:

a. ______________________________

____

b. ______________________________

____

c. ______________________________

____

2. I can't help stopping in the bakery every Sunday morning because the smells are so good.

Three sentences with sensory images:

a. ______________________________

____

b. ______________________________

____

c. ______________________________

____

3. The best part of my vacation last year was the sight that greeted me when I got up in the morning.

Three sentences with sensory images:

a. ______________________________

____

b. ______________________________

____

c. ______________________________

____

EXERCISE 9 Creating Sensory Images

Each of the following topic sentences contains an underlined word that identifies a physical sense. For each topic sentence, write three sentences that give examples of sensory images.

1. It is a luxury to wear clothing made with natural fibers because the feeling is quite different from polyesters.

Three sentences with sensory images:

a. ______________________________

____

b. ______________________________

____

c. ______________________________

____

2. I knew the garbage strike had gone on for a long time when I had to hold my nose walking down some streets.

Three sentences with sensory images:

a. ______________________________

____

b. ______________________________

____

c. ______________________________

____

3. A lake in the summertime is a relaxing place to be because the sounds you hear all day are so subdued.

Three sentences with sensory images:

a. ______________________________

____

b. ______________________________

____

c. ______________________________

____

EXERCISE 10 Creating Sensory Images

Each of the following topic sentences contains an underlined word that identifies a physical sense. For each topic sentence, write three sentences that give examples of sensory images.

1. Going to a disco is an overwhelming experience because of the different sounds you hear there.

Three sentences with sensory images:

a. ______________________________

____

b. ______________________________

____

c. ______________________________

____

2. My friend Bill says he loves the feel of the chocolate, the nuts, and the coconut when he eats that candy bar.

Three sentences with sensory images:

a. ______________________________

____

b. ______________________________

____

c. ______________________________

____

3. I could see that the old woman standing on the corner was very poor.

Three sentences with sensory images:

a. ______________________________

____

b. ______________________________

____

c. ______________________________

____

Coherence in Description: Putting Details in Spatial Order

In descriptive paragraphs, the writer often chooses to arrange supporting details according to space. With this method, you place yourself at the scene and then use a logical order such as moving from nearby to farther away, right to left, or top to bottom. Often you move in such a way that you save the most important detail until last in order to achieve the greatest effect.

> **Order** in descriptive writing is often a *spatial order.* Details can be given as one's eyes might move, for example, from top to bottom, left to right, outside to inside, or around in a circle.

Here is a description of a hotel room by the writer Virginia Paxton:

> The room was about the size of New York's Grand Central Station. It had been painted a fiendish dark-green. A single light bulb hung from the thirteen foot high ceiling. The bed was oversized. The desk was gigantic, and the leather-covered chairs engulfed us. Although hot water ran from the cold faucet and cold from the hot, we were delighted.

Notice how the writer begins with a general description of the room, including its size and color, the height of the ceiling, and the light. Then the writer moves on to give details about the furniture. A final detail is given, one that is meant to be humorous (the mix-up with the hot and cold water); the writer wants to amuse us and convince us that she enjoys the adventure of staying in an unusual hotel room. You might say the order of details here goes from the outer edges of the room to the center. A careful reader may also notice that the details proceed from more general description (size and color of room) to more specific items (chairs and faucets). When writing a descriptive paragraph, no matter which method of spatial order you choose, the details should be in a certain sequence that will allow your reader to visualize the scene in a logical order.

EXERCISE 11 **Working for Coherence: Using Spatial Order**

Each of the following topic sentences is followed by four or more descriptive sentences that are not in order. Put these descriptive sentences in order by placing a number (1, 2, 3, 4, or 5) in the space provided before each sentence.

1. The Statue of Liberty, now completely restored, is a marvel to visitors from all over the world.

(Order the material from the bottom to top.)

__________ With current restoration finished, the crown continues to be used as a place where visitors can get a good view of New York Harbor.

__________ The granite base of the statue was quarried and cut many miles from New York City and then taken by boat to Bedloe's Island, where the statue was built.

__________ The torch has been repaired and will now be illuminated by outside lights, not lights from inside the torch itself.

__________ The seven spikes that rise above the crown represent the seven seas of the world.

__________ The body was covered with sheets of copper that was originally mined on an island off the coast of Norway.

2. French women are distinguishable by their good taste in dress.

(Order the material from the top to bottom.)

__________ Their skirts are handsomely cut.

__________ Shoes are sensible but beautiful.

__________ Around their necks are exquisite silk scarves.

__________ They pay meticulous attention to their hairstyles and makeup.

__________ Their blouses and sweaters fit perfectly.

3. My aunt's kitchen is a very orderly place.

(Order the material from near to far.)

__________ As usual, in the center of the table sits a vase with a fresh yellow daffodil.

__________ Nearby on the refrigerator, a magnet holds the week's menu.

_______ Sitting at the kitchen table, I am struck by the freshly pressed linen tablecloth.

_______ Looking across the room through the stained glass doors of her kitchen cupboards, I can see neat rows of dishes, exactly eight each, matching the colors of the tablecloth and wallpaper.

EXERCISE 12 Working for Coherence: Using Spatial Order

Each of the following topic sentences could be expanded into a fully developed paragraph. In the spaces provided, give the appropriate supporting details for the topic sentence. Be sure to give your supporting details in a particular order. That is, the details should go from top to bottom, from outside to inside, from close to far, or around the area you are describing.

1. The airport terminal was as busy inside as it was outside.

a. ______________________________

____

b. ______________________________

____

c. ______________________________

____

d. ______________________________

____

2. The student lounge is a quiet and relaxing place in our school.

a. ______________________________

____

b. ______________________________

____

c. ______________________________

____

d. ______________________________

____

3. The motel lobby had once been very beautiful, but now it was beginning to look shabby.

a. ______________________________

____

b. ______________________________

____

c. ______________________________

____

d. ______________________________

____

EXERCISE 13 **Working for Coherence: Using Spatial Order**

Each of the following topic sentences could be expanded into a fully developed paragraph. In the spaces provided, give the appropriate supporting details for the topic sentence. Be sure to give your supporting details in a particular order. That is, the details should go from top to bottom, from outside to inside, from close to far, or around the area you are describing.

1. The shopping mall was supposed to be enjoyable, but the noise and the bright lights gave me a headache.

a. ______________________________

____

b. ______________________________

____

c. ______________________________

____

d. ______________________________

____

2. The pizza shop is so tiny that people are not likely to stay and eat.

a. ______________________________

____

b. ______________________________

____

c. ______________________________

____

d. ______________________________

____

3. The bus was filled with a strange assortment of people.

a. ______________________________

____

b. ______________________________

____

c. ______________________________

____

d. ______________________________

____

Writing the Descriptive Paragraph Step-by-Step

To learn a skill with some degree of ease, it is best to follow a step-by-step approach so that various skills are isolated. This will ensure that you are not missing a crucial point or misunderstanding a part of the whole. There certainly are other ways to go about writing an effective paragraph, but here is one method you can use to achieve successful results. You will learn that writing, like most skills, can be developed by using a logical process.

STEPS FOR WRITING THE DESCRIPTIVE PARAGRAPH

1. Study the given topic, and then plan your topic sentence, especially the dominant impression.
2. List at least ten details that come to your mind when you think about the description you have chosen.
3. Then choose the five or six most important details from your list. Be sure these details support the dominant impression.
4. Put your list in order.
5. Write one complete sentence for each of the details you have chosen from your list.
6. Write a concluding statement that offers some reason for describing this topic.
7. Finally, copy your sentences into standard paragraph form.
8. Always make a final check for spelling errors and other mistakes, such as omitted words. When you use a computer spellcheck feature, keep in mind that this feature will only alert you to spellings that do not match words in its dictionary. If you type *there* when you mean *their,* the spellchecker will see an acceptable word. When it comes to a final editing, there is no substitute for your own careful reading.

EXERCISE 14 **Writing the Descriptive Paragraph Step-by-Step**

The following exercise will guide you through the construction of a descriptive paragraph. Start with the suggested topic. Use the eight steps to help you work through each stage of the writing process.

Topic: A place you have lived

1. Topic sentence: ______________________________

____

2. Make a list of possible supporting details.

a. ______________________________

b. ______________________________

c. ______________________________

d. ______________________________

e. ______________________________

f. ______________________________

g. ______________________________

h. ______________________________

i. ______________________________

j. ______________________________

3. Circle the five or six details you believe are the most important for the description.

4. Put your selected details in order by numbering them.

5. Using your final list, write at least one sentence for each detail you have chosen.

a. ______________________________

____

b. ______________________________

____

c. ______________________________

____

d. ______________________________

____

e. ______________________________

____

f. ______________________________

____

g. ______________________________

____

6. Write a concluding statement. ______________________________

____

7. Copy your sentences into standard paragraph form.

8. Do a final reading to check for errors and omissions.

EXERCISE 15 **Writing the Descriptive Paragraph Step-by-Step**

The following exercise will guide you through the construction of a descriptive paragraph. Start with the suggested topic. Use the eight steps to help you work through each stage of the writing process.

Topic: A person you admire

1. Topic sentence: ______________________________

____

2. Make a list of possible supporting details.

a. ____

b. ____

c. ____

d. ____

e. ____

f. ____

g. ____

h. ____

i. ____

j. ____

3. Circle the five or six details you believe are the most important for the description.

4. Put your selected details in order by numbering them.

5. Using your final list, write at least one sentence for each detail you have chosen.

a. ____
____

b. ____
____

c. ____
____

d. ____
____

e. ____
____

f. ____
____

g. ____
____

6. Write a concluding statement. ________________________
____

7. Copy your sentences into standard paragraph form.

8. Do a final reading to check for errors and omissions.

EXERCISE 16 **Writing the Descriptive Paragraph Step-by-Step**

The following exercise will guide you through the construction of a descriptive paragraph. Start with the suggested topic. Use the eight steps to help you work through each stage of the writing process.

Topic: An ideal gift for a child

1. Topic sentence: ______________________________

____

2. Make a list of possible supporting details.

a. ______________________________

b. ______________________________

c. ______________________________

d. ______________________________

e. ______________________________

f. ______________________________

g. ______________________________

h. ______________________________

i. ______________________________

j. ______________________________

3. Circle the five or six details you believe are the most important for the description.

4. Put your selected details in order by numbering them.

5. Using your final list, write at least one sentence for each detail you have chosen.

a. ______________________________

____

b. ______________________________

____

c. ______________________________

____

d. ______________________________

____

e. ______________________________

____

f. ______________________________

____

g. ______________________________

____

6. Write a concluding statement. ______________________________

____

7. Copy your sentences into standard paragraph form.
8. Do a final reading to check for errors and omissions.

On Your Own: Writing Descriptive Paragraphs from Model Paragraphs

A Description of a Home

Assignment 1

Write a paragraph in which you describe a house or room that you remember clearly. Choose your dominant impression carefully and then make your sensory images support that impression. In your description you may want to include the person who lives in the house or room. In the following model paragraph from Charles Chaplin's *My Autobiography,* notice the importance of the last sentence, in which the writer gives his paragraph added impact by naming the person who lives in the house he has described.

MODEL PARAGRAPH: THE BUNGALOW

It was dark when we entered his bungalow, and when we switched on the light I was shocked. The place was empty and drab. In his room was an old iron bed with a light bulb hanging over the head of it. A rickety old table and one chair were the other furnishings. Near the bed was a wooden box upon which was a brass ashtray filled with cigarette butts. The room allotted to me was almost the same, only it was minus a grocery box. Nothing worked. The bathroom was unspeakable. One had to take a jug and fill it from the bath tap and empty it down the flush to make the toilet work. This was the home of G. M. Anderson, the multimillionaire cowboy.

Ten suggested topics

1. A student's apartment
2. A vacation cottage
3. A dormitory
4. The house of your dreams
5. Your bedroom
6. A kitchen
7. The messiest room you ever saw
8. The strangest room you ever saw
9. A house you will never forget
10. A house that did not fit the character of the person living there

A Description of a Person

Assignment 2

Describe a person whose appearance made a deep impression on you. If you saw this person only once, indicate the details that made him or her stay in your mind. If you choose to describe a person with whom you are more familiar, select the most outstanding details that will help your reader have a single, dominant impression. In the model paragraph, Scott Russell Sanders remembers the men from his rural and working class childhood in Tennessee.

MODEL PARAGRAPH: WORKING MEN

The bodies of the men I knew were twisted and maimed in ways visible and invisible. The nails of their hands were black and split, the hands tattooed with scars. Some had lost fingers. Heavy lifting had given many of them finicky backs and guts weak from hernias. Racing against conveyor belts had given them ulcers. Their ankles and knees ached from years of standing on concrete. Anyone who had worked for long around machines was hard of hearing. They squinted, and the skin of their faces was creased like the leather of old work gloves. There were times, studying them, when I dreaded growing up. Most of them coughed, from dust or cigarettes, and most of them drank cheap wine or whiskey, so their eyes looked bloodshot and bruised. The fathers of my friends always seemed older than the mothers. Men wore out sooner. Only women lived into old age.

Ten suggested topics

1. An elderly relative
2. A hard-working student
3. An outstanding athlete
4. A loyal friend
5. An overworked waitress
6. A cab driver
7. A fashion model
8. A gossipy neighbor
9. A street vendor
10. A rude salesperson

A Description of a Time of Day

Assignment 3

Write a paragraph in which you describe the sights, sounds, and events of a particular time of day in a place you know well. In the model paragraph that follows, the writer has chosen to describe an especially busy time of day, the morning, when activity can be frantic in a household.

MODEL PARAGRAPH: GROWING UP IN CLEVELAND

I remember the turmoil of mornings in our house. My brothers and sisters rushed about upstairs and down trying to get ready for school. Mom would repeatedly tell them to hurry up. Molly would usually scream down from her bedroom, "What am I going to do? I don't have any clean underwear!" Amy, often in tears, sat at the kitchen table still in her pajamas trying to do her math. Paul paced back and forth in front of the mirror angrily combing his unruly hair which stuck up in all directions while Roland threatened to punch him if he didn't find the pen he had borrowed the night before. Mother was stuffing sandwiches into bags while she sighed, "I'm afraid there isn't anything for dessert today." No one heard her. Then came the yelling up the stairs, "You should have left ten minutes ago." One by one, these unwilling victims were packed up and pushed out the door. Mother wasn't safe yet. Somebody always came back frantic and desperate. "My flute, Mom, where's my flute, quick! I'll get killed if I don't have it today." Every crisis apparently meant the difference between life and death. Morning at our house was like watching a troop preparing for battle. When they had finally gone, I was left in complete silence while my mother slumped on a chair at the kitchen table. She paid no attention to me.

Ten suggested topics

1. A Saturday filled with errands
2. The dinner hour at my house
3. Lunchtime in a cafeteria
4. A midnight raid on the refrigerator
5. Christmas morning
6. TGIF (Thank God It's Friday)
7. Getting ready to go out on a Friday night
8. My Sunday morning routine
9. Coming home from school or work
10. Watching late-night movies

A Description of a Place

Assignment 4 Write a paragraph in which you describe a place you know well or remember clearly. The model paragraph that follows is from *The Airtight Cage,* a classic study by Joseph Lyford of an urban neighborhood in a state of change.

MODEL PARAGRAPH: THE CONDEMNED BUILDING

The wreckers would put a one-story scaffold in front of the building to protect automobiles and pedestrians, then begin at the top, working down story by story, gutting the rooms, ripping out woodwork, electrical wiring, plumbing, and fixtures. Once this was done, the men would hammer the shell of the house with sledges. Sections of brick wall would shudder, undulate for a second and dissolve into fragments that fell in slow motion. When the fragments hit the ground, the dust rocketed several feet into the air. The heaps of brick and plaster, coils and stems of rusty pipe attracted children from all over the area. On weekends and after 4 P.M. on weekdays, they would scamper from building to building, dancing in the second-, third-, and fourth-story rooms where fronts and backs had been knocked out, bombing each other with bricks and bits of concrete. Sometimes when they were dashing in and out of clouds of smoke and dust, with ruined buildings in the background, the children looked as if they were taking a town over under heavy artillery fire. The city eventually assigned a guard to stop the children but apparently there were too many of them to handle and the pandemonium continued.

Ten suggested topics

1. A large department store
2. A sports stadium
3. A coffee shop
4. A pizza parlor
5. A shoe store
6. A night spot
7. A lively street corner
8. A college bookstore
9. A gymnasium
10. A medical clinic

A Description of a Time of Year

Assignment 5

Write a paragraph in which you describe a particular time of year. Make sure that all of the details you choose relate specifically to that time of year. In the model paragraph that follows, from "Boyhood in Jamaica" by Claude McKay, the writer remembers springtime on his native island.

MODEL PARAGRAPH: SEASONS IN JAMAICA

Most of the time there was hardly any way of telling the seasons. To us in Jamaica, as elsewhere in the tropics, there were only two seasons—the rainy season and the dry season. We had no idea of spring, summer, autumn, and winter like the peoples of northern lands. Springtime, however, we did know by the new and lush burgeoning of grasses and the blossoming of trees, although we had blooms all the year round. The mango tree was especially significant of spring, because it was one of the few trees that used to shed its leaves. Then, in springtime, the new leaves sprouted—very tender, a kind of sulphur brown, as if they had been singed by fire. Soon afterwards the white blossoms came out and we knew that we would be eating juicy mangoes by August.

Ten suggested topics

1. A winter storm
2. A summer picnic
3. Summer in the city
4. A winter walk
5. Jogging in the spring rain
6. Sunbathing on a beach
7. Signs of spring in my neighborhood
8. The woods in autumn
9. Ice skating in winter
10. Halloween night

EXPLORING ONLINE

For further reading about description, see

http://www.morrisville.edu/~hildebfl/rdsindex.html

WORKING TOGETHER

WRITING A CHARACTER SKETCH

The following personal advertisement appeared in a local newspaper:

> Young man seeks neat, responsible roommate to share off-campus apartment for next academic year. Person must be a nonsmoker and respect a vegetarian who cooks at home. Furniture not needed, but CD player would be welcome!

Personal habits have a way of causing friction between people who share the same living space. For this reason, finding the right roommate in a college dormitory, finding the right person with whom to share an apartment, or finding the right long-term companion can be very difficult.

Divide into groups. Develop a random list of habits that can become problems when people share living space. Then, working together, group the items on your list into categories with general headings. For instance, one general heading might be called *eating patterns.*

Portfolio Suggestions

1. Write a paragraph or two in which you provide a character description of yourself for an agency that will match you up with a roommate. As you write, be sure you include information about your hobbies, habits, attitudes, and any other personal characteristics that could make a difference in the kind of person the agency will select for you.

2. Write a paragraph or two in which you provide a character sketch of the roommate you would like the agency to find for you.
3. Write your own description of what you imagine would be the "roommate from Hell."

Online Activity

Read and discuss the summaries of *The Seven Habits of Highly Effective People:*

http://www.profitadvisors.com/7HABITSLIST.HTM

Chapter 21 Developing Paragraphs: Process

Preview

Giving instructions or explaining how something is done involves a careful reconstructing of a sequence of steps. With a careless omission, an entire process can be misunderstood. In this chapter, you will learn the elements of writing a good process paragraph:

- Understanding the difference between *directional* and *informational* process writing
- Learning about the importance of *completeness*
- Achieving coherence through *logical sequence* and the use of *transitions*
- Practice your own process paragraphs
  - Using a step-by-step approach
  - Using model paragraphs with suggested topics

Key Term

Process

Charts

List of transitions used in process
Steps for writing process paragraphs

What Is Process?

Process is a method of development that provides a step-by-step explanation of how something is done or how something works.

A paragraph using process analysis may be **directional;** that is, the paragraph is intended for a reader who needs to follow the directions in order to perform a task.

Example of a **directional** process paragraph:

What to Do If You Are Bitten by a Tick

Remove the tick with a pair of tweezers. Put the tweezers as close to the skin as possible and pull straight out. Don't twist as you pull and don't squeeze its bloated body or the bacteria may be injected into the skin. Thoroughly wash your hands and the bite area and apply a topical

> antiseptic such as rubbing alcohol to the bite area. Don't use a match to try to burn the tick out or any other home remedy like kerosene or petroleum jelly. Try to save the tick. Then call your physician and ask for an appointment as quickly as possible. Bring the tick so that it may be identified. For the next three weeks, look for small raised bumps on the skin, rash, fever, chills, severe headaches, backache, stiff neck, or swelling painful joints. Remember: time is crucial because the longer the tick is attached, the greater the risk of Lyme disease.

Your daily life is filled with activities that involve directional process. Instructions on a test, directions on how to get to a wedding reception, or your favorite spaghetti recipe are a few examples of the kinds of process writing you see and use regularly. You can find examples of directional process writing everywhere you look, in newspapers, magazines, and books, as well as on the containers and packages of products you use every day.

The other type of process writing is **informational.** In this case, you explain how something works or how something was done in the past. There is no expectation or even the possibility that you would or could act upon it. The purpose of describing the process is purely for information. History lessons are filled with such writing. For instance, if you learned how a Civil War general planned his battle strategy, this would be informational process writing. Notice in the following example the various steps the writer and public speaker Malcolm X went through in the process of his self-education. In the paragraph, the transitional words that signal the steps or stages of the process have been italicized.

Example of an **informational** process paragraph:

> When Malcolm X was in prison, he became very frustrated because he could not express his thoughts in letters written to his family and friends. Nor could he read well enough to be able to get the meaning from a book. He decided upon a program to change this situation. *First,* he got hold of a dictionary along with some paper and pencils. He was astounded at how many words there were. Not knowing what else to do, he turned to the first page and *began* by copying words from the page. It took him the entire day. *Next,* he read what he had written aloud, over and over again. He was excited to be learning words he never knew existed. *The next morning,* he reviewed what he had forgotten and *then* copied the next page. He found he was learning about people, places, and events from history. This process *continued until* he had filled a tablet with all the A's and *then* all the B's. *Eventually,* Malcolm X copied the entire dictionary!

Working with Process: Don't Overlook Any One of the Steps

The writer of the process essay is almost always more of an authority on the subject than the person reading the essay. In giving directions or information on how something was done or is to be done, it is possible to leave out a step that you think is so obvious that it is not worth mentioning. The reader, on the other hand, does not necessarily fill in the missing step as you did. An important part of process writing, therefore, is understanding your reader's level of ability. All of us have been given directions that, at first, seemed very clear. However, when we actually tried to carry out the process, something went wrong. A step in the process was misunderstood or missing. The giver of the information either assumed we would know certain parts of the process or didn't stop to think through the process completely. Also, keep in mind that any special equipment needed must be included. Directions must be complete and accurate.

EXERCISE 1 **Is the Process Complete?**

In each of the following processes, decide if any important steps of information have been omitted. Imagine yourself going through the process using only the information provided.

How to make a Swedish spice cake

1. Butter an 8-inch tube pan and sprinkle with 2 tbsp. of fine dry bread crumbs.
2. Cream ½ cup of butter; add 1 cup of firmly packed brown sugar and cream until light and fluffy.
3. In a small bowl beat 2 egg yolks until light and add to the creamed mixture.
4. Sift together 1½ cups all purpose flour, 1 tsp. baking power, 2 tsp. ground cardamon, and 2 tsp. of ground cinnamon.
5. Add the dry ingredients to the creamed ingredients mixing alternately with ½ cup of light cream.
6. Beat egg whites stiff and fold into batter.
7. Turn in prepared pan, bake, and serve unfrosted.

Missing step or steps: ______________________________

____

____

____

How to plan a wedding

1. Make an appointment with the minister or other authority involved, to set a date for the wedding.
2. Discuss plans with both families as to the budget available for the wedding; this will determine the size of the party and where it is to be held.
3. Reserve the banquet hall up to eight months in advance.
4. Choose members of the wedding party and ask them whether they will be able to participate in the ceremony.
5. Begin to choose the clothing for the wedding party, including your own wedding gown or suit.
6. Enjoy your wedding!

Missing step or steps: ______________________________

____

____

____

EXERCISE 2 **Is the Process Complete?**

In each of the following processes, decide if any important steps of information have been omitted. Imagine yourself going through the process using only the information provided.

How to prepare for an essay exam

1. Read the chapters as they are assigned, well in advance of the test.
2. Take notes in class.
3. Ask the teacher what format the test will take.
4. Get a good night's sleep the night before.
5. Bring any pens or pencils that you might need.
6. Arrive at the classroom a few minutes early in order to get yourself settled and to keep yourself calm.

Missing step or steps: ______________________________

____

____

____

How to wrap a present

1. Gather all the materials needed: box for gift, wrapping paper, tape, scissors, and ribbon.
2. Measure the amount of paper needed and cut off excess.
3. Place box top side down on paper.
4. Bring one long side of wrapping paper up and tape it to the box.
5. Bring the other long side of the paper up over the box to the far edge. Pull tight. Fold the paper under so that it fits exactly along the far edge of the box. Tape securely.
6. Tie ribbon, make bow, and attach the card.

Note: Many instructions include pictures to make the process easier to follow.

Missing step or steps: ______________________________

____

____

____

Working for Coherence: Order in Logical Sequence

When you are working with process, it is important not only to make sure the steps in the process are complete but also to present the steps in the right sequence. For example, if you are describing the process of cleaning a mixer, it is important to point out that you must first unplug the appliance before you actually remove the blades. The importance of this step is clear when you realize that a person could lose a finger if this part of the process were missing. Improperly written instructions have caused serious injuries and even death.

EXERCISE 3 **Coherence in Process: Order in Logical Sequence**

The following steps describe the process of refinishing hardwood floors. Put the steps into their proper sequence.

__________ Keep sanding until you expose the hard wood.

__________ Apply a coat of polyurethane finish.

__________ When the sanding is done, clean the floor thoroughly with a vacuum sweeper to remove all the sawdust.

__________ Allow the finish to dry for three days before waxing and buffing.

__________ Take all furnishings out of the room.

__________ Do the initial sanding with a coarse sandpaper on the sanding machine.

__________ The edger and hand sander are used after the machine sanding to get to those hard-to-reach places.

__________ Put the second coat of polyurethane finish on the following day, using a brush or a roller.

__________ Change the machine to a fine sandpaper for the final sanding.

__________ Any nails sticking out from the floor should be either pulled out or set below the surface of the boards before you start the sanding machine.

EXERCISE 4 **Coherence in Process: Order in Logical Sequence**

The following steps describe the process of devising a filing system. Put the steps into their proper sequence.

__________ When your mind begins to blur, stop filing for that day.

__________ Now label the file folder and slip the piece of paper in.

__________ Gather together all materials to be filed so that they are all in one location.

__________ Alphabetize your file folders and put them away into your file drawer, and you are finished for that session.

__________ Add to these materials a wastebasket, folders, labels, and a pen.

__________ Pick up the next piece of paper and go through the same procedure, the only variation being that this new piece of paper might fit into an existing file, rather than one with a new heading.

__________ Pick up an item on the top of the pile and decide whether this item has value for you. If it does not, throw it away. If it does, go on to the next step.

__________ Finally, to maintain your file once it is established, each time you consult a file folder, riffle through it quickly in order to throw out material no longer useful.

__________ If the piece of paper is worth saving, ask yourself the question, "What is this paper about?"

Working for Coherence: Using Transitions

Writers of process, like writers of narration, usually order their material by using time sequence. Although it would be tiresome to use "and then" for each new step, a certain number of transitions are necessary for the process to read smoothly and coherently. Here is a list of transitions frequently used in a process paragraph.

TRANSITIONS COMMONLY USED IN *PROCESS*

the first step	while you are . . .	the last step
in the beginning	as you are . . .	the final step
to start with	next	finally
to begin with	then	at last
first of all	the second step	eventually
	after you have . . .	

EXERCISE 5 **Using Transitions to Go from a List to a Paragraph**

Select one of the four processes given on pages 385–386. Use the list to write a process paragraph. Be sure to include transitional devices to make the paragraph read smoothly and coherently.

____

____

____

____

____

____

____

____

EXERCISE 6 **Using Transitions to Go from a List to a Paragraph**

Select one of the four processes listed on pages 385–386. Use the list to write a process paragraph. Be sure to include transitional devices to make the paragraph read smoothly and coherently.

Writing the Process Paragraph Step-by-Step

Writing a process paragraph is a task with several special requirements. One approach is to work step-by-step so that each requirement can be given enough thought before you go on to the next part. Although there is more than one way to approach a writing task, here is one plan you can use to achieve good results.

STEPS FOR WRITING THE PROCESS PARAGRAPH

1. After you have chosen your topic and controlling idea, plan your topic sentence.
2. List as many steps or stages in the process as you can.
3. Eliminate any irrelevant steps, add equipment needed, or explain any special circumstances of the process.
4. Put the steps in order.
5. Write at least one complete sentence for each of the steps you have chosen from your list.
6. Write a concluding statement that says something about the results of completing the process.
7. Finally, copy your sentences into standard paragraph form.
8. Make a final check for spelling errors and other mistakes, such as omitted words.

EXERCISE 7 **Writing the Process Paragraph Step-by-Step**

This exercise will guide you through the construction of a complete process paragraph. Start with the topic suggested below. Use the eight steps to help you work through each stage of the writing process.

Topic: How to lose weight

Perhaps no topic has filled more bookstores or magazine pages than the "lose five pounds in one week" promise. The wide variety of diet plans boggles the mind. Here is your chance to add your own version.

1. Topic sentence: ______________________________

____

2. Make a list of possible steps.

a. ______________________________

b. ______________________________

c. ______________________________

d. ______________________________

e. ______________________________

f. ______________________________

g. ______________________________

h. ______________________________

i. ______________________________

j. ______________________________

3. Eliminate any irrelevant steps, point out any equipment needed, or explain any special circumstances.

4. Put your steps in order by numbering them.

5. Using your final list, write at least one sentence for each step you have chosen.

a. ______________________________

____

b. ______________________________

____

c. ______________________________

____

d. ______________________________

____

e. ______________________________

____

f. ______________________________

____

g. ______________________________

____

6. Write a concluding statement. ______________________________

____

____

7. On a separate piece of paper, copy your sentences into standard paragraph form.

8. Do a final reading to check for errors and omissions.

EXERCISE 8 **Writing the Process Paragraph Step-by-Step**

This exercise will guide you through the construction of a complete process paragraph. Start with the topic suggested below. Use the eight steps to help you work through each stage of the writing process.

Topic: How to choose a college

The factors that go into selecting a college can be extremely complicated. Sometimes an individual goes through an agonizing process before he or she is finally seated in a college classroom. Give advice to a prospective college student on how to go about finding the right college.

1. Topic sentence: ______________________________

____

2. Make a list of possible steps.

a. ______________________________

b. ______________________________

c. ______________________________

d. ____________________

e. ____________________

f. ____________________

g. ____________________

h. ____________________

i. ____________________

j. ____________________

3. Eliminate any irrelevant steps, point out any equipment needed, or explain any special circumstances.

4. Put your steps in order by numbering them.

5. Using your final list, write at least one sentence for each step you have chosen.

a. ____________________

____

b. ____________________

____

c. ____________________

____

d. ____________________

____

e. ____________________

____

f. ____________________

____

g. ____________________

____

6. Write a concluding statement. ____________________

____

____

7. On a separate piece of paper, copy your sentences into standard paragraph form.

8. Do a final reading to check for errors and omissions.

EXERCISE 9

Writing the Process Paragraph Step-by-Step

This exercise will guide you through the construction of a complete process paragraph. Start with the topic suggested below. Use the eight steps to help you work through each stage of the writing process.

Topic: How to set up a budget

Imagine you are the expert who has been hired by a couple to help them sort out their money problems. Together they bring in a reasonable salary, but in spite of this, they are always spending more than they earn.

1. Topic sentence: ______________________________

____

2. Make a list of possible steps.

a. ______________________________

b. ______________________________

c. ______________________________

d. ______________________________

e. ______________________________

f. ______________________________

g. ______________________________

h. ______________________________

i. ______________________________

j. ______________________________

3. Eliminate any irrelevant steps, point out any equipment needed, or explain any special circumstances.

4. Put your steps in order by numbering them.

5. Using your final list, write at least one sentence for each step you have chosen.

a. ______________________________

____

b. ______________________________

____

c. ______________________________

____

d. ______________________________

____

e. ______________________________

____

f. ____

____

g. ____

____

6. Write a concluding statement. ______________________________

____

____

7. On a separate piece of paper, copy your sentences into standard paragraph form.

8. Do a final reading to check for errors and omissions.

On Your Own: Writing Process Paragraphs from Model Paragraphs

Directional: How to Accomplish a Daily Task

Assignment 1 Write a paragraph in which you describe the process of doing a daily task of some kind. For example, you might have learned how to antique an old piece of furniture in order to save money, or you might have learned how to drive so that you would be in a better position to get a job. The following paragraph shows the correct process for making a common beverage, one used by millions of people every day: the ordinary cup of tea.

MODEL PARAGRAPH: HOW TO MAKE A GOOD CUP OF TEA

Making a good cup of tea is exquisitely simple. First, heat the teapot by filling it with water that has just come to a boil. Discard this water, and place 1 teaspoon of loose tea per cup in the teapot (the exact amount may vary according to taste). Pour in fresh water that has just come to a boil, 6 ounces for each cup of tea. Allow the tea to steep for 3 to 5 minutes; then, pour it through a strainer into a cup or mug. A pound of loose tea will yield about 200 cups of brewed tea. Using a tea bag eliminates the strainer, but it is still best to make the tea in a teapot so the water stays sufficiently hot. The typical restaurant service, a cup of hot water with the tea bag on the side, will not produce the best cup of tea because the water is never hot enough when it reaches the table and because the tea should not be dunked into the water; the water should be poured over the tea. Tea in a pot often becomes too strong, but that problem can be dealt with by adding boiling water.

Ten suggested topics

1. How to move from one city to another
2. How to install your own telephone
3. How to install a stereo system
4. How to lay a carpet
5. How to make homemade ice cream
6. How to prepare a package for mailing
7. How to pack a suitcase
8. How to furnish an apartment inexpensively
9. How to wallpaper a room
10. How to care for a lawn

Directional: How to Care for Your Health

Assignment 2

Write a paragraph in which you show steps you could take for your mental or physical health. Concern for health and physical fitness is enjoying great popularity, bringing in big profits to health-related magazines, health clubs, health-food producers, and sports equipment manufacturers. The following paragraph tells us how to get a good night's sleep.

MODEL PARAGRAPH: HOW TO GET A GOOD NIGHT'S SLEEP

The process of getting a good night's sleep depends on several factors. First, the conditions in your bedroom must be correct. Be sure that the room temperature is around sixty-five degrees and that the room is as quiet as possible. Next, pay attention to your bed and how it is furnished. A firm mattress is best and wool blankets are better than blankets made of synthetic material. In addition, pillows that are too soft can cause stiffness of the neck and lead to a poor night's sleep. Also, keep in mind that what you eat and how you eat are part of the process of preparing for bed. Do not go to bed hungry, but do not overeat, either. Avoid candy bars or cookies; the sugar they contain acts as a stimulant. Finally, do not go to bed until you are sleepy; do something relaxing until you are tired.

Ten suggested topics

1. How to plan a healthful diet
2. How to care for someone who is ill
3. How to plan a daily exercise program
4. How to choose a sport that is suitable for you
5. How to live to be one hundred
6. How to pick a doctor
7. How to make exercise and diet foods fun
8. How to stop eating junk food
9. How to deal with depression
10. How to find a spiritual side to life

Directional: How to Write School Assignments

Assignment 3 Your writing in school takes many forms. Write a paragraph in which you show the process of writing a specific assignment related to school. The following paragraph, adapted from Donald Murray's *Write to Learn,* shows the several steps you need to follow in the writing of a term paper.

MODEL PARAGRAPH: WRITING A TERM PAPER

Doing a term paper involves both careful research on a topic and a methodical approach to the writing of the material. First, consult the important and up-to-date books and articles related to your subject. Next, find out the style of writing that your instructor wants; also find out details about length, organization, footnoting, and bibliography that will be part of the presentation of your paper. Then write a draft of the paper as quickly as you can, without using notes or bibliography; this will help you see your ideas and how they can be further developed. Before you go any further, review what you have written to see if you have begun to develop a point of view about your subject or an attitude toward your topic. Finally, write a draft of your paper that includes all of the important information about your subject, a draft that includes your footnotes and your bibliography.

Ten suggested topics

1. How to prepare an oral report
2. How to write a résumé
3. How to write a letter of application (for a school or for a job)
4. How to report a science experiment
5. How to write a book review
6. How to revise an essay
7. How to take classroom notes
8. How to take notes from a textbook
9. How to write a letter home, asking for money
10. How to write a story for the school newspaper

Informational: How Something Happens in the World of Nature

Assignment 4 Write a paragraph in which you show how a natural occurrence takes place in nature. It might be an interesting phenomenon with humans, it could be an example of instinctive animal behavior, or it could be any other phenomenon in the natural world. The paragraph on page 397, describing how a kitten instinctively practices the necessary skills for hunting its prey, is an example of informational process writing.

MODEL PARAGRAPH: HOW A KITTEN INSTINCTIVELY LEARNS TO HUNT

A kitten is playing with its classical plaything, a ball of wool. Unfailingly, it begins to paw at the object, first gently and enquiringly with outstretched forearm and inwardly flexed paw. Now with extended claws, it draws the ball toward itself, pushes it away again or jumps a few steps backward, crouching. It lies low, raises its head with tense expression, glaring at the plaything. Then its head drops so suddenly that you expect its chin to bump the floor. The hind feet perform peculiar, alternately treading and clawing movements as though the kitten were seeking a firm hold from which to spring. Suddenly it bounds in a great semicircle and lands on its toy with stiff forepaws pressed closely together. It will even bite it, if the game has reached a pitch of some intensity. Again it pushes the ball and this time it rolls under a cupboard which stands too close to the floor for the kitten to get underneath. With an elegant "practiced" movement, it reaches with one arm into the space and fishes its plaything out again. It is at once clear to anyone who has ever watched a cat hunting a mouse, that our kitten, which we have reared apart from its mother, is performing all those highly specialized movements which aid the cat in the hunting of its most important prey—the mouse. In the wild state, this constitutes its "daily bread."

Ten suggested topics

1. How an earthquake occurs
2. How the hole in the ozone layer has occurred
3. How scientists explain global warming
4. How life can exist at great ocean depths
5. How pearls are formed
6. How certain birds migrate
7. How the human heart works
8. How metamorphosis happens
9. How a cut heals
10. How the bee makes honey

EXPLORING ONLINE

For further reading about the properties of process analysis, see

http://www.morrisville.edu/~hildebfl/rprindex.htm

WORKING TOGETHER

BUILDING A TEAM

Working well in groups or teams is important, not only in many college situations, but also increasingly in the workplace. Group work, however, may have its problems if not approached with a careful understanding of how groups work. Appoint one person in your class to direct the discussion and then choose another person to put on the board the main ideas that come out of the discussion. Your class may want to consider some of the following issues often encountered when people work in groups:

1. How important is it that everybody first understand the task?
2. How can you avoid a situation where one person seems to be doing all the work?
3. What can be done about the person who dominates all the discussions?
4. What can be done about the person who is very shy?
5. What can be done about the person has an "attitude"?
6. How can you be sure the group meeting does not end up with people chatting and not focusing on the task?
7. How do you avoid personality conflicts?
8. How can you avoid disagreements later on about the decisions that were made?
9. What procedure should be followed when the group meets?

Portfolio Suggestion

Use the material from the classroom discussion to write a process essay. In your essay, give the procedure to be followed when a team meets to work on a project. Even though you are giving general rules to be followed, it might be helpful to give an example of a project that could be assigned to a group of workers doing a particular job, such as a group of teachers who are meeting to design a new curriculum for a course, or a group of magazine writers who are trying to decide on a theme for the next issue of their magazine.

Online Activity

Read and discuss the principles of teamwork:

http://www.smartbiz.com/sbs/arts/exe71.htm

Chapter 22 Developing Paragraphs: Comparison/Contrast

Preview

This form of development is unusual in that you have two topics to balance at the same time. This chapter will look at the special areas of developing such a paragraph:

- The two-part topic
- Ordering material using the point-by-point method or the block method
- Improving coherence by using transitional phrases common to comparison/contrast writing
- Practice your own comparison/contrast paragraphs
    - Using a step-by-step approach
    - Using model paragraphs with suggested topics

Key Terms

Comparison/contrast
Point-by-point method
Block method

Charts

List of transitions used in comparison/contrast
Steps for writing comparison/contrast paragraphs

What Is Comparison/Contrast?

We use comparison or contrast in a variety of ways every day. In the grocery store, we consider similar products before we decide to buy one of them; we listen to two politicians on television and think about the differences between their positions before we vote for one of them; and we read college catalogues and talk to our friends before we make a final choice as to which school we should attend.

When we compare or contrast two items, we want to be able to see very clearly the points of comparison or contrast so that we may judge which item is better or worse than the other in some respect. The process of comparison gives us a deeper understanding of the subject and enables us to make well-researched decisions rather than being at the mercy of a clever salesperson or being convinced by a good price or some other feature that might strike us at first glance.

Let's think about the selection of a word processing program, an expensive purchase that many individuals and companies will make. A shopper must consider price, availability of help for installing and troubleshooting, compatibility with available computers, specific features that differentiate the package from other programs available, how "user-friendly" the program is, what the specific needs are now and what they might be in the future, and how current or popular the program is among other software users. Also, it is a good idea to seek out advice from others who are more expert on the available programs. All of this research is basically comparison and contrast. Especially with such a complex and expensive purchase as computer software, we can see that comparison and contrast becomes not only a useful tool, but an essential one.

Comparison/contrast, a method for developing ideas, is the examination of similarities and/or differences between people, objects, or ideas, in order to arrive at a judgment or conclusion.

Working with Comparison or Contrast: Choosing the Two-Part Topic

The problem with writing a good comparison or contrast paragraph usually centers on the fact that you now have a two-part topic. This demands very careful attention to the topic sentence. While you must be careful to choose two subjects that have enough in common to make them comparable, you must also not choose two things having so much in common that you cannot possibly handle all the comparable points in one paragraph or even ten paragraphs. For example, a student trying to compare the French word *chaise* with the English word *chair* might be able to come up with only two sentences of material. With only a dictionary to consult, it is unlikely that the student would find enough material for several points of comparison. On the other hand, contrasting the United States with Europe would present such an endless supply of points to compare that the tendency would be to give only general facts that your reader would already know. When the subject is too broad, the writing is often too general. A better two-part topic might be to compare traveling by train in Europe with traveling by train in the United States.

Once you have chosen a two-part topic that you feel is not too limiting and not too broad, you must remember that a good comparison or contrast paragraph should devote an equal or nearly equal amount of space to each of the two parts. If the writer is only interested in one of the topics, the danger is that the paragraph will end up being very one-sided.

Here's an example of a one-sided contrast:

> While American trains go to only a few towns, are infrequent, and are often shabby and uncomfortable, the European train is much nicer.

The following example is a better written contrast that gives attention to both topics:

> While American trains go to only a few large cities, run very infrequently, and are often shabby and uncomfortable, European trains go to virtually every small town, are always dependable, and are clean and attractive.

EXERCISE 1 Evaluating the Two-Part Topic

Study the following topics and decide whether each topic is *too broad* for a paragraph, or whether it is *suitable* as a topic for a paragraph of comparison or contrast. Mark your choice in the appropriate space to the right of each topic.

Topic	Too broad	Suitable
1. Australia and England	________	________
2. Indian elephants and African elephants	________	________
3. California champagne and French champagne	________	________
4. Wooden furniture and plastic furniture	________	________
5. Wood and plastic	________	________
6. Paperback books and hardcover books	________	________
7. Mothers and fathers	________	________
8. Taking photographs with a flash and taking photographs using available light	________	________
9. Doctors and lawyers	________	________
10. Trains and airplanes	________	________

EXERCISE 2 Working with Comparison or Contrast

For each of the following comparison or contrast topics, complete both parts of the topic by supplying details of your own. Each topic you complete should be one that you could develop as an example of comparison or contrast.

1. Compare two friends:

   My friend ______________ with my friend ______________

2. Compare two kinds of coats:

   ______________ coats with ______________ coats

3. Compare two kinds of diets:

   The ______________ diet and the ______________ diet

4. Compare two kinds of floors:

   ______________ floors with ______________ floors

5. Compare two kinds of entertainment:

   Watching ______________ with looking at ______________

6. Compare two kinds of rice:

   ______________ rice with ______________ rice

7. Compare two places where you can study:

   Studying in the ______________ with studying in the ______________

8. Compare the wedding customs of two groups:

   What ________ do at a wedding with what ________ do at a wedding

9. Compare two textbooks:

   A textbook that has ________ with a textbook that contains ________

10. Compare two politicians:

   A local politician who ____________ with a national politician who ____________

EXERCISE 3 **Working with Comparison or Contrast**

For each of the following comparison or contrast topics, complete both parts of the topic by supplying details of your own. Each topic you complete should be one that you could develop as an example of comparison or contrast.

1. Compare two kinds of popular board games people play:

   Playing ____________ with playing ____________

2. Compare two ways of looking at movies:

   Watching movies on ____________ with going to ____________

3. Compare two careers:

   A career in ____________ with a career as a ____________

4. Compare two ways of paying for a purchase:

   Using ________ to buy something, with using ________ to buy something

5. Compare two different lifestyles:

   Living the life of a ____________ with living as a ____________

6. Compare two places to go swimming:

   Swimming in a ____________ with swimming in a ____________

7. Compare a no-frills product with the same product sold under a standard brand name (such as no-frills corn flakes with Kellogg's corn flakes):

   A no-frills ____________ with ____________

8. Compare two popular magazines:

   ____________ with ____________

9. Compare two hobbies:

   Collecting ____________ with ____________

10. Compare two kinds of tests given in school:

   The ____________ kind of test with the ____________ kind of test

Coherence in Comparison or Contrast: Two Approaches to Ordering Material

Point-by-Point Method

The first method for ordering material in a paragraph of comparison or contrast is known as the **point-by-point method.** When you use this method, you compare a point of one topic with a point of the other topic. For example, here is a paragraph from Julius Lester's *All Is Well.* In the paragraph, the writer uses the point-by-point method to compare the difficulties of being a boy with the difficulties of being a girl:

> Now, of course, I know that it was as difficult being a girl as it was a boy, if not more so. While I stood paralyzed at one end of a dance floor trying to find the courage to ask a girl for a dance, most of the girls waited in terror at the other, afraid that no one, not even I, would ask them. And while I resented having to ask a girl for a date, wasn't it also horrible to be the one who waited for the phone to ring? And how many of those girls who laughed at me making a fool of myself on the baseball diamond would have gladly given up their places on the sidelines for mine on the field?

Notice how, after the opening topic sentence, the writer uses half of each sentence to describe a boy's situation growing up and the other half of the same sentence to describe a girl's experience. This technique is effective in such a paragraph, and it is most often used in longer pieces of writing in which many points of comparison are made. This method helps the reader keep the comparison or contrast carefully in mind at each point.

If the paragraph is broken down into its parts, this is how the point-by-point method would appear.

Topic sentence: "Now, of course, I know that it was as difficult being a girl as it was a boy, if not more so."

First point, first topic: "While I stood paralyzed at one end of a dance floor trying to find the courage to ask a girl for a dance . . ."

First point, second topic: ". . . most of the girls waited in terror at the other, afraid that no one, not even I, would ask them."

Second point, first topic: "And while I resented having to ask a girl for a date, . . ."

Second point, second topic: ". . . wasn't it also horrible to be the one who waited for the phone to ring?"

Third point, first topic: "And how many of those girls who laughed at me making a fool of myself on the baseball diamond . . ."

Third point, second topic: ". . . would have gladly given up their places on the sidelines for mine on the field?"

Block Method

The second method for ordering material in a paragraph of comparison or contrast is known as the **block method.** When you use this approach, you present all of the facts and supporting details about your first topic, and then you give all of the facts and supporting details about your second topic.

Here, for example, is another version of the paragraph you studied on page 405, but this time it is written according to the block method:

> Now, of course, I know that it was as difficult being a girl as it was being a boy, if not more so. I stood paralyzed at one end of the dance floor trying to find the courage to ask a girl for a dance. I resented having to ask a girl for a date, just as I often felt foolish on the baseball diamond. On the other hand, most of the girls waited in terror at the other end of the dance floor, afraid that no one, not even I, would ask them to dance. In addition, it was a horrible situation for the girls who had to wait for the phone to ring. And how many of those girls who waited on the sidelines would have traded places with me on the baseball diamond?

Notice how the first half of this version presents all of the details about the boy, while the second part of the paragraph presents all of the information about the girls. This method is often used in shorter pieces of writing because with a shorter piece it is possible for the reader to keep the blocks of information in mind.

If the paragraph is broken down into its parts, this is how the block method would appear.

Topic sentence: "Now, of course, I know that it was as difficult being a girl as it was a boy, if not more so."

First topic, points one, two, and three: "I stood paralyzed at one end of the dance floor trying to find the courage to ask a girl for a dance. I resented having to ask a girl for a date, just as I often felt foolish on the baseball diamond."

Second topic, points one, two, and three: "On the other hand, most of the girls waited in terror at the other end of the dance floor, afraid that no one, not even I, would ask them to dance. In addition, it was a horrible situation for the girls who had to wait for the phone to ring. And how many of those girls who waited on the sidelines would have traded places with me on the baseball diamond?"

You will want to choose one of these methods before you write a comparison or contrast assignment. Keep in mind that although the block method is most often used in shorter writing assignments, such as a paragraph, you will have the chance to practice the point-by-point method as well.

EXERCISE 4

Working for Coherence: Recognizing the Two Approaches to Ordering Material

Each of the following passages is an example of comparison or contrast. Read each paragraph carefully and decide whether the writer has used the point-by-point method or the block method. Also indicate whether the piece emphasizes similarities or differences. Indicate your choices in the spaces provided after each example.

1. Female infants speak sooner, have larger vocabularies, and rarely demonstrate speech defects. (Stuttering, for instance, occurs almost exclusively among boys.) Girls exceed boys in language abilities, and this early linguistic bias often prevails throughout life. Girls read sooner, learn foreign languages more easily, and, as a result, are more

likely to enter occupations involving language mastery. Boys, in contrast, show an early visual superiority. They are also clumsier, performing poorly at something like arranging a row of beads, but excel at other activities calling on total body coordination. Their attentional mechanisms are also different. A boy will react to an inanimate object as quickly as he will to a person. A male baby will often ignore the mother and babble to a blinking light, fixate on a geometric figure, and, at a later point, manipulate it and attempt to take it apart.

__________ Point-by-Point __________ Block

__________ Similarities __________ Differences

2. Each man had, to begin with, the great virtue of utter tenacity and fidelity. Grant fought his way down the Mississippi Valley in spite of acute personal discouragement and profound military handicaps. Lee hung on in the trenches at Petersburg after hope itself had died. In each man there was an indomitable quality . . . the born fighter's refusal to give up as long as he can still remain on his feet and lift his two fists. Daring and resourcefulness they had, too; the ability to think faster and move faster than the enemy. These were the qualities which gave Lee the dazzling campaigns of Second Manassas and Chancellorsville and won Vicksburg for Grant.

__________ Point-by-Point __________ Block

__________ Similarities __________ Differences

3. I first realized that the act of writing was about to enter a new era five years ago when I went to see an editor at *The New York Times.* As I was ushered through the vast city room I felt that I had strayed into the wrong office. The place was clean and carpeted and quiet. As I passed long rows of desks, I saw that almost every desk had its own computer terminal and its own solemn occupant—a man or a woman typing at the computer keyboard or reading what was on the terminal screen. I saw no typewriters, no paper, no mess. It was a cool and sterile environment; the drones at their machines could have been processing insurance claims or tracking a spacecraft in orbit. What they didn't look like were newspaper people, and what the place didn't look like was a newspaper office. I knew how a newspaper office should look and sound and smell—I worked in one for thirteen years. The paper was the *New York Herald Tribune,* and its city room, wide as a city block, was dirty and disheveled. Reporters wrote on ancient typewriters that filled the air with clatter; copy editors labored on coffee-stained desks over what the reporters had written. Crumpled balls of paper littered the floor and filled the wastebaskets—failed efforts to write a good lead or a decent sentence. The walls were grimy—every few years they were painted over in a less restful shade of eye-rest green—and the atmosphere was hazy with the smoke of cigarettes and cigars. At the very center the city editor, a giant named L. L. Engelking, bellowed his displeasure with the day's work, his voice a rumbling volcano in our lives. I thought it was the most beautiful place in the world.

__________ Point-by-Point __________ Block

__________ Similarities __________ Differences

4. We went fishing the first morning. I felt the same damp moss covering the worms in the bait can, and saw the dragonfly alight on the tip of my rod as it hovered a few inches from the surface of the water. It was the arrival of this fly that convinced me beyond any doubt that everything was as it always had been, that the years were a mirage and there had been no years. The small waves were the same, chucking the rowboat under the chin as we fished at anchor, and the boat was the same boat, the same color green and the ribs broken in the same places, and under the floor-boards the same freshwater leavings and debris—the dead helgramite, the wisps of moss, the rusty discarded fishhook, the dried blood from yesterday's catch. We stared silently at the tips of our rods, at the dragonflies that came and went. I lowered the tip of mine into the water, tentatively, pensively dislodging the fly, which darted two feet away, poised, darted two feet back, and came to rest again a little farther up the rod. There had been no years between the ducking of this dragonfly and the other one—the one that was part of memory. I looked at the boy, who was silently watching his fly, and it was my hands that held his rod, my eyes watching. I felt dizzy and didn't know which rod I was at the end of.

__________ Point-by-Point __________ Block

__________ Similarities __________ Differences

5. The streets are littered with cigarette and cigar butts, paper wrappings, particles of food, and dog droppings. How long before they become indistinguishable from the gutters of medieval towns when slop pails were emptied from the second-story windows? Thousands of New York women no longer attend evening services in their churches. They fear assault as they walk the few steps from bus or subway station to their apartment houses. The era of the medieval footpad has returned, and, as in the Dark Ages, the cry for help brings no assistance, for even grown men know they would be cut down before the police could arrive.

__________ Point-by-Point __________ Block

__________ Similarities __________ Differences

EXERCISE 5 **Using the Point-by-Point and Block Methods for Comparison or Contrast**

Passage number three, given on page 407, uses the block method to make its points of contrast. Rewrite the material using the point-by-point approach.

EXERCISE 6 **Using the Point-by-Point and Block Methods for Comparison or Contrast**

Use the list below to write a comparison or contrast paragraph on life in the city compared with life in a suburban area. Review the list provided and add to it any of your own ideas. Omit any you do not wish to use. Then, selecting either the block method or the point-by-point method, write a comparison or contrast paragraph.

Topic sentence: If I could move back to the city from the suburbs, I know I would be happy.

The following points provide details that relate to living in the city and living in a suburban community:

Topic I **Advantages of the city**	**Topic II** **Disadvantages of the suburbs**
a. A short ride on the bus or subway gets you to work.	a. Commuting to work from th suburb to the city is often long and exhausting.
b. Men are as visible as women in the neighborhood.	b. Because most men in the suburbs work in the city, few of them are active in the suburban community.
c. The architecture and ethnic diversity is stimulating.	c. The sameness of people and streets is monotonous.
d. Local shopping for nearly everything can be done on foot.	d. Highway shopping requires a car.
e. People walk in their neighborhoods.	e. People use cars to go everywhere.

Notice that the writer who created this list emphasized the disadvantages of the suburbs, in contrast to the advantages of the city. No mention was made, for example, of crime in the city. A writer could create another list, this time from the point of view of a person who prefers the suburbs.

Working for Coherence: Using Transitions

A number of words and phrases are useful to keep in mind when writing the comparison or contrast paper. Some of them are used in phrases, some in clauses.

TRANSITIONS COMMONLY USED IN *COMPARISON/CONTRAST*

Transitions for Comparison	*Transitions for Contrast*	
similar to	on the contrary	though
similarly	on the other hand	unlike
like	in contrast with	even though
likewise	in spite of	nevertheless
just like	despite	however
just as	instead of	but
furthermore	different from	otherwise
moreover	whereas	except for
equally	while	and yet
again	although	still
also		
too		
so		

Notice the different uses of *like* and *as:*
Like is a preposition and is used in the prepositional phrase *like me.*

My sister is just *like* me.

As is a subordinate conjunction and is used in the clause below with a subject and a verb.

My sister sews every evening, *as* does her older daughter.

EXERCISE 7 Using Transitions in Comparisons and Contrasts

Each of the following examples is made up of two sentences. Read both sentences and decide whether the idea being expressed is one of comparison or contrast. Next, combine the two sentences by using a transition you have chosen from the list at the top of the page. Then write your new sentence on the lines provided. You may reword your new sentence slightly in order to make it grammatically correct. An example has been done for you.

Mr. Johnson is a teacher.

His wife is a teacher.

First you decide that the two sentences show a comparison. Then you combine the two by using an appropriate transition:

Mr. Johnson is a teacher just like his wife.
or
Mr. Johnson is a teacher; his wife is too.

1. Dr. Rappole has a reputation for excellent bedside manners.

Dr. Connolly is very withdrawn and speaks so softly that it is almost impossible to understand what he has said.

Your combined sentence: ____

____

____

2. In the United States, interest in soccer has become apparent only in recent years.

Soccer has always been immensely popular in Brazil.

Your combined sentence: ____

____

____

3. Hemingway's book *Death in the Afternoon* deals with the theme of man against nature.

The same writer's novel *The Old Man and the Sea* deals with the theme of man against nature.

Your combined sentence: ____

____

____

4. Amy is carefree and fun-loving, with little interest in school.

Janet, Amy's sister, is so studious and hard-working that she is always on the honor roll.

Your combined sentence: ______________________________

____

____

5. The apartment had almost no furniture, was badly in need of painting, and felt chilly even though I was wearing a coat.

The other apartment was attractively furnished, had been freshly painted, and was warm enough so that I had to take off my coat.

Your combined sentence: ______________________________

____

____

EXERCISE 8 Using Transitions in Comparisons and Contrasts

First, identify each of the following examples as comparison or contrast. Then combine the two sentences by using a transition from the list on page 409. Finally, write your new sentence on the lines provided.

1. Oprah Winfrey's daytime talk show deals with current controversial issues that are of importance to society.

David Letterman's program gives people light entertainment in the evening.

Your combined sentence: ______________________________

____

____

2. Shakespeare's *Romeo and Juliet* is a famous love story that takes place in Italy.

West Side Story is a modern-day version of Shakespeare's love story that takes place in New York City.

Your combined sentence: ______________________________

____

____

3. The French Revolution was directed by the common people.

The Russian Revolution was directed by an elite group of thinkers.

Your combined sentence: ______________________________

____

____

4. Some scientists believe that dinosaurs became extinct because they ran out of food.

Some scientists think that dinosaurs were victims of radiation from a meteor from outer space.

Your combined sentence: ______________________________

____

____

5. The Museum of Modern Art in New York City shows paintings, photographs, movies, and many other forms of twentieth-century art.

The Metropolitan Museum of Art in New York City contains sculptures, paintings, and other forms of art that date from the beginning of recorded history.

Your combined sentence: ______________________________

____

____

EXERCISE 9 Using Transitions in Comparisons and Contrasts

First, identify each of the following examples as comparison or contrast. Then combine the two sentences by using a transition from the list on page 409. Finally, write your new sentence on the lines provided.

1. A ballet dancer trains for years in order to master all aspects of dancing.

A football player puts in years of practice in order to learn the game from every angle.

Your combined sentence: ______________________________

____

____

2. The University of Chicago is a large urban university that has the resources of a big city as part of its attraction for faculty and students.

Fredonia State College is a small rural college that has beautiful surroundings as part of its attraction.

Your combined sentence: ______________________________

____

____

3. Ice cream, a popular dessert for many years, has many calories and added chemicals to give it more flavor.

Tofutti is a dessert made of processed soybeans that is low in calories and contains no harmful additives.

Your combined sentence: ______________________________

____

____

4. Nelson Rockefeller gave much of his time and money for education and the arts.

Andrew Carnegie set up a famous foundation to support learning and artistic achievement.

Your combined sentence: ____

____

____

5. *A Soldier's Play* is a play that has a single setting for all of its action.

A Soldier's Story, a film based on the play, is a movie that is able to use many different settings to present all of its action.

Your combined sentence: ____

____

____

Writing the Comparison or Contrast Paragraph Step-by-Step

To learn a skill that has so many different demands, the best approach is to work step-by-step so that one aspect can be worked on at a time. This will ensure that you are not missing a crucial point or misunderstanding a part of the whole. There certainly are other ways to go about writing an effective paragraph, but here is one logical method you can use to achieve results.

STEPS FOR WRITING THE COMPARISON OR CONTRAST PARAGRAPH

1. After you have chosen your two-part topic, plan your topic sentence.
2. List all your ideas for points that could be compared or contrasted.
3. Then choose the three or four most important points from your list.
4. Decide whether you want to use the point-by-point method or the block method of organizing your paragraph.
5. Write at least one complete sentence for each of the points you have chosen from your list.
6. Write a concluding statement that summarizes the main points, makes a judgment, or emphasizes what you believe is the most important point.
7. Finally, copy your sentences into standard paragraph form.
8. Always make a final check for spelling errors and other mistakes, such as omitted words. When you use a computer spellcheck feature, keep in mind that this feature will only alert you to spellings that do not match words in its dictionary. If you type *there* when you mean *their,* the spellchecker will see an acceptable word. When it comes to a final editing, there is no substitute for your own careful reading.

EXERCISE 10 **Writing the Comparison or Contrast Paragraph Step-by-Step**

This exercise will guide you through the construction of a comparison or contrast paragraph. Start with the suggested topic. Use the eight steps to help you work through each stage of the writing process.

Topic: Compare or contrast how you spend your leisure time with how your parents or a friend spends leisure time.

1. Topic sentence: ______________________________

____

2. Make a list of possible comparisons or contrasts.

a. ______________________________

b. ______________________________

c. ______________________________

d. ______________________________

e. ______________________________

f. ______________________________

g. ______________________________

h. ______________________________

i. ______________________________

j. ______________________________

3. Circle the three or four comparisons or contrasts that you believe are most important and put them in order.

4. Choose either the point-by-point method or the block method.

5. Using your final list, write at least one sentence for each comparison or contrast you have chosen.

a. ______________________________

____

b. ______________________________

____

c. ______________________________

____

d. ______________________________

____

e. ______________________________

____

f. ______________________________

____

g. ______________________________

____

6. Write a concluding statement. ______________________________

____

____

7. On a separate piece of paper, copy your sentences into standard paragraph form.

8. Do a final reading to check for errors and omissions.

EXERCISE 11 **Writing the Comparison or Contrast Paragraph Step-by-Step**

This exercise will guide you through the construction of a comparison or contrast paragraph. Start with the suggested topic. Use the eight steps to help you work through each stage of the writing process.

Topic: Compare or contrast going to work with going on to college immediately after high school.

1. Topic sentence: ______________________________

____

2. Make a list of possible comparisons or contrasts.

a. ______________________________
b. ______________________________
c. ______________________________
d. ______________________________
e. ______________________________
f. ______________________________
g. ______________________________
h. ______________________________
i. ______________________________
j. ______________________________

3. Circle the three or four comparisons or contrasts that you believe are most important and put them in order.

4. Choose either the point-by-point method or the block method.

5. Using your final list, write at least one sentence for each comparison or contrast you have chosen.

a. ______________________________

____

b. ______________________________

____

c. ______________________________

____

d. ______________________________

____

e. ______________________________

____

f. ______________________________

____

g. ______________________________

____

6. Write a concluding statement. ______________________________

____

____

7. On a separate piece of paper, copy your sentences into standard paragraph form.

8. Do a final reading to check for errors and omissions.

EXERCISE 12 **Writing the Comparison or Contrast Paragraph Step-by-Step**

This exercise will guide you through the construction of a comparison or contrast paragraph. Start with the suggested topic. Use the eight steps to help you work through each stage of the writing process.

Topic: Compare or contrast the styles of two television personalities (or two public figures often in the news).

1. Topic sentence: ______________________________

____

2. Make a list of possible comparisons or contrasts.

a. ______________________________

b. ______________________________

c. ______________________________

d. ______________________________

e. ______________________________

f. ______________________________

g. ______________________________

h. ______________________________

i. ______________________________

j. ______________________________

3. Circle the three or four comparisons or contrasts that you believe are most important and put them in order.

4. Choose either the point-by-point method or the block method.

5. Using your final list, write at least one sentence for each comparison or contrast you have chosen.

a. ______________________________

____

b. ______________________________

____

c. ______________________________

____

d. ______________________________

____

e. ______________________________

____

f. ______________________________

____

g. ______________________________

____

6. Write a concluding statement. ______________________________

____

____

7. On a separate piece of paper, copy your sentences into standard paragraph form.

8. Do a final reading to check for errors and omissions.

On Your Own: Writing Comparison or Contrast Paragraphs

Contrasting Two Different Perceptions toward a Topic

Assignment 1 Write a paragraph in which you contrast two perceptions toward a topic. The paragraph on page 418 contrasts the Disney film depiction of the Pocahontas story with what we know to be more historically correct about the real Pocahontas.

MODEL PARAGRAPH: TWO VERSIONS OF THE POCAHONTAS STORY

The Disney version of the Pocahontas story is not an accurate portrayal of what we know to be true. A seventeenth-century portrait of Pocahontas reveals her to be buxom, full-faced, and strong, not the Barbie-like glamour girl of Disney. John Smith, too, is portrayed inaccurately in the film. Far from the young blond heroic figure shown in the movie, John Smith was in actuality a bearded and weathered-looking man of thirty when he met Pocahontas. The dramatic version of romance and rescue is another historical inaccuracy of the Disney film. Most historians contend that the supposed "rescue" of John Smith was in fact a farce. The Powhatans, historians claim, may have been adopting Smith into their tribe through a ritual that required a little play acting. So, while Pocahontas may have rescued Smith, the circumstances of that rescue may have been very different from the film's depiction. Furthermore, there is no historical evidence to support a romance between Pocahontas and John Smith as the movie shows. The unfortunate reality was that Pocahontas was taken captive by the English and forced to marry an English tobacco planter named John Rolfe. The ending of the film is certainly the final blow to what we know to be fact. Pocahontas did not, as Disney suggests, stay in North America while John Smith sailed into the distance toward his native England. Instead, she traveled to England with Rolfe, her new husband. On the return trip to her native North America, at the young age of twenty-two, Pocahontas fell ill, probably with smallpox, and died.

Compare or contrast two perceptions you have had of the same topic. Choose from one of the topics suggested below or a topic you think of yourself.

Ten suggested topics

1. A sports figure's public image, versus details of his or her private life, exposed by the media
2. A politician's promises before an election with those after an election
3. A "friend" before you win the lottery and after
4. Attitudes toward smoking twenty years ago contrasted with attitudes today
5. A person's reputation in the past with his or her reputation today
6. An actor or musician on television or stage with the same actor off-stage
7. Baseball years ago and baseball now
8. Attitudes toward AIDS when the virus was first discovered contrasted with attitudes toward the disease today
9. Traditional portrayal of Native Americans (in old films, for example) with portrayals today

10. How a member of your family acts at home, contrasted with how that same person acts in public

Comparing Two Cultures

Assignment 2

Write a paragraph in which you compare two cultures, or an aspect of culture that may be observed in two societies. The following paragraph was written by Brenda David, an American teacher who worked with schoolchildren in Milan, Italy, for several years.

MODEL PARAGRAPH: CHILDREN OF TWO NATIONS

All young children, whatever their culture, are alike in their charm and innocence—in being a clean slate on which the wonders and ways of the world are yet to be written. But during the three years I worked in a school in Milan, I learned that American and Italian children are different in several ways. First, young American children tend to be active, enthusiastic, and inquisitive. Italian children, on the other hand, tend to be passive, quiet, and not particularly inquisitive. They usually depend on their parents to tell them what to do. Second, American children show their independence while their Italian counterparts are still looking to their parents and grandparents to tell them what to do or not do. Third, and most important to those who question the influence of environment on a child, the American children generally surpass their Italian schoolmates in math, mechanical, and scientific abilities. But American children are overshadowed by their Italian counterparts in their language, literature, art, and music courses. Perhaps the differences, which those of us at the school confirmed in an informal study, were to be expected. After all, what priority do Americans give to the technological skills? And what value do Italians—with the literature of poets and authors like Boccaccio, the works of Michelangelo, and the music of the world-famous La Scala opera at Milan—place on the cultural arts?

Ten suggested topics

Compare or contrast:

1. Mexican cooking with Chinese cooking
2. Marriage customs in Africa and in the United States
3. Attitudes toward women's roles in Saudi Arabia and in the United States
4. Folk dancing in two countries
5. Raising children in China and raising them in the United States
6. Urban people with small-town people
7. The reputation of a place with the reality of the place as you found it
8. The culture of your neighborhood with the general culture of our society

9. The culture you live in now with the culture in which your parents were raised
10. Medical care in our society with the medical care of another society

Comparing a Place Then and Now

Assignment 3 Write a paragraph in which you compare the appearance of a place you knew when you were growing up with the appearance of that same place now. The following paragraph compares a small city as it was some years ago and how it appeared to the writer on a recent visit.

MODEL PARAGRAPH: THIRTY YEARS LATER

As I drove up Swede Hill, I realized that the picture I had in my mind all these years was largely a romantic one. It was here that my father had boarded, as a young man of eighteen, with a widow who rented rooms in her house. Now the large old wooden frame houses were mostly two-family homes; no single family could afford to heat them in the winter. The porches which had once been beautiful and where people had passed their summer evenings had peeling paint and were in poor condition. No one now stopped to talk; the only sounds to be heard were those of cars whizzing past. The immigrants who had come to this country and worked hard to put their children through school were now elderly and mostly alone, since their educated children could find no jobs in the small upstate city. From the top of the hill I looked down fondly upon the town built on the hills and noticed that a new and wider highway now went through the town. My father would have liked that; he would not have had to complain about Sunday drives on Foote Avenue. In the distance I could see the large shopping mall which now had most of the business in the surrounding area and which had forced several local businesses to close. Now the center of town no longer hummed with activity, as it once had. My town was not the same place I had known, and I could see that changes were taking place that would eventually transform the entire area.

Ten suggested topics Compare or contrast a place as it appears now with how it appeared some years ago:

1. A barber shop or beauty salon
2. A house of worship
3. A local "corner store"
4. A friend's home
5. Your elementary school
6. A local bank
7. A downtown shopping area
8. A restaurant or diner

9. An undeveloped place such as an open field or wooded area
10. A favorite local gathering place

Comparing Two Approaches to a Subject

Assignment 4

Write a paragraph in which you compare two ways of considering a particular topic. The following paragraph compares two approaches to the art of healing—the traditional medical approach and the approach that involves less dependence on chemicals and more reliance on the body's natural defense system.

MODEL PARAGRAPH: THE MEDICAL PROFESSION AND NATURAL HEALING

Natural healing is basically a much more conservative approach to health care than traditional medical practice. Traditional medical practice aims for the quick cure by means of introducing substances or instruments into the body which are highly antagonistic to whatever is causing the disease. A doctor wants to see results, and he or she wants you to appreciate the fact that traditional medicine is what is delivering those results to you. Because of this desire for swift, decisive victories over disease, traditional medicine tends to be dramatic, risky, and expensive. Natural healing takes a slower, more organic approach to the problem of disease. It first recognizes that the human body is superbly equipped to resist disease and heal injuries. But when disease does take hold or an injury occurs, the first instinct in natural healing is to see what might be done to strengthen that natural resistance and those natural healing agents so that they can act against the disease more effectively. Results are not expected to occur overnight, but neither are they expected to occur at the expense of the body, which may experience side effects or dangerous complications.

Ten suggested topics

Compare or contrast:

1. Retiring or working after age sixty-five
2. Owning your own business or working for someone else
3. Two views on abortion
4. Two attitudes toward divorce
5. Two political viewpoints
6. Your lifestyle today and five years ago
7. Mothers who stay home and those who work away from home
8. Buying U.S.–made products or buying foreign-made goods
9. Two attitudes on the "right to die" issue
10. Two attitudes toward religion

Comparing Male Attitudes and Female Attitudes

Assignment 5

Some observers believe that males share similar attitudes toward certain subjects, while females seem to have a similar way of thinking on certain other topics. Some observers believe that such conclusions are nothing more than stereotypes and that people should not be divided in this way. The following paragraph reports that recent studies indicate a possible biological basis for some of the differences between males and females.

MODEL PARAGRAPH: DIFFERENCES BETWEEN BOYS AND GIRLS

Recent scientific research has shown that differences in behavior between males and females may have their origins in biological differences in the brain. Shortly after birth, females are more sensitive than males to certain types of sounds, and by the age of five months a female baby can recognize photographs of familiar people, while a boy of that age can rarely accomplish this. Researchers also found that girls tend to speak sooner than boys, read sooner than they do, and learn foreign languages more easily than boys do. On the other hand, boys show an early visual superiority over girls and they are better than girls at working with three-dimensional space. When preschool girls and boys are asked to mentally work with an object, the girls are not as successful as the boys. In this case, as in several others, the girls are likely to give verbal descriptions while the boys are able to do the actual work in their minds.

Ten suggested topics

In a paragraph, compare or contrast what you believe are male and female attitudes on one of the following topics:

1. Cooking
2. Sports
3. The nursing profession
4. Child care
5. The construction trade
6. Military careers
7. A career in science
8. Hobbies
9. Friendship
10. Clothing

EXPLORING ONLINE

Read further about the structure of comparison/contrast paragraphs:

http://www.powa.org/thesfrms.htm

WORKING TOGETHER

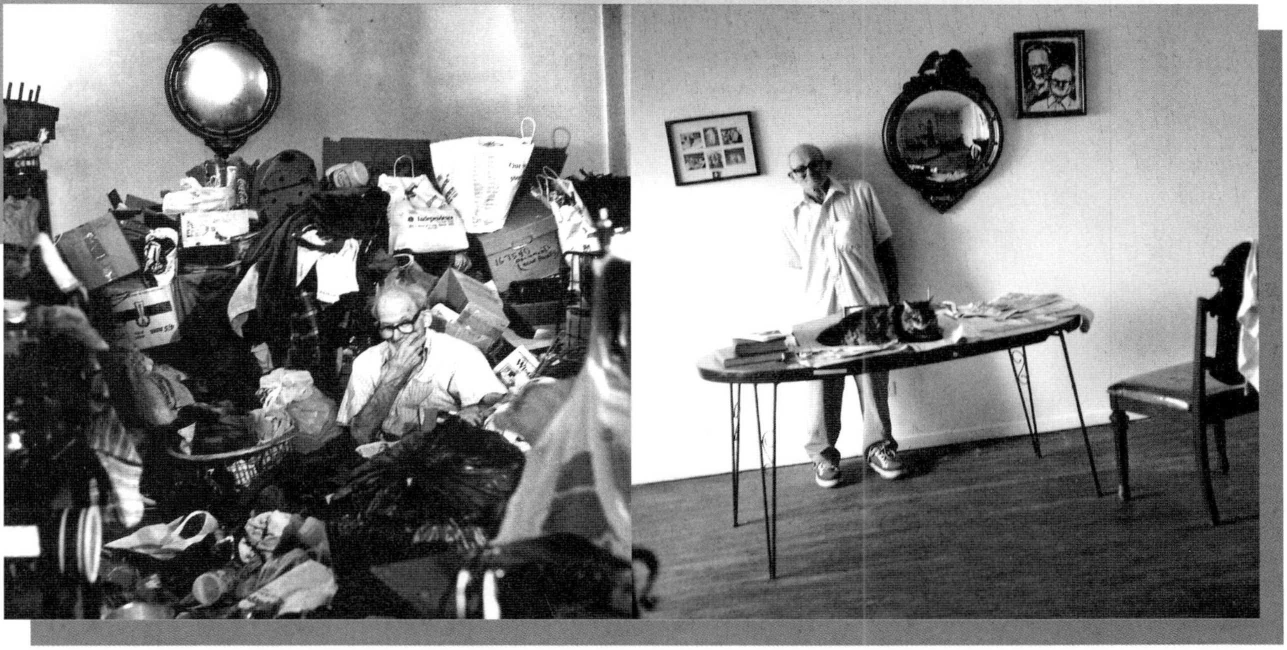

A BEFORE AND AFTER STORY

Below is an account of a radical change in one man's life. When you have read this before and after report (which uses the block method), share with your classmates some stories you recall that tell of changes in the lives of people you have known. Then write a before and after story of your own. Use the chart provided on the next page to help plan your response to the two-part topic.

Before

Since I was 15, I've saved all kinds of stuff: bureau handles, small bottles, marbles, mirrors, nuts, screws, wire, cord, bathtub stoppers, mothballs, empty cigarette packs, frying pans, pencils that say different things on them, trusses, parking tickets. In 1997, my brother Harry, with whom I lived, slipped on some of my papers and got brought to a nursing home. The social worker wouldn't let him come back unless I got rid of my collections. So I bought a bus pass and visited him once a week. He died last year at 85. If he'd had a hobby like me, he might have lived longer. I liked living in my junk, and I always knew where everything was. In the living room, the junk came up to about my chest. In the bedroom, it wasn't too bad; it just came up to my knees. I made paths to get around. It made me feel important. But I guess I overdid it. The landlord wanted me to get rid of my junk. A third of my neighbors wouldn't talk to me. I suspected I might get evicted. So this summer I had to let my junk go.

After

My nephew cleaned it out with some friends of his. It took 10 days. I wasn't there. When I came back, I was disappointed. I thought more stuff would be saved. I had an empty feeling, like I was robbed. I lost memories of my four brothers and my mother. But things happen—what can you do? I'm too old to worry anymore. All that's left is my necktie collection and my cat, Wagging. The emptiness is a little hard to get used to. For one thing, the traffic noise is very loud now. And I feel hollow. My junk was sort of a freedom. I put so much work into saving—years and years—and it's suddenly gone. It's like somebody had died, a fire or an earthquake. It's like the change from hot to cold water. I may start saving certain things, like books, but I don't go out as much as I used to, so I can't collect as much. From now on, I'll have fewer hobbies.

Photographs by Gigi Cohen

continued on next page

Prepare to write a comparison and contrast paragraph by noting points of comparison and contrast. Use the chart provided below.

Points to Compare or Contrast	*Before*	*After*
Point 1		
Point 2		
Point 3		
Point 4		
Point 5		

Online Activity

Type "Before and After Photos" into your search engine, and find one pair of photos that appeals to you. Write a paragraph comparing the two photos.

Chapter 23 Developing Paragraphs: Cause and Effect

Preview

What is the connection between two events? Are they coincidental, accidental, or somehow connected? With cause and effect, the writer considers these relationships. In this chapter, you will focus on the following:

- Avoiding errors in *logic*
- If the connection is causal, what are the *immediate causes or underlying causes?*
- If the connection is causal, what are the *immediate effects or long-term effects?*
- Improving coherence by using transitional phrases common to cause and effect
- Practice your own cause or effect paragraphs
    - Using a step-by-step approach
    - Using model paragraphs with suggested topics

Key Term

Cause and effect

Charts

List of transitions used in cause and effect
Steps for writing cause and effect paragraphs

What Is Cause and Effect?

Cause and effect is the method of developing ideas that looks for the relationship between two actions or two events, one of which we conclude is the reason for the other.

People have always looked at the world and asked the questions, "Why did this happen?" or "What will be the result?" Ancient societies created beautiful myths and legends to explain the origin of the universe and our place in it, while modern civilization has emphasized scientific methods of observation to find the cause of a disease or to determine why the planet Mars appears to be covered by canals. When we examine the spiritual or physical mysteries of our world, we are trying to discover the connections or links between events. In this chapter, we will refer to connections between events as ***causal relationships.***

Causal relationships are part of our daily lives and provide a way of understanding the cause, result, or consequence of a particular event. The search for cause or effect is a bit like detective work. Probing an event is a way of searching for clues to discover what caused an event or what result it will have in the future.

For example, we might ask the question, "Why did the car break down just after it came back from the garage?" as a way of searching for the cause of the car's new problem. Or we might ask, "What will be the side effects of taking a certain medicine?" This search for connections can be complex. Often the logical analysis of a problem reveals more than one possible explanation. Sometimes the best one can do is find possible causes or probable effects. In the exercises that follow, you will be asked to search for causal relationships.

Practice Become familiar with causal relationships by thinking through a few typical situations signaled by the following expressions:

1. If . . . . then

If you ____________, **then** you will ____________

____.

2. The cause or reason . . . . the result, consequence, or effect

Because I ____________, the **result** was that I ____________

____.

3. The problem . . . . the solution ____________

____________ could be **solved** by ____________.

EXERCISE 1

Finding Causes and Effects in Paragraphs

Below are two paragraphs about the same topic: headaches. One paragraph considers causes and the other looks at some of the effects that recurring headaches have on people's lives. In each case, list the causal relationships suggested in the paragraph.

1. CAUSE: Explaining WHY

Headaches can have several causes. Many people think that the major cause of headache is nervous tension, but there is strong evidence that suggests diet and environment as possible factors. Some people get headaches because they are dependent on caffeine. Other people may be allergic to salt, or they may have low blood sugar. Still other people are allergic to household chemicals including polishes, waxes, bug killers, and paint. If they can manage to avoid these substances, their headaches tend to go away. When a person has recurring headaches, it is worthwhile to look for the underlying cause, especially if the result of that search is freedom from pain.

What causes a headache?

1. ______________________________

2. ______________________________

a. ______________________________

b. ______________________________

c. ______________________________

3. ______________________________

a. ______________________________

b. ______________________________

c. ______________________________

d. ______________________________

2. EFFECT: Understanding or predicting RESULTS, CONSEQUENCES, EFFECTS, SOLUTIONS

Recurring headaches can have several disruptive effects on a person's life. Severe headaches are more than temporary inconveniences. In many cases, these headaches make a person nauseous to the point that he or she must go to bed. Sleep is often interrupted because of the pain. This worsens the physical and emotional state of the sufferer. For those who try to maintain a normal lifestyle, drugs are often relied on to get through the day. Such drugs, of course, can have negative side effects. Productivity on a job can certainly be reduced, even to the point of regular absences. Finally, perhaps the most distressing aspect of all this is the seemingly unpredictable occurrence of these headaches. The interruption to a person's family life is enormous: cancelling plans in the last minute and straining relationships with friends and family. It is no wonder that many of these people feel discouraged and even depressed.

What are some of the effects of headaches?

1. ______________________________

2. ______________________________

3. ______________________________

4. ______________________________

5. ______________________________

EXPLORING ONLINE

Explore the causes and effects of feline diabetes:

http://www.netpets.com/cats/reference/diabetes.html

EXERCISE 2 **Separating the Cause from the Effect**

In each sentence, separate the cause, problem, or reason from the effect, solution or result. Remember the cause is not necessarily given first.

1. More than half of the mothers with children under one year of age work outside the home which has resulted in the unprecedented need for day-care in this country.

   cause ______________________________

   ____

   effect ______________________________

   ____

2. In 1995, two-thirds of all preschool children had mothers who worked, and four out of five school-age children had working mothers, facts that led to increased strains on the day-care system.

   cause ______________________________

   ____

   effect ______________________________

   ____

3. In one national survey, over half the working mothers reported that they had either changed jobs or cut back on their hours in order to be more available for their children.

   problem ______________________________

   ____

   solution ______________________________

   ____

4. Many mothers who work do so only when their children are in school, while other mothers work only occasionally during the school year because they feel their children need the supervision of a parent.

   cause ______________________________

   ____

   effect ______________________________

   ____

5. Many mothers experience deep emotional crises as a result of their need to combine the financial obligations of their home with their own emotional needs as parents.

   problem ______________________________

   ____

   result ______________________________

   ____

Working with Cause and Effect: Recognizing Connections between Events

Here is an example of a possible error in logic:

> Every time I try to write an essay in the evening, I have trouble getting to sleep. Therefore, writing must prevent me from sleeping.

In this case, writing may indeed be a stimulant that prevents the person from sleeping. However, if the person is serious about finding the cause of insomnia, he or she must observe whether any other ***factors*** may be to blame. For instance, if the person is drinking several cups of coffee while writing each evening, this could be a more likely cause of why the person is not sleeping.

AVOID THESE COMMON ERRORS IN LOGIC

1. Do not confuse coincidence or chronological sequence with evidence.
2. Look for underlying causes beneath the obvious ones and for far-reaching effects beyond the ones that first come to mind. Often what appears to be a single cause or a single effect is a much more complex problem.

EXERCISE 3 **Looking for the Causal Relationship**

Study each of the following situations. In each case, if the sequence of events is merely coincidental or chronological, put a "T" for "time" in the space provided. If the relationship is most likely causal, put a "C." Be prepared to explain your answers in class.

______ **1.** Every time I carry my umbrella, it doesn't rain. I am carrying my umbrella today; therefore, it won't rain.

______ **2.** We put the fertilizer on the grass. A week later the grass grew two inches and turned a deeper green.

______ **3.** On Tuesday morning, I walked under a ladder. On Wednesday morning, I walked into my office and was told I had lost my job.

______ **4.** The child grew up helping her mother cook. In adulthood, she became a famous chef.

______ **5.** Tar and nicotine from cigarettes damage the lungs. People who smoke cigarettes increase their chances of dying from lung cancer.

______ **6.** A political scandal was exposed in the city on Friday. On Saturday night, only twenty-four hours later, a power blackout occurred in the city.

______ **7.** Increasing numbers of tourists came to the island last year. The economy of the island reached new heights.

______ **8.** Many natural disasters have occurred this year. The world must be coming to an end.

_______________ **9.** The factory in a certain town decided to relocate to another country. The town officials invited different industries to consider moving to the town.

_______________ **10.** That woman sings beautifully. She must have an equally beautiful personality.

EXERCISE 4 **Underlying Causes**

Below are five topics. For each topic, give a possible immediate or direct cause and then give a possible underlying cause. Discuss your answers in class. An example has been done for you.

Causes of a particular disease, such as tuberculosis

Immediate or direct cause: contact with a carrier of the disease

Underlying cause: weakened immune system due to poor nutrition

1. Causes for being selected out of several candidates for a position

Immediate cause _______________

Underlying cause _______________

2. Causes for immigrants coming to the United States

Immediate cause _______________

Underlying cause _______________

3. Causes for spanking a child

Immediate cause _______________

Underlying cause _______________

4. Causes for an unreasonable fear you have

Immediate cause _______________

Underlying cause _______________

5. Causes for a bad habit you have

Immediate cause _______________

Underlying cause _______________

EXERCISE 5 **Immediate or Long-Term Effects**

Below are five topics. For each topic give an immediate effect and then give a possible long-term effect. Discuss your answers in class. An example has been done for you.

Possible effects of using credit cards

Immediate effect: money available on the spot for purchases

Long-term effect: greater cost due to interest payments

1. Effects of horror movies on young children

Immediate effect _______________

Long-term effect _______________

2. Effects of tuition increases in four-year colleges

Immediate effect ______________________________

Long-term effect ______________________________

3. Effects of increased carjackings on people's driving habits

Immediate effect ______________________________

Long-term effect ______________________________

4. Effects of a microwave oven on how a family lives

Immediate effect ______________________________

Long-term effect ______________________________

5. Effects of having a family member with special needs

Immediate effect ______________________________

Long-term effect ______________________________

Working for Coherence: Using Transitions

Several transitional words and expressions are particularly useful when writing about causes or effects. You will need to feel comfortable using these words and expressions, and you will need to know what punctuation is required.

TRANSITIONS COMMONLY USED IN *CAUSE* AND *EFFECT*

common transitions for *cause:*

because
caused by
results from
the reason is that . . . (followed by an independent clause)
since

common transitions for *effect:*

accordingly
as a result, resulted in
consequently
for this reason
so, so that
then, therefore, thus

EXERCISE 6 **Using Transitional Words and Expressions for Cause**

Use each of the following words or phrases in a sentence that demonstrates your understanding of its use for expressing **causal** relationships.

1. to be caused by

2. because (of)

3. resulted from

4. the reason is that (followed by an independent clause)

5. since

EXERCISE 7 **Using Transitional Words and Expressions for Effect**

Use each of the following words or phrases in a complete sentence. This will demonstrate your understanding of how the word or phrase is used to point to an effect.

1. accordingly

2. as a result

3. results in

4. consequently

5. for this reason

6. so

____

____

7. therefore

____

____

Writing the Cause or Effect Paragraph Step-by-Step

To learn a skill that has so many different demands, the best approach is to work step-by-step so that one aspect can be worked on at a time. This will ensure that you are not missing a crucial point or misunderstanding a part of the whole. There certainly are other ways to go about writing an effective paragraph, but here is one logical method you can use to achieve results.

STEPS FOR WRITING THE CAUSE OR EFFECT PARAGRAPH

1. After you have chosen your topic, plan your topic sentence.
2. Brainstorm by jotting down all possible causes or effects. Ask others for their thoughts. Do research if necessary. Consider long-range effects or underlying causes.
3. Then choose the three or four best points from your list.
4. Decide on the best order for these points. (One way to organize them is from least important to most important.)
5. Write at least one complete sentence for each of the causes or effects you have chosen from your list.
6. Write a concluding statement.
7. On a separate piece of paper or on the computer, copy your sentences into standard paragraph form.
8. Always make a final check for spelling errors and other mistakes, such as omitted words. When you use a computer spellcheck feature, keep in mind that this feature will only alert you to spellings that do not match words in its dictionary. If you type *there* when you mean *their,* the spellchecker will see an acceptable word. When it comes to a final editing, there is no substitute for your own careful reading.

EXERCISE 8 **Writing the Causal Paragraph Step-by-Step**

This exercise will guide you through the causal paragraph. Start with the suggested topic. Use the eight steps to help you work through each stage of the writing process.

Topic: Why do so few Americans want to learn a second language?

1. Topic sentence: ____

____

2. Make a list of possible causes. (Consider underlying causes.)

   a. ______
   b. ______
   c. ______
   d. ______
   e. ______

3. Cross out any points that may be illogical or merely coincidental.
4. Put your list in order.
5. Using your final list, write at least one sentence for each of the causes you have found.

   a. ______
   b. ______
   c. ______
   d. ______
   e. ______

6. Write a concluding statement. ______
7. On a separate piece of paper, copy your sentences into standard paragraph form.
8. Do a final reading to check for errors and omissions.

EXERCISE 9 **Writing the Effect Paragraph Step-by-Step**

This exercise will guide you through the effect paragraph. Start with the suggested topic. Use the eight steps to help you work through each stage of the writing process.

Topic: What are the effects of teenagers having part-time jobs after school?

1. Topic sentence: ______
2. Make a list of possible effects. (Consider long-range effects.)

   a. ______
   b. ______

c. ______________________________

d. ______________________________

e. ______________________________

3. Cross out any points that may be illogical or merely coincidental, or the result of only time sequence.

4. Put your list in order.

5. Using your final list, write at least one sentence for each of the effects you have found.

a. ______________________________

____

b. ______________________________

____

c. ______________________________

____

d. ______________________________

____

e. ______________________________

____

6. Write a concluding statement. ______________________________

____

____

7. On a separate piece of paper or on the computer, copy your sentences into standard paragraph form.

8. Do a final reading to check for errors and omissions.

On Your Own: Writing Cause and Effect Paragraphs from Model Paragraphs

The Causes of a Social Problem

Assignment 1

Write a paragraph about the causes of a social problem that is of concern to you. The following paragraph looks at possible causes for placing an elderly relative in a nursing home.

MODEL PARAGRAPH: OLD AGE IN MODERN SOCIETY

Industrialized societies have developed homes for the elderly who are unable to care for themselves. In spite of much criticism, these homes have a growing percentage of our nation's elderly. Why do some people feel forced into placing parents into a nursing home? The most immediate cause is that following some serious illness, there is often no place for the elderly person to go where he or she can be cared for. In the family of today, it is often the case that both partners work outside the home, so no one is home during the day to care for the person. Hiring a nurse to be in the home every day is beyond the budget of nearly every family. Even when a family member can be home to care for the elderly person, the problems can be overwhelming. The older person can be too heavy for one or even two to manage. Bathing, particularly, can be dangerous in these circumstances. In addition, many elderly people have to be watched very carefully because of their medical condition. Many families do not have the proper training to meet these needs. Finally, elderly people who may be senile and difficult can often intrude on a family's life to the point that a caregiver may never be able to leave the house or get a proper night's rest. Perhaps a better system of visiting nursing care could help some families keep their loved ones in their homes longer.

Ten suggested topics

1. The causes of homelessness
2. The causes of prostitution
3. The causes of teenage runaways
4. The causes of high school dropouts
5. The causes of divorce
6. The causes of child abuse
7. The causes of white-collar crime
8. The causes of high stress among college students
9. The causes of road rage
10. The causes of the increase in childless couples

The Causes that Led to a Particular Historical Event

Assignment 2

Write a paragraph about the causes that led to a particular event in history. The following model paragraph looks at the causes for the loss of life in the sinking of a supposedly unsinkable ship on its maiden voyage over 80 years ago.

MODEL PARAGRAPH: THE SINKING OF THE TITANIC

One of the most tragic events of the twentieth century was the sinking of the British ship *Titanic* in the Atlantic Ocean on April 15, 1912, with the loss of over 1500 lives. The immediate cause of this terrible loss of life was a large iceberg that tore a three-hundred-foot gash in the side of the ship, flooding five of its watertight compartments. Some believe that the tragedy took place because the crew members did not see the iceberg in time, but others see a chain of different events that contributed to the tragedy. First was the fact that the ship was not carrying enough lifeboats for all of its passengers: It had enough boats for only about half of the people on board. Furthermore, the ship's crew showed a clear lack of caring about the third class or "steerage" passengers, who were left in their cramped quarters below decks with little or no help as the ship went down. It has often been said that this social attitude of helping the wealthy and neglecting the poor was one of the real causes of the loss of life that night. Indeed, some of the lifeboats that were used were not filled to capacity when the rescue ships eventually found them. Finally, the tragedy of the Titanic was magnified by the fact that some ships nearby did not have a radio crew on duty and therefore missed the distress signals sent by the Titanic. Out of all this, the need to reform safety regulations on passenger ships became obvious.

Ten suggested topics

1. Causes for the decline of the Roman Empire
2. Causes for the growth of the Civil Rights Movement in the 1960s in the United States
3. Causes for the Gulf War in 1991
4. Causes for the reductions in the United States military budget in the 1990s
5. Causes for the victory (or loss) of a particular political candidate in a recent election
6. Causes for the Dust bowl in the western United States in the 1930s
7. Causes for the growth of the feminist movement during the 1970s in the United States
8. Causes for the Depression of 1929
9. Causes for the rise to power of Adolf Hitler
10. Causes for the economic growth during the 1990s in the United States

The Effects of a Substance or Activity on the Human Body

Assignment 3

Write a paragraph about what happens to the human body when it uses a substance or engages in some activity. The following model paragraph is from Norman Taylor's *Plant Drugs That Changed the World.*

MODEL PARAGRAPH: EFFECTS OF CAFFEINE

The ordinary cup of coffee, of the usual breakfast strength, contains about one and a half grains of caffeine (100 mg.). That "second cup of coffee" hence means just about three grains of caffeine at one sitting. Its effects upon the nervous system, the increased capacity for thinking, its stimulating effects on circulation and muscular activity, not to speak of its sparking greater fluency—these are attributes of the beverage that few will give up. If it has any dangers, most of us are inclined to ignore them. But there is no doubt that excessive intake of caffeine at one time, say up to seven or eight grains (*i.e.,* 5 or 6 cups), has harmful effects such as restlessness, nervous irritability, insomnia, and muscular tremor. The lethal dose in man is unknown, for there are no records of it. Experimental animals die in convulsions after overdoses and from such studies it is assumed that a fatal dose of caffeine in man may be about 150 grains (*i.e.,* one-half ounce). That would mean about one hundred cups of coffee!

Ten suggested topics

1. The effects of alcohol on the body
2. The effects of regular exercise
3. The effects of overeating
4. The effects of a strict diet
5. The effects of fasting
6. The effects of drug abuse
7. The effects of sunburn
8. The effects of allergies
9. The effects of a sedentary lifestyle
10. The effects of vitamins

The Effects of a Community Disaster

Assignment 4

Think of a disaster that took place in or around your community, a disaser you either witnessed or heard about in the media. Describe the effects this disaster had on you or on the people involved. The following model paragraph describes the effects of an incident that began with an ordinary traffic procedure in California a decade ago.

MODEL PARAGRAPH: A ROUTINE TRAFFIC STOP

In 1991, a routine traffic stop on a street in Los Angeles led to a number of unexpected results. Motorist Rodney King was said to have refused to follow police instructions; what is certain is that a videotape showed King being beaten by four police officers. After a three-month trial, the officers were found not guilty of any wrongdoing, a verdict that had several effects, both in Los Angeles and in the rest of the nation. The city of Los Angeles immediately erupted with over 150 fires, extensive looting, and many senseless beatings of innocent people. The smoke from the fires became so thick that aviation officials would not allow incoming flights to land at the Los Angeles airport. As the violence and looting went into a second day, the mayor announced a curfew and the governor of California called in the National Guard. The U.S. Post Office suspended mail delivery, all city schools were closed, and garbage collection was delayed. Professional sports teams canceled their games, and university classes and final examinations were postponed. Although incidents of rioting and looting took place in other cities, Los Angeles experienced the worst of the violence, with fifty deaths, two thousand injuries, seven hundred arrests, and nearly a billion dollars in property damage. Looking at the long-term effects, the worst result has been a diminished sense of trust in the fairness of law enforcement. A better result is that the use of videotapes as a part of courtroom evidence has become more commonplace. Most importantly, communities have become increasingly aware that officials must be held more accountable for showing restraint as they deal with law enforcement situations.

Ten suggested topics

1. The effects of a hurricane
2. The effects of a power blackout on a town
3. The effects of a flood or other extensive water damage on a home or community
4. The effects of a long dark winter or other lengthy bad weather
5. The effects of a bus, train, or taxi strike on a community
6. The effects of a major fire to a downtown block
7. The effects of the loss of small businesses in a community

8. The effects of the loss of an important community leader
9. The effects decreased (or increased) services in communities
10. The effects of civil unrest in a city neighborhood

EXPLORING ONLINE

For more information about cause and effect paragraphs, see:

http://www.wuacc.edu/services/zzcwwctr/org~cause.wm.txt

WORKING TOGETHER

LOOKING AT IMMEDIATE AND LONG-TERM EFFECTS: THE STORY OF ROSA PARKS

Read the following excerpt taken from an article on the life of Rosa Parks, the Alabama woman who showed incredible courage during the earliest years of the civil rights struggle.

The incident that changed Parks' life occurred on Thursday, December 1, 1955, as she was riding home on the Cleveland Avenue bus from her job at Montgomery Fair, a downtown department store where she worked as an assistant tailor. The first ten seats on the city buses, which were always reserved for whites, soon filled up. She sat down next to a man in the front of the section designated for blacks, when a white male got on and looked for a seat. In such situations, the black section was made smaller. The driver, who was white, requested that the four blacks move. The others complied, but Parks refused to surrender her seat, so the driver called the police. Parks had been evicted from a bus twelve years earlier by the same driver, but this time it was different. In a *Black Women Oral History Project* interview, she said, "I didn't consider myself breaking any segregation laws . . . because he was extending what we considered our section of the bus." And in *Black Women* she explained, "I felt just resigned to give what I could to protest against the way I was being treated."

At this time there had been fruitless meetings with the bus company about the rudeness of the drivers and other issues—including trying to get the bus line extended farther into the black community, since three-quarters of the bus riders were from there. In the previous year three black women, two of them teenagers, had been arrested for defying the seating laws on the Montgomery buses. The community had talked many times about a citywide demonstration, such as boycotting the bus line, but it never developed. The Women's Political Council already had a network of volunteers in place and had preprinted flyers; they needed only a time and place for a meeting.

About six o'clock that evening, Parks was arrested and sent to jail. She was later released on a one-hundred-dollar bond, and her trial was scheduled for December 5. Parks agreed to allow her case to become the focus for a struggle against the system of segregation. On December 2, the Women's Political Council distributed more than 52,000 flyers throughout Montgomery calling for a one-day bus boycott on the day of Parks' trial. There was a mass meeting of more than 7,000 blacks at the Holt Street Baptist Church. The black community formed the Montgomery Improvement Association and elected Martin Luther King Jr. president. The success of the bus boycott on December 5 led to its continuation. In the second month

continued on next page

it was almost one hundred percent effective, involving 30,000 black riders. When Parks was tried, she was found guilty and fined ten dollars plus court costs of four dollars. She refused to pay and appealed the case to the Montgomery Circuit Court.

Following her release from jail, Parks went back to work but later lost her job, as did her husband. At home, the couple had to deal with threatening telephone calls. Rosa Parks devoted her time to arranging rides in support of the boycott. Blacks were harassed and intimidated by the authorities in Montgomery, and there was an attempt to break up their carpools. Parks served for a time on the board of directors of the Montgomery Improvement Association, and often was invited elsewhere to speak about the boycott.

On February 1, 1956, in an attempt to have the Alabama segregation laws declared unconstitutional, the Montgomery Improvement Association filed a suit in the United States District Court in the names of four women and on behalf of all who had suffered indignities on the buses. On June 2 the lower court declared segregated seating on the buses unconstitutional. The Supreme Court upheld the lower court order that Montgomery buses must be integrated, and on December 20, 1956, the order was served on Montgomery officials. After 381 days of boycotting, resulting in extreme financial loss to the bus company, segregation and other discriminatory practices were outlawed on the city buses. Parks's refusal to give up her seat on a bus was the beginning of the civil rights movement of the 1950s and 1960s. Her action marked the beginning of a time of struggle by black Americans and their supporters as they sought to become an integral part of America.

With the notoriety surrounding her name, Parks was unable to find employment in Montgomery. Her husband became ill and could not work, so Parks, her husband, and mother moved to Detroit in 1957 to join Parks' brother. Since Raymond did not have a Michigan barber's license, he worked in a training school for barbers. In 1958 Parks accepted a position at Hampton Institute in Virginia for one year, after which she returned to Detroit and worked as a seamstress. She continued her efforts to improve life for the black community, working with the Southern Christian Leadership Conference in Detroit. In 1965 Parks became a staff assistant in the Detroit office of United States Representative John Conyers; she retired in 1988.

The entire class should listen as the excerpt is read out loud. Divide into groups. Then, work together to make two lists: immediate effects and long-term effects of the decision Rosa Parks made on December 1, 1955, in Montgomery, Alabama.

Come together as a class and check to see if each group has the same items on the list of immediate effects and the same items on the list of long-term effects.

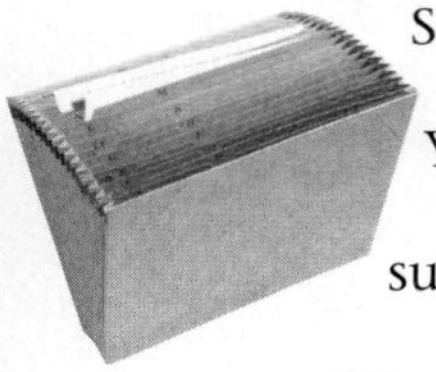

Portfolio Suggestion

Since Rosa Parks took her historic stand in 1955, many changes have taken place in the area of civil rights in our society. Write an essay in which you detail several of these changes. You may want to do some research on the topic.

Another idea for an essay would be to look at the effects of current laws or social pressures on one of the following groups:

- Women; men; children; teens
- A particular religious group
- A particular ethnic group
- The elderly

Online Activity

Read about the life and work of Cesar Chavez, who founded the United Farm Workers Union. How did his contributions impact the lives of Americans who work in the fields?

http://www.ufw.org/cecstory.htm

Chapter 24 Developing Paragraphs: Definition; Classification

Preview

Definition and **classification** are two more methods you can use to develop ideas. This chapter will give you an overview of both of these methods and suggest topics for writing.

Definition

steps for writing a definition:

- place the term in a larger class
- identify the term's characteristics
- provide examples
- use negation

Practice your own paragraphs using extended definition

Classification

steps for classifying items:

- find a basis for classifying
- make distinct categories
- check for completeness
- check for usefulness

Practice your own classification paragraphs

Key Terms

Definition
Extended definition or analysis
Classification

Charts

Transitions for definition
Transitions for classification

What Is Definition?

Definition, as a method of developing ideas, is the exploration of the meaning or significance of a term.

The starting point for any good definition is to group the word into a larger **category** or **class.** For example, a *trout* is a kind of fish; a *doll* is a kind of toy; a *shirt* is an article of clothing. Here is a dictionary entry for the word *family.*

> **family** (fam´e -le, fam´le) *n., pl.* **-lies.** *Abbr.* **fam.** 1. The most instinctive, fundamental social or mating group in man and animal, especially the union of man and woman through marriage and their offspring; parents and their children. 2. One's spouse and children. 3. Persons related by blood or marriage; relatives; kinfolk. 4. Lineage; especially, upper-class lineage. 5. All the members of a household; those who share one's domestic home.

To what larger category does the word *family* belong? According to this dictionary entry, the *family* is the most basic of *social groups.*

Once a word has been put into a larger class, the next step is to provide the **identifying characteristics** that make the word different from other members in that class. What makes a *trout* different from a *bass,* a *doll* different from a *puppet,* a *shirt* different from a *sweater?* Here a definition can give examples. The dictionary definition of *family* identifies the family as a married man and woman and their children. Four additional meanings provide a suggestion for some variations.

When you write a paragraph or an essay that uses definition, the dictionary entry is only the beginning. It is not the function of a dictionary to go into great depth. It can only provide the basic meanings and synonyms. In order for your reader to understand a difficult term or idea, you will need to expand this definition into what is called ***extended definition.*** *Extended definition* seeks to analyze a concept so that the reader will have a more complete understanding of a term. For instance, you might include a historical perspective. When or how did the concept begin? How did the term change or evolve over the years, or how do different cultures understand the term? You will become involved in the word's connotations. ***Extended definition,*** or ***analysis*** as it is sometimes called, uses more than one method to arrive at an understanding of a term.

> **Extended definition** is an expanded definition or analysis of a concept or term, giving additional information in order to convey a fuller meaning.

The following paragraph, taken from *Sociology: An Introduction* by John E. Conklin, is the beginning of a chapter on the family. The author's starting point is very similar to the dictionary entry.

> In every society, social norms define a variety of relationships among people, and some of these relationships are socially recognized as family or kinship ties. A *family* is a socially defined set of relationships between at least two people who are related by birth, marriage, or adoption. We can think of a family as including several possible relationships, the most common being between husband and wife, between parents and children, and between people who are related to each other by birth (siblings, for example) or by marriage (a woman and her mother-in-law, perhaps). Family relationships are often

defined by custom, such as the relationship between an infant and godparents, or by law, such as the adoption of a child.

The author began this definition by putting the term into a larger class. *Family* is one type of social relationship among people. The writer then identifies the people who are members of this group. Family relationships can be formed by marriage, birth, adoption, or custom. The author does not stop here. The extended definition explores the functions of the family, conflicts in the family, the structure of the family, and the special characteristics of the family.

The writer could also have defined *family* by ***negation.*** That is, he could have described what a family is *not:*

A family is not a corporation.

A family is not a formal school.

A family is not a church.

When a writer defines a concept using negation, the definition should be completed by stating what the subject *is:*

A family is not a corporation, but it is an economic unit of production and consumption.

A family is not a formal school, but it is a major center for learning.

A family is not a church, but it is where children learn their moral values.

EXERCISE 1

Working with Definition: Class

Define each of the following terms by placing it in a larger class. Keep in mind that when you define something by class, you are placing it in a larger category so that the reader can see where it belongs. Use the dictionary if you need help. An example has been done for you.

Chemistry is *one of the branches of science* that deals with a close study of the natural world.

1. Mythology is ______________________________
2. Nylon is ______________________________
3. An amoeba is ______________________________
4. A tricycle is ______________________________
5. Cabbage is ______________________________
6. Democracy is ______________________________
7. Asbestos is ______________________________
8. A piccolo is ______________________________
9. Poetry is ______________________________
10. A university is ______________________________

EXERCISE 2

Working with Definition: Distinguishing Characteristics

Using the same terms as in Exercise 1, give one or two identifying characteristics that differentiate your term from other terms in the same class. An example is done for you.

Chemistry studies the structure, properties, and reactions of matter.

1. Mythology ______________________________

____

2. Nylon ______________________________

____

3. An amoeba ______________________________

____

4. A tricycle ______________________________

____

5. Cabbage ______________________________

____

6. Democracy ______________________________

____

7. Asbestos ______________________________

____

8. A piccolo ______________________________

____

9. Poetry ______________________________

____

10. A university ______________________________

____

EXERCISE 3

Working with Definition: Example

Help define each of the following terms by providing one example. Examples always make writing more alive. An example has been done for you.

Term: Chemistry

Example: Chemistry studies an element like hydrogen. This element is the simplest in structure of all the elements, with only one electron and one proton; it is colorless, highly flammable, the lightest of all gases, and the most abundant element in the universe.

1. Mythology

____

____

2. Friendship

____

____

3. Philanthropist

____

____

4. Planet

____

____

5. Gland

____

____

6. Greed

____

____

7. Volcano

____

____

8. Patriotism

____

____

9. Terrorism

____

____

10. Equality

____

____

EXERCISE 4 **Working with Definition: Negation**

Define each of the following terms by using negation to construct your definition. Keep in mind that such a definition is not complete until you have also included what the topic is that you are defining.

1. A *disability* is not ______________________________

but it is ______________________________

2. The *perfect car* is not ______________________________

but it is ______________________________

3. *Drugs* are not ______________________
but they are ______________________
4. *Freedom* is not ______________________
but it ______________________
5. A *good job* is not ______________________
but it is ______________________
6. *Exercise* is not ______________________
but it is ______________________
7. A *university* is not ______________________
but it is ______________________
8. A *legislator* is not ______________________
but he or she is ______________________
9. The *ideal pet* is not ______________________
but it is ______________________
10. A *boring person* is not ______________________
but he or she is ______________________

TRANSITIONS FOR DEFINITION

is defined as
is understood to be
means that
is sometimes thought to be
signifies

Writing a Paragraph Using Definition

Here is a list of topics for possible paragraph assignments. For each topic that you choose to write about, develop a complete paragraph of definition by using more than one of the techniques you have studied—***class, identifying characteristics, example,*** and ***negation***—as well as any further analysis, historical or cultural, that would help the reader.

Ten suggested topics

1. Photosynthesis
2. Ecology
3. Symphony
4. Football
5. Paranoia
6. Courage
7. Algebra
8. Democracy
9. Masculinity or femininity
10. Justice

EXPLORING ONLINE

For further reading about definition paragraphs, go to

http://www.wuacc.edu/services/zzcwwctr/org-definition.wm.txt

What Is Classification?

Classification is the placing of items into separate categories for the purpose of helping us to think about these items more clearly. This can be extremely useful and even necessary when large numbers of items are being considered.

In order to classify things properly, you must always take the items you are working with and put them into ***distinct categories,*** making sure that each item belongs in only one category. For example, if you tried to classify motorcycles into imported motorcycles, U.S.–made motorcycles, and used motorcycles, this would not be an effective use of classification because an imported motorcycle or a U.S.–made motorcycle could also be a used motorcycle. When you classify, you want each item to belong in only one category.

A classification should also be ***complete.*** For example, if you were classifying motorcycles into the two categories of new and used, your classification would be complete because any item can only be new or used. Finally, a classification should be ***useful.*** If you are thinking of buying a motorcycle, or if a friend is thinking of buying one, then it might be very useful to classify them in this way because you or your friend might save a great deal of money by deciding to buy a used machine.

The following paragraph is taken from Judith Viorst's essay "Friends, Good Friends—and Such Good Friends" and shows the writer classifying different kinds of friends.

> There are medium friends, and pretty good friends, and very good friends indeed, and these friendships are defined by their level of intimacy. And what we'll reveal at each of these levels of intimacy is calibrated with care. We might tell a medium friend, for example, that yesterday we had a fight with our husband. And we might tell a pretty good friend that this fight with our husband made us so mad that we slept on the couch. And we might tell a very good friend that the reason we got so mad in that fight that we slept on the couch had something to do with that girl who works in his office. But it's only to our very best friends that we're willing to tell all, to tell what's going on with that girl in his office.

In this paragraph, the writer gives us four distinct types of friends, beginning with "medium friends," going on to "pretty good friends" and "very good friends," and ending with "very best friends." Her classification is complete because it covers a full range of friendships, and it is useful because people are naturally interested in the types of friends they have.

EXERCISE 5 Working with Classification: Finding the Basis for a Classification

For each of the following topics, pick three different ways the topic could be classified. You may find the following example helpful.

Topic:	Ways to choose a vacation spot
Basis for classification:	By price (first class, medium price, economy), by its special attraction (the beach, the mountains, the desert, etc.), by the accommodations (hotel, motel, cabin, trailer)

1. Topic: Cars

Ways to divide the topic: ______________________________

____

2. Topic: Houses

Ways to divide the topic: ______________________________

____

3. Topic: Neighborhoods

Ways to divide the topic: ______________________________

____

4. Topic: Religions

Ways to divide the topic: ______________________________

____

5. Topic: Soft drinks

Ways to divide the topic: ______________________________

____

6. Topic: Dating

Ways to divide the topic: ______________________________

____

7. Topic: Floor coverings

Ways to divide the topic: ______________________________

____

8. Topic: Medicines

Ways to divide the topic: ______________________________

9. Topic: Snack foods

Ways to divide the topic: ______________________________

____

10. Topic: Relatives

Ways to divide the topic: ______________________________

____

EXERCISE 6 **Working with Classification: Making Distinct Categories**

For each of the following topics, choose a basis for classification. Then break it down into distinct categories. Divide the topic into as many distinct categories as you think the classification requires.

Keep in mind that when you divide your topic, each part of your classification must belong to only one category. For example, if you were to classify cars, you would not want to make *sports cars* and *imported cars* two of your categories because several kinds of sports cars are also imported cars.

1. Clothing stores

Distinct categories:

______________ ______________ ______________

______________ ______________ ______________

2. Television commercials

Distinct categories:

______________ ______________ ______________

______________ ______________ ______________

3. College sports

Distinct categories:

______________ ______________ ______________

______________ ______________ ______________

4. Doctors

Distinct categories:

______________ ______________ ______________

______________ ______________ ______________

5. Hats

Distinct categories:

______________ ______________ ______________

______________ ______________ ______________

6. Courses in the English department of your college

Distinct categories:

______________ ______________ ______________

______________ ______________ ______________

7. Pens

Distinct categories:

______________ ______________ ______________

______________ ______________ ______________

8. Dances

Distinct categories:

______________ ______________ ______________

______________ ______________ ______________

9. Mail

Distinct categories:

______________ ______________ ______________

______________ ______________ ______________

10. Music

Distinct categories:

______________ ______________ ______________

______________ ______________ ______________

TRANSITIONS FOR CLASSIFICATION

divisions, divided into
categories, categorized by
types, kinds
groups, groupings, grouped into
areas, fields, sections, parts

Writing a Paragraph Using Classification

Here is a list of topics for possible paragraph assignments using classification. As you plan your paragraph, keep in mind the following points. Does the classification help to organize the material? Are you sure the classification is complete and that no item could belong to more than one category? Is there some purpose for your classifying the items as you did? (For example, will it help someone make a decision or understand a concept?)

Ten suggested topics

1. Parents
2. Governments
3. Dogs
4. Careers
5. Parties
6. Summer jobs
7. Movies
8. Classmates
9. Coworkers
10. Restaurants

WORKING TOGETHER

WHAT IS A HERO?

Some words or ideas are hard to define, either because they are complicated, or they are controversial. One such idea is the concept of *heroism.*

Working together as a class, make a list of ten people you believe are heroes or role models. What has each of them done to deserve the title of hero or role model? Once you have decided on your examples, note the qualities shared by these people. In your view, do these qualities define *heroism?* Finally, develop a single sentence to define the term. After working out a definition in the class, look up the dictionary definition. How close is the classroom definition to the dictionary definition?

Portfolio Suggestion

Using the conclusions you and your classmates have come to, look up some famous historical figures in an encyclopedia. Your choices could come from any period of history, from the ancient world (Cleopatra or Alexander the Great) to our own time (Mother Teresa, Martin Luther King Jr. or Amelia Earhart). Examine these persons' lives and then make judgments about them. Are they true heroes or role models?

Online Activity

Read and discuss accounts of "Modern Day Heroism":

http://www.rev.net/~aloe/heroism

PART V STRUCTURING THE COLLEGE ESSAY

In earlier parts of the book, when you learned how to master sentence mechanics and write well developed paragraphs, you were creating the basic supports needed to construct college essays of more than a few paragraphs. Part 5 will take you through the more demanding requirements of essay writing, including the careful construction of the thesis statement. Part of learning the process of essay writing is practicing different modes of development. In working with each of these modes, you will learn how to organize material in greater depth, how to make effective transitions among your ideas, and how to arrive at logical and convincing conclusions.

Chapter 25 Moving from the Paragraph to the Essay

Preview

Before you begin to write your own college essays, study this chapter to become familiar with these special essay features:

- The three kinds of paragraphs in an essay
- Recognizing and writing the **thesis statement**
- Ways to write **introductory paragraphs**
- What *not* to say in an introductory paragraph
- **Transitions** between **body paragraphs**
- Ways to write **concluding paragraphs**
- What *not* to say in a concluding paragraph
- A note about titles

Key Terms

College essay
Thesis
Introduction
Conclusion

What Is the *College Essay?*

No matter what major a student chooses in college, developing as a writer is an important part of that student's growth and progress. Becoming skilled in the writing of college essays (also called *compositions, themes,* or simply *papers*) is a necessary tool to have for nearly every college course, not only English Composition.

In Part 4 you learned that the paragraph, with its topic sentence and supporting details, must have a unified and coherent organization. The full-length essay must also have the same characteristics. Since topics for essays are developed at greater length and depth than paragraphs, the challenge is greater to make all parts of the essay work together.

The **college essay** is a piece of nonfiction writing that uses five or more paragraphs to develop a single topic. The essay usually includes an introductory paragraph that states the thesis, three or more supporting paragraphs that develop the topic, and a concluding paragraph.

What Kinds of Paragraphs Are in an Essay?

In addition to the support paragraphs that you studied in Part 4, the essay has two new kinds of paragraphs:

1. The **introductory paragraph** is the first paragraph of the essay. Its purpose is to be so inviting that the reader will not want to stop reading. In most essays, this introduction contains a **thesis statement.**
2. **Support paragraphs** (sometimes called **body paragraphs**) provide the evidence that shows your thesis is valid. An essay must have at least three well-developed support paragraphs. (You have studied these kinds of paragraphs in Part 4.) One paragraph must flow logically into the next. This is accomplished by the careful use of **transitional expressions.**
3. The **concluding paragraph** is the last paragraph of the essay. Its purpose is to give the reader a sense of coming to a satisfying conclusion. By this point the reader should have the feeling that everything has been said that needed to be said.

What Is a Thesis?

A **thesis** is a statement of the main idea of an essay.

The thesis states what you are going to explain, defend, or prove about your topic. It is usually placed at the end of the introductory paragraph.

How to Recognize the Thesis Statement

A thesis statement is always expressed in a complete sentence, and it usually presents a viewpoint about a topic that can be defended or explained in the essay that follows.

Be careful not to confuse a title or a simple fact with a thesis. Remember that a **title** is usually a phrase, not a complete sentence. A **fact** is something known for certain—it can be verified. A fact does not give a personal viewpoint.

Thesis: Most children at five years of age should not be in school more than half the day.

or

Schools should offer parents the option of an all-day kindergarten program which would benefit the children as well as the working parents.

Title: The Disadvantages of All-Day Kindergarten

or

The Advantages of All-Day Kindergarten

Fact: Nearly all kindergartens in the United States offer only a half day of instruction.

Practice

Read each of the following statements. If you think the statement is a thesis, mark (TH) on the blank line. If you think the statement is a title, mark (T). If you think the statement is a fact, mark (F).

_______________ **1.** In the United States, kindergarten is not compulsory.

_______________ **2.** Children should begin learning to read in kindergarten.

_______________ **3.** Putting a child into kindergarten before he or she is ready can have several unfortunate effects on that child.

_______________ **4.** Learning to read in kindergarten

_______________ **5.** In some European countries, children do not begin formal schooling until the age of seven.

EXERCISE 1 Recognizing the Thesis Statement

Identify each of the following as (T) a *title,* (TH) a *thesis,* or (F) a *fact* that could be used to support a thesis.

_______________ **1.** The personal interview is the most important step in the employment process.

_______________ **2.** Looking for a job

_______________ **3.** Sixty percent of all jobs are obtained through newspaper advertisements.

_______________ **4.** The best time to begin a foreign language is in grade school.

_______________ **5.** The importance of learning a foreign language

_______________ **6.** In the 1970s, the number of students studying foreign languages declined dramatically.

_______________ **7.** Most Americans doing business with Japan do not know a word of Japanese.

_______________ **8.** Working and studying at the same time

_______________ **9.** Many students in community colleges have part-time jobs while they are going to school.

_______________ **10.** Working a part-time job while going to school puts an enormous strain on a person.

EXERCISE 2 Recognizing the Thesis Statement

Identify each of the following as (T) a *title,* (TH) a *thesis,* or (F) a *fact* that could be used to support a thesis.

_______________ **1.** It is estimated that approximately 200 grizzly bears live in Yellowstone National Park.

_______________ **2.** The survival of grizzly bears in our country should be a top priority.

_______________ **3.** When bears are young cubs, there are twice as many males as females.

_______________ **4.** Only about 60 percent of bear cubs survive the first few years of life.

_______________ **5.** Bears, a precious natural resource

_______________ **6.** The average life span of a bear today is only five or six years.

_______________ **7.** The sad plight of the American grizzly bear

_______________ **8.** Five actions need to be taken to save the grizzly bear from extinction.

_______________ **9.** To save the grizzly bear, we need laws from Congress, the cooperation of hunters and campers, and an educated general public.

_______________ **10.** A decision to save the grizzly bear

EXERCISE 3 **Recognizing the Thesis Statement**

Identify each of the following as (T) a *title,* (TH) a *thesis,* or (F) a *fact* that could be used to support a thesis.

_______________ **1.** Tons of ancient material have been taken out of Russell Cave.

_______________ **2.** The opening of the cave is 107 feet wide and 26 feet high.

_______________ **3.** People lived in this cave more than nine thousand years ago.

_______________ **4.** Russell Cave in Jackson County, Alabama, should be preserved as an important source of information about the ancient people of North America.

_______________ **5.** The way ancient people lived

_______________ **6.** All kinds of articles, from fish hooks to human skeletons, have been found in Russell Cave.

_______________ **7.** Learning about the diet of an ancient people of North America

_______________ **8.** An archaeologist discovers Russell Cave

_______________ **9.** Some of the theories previously held about life in North America thousands of years ago must now be changed because of the discoveries made in Russell Cave.

_______________ **10.** Russell Cave is the oldest known home of human beings in the southeastern United States.

Writing the Effective Thesis Statement

An effective thesis statement has the following parts:

1. **A topic that is not too broad:** Broad topics must be narrowed in scope. You can do this by *limiting the topic* (changing the term to cover a smaller part of the topic), or *qualifying the topic* (adding phrases or words to the general term that will narrow the topic).

   Broad topic: Swimming

   Limited topic: Floating (*Floating* is a kind of swimming, more specialized than the term *swimming*.)

   Qualified topic: Swimming for health two hours a week (The use of the phrase *for health two hours a week* narrows the topic down considerably. Now the topic concentrates on the fact that the *time* and the *reason* spent swimming are important parts of the topic.)

   There are a number of ways to narrow a topic in order to make it fit into a proper essay length, as well as make it fit your experience and knowledge.

2. **A controlling idea that you can defend:** The controlling idea is what you want to show or prove about your topic; it is your attitude about that topic. Often the word is an adjective such as *beneficial, difficult,* or *unfair.*

   Learning to float at the age of twenty was a *terrifying* experience.

   Swimming two hours a week brought about a *dramatic change* in my health.

3. **An indication of what strategy of development is to be used:** (Often you can use words such as the following: *description, steps, stages, comparison, contrast, causes, effects, reasons, advantages, disadvantages, definition, analysis,* or *argument.*)
   Although not all writers include the strategy in the thesis statement, they must always have in mind what major strategy they plan to use to prove their thesis. Professional writers often use more than one strategy to prove their thesis. However, in this book you are asked to develop your essays by using one major strategy at a time. By working in this way, you can concentrate on understanding and developing the skills needed for each specific strategy.

Study the following thesis statement:

Although a date with the right person is marvelous, going out with a group can have many advantages.

Now look back and check the parts of this thesis statement.

General topic:	Going out
Qualified topic:	Going out in a group (as opposed to a single date)
Controlling idea:	To give the advantages of going out in a group
Strategy of development:	Contrast between the single date and the group date

EXERCISE 4 **Writing the Thesis Statement**

Below are four topics. For each one, develop a thesis sentence by (1) limiting or qualifying the general topic, (2) choosing a controlling idea (what you want to explain or prove about the topic), and (3) selecting a strategy that you could use to develop that topic. An example is done for you.

General topic: Senior citizens

a. *Limit or qualify the subject:*

Community services available to the senior citizens in my town

b. *Controlling idea:*

To show the great variety of programs

c. *Strategy for development* (narration, process, cause and effect, definition and analysis, comparison or contrast, classification, argument):

Classify the services into major groups

Thesis statement:

The senior citizens of Ann Arbor, Michigan, are very fortunate to have three major kinds of programs available that help them deal with health, housing, and leisure time.

1. Miami (or another city with which you are familiar)

a. Limit or qualify the subject:

____

b. Controlling idea:

____

c. Strategy for development *(narration, process, cause and effect, definition and analysis, comparison/contrast, classification,* or *argument):*

____

Thesis statement:

____

____

____

2. Female vocalist

a. Limit or qualify the subject:

____

b. Controlling idea:

____

c. Strategy for development *(narration, process, cause and effect, definition and analysis, comparison/contrast, classification,* or *argument):*

____

Thesis statement:

____

____

____

3. Shopping

a. Limit or qualify the subject:

____

b. Controlling idea:

____

c. Strategy for development *(narration, process, cause and effect, definition and analysis, comparison/contrast, classification,* or *argument):*

____

Thesis statement:

____

____

____

4. The library

a. Limit or qualify the subject:

____

b. Controlling idea:

____

c. Strategy for development *(narration, process, cause and effect, definition and analysis, comparison/contrast, classification,* or *argument):*

____

Thesis statement:

____

____

____

EXERCISE 5 **Writing the Thesis Statement**

Below are five topics. For each one, develop a thesis sentence by (1) limiting or qualifying the general topic, (2) choosing a controlling idea (what you want to explain or prove about the topic), and (3) selecting a strategy that you could use to develop that topic. Review the example in Exercise 4 (page 462).

1. Television

a. Limit or qualify the subject:

____

b. Controlling idea:

____

c. Strategy for development *(narration, process, cause and effect, definition and analysis, comparison/contrast, classification,* or *argument):*

____

Thesis statement:

____

____

____

2. Soccer (or another sport)

a. Limit or qualify the subject:

____

b. Controlling idea:

____

c. Strategy for development *(narration, process, cause and effect, definition and analysis, comparison/contrast, classification,* or *argument):*

____

Thesis statement:

____

____

____

3. Math (or another field of study)

a. Limit or qualify the subject:

____

b. Controlling idea:

____

c. Strategy for development *(narration, process, cause and effect, definition and analysis, comparison/contrast, classification,* or *argument):*

____

Thesis statement:

____

____

____

4. Games

a. Limit or qualify the subject:

____

b. Controlling idea:

____

c. Strategy for development *(narration, process, cause and effect, definition and analysis, comparison/contrast, classification,* or *argument):*

____

Thesis statement:

____

____

____

5. Clubs

a. Limit or qualify the subject:

____

b. Controlling idea:

____

c. Strategy for development *(narration, process, cause and effect, definition and analysis, comparison/contrast, classification,* or *argument):*

____

Thesis statement:

____

____

____

Ways to Write an Effective Introductory Paragraph

An **introduction** has one main purpose: to "grab" your readers' interest so that they will keep reading.

There is no one way to write an introduction. However, since many good introductions follow the same common patterns, you will find it helpful to look at a few examples of the more typical patterns. When you are ready to create your own introductions, you can consider trying out some of these patterns.

1. ***Begin with a general subject that can be narrowed down into the specific topic of your essay.*** Here is an introduction to an essay about a family making cider on their farm:

    The number of children who eagerly help around a farm is rather small. Willing helpers do exist, but many more of them are five years old than fifteen. In fact, there seems to be a general law that says as long as a kid is too little to help effectively, he or she is dying to. Then, just as they reach the age when they really could drive a fence post or empty a sap bucket without spilling half of it, they lose interest. Now it's cars they want to drive, or else they want to stay in the house and listen for four straight hours to The Who. There is one exception to this rule. Almost no kid that I have ever met outgrows an interest in cidering.

    FROM NOEL PERRIN,
    "Falling for Apples"

2. ***Begin with specifics (a brief anecdote, a specific example or fact) that will broaden into the more general topic of your essay.*** Here is the introduction to an essay on the place of news programs in our lives:

    Let me begin with a confession. I am a news addict. Upon awakening I flip on the *Today* show to learn what events transpired during the night. On the commuter train which takes me to work, I scour *The New York Times,* and find myself absorbed in tales of earthquakes, diplomacy and economics. I read the news paper as religiously as my grandparents read their prayerbooks. The sacramental character of the news extends into the evening. The length of my workday is determined precisely by my need to get home in time for Walter Cronkite. My children understand that my communion with Cronkite is something serious and cannot be interrupted for light and transient causes. What is news, and why does it occupy a place of special significance for so many people?

    FROM STANLEY MILGRAM,
    "Confessions of a News Addict"

3. ***Give a definition of the concept that will be discussed.*** Here is the introduction to an essay about the public's common use of two addictive drugs, alcohol and cigarettes:

Our attitude toward the word "drug" depends on whether we are talking about penicillin or heroin or something in-between. The unabridged three-volume Webster's says a drug is "a chemical substance administered to prevent or cure disease or enhance physical and mental welfare" or "a substance affecting the structure or function of the body." Webster's should have added "mind," but they probably thought that was part of the body. Some substances that aren't drugs, like placebos, affect "the structure or function of the body," but they work because we *think* they're drugs.

FROM ADAM SMITH,
"Some American Drugs Familiar to Everybody"

4. ***Make a startling statement:***

Man will never conquer space. Such a statement may sound ludicrous, now that our rockets are already 1 million miles beyond the moon and the first human travelers are preparing to leave the atmosphere. Yet it expresses a truth which our forefathers knew, one we have forgotten—and our descendants must learn again, in heartbreak and loneliness.

FROM ARTHUR C. CLARKE,
"We'll Never Conquer Space"

5. ***Start with an idea or statement that is a widely held point of view. Then surprise the reader by stating that this idea is false or that you hold a different point of view:***

Tom Wolfe has christened today's young adults as the "me" generation, and the 1970s—obsessed with things like consciousness expansion and self-awareness—have been described as the decade of the new narcissism. The cult of "I," in fact, has taken hold with the strength and impetus of a new religion. But the joker in the pack is that it is all based on a false idea.

FROM MARGARET HALSEY,
"What's Wrong with 'Me, Me, Me'?"

6. ***Start with a familiar quotation or a quotation by a famous person:***

"The very hairs of your head," says Matthew 10:30, "are all numbered." There is little reason to doubt it. Increasingly, everything tends to get numbered one way or another, everything that can be counted, measured, averaged, estimated or quantified. Intelligence is gauged by a quotient, the humidity by a ratio, pollen by its count, and the trends of birth, death, marriage and divorce by rates. In this epoch of runaway demographics, society is as often described and analyzed with statistics as with words. Politics seems more and more a game played with percentages turned up by pollsters, and economics a learned babble of ciphers and indexes that few people can translate and apparently

nobody can control. Modern civilization, in sum, has begun to resemble an interminable arithmetic class in which, as Carl Sandburg put it, "numbers fly like pigeons in and out of your head."

FROM FRANK TRIPPETT,
"Getting Dizzy by the Numbers"

7. ***Give a number of descriptive images that will lead to the thesis of your essay.*** Here is the opening of a lengthy essay about the importance of sports in our lives:

I cannot remember when I was not surrounded by sports, when talk of sports was not in the air, when I did not care passionately about sports. As a boy in Chicago in the late Forties, I lived in the same building as the sister and brother-in-law of Barney Ross, the welterweight champion. Half a block away, down near the lake, the Sullivan High School football team worked out in the spring and autumn. Summers the same field was given over to baseball and men's softball on Sundays. A few blocks to the north was the Touhy Avenue Fieldhouse, where basketball was played, and lifeguards trained, and behind which, in a softball field frozen over in winter, crack-the-whip, hockey, and speed skating took over. To the west, a block or so up Morse Avenue, was the Morse Avenue "L" Recreations, a combined pool hall and bowling alley. Life, in short, was games.

FROM JOSEPH EPSTEIN,
"Obsessed with Sport: On the Interpretation of a Fan's Dreams"

8. ***Ask a question that you intend to answer.*** Many essays you will read in magazines and newspapers use a question in the introductory paragraph to make the reader curious about the author's viewpoint. Some writing instructors prefer that students do not use this method. Check with your instructor for his or her viewpoint. Here is an example of such an introduction:

Suppose there were no critics to tell us how to react to a picture, a play, or a new composition of music. Suppose we wandered innocent as the dawn into an art exhibition of unsigned paintings. By what standards, by what values would we decide whether they were good or bad, talented or untalented, successes or failures? How can we ever know that what we think is right?

FROM MARYA MANNES,
"How Do You Know It's Good?"

9. ***Use classification to indicate how your topic fits into the larger class to which it belongs, or how your topic can be divided into categories that you are going to discuss.*** Here is how Aaron Copland began an essay on listening to music:

We all listen to music according to our separate capacities. But, for the sake of analysis, the whole listening process may become clearer if we break it up into its component parts, so to speak. In a certain sense we all listen to music on three separate planes. For lack of a better terminology, one might name these: the sensuous plane, the expressive plane, the sheerly musical plane. The only advantage to be gained from mechanically splitting up the listening process into these hypothetical planes is the clearer view to be had of the way in which we listen.

FROM AARON COPLAND,
What to Listen For in Music

What Not to Say in Your Introduction

1. ***Avoid telling your reader that you are beginning your essay:***

   In this essay I will discuss . . .

   I will talk about . . .

   I am going to prove . . .

2. ***Don't apologize:***

   Although I am not an expert . . .

   In my humble opinion . . .

3. ***Do not refer to later parts of your essay:***

   By the end of this essay you will agree . . .

   In the next paragraph you will see . . .

4. ***Don't use trite expressions.*** Since these expressions have been so overused, they have lost all interest and effectiveness. Using such expressions shows that you have not taken the time to use your own words to express your ideas. The following are some examples of trite expressions:

   busy as a bee

   you can't tell a book by its cover

   haste makes waste

Using Transitions to Move the Reader from One Idea to the Next

Successful essays help the reader understand the logic of the writer's thinking by using transitional expressions when needed. Usually this occurs when the writer is moving from one point to the next. It can also occur whenever the idea is complicated. The writer may need to summarize the points so far; the writer may need to emphasize a point already made; or the writer may want to repeat an important point. The transition may be a word, a phrase, a sentence, or even a paragraph.

- Here are some of the transitional expressions that might be used to help the reader make the right connections:

1. To make your points stand out clearly:

the first reason	second, secondly	finally
first of all	another example	most important
in the first place	even more important	all in all
	also, next	in conclusion
	then	to summarize

2. To provide an example of what has just been said:

   for example
   for instance

3. To show the consequence of what has just been said:

   therefore
   as a result
   then

4. To make a contrasting point clear:

   on the other hand
   but
   contrary to current thinking
   however

5. To admit a point:

   of course
   granted

6. To resume your argument after admitting a point:

   nevertheless
   even though
   nonetheless
   still

7. To call the reader's attention to your organization:

   Before attempting to answer these questions, let me . . .
   In our discussions so far, we have seen that . . .
   At this point, it is necessary to . . .
   It is beyond the scope of this paper to . . .

- A more subtle way to link one idea to another in an essay is to repeat a word or phrase from the preceding sentence. Sometimes a pronoun, instead of the actual word, will take the place of the word.

8. To repeat a word or phrase from a preceding sentence:

   I have many memories of my childhood in Cuba. These *memories* include the aunts, uncles, grandparents, and friends I had to leave behind.

9. To use a pronoun to refer to a word or phrase from a preceding sentence:

    Like all immigrants, my family and I have had to build a new life from almost nothing. *It* was often difficult, but I believe the struggle made us strong.

EXERCISE 6 **Finding Transitional Expressions**

Below are the first three paragraphs of an essay on African art. Circle all the transitional expressions including repeated words that are used to link one sentence to another or one idea to the next.

Like language and social organization, art is essential to human life. As embellishment and as creation of objects beyond the requirements of the most basic needs of living, art has accompanied man since prehistoric times. Because of its almost unfailing consistency as an element of many societies, art may be the response to some biological or psychological need. Indeed, it is one of the most constant forms of human behavior.

However, use of the word *art* is not relevant when we describe African "art" because it is really a European term that at first grew out of Greek philosophy and was later reinforced by European culture. The use of other terms, such as *exotic art, primitive art, art sauvage,* and so on, to delineate differences is just as misleading. Most such terms are pejorative—implying that African art is on a lower cultural level. Levels of culture are irrelevant here, since African and European attitudes toward the creative act are so different. Since there is no term in our language to distinguish between the essential differences in thinking, it is best then to describe standards of African art.

African art attracts because of its powerful emotional content and its beautiful abstract form. Abstract treatment of form describes most often—with bare essentials of line, shape, texture, and pattern—intense energy and sublime spirituality. Hundreds of distinct cultures and languages and many types of people have created over one thousand different styles that defy classification. Each art and craft form has its own history and its own aesthetic content. But there are some common denominators (always with exceptions).

EXPLORING ONLINE

For further explanation of transitional words and phrases, see

http://www.wisc.edu/writing/Handbook/Transitions.html

Ways to Write an Effective Concluding Paragraph

A concluding paragraph has one main purpose: to give the reader the sense of reaching a satisfying ending to the topic discussed. Students often feel they have nothing to say at the end. A look at how professional writers frequently end their essays can ease your anxiety about writing an effective conclusion. You have more than one possibility. Here are some of the most frequently used patterns for ending an essay:

1. ***Come full circle. That is, return to the material in your introduction.*** Finish what you started there. Remind the reader of the thesis. Be sure to restate the main idea using a different wording. Here is the conclusion to an essay "Confessions of a News Addict." (The introductory paragraph appears on page 466.)

   Living in the modern world, I cannot help but be shaped by it, suckered by the influence and impact of our great institutions. *The New York Times, CBS,* and *Newsweek* have made me into a news addict. In daily life I have come to accept the supposition that if *The New York Times* places a story on the front page, it deserves my attention. I feel obligated to know what is going on. But sometimes, in quieter moments, another voice asks: If the news went away, would the world be any worse for it?

2. ***Summarize by repeating the main points.*** This example is the concluding paragraph to an essay on African art. (The first three paragraphs appear on page 471.)

   In summary, African art explains the past, describes values and a way of life, helps man relate to supernatural forces, mediates his social relations, expresses emotions, and enhances man's present life as an embellishment denoting pride or status as well as providing entertainment such as with dance and music.

3. ***Show the significance of your thesis by making predictions, giving a warning, giving advice, offering a solution, suggesting an alternative, or telling the results.*** This example is the concluding paragraph to "Falling for Apples." (The introductory paragraph appears on page 466.)

   This pleasure goes on and on. In an average year we start making cider the second week of September, and we continue until early November. We make all we can drink ourselves, and quite a lot to give away. We have supplied whole church suppers. One year the girls sold about ten gallons to the village store, which made them some pocket money they were prouder of than any they ever earned from baby-sitting. Best of all, there are two months each year when all of us are running the farm together, just like a pioneer family.

4. ***End with an anecdote that illustrates your thesis.*** This example is the concluding paragraph to the essay "Obsessed with Sport . . ." (The introductory paragraph appears on page 468.)

> When I was a boy I had a neighbor, a man who, after retirement, had a number of strokes. An old man and a young boy, we had in common a love of sports, which, when we met on the street, was our only topic of conversation. He once inspected a new glove of mine, and instructed me to rub it down with neat's-foot-oil, place a ball firmly in the pocket, wrap string tightly around the glove, and leave it like that for the winter. I did, and it worked. After his last stroke but one, he seldom left his house. Afternoons he spent in a chair in his bedroom, a blanket over his lap, listening to Cub games over the radio. It was while listening to a ball game that he quietly died. I cannot imagine a better way.

What *Not* to Say in Your Conclusion

1. **Do not introduce a new point.**
2. **Do not apologize.**
3. **Do not end up in the air, leaving the reader feeling unsatisfied. This sometimes happens if the very last sentence is not strong enough.**

A Note about Titles

Be sure to follow the standard procedure for writing your title.

1. **Capitalize all words except articles *(the, a, an)* and prepositions.**
2. **Do not underline the title or put quotation marks around it.**
3. **Try to think of a short and catchy phrase (three to six words). Often writers wait until they have written a draft before working on a title. A phrase taken from the essay might be perfect. If you still cannot think of a clever title after you have written a draft, choose some key words from your thesis statement.**
4. **Center the title at the top of the page, and remember to leave about an inch of space between the title and the beginning of the first paragraph.**

EXPLORING ONLINE

For a thumbnail explanation of the principles of the essay, go to:

http://twc.cc.duq.edu/Grammar/writing.htm

WORKING TOGETHER

TOM TOLES
Pop Quiz
1. Which gets more status?
a. learning
b. sports
2. Which gets more hours?
a. reading
b. TV
3. Which gets more attention?
a. a new idea
b. a new car
4. Which gets more promotion?
a. studying
b. shopping
5. Essay Question:
Why do you think there's an education problem in this country?
THINK?
TOLES

PLANNING THE PARTS OF AN ESSAY

The cartoon uses the technique of a multiple choice quiz to suggest some of the possible reasons why education in America is in trouble. As a class, discuss each of the four areas of concern raised by the cartoonist. What do you think is the *thesis* for this cartoon?

Break into groups of five or six. Work together to produce a five or six paragraph essay using the organization and content suggested by Tom Toles. Use any ideas that were presented in the class discussion or in your group. Assign each person in your group to one of the following paragraphs:

Introductory paragraph

Four paragraphs of support:

1. Learning vs. sports
2. Reading vs. television
3. A new idea vs. a new car
4. Studying vs. shopping

Concluding paragraph

Before you write, review the basic content for each paragraph so that each group member understands what should be in his or her paragraph.

Portfolio Suggestion

Keep this group essay effort in your portfolio. How well did the members of your group succeed in helping each other build one unified essay? Many people in their jobs are expected to work with their colleagues to produce annual reports, write-ups of experiments, or brochures that advertise their products or services. Seek to improve your ability to work with others in school and on the job.

Online Activity

Education often takes a back seat to other activities. Read about how middle school students deal with the competing pressures of social life and school in the article "Competing Forces" by Jessica Portner, found in *Education Week,* October 4, 2000.

http://www.edweek.org/ew/ewstory.cfm?slug=05MSCulture.h20

Chapter 26 Watching a Student Essay Take Form

Preview

In this chapter, you will follow a student writer as she works through the writing process to produce an essay. The sequence of steps begins with the initial assignment and ends with the final proofreading of the essay.

1. The student selects the topic and controlling idea for the thesis statement.
2. She gathers the information using brainstorming techniques.
3. She selects and organizes the material.
4. She writes a rough draft.
5. She revises the rough draft for greater clarity of ideas. (Many writers work on several drafts before a satisfactory final version is reached.)
6. The revised draft is edited for correctness. (The student corrects errors such as misspellings or faulty grammar.)
7. She prepares the final copy by saving the file on a disk, printing out two copies, and proofreading it one last time.

As you follow the student's progress through this chapter, you should maintain a critical attitude. That is, you should be prepared to analyze how well the student succeeds in producing a finished essay. Ask yourself what you might have done with the same topic. You may eventually want to write your own essay on the same topic, but with a very different controlling idea.

Choosing a Topic and a Controlling Idea for the Thesis Statement

The student's first task is to think over what topic would be appropriate and what approach should be taken. This leads the writer in the direction of developing a tentative thesis—the sentence that states the main idea—for the entire essay. Although not all essays come right out and state the thesis directly, the writer must always have a main idea if the writing is to be focused. A reader should never have to wonder what your main idea is.

In this case, the student has been asked to write an essay about a social issue using cause or effect as the method of development. Having this assignment from the beginning is helpful because it gives the student a good sense of direction. With the help of several members of the class, she begins by making a list of possible topics on social issues that come to mind.

The causes of children failing in school

The causes of children succeeding in school

The effects of dishonesty in business

The causes of couples choosing to have small families

The effects of growing up in a large city

The effects of consumerism on the environment

The effects on the family when both parents work

The effects of being an only child

The topic she chooses is important because her success will depend on selecting a topic that is of interest to her. Writing on a topic that you don't care about will not produce a very creative result.

The student reviews the list, talks over the ideas with others and finds herself responding most directly to the topic of families with two wage earners. Although she doesn't work at present and her mother never worked outside the home, she intends to find a job as soon as she finishes her education. She has been thinking about the changes that going to work might mean for her family, particularly her husband. Not only is the topic of real interest to her, but she suspects most people in her class, many of whom are young mothers, will also have a strong interest in the topic.

Once a student knows the subject for the essay, there still is the question about what the point should be for this essay. Many students may find it difficult to figure this out before they actually do some brainstorming and see what material they have to develop. In this case, the instructor has already asked the students in the class to develop their essay by discussing the causes or the effects. This limits how our student can handle the material. Her main form of development will not be to tell a story about a friend who works (narration). She will not contrast a woman who works outside the home to a woman who stays at home (comparison and contrast); she will not give advice on how a woman can manage a job and a family at the same time (process). Although writing often can combine methods of development, she will focus on the *effects* on the family when both parents work.

Gathering Information Using Brainstorming Techniques

Here is what the student listed when she thought about her topic, *Working Parents:*

```
no time to cook
more microwavable dinners
more fast food
no hot meals for children
nobody at home for deliveries
hard to get to bank and to medical appointments
grocery shopping on weekends
```

```
no time to entertain
dads have to do more household chores—more than just take
out the garbage
dads may be resentful
some marriages could fail
moms have to clean house at night
mom not home for children's emergencies
```

Some writers like to cluster their ideas when they brainstorm. **Clustering** is a *visual map* of your ideas rather than a *list*. Had the student clustered her ideas, they might have looked like this:

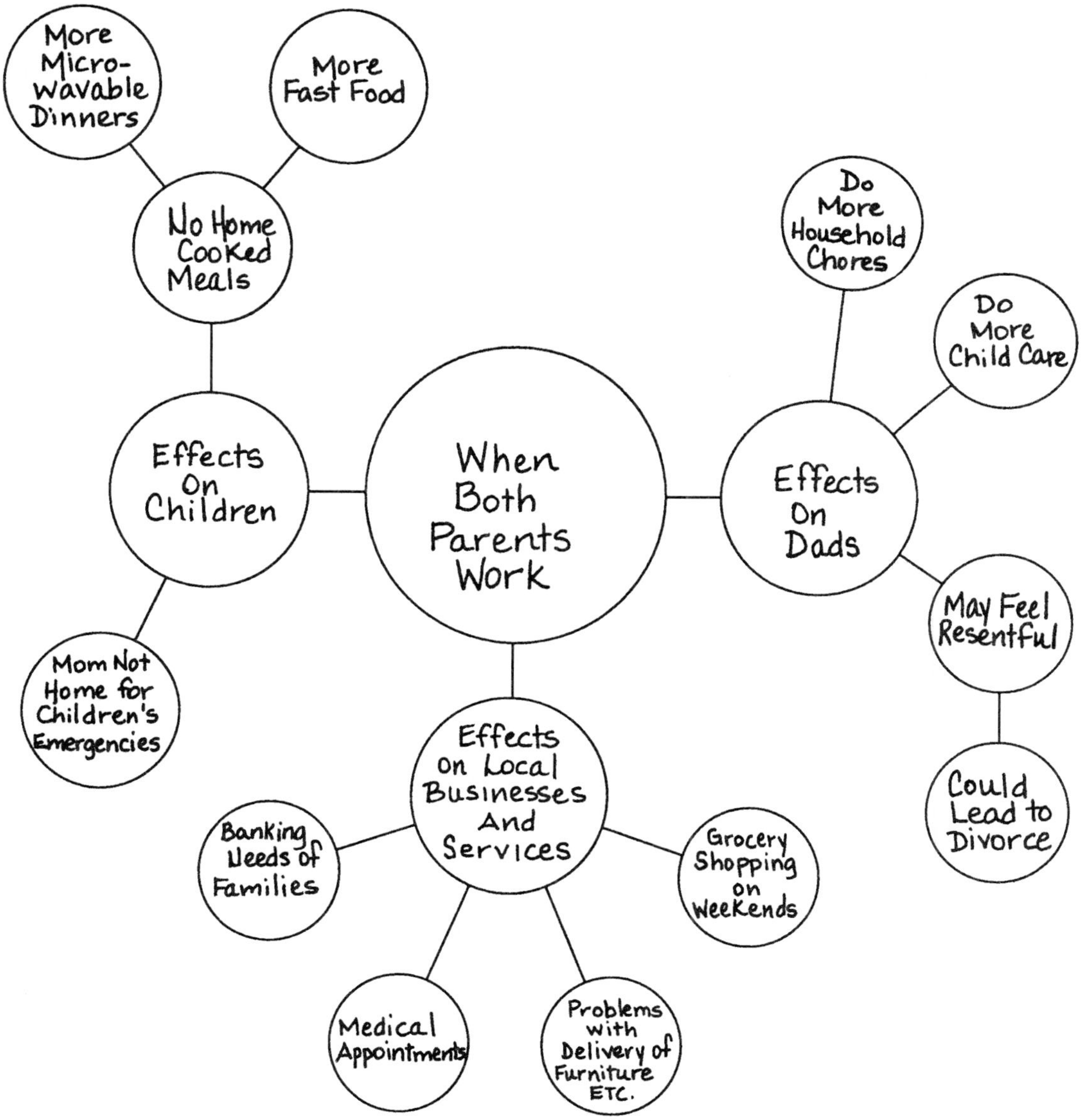

You might want to try both ways of generating ideas to see which approach works better for you.

Selecting and Organizing the Material

When the student has listed as many ideas as she can think of and has also asked her classmates for their ideas, she then looks over the list to see how she might group the words, phrases, or ideas into sections. Perhaps some ideas should be crossed out and not used at all. Maybe other ideas could be further developed. The student must also remember that once she starts to write, some creative flow may also direct her writing away from the exact outline she has developed by this point. That is fine. The outline is useful if it keeps the focus of the essay in mind.

Many instructors require the student to write a tentative thesis statement and an outline at this point so the instructor can verify that the student is on the right track.

Here is the outline the student wrote:

Topic: Parents who work outside the home

Method of Development: Discuss the effects on the family

Tentative Thesis: When economic needs force both parents to work, the effects on the family are noticeable.

I. Introductory paragraph: Economy makes it necessary for both parents to work

II. Support paragraphs: Effects on the family

  A. Effects on children

    1. No hot meals

    2. No sympathetic ear

  B. Effects on local businesses and services

    1. Medical appointments

    2. Banking and other businesses

    3. Grocery shopping

  C. Effects on dads

    1. More household chores

    2. More child care

    3. More meal preparation

  D. Effects on family eating habits

    1. More convenience foods

    2. More microwavable foods

III. Concluding paragraph: Marriage could end in divorce

Writing the Rough Draft

This student went to the computer lab where she knew she could work without interruption. With her outline and brainstorming list in front of her, she wrote the first draft of her essay. At this point, she was not concerned about a polished piece of work. The writer's goal was to get all her thoughts written down as a first draft. When she finished this rough draft, she not only saved it on a diskette of her own, she also printed out her draft so she could take the hard copy (actual printed pages) with her for later review. At that time, she would be ready to consider making revisions.

Read the student's rough draft and discuss your first impressions of it with your classmates. What are the strengths and weaknesses of this draft?

When Both Parents Work

1 The economy today has made it necessary for both parents to work. Rising prices have made two-income families the norm. What has been the effect?

2 The most noticeable change for most families is that Mom is no longer home during the day. She is not there to fix hot lunches or to soothe scraped knees and bruised egos.

3 Another effect of Mom's absence from the home is that businesses are discovering that she is no longer available to let meter readers in, accept furniture deliveries, take children to the doctor and dentist, or take care of banking needs. Just as many supermarkets have changed to a twenty-four-hour selling day, retail stores and service industries are beginning to realize that they must also adapt if they want to keep the working woman's business.

4 Even when Mom comes home in the evening, life is still not normal. Housecleaning is becoming a shared activity, when it gets done at all. Dad's duties are no longer confined to mowing the lawn and taking out the garbage, he is now expected to do lots of other things.

5 It's always a pleasure to see fathers taking their children out on weekends. Sometimes they are trying to give their wives a break, so they take the children out for a few hours or even for an entire day. This is a positive experience for the children, for they will remember these as happy hours spent with the exclusive attention of one parent.

6 So now we have Dad helping with the household chores and with the children. What about meals? Again, Dad may be asked to help out. But many men (and women) still feel the kitchen is the woman's domain. The idea that women belong in the kitchen is a popular one. Enter time-saving appliances, such as the microwave oven and convenience foods such as boil-in-the-bag frozen entrees. Mom simply doesn't have the time or the energy to prepare traditional meals.

```
Instant meals are no longer considered a luxury and the
food industry is cashing in on the demand. Even old standby
items on the grocery shelves now proclaim that they are mi-
crowavable. A fact that is not hurting their sales one bit.
7  How does the family feel about Mom as a late bloomer?
Dad may feel somewhat threatened, especially if he was
raised to believe that a womans place is in the home. He
may resent her working even more when the financial need is
severe. Because he feels it announces to the world that he
cannot provide for his family. In marriages that are not
solid to begin with, this perceived loss of dominance by
the husband may lead to divorce.
```

Revising the Rough Draft for Greater Clarity of Ideas

When the student has left the rough draft for a day or more and then returns to make revisions, she must consider what needs to be changed. Some of the questions that follow should help in the revision process. Go through these questions with your classmates and discuss what revisions need to be made. Remember that at this stage the writer should be concerned about the ideas and the organization of the ideas, not how a word is spelled or where a comma belongs.

1. **Is the essay unified? Does she stick to the topic? Does any material need to be cut?**
2. **Does she repeat herself anywhere? If so, what needs to be cut?**
3. **Does the essay make sense? Can you follow her logic? If any spot is confusing, how could she make her idea clear? Sometimes the use of transitional expressions such as *another effect, the most important effect,* or *the second effect* will help show the writer is moving to the next point.**
4. **Are the paragraphs roughly the same length? If you see one sentence presented as a paragraph, you know something is wrong.**
5. **Does the essay follow essay form? Is there an introductory paragraph with the thesis statement? Are there at least three supporting paragraphs in the body of the essay? Is there a concluding paragraph?**
6. **Are there places where more specific details could be added to develop an idea further or to add more interest?**
7. **Could the introduction, conclusion, or title be more creative?**

Now let's look at what the student's writing instructor suggested. Here is the rough draft again with the instructor's comments written in the margins. Notice that no corrections of punctuation, spelling, or grammar have yet been considered. See if you agree with the instructor's comments. Think about what other comments you would have added if you had been the instructor.

You might be able to think of a more catchy title.

Introductory paragraph needs more development. You might tell us more about the economy.

¶2 Is anyone available for this? More development please!

¶3 good specific details

¶4 What exactly does Dad do now? Be more specific. Give examples.

¶5 is not relevant to this essay, is it? Omit it in your next draft or revise it.

In ¶6, which two sentences say the same thing?

¶7 presents another effect. It is not a conclusion to the essay.

In your concluding ¶, you might look to the future for more positive solutions or summarize all your points.

When Both Parents Work

1 The economy today has made it necessary for most women to work. What has been the effect?

2 The most noticeable change for most families is that Mom is no longer home during the day. She is not there to fix hot lunches or to soothe scraped knees and bruised egos.

3 Another effect of Mom's absence from the home is that businesses are discovering that she is no longer available to let meter readers in, accept furniture deliveries, take children to the doctor and dentist, or take care of banking needs. Just as many supermarkets have changed to a twenty-four-hour selling day, retail stores and service industries are beginning to realize that they must also adapt if they want to keep the working woman's business.

4 Even when Mom comes home in the evening, life is still not normal. Housecleaning is becoming a shared activity, when it gets done at all. Dad's duties are no longer confined to mowing the lawn and taking out the garbage, he is now expected to do lots of other things.

5 It's always a pleasure to see fathers taking their children out on weekends. Sometimes they are trying to give their wives a break, so they take the children out for a few hours or even for an entire day. This is a positive experience for the children, for they will remember these as happy hours spent with the exclusive attention of one parent.

6 So now we have Dad helping with the household chores and with the children. What about meals? Again, Dad may be asked to help out. But many men (and women) still feel the kitchen is the woman's domain. The idea that women belong in the kitchen is a popular one. Enter time-saving appliances, such as the microwave oven and convenience foods such as boil-in-the-bag frozen entrees. Mom simply doesn't have the time or the energy to prepare traditional meals. Instant meals are no longer considered a luxury and the food industry is cashing in on the demand. Even old standby items on the grocery shelves now proclaim that they are microwavable. A fact that is not hurting their sales one bit.

7 How does the family feel about Mom as a late bloomer? Dad may feel somewhat threatened, especially if he was raised to believe that a womans place is in the home. He may resent her working even more when the financial need is severe. Because he feels it announces to the world that he cannot provide for his family. In marriages that are not solid to begin with, this perceived loss of dominance by the husband may lead to divorce.

Editing the Revised Draft for Correctness

Until now, the student has been concerned with the content and organization of the essay. After the student is satisfied with these revisions, it is time to look at the sentences themselves for errors such as faulty grammar, misspelling, incorrect punctuation, and inappropriate diction.

Now she should take each sentence by itself, perhaps starting with the last sentence and working backwards. (This will help her focus on the correctness of the sentences and words themselves rather than on the ideas.) She should concentrate on any weaknesses that usually cause problems for her. Many of the errors we make are unconscious and therefore hard for us to spot. Some attention from another student may be helpful and may lead to finding some of her particular errors.

When you edit your draft, look for problems such as those suggested in the following list:

1. **Sentence level errors: run-ons and fragments, often corrected by use of the proper punctuation.**
2. **Misspellings.**
3. **Lack of understanding about when to use the comma.**
4. **Possessives: *dog's* collar, but *its collar.***
5. **Diction: wordiness, use of slang, informal language or abbreviated forms, wrong word.**
6. **Grammar errors: subject-verb agreement, parallel structure, pronoun consistency.**

Practice.......... Here is the fourth paragraph from the student's revised draft. The student has responded to the instructor's comments and has added more specific details along with examples. Edit the paragraph for correctness, finding at least one mistake from each of the six problem areas listed.

Even when Mom comes home in the evening, life is still not normal. Housecleaning is becoming a shared activity, when it gets done at all. Dads duties are no longer confined to mowing the lawn and taking out the garbage, he is now expected to vacuum wash dishes bathe children fold laundry—chores that no self-respecting man of a generation ago would have done. Has Dad's ego suffered? Maybe. But possibly, just possibly, his sense of being part of a family unit, not just the bread winner and disciplinarian, have increased. Because he is now forced to deal with his kids on a less exalted level, he may find that he is closer to them and they to him. Certainly, both parent and kid will be effected by this more active fathering.

Preparing the Final Copy

Read the student's final version which she has typed, printed, and proofread. Compare it to the rough draft. Did the student make the changes suggested by the instructor? In what ways has the essay improved? What criticisms do you still have?

Goodbye, Mom's Apple Pie

1 Inflation. Stagflation. Recession. No matter what you call the current state of our economy, virtually all of us have been touched by its effects. Rising prices and the shrinking dollar have made two-income families, once a rarity, now almost the norm. Besides fattening the family pocketbook (if only to buy necessities), how else has this phenomenon changed our lives?

2 The most noticeable change for most families is that Mom is no longer home during the day. She is not there to fix hot lunches or to soothe scraped knees and bruised egos. So who does? The answer, unfortunately, often is "No one." Countless numbers of children have become "latchkey children," left to fend for themselves after school because there aren't enough dependable, affordable babysitters or after-school programs for them. Some children are able to handle this early independence quite well and may even become more resourceful adults because of it, but many are not. Vandalism, petty thievery, alcohol and drug abuse may all be products of this unsupervised life, problems that society in general must deal with eventually. Some companies (although too few) have adapted to this changing lifestyle by instituting on-site childcare facilities and/or "flextime" schedules for working mothers and fathers. Schools have begun to provide low-cost after-school activities during the schoolyear, and summer day camps are filling the need during those months.

3 Another effect of Mom's absence from the home is that businesses are discovering that she is no longer available to let meter readers in, accept furniture deliveries, take children to the doctor and dentist, or take care of banking needs. Just as many supermarkets have changed to a twenty-four-hour selling day, retail stores and service industries are beginning to realize that they must also adapt if they want to keep the working woman's business.

4 Even when Mom comes home in the evening, life is still not normal. Housecleaning is becoming a shared activity, when it gets done at all. Dad's duties are no longer confined to mowing the lawn and taking out the garbage. He is now expected to vacuum, wash dishes, bathe children, fold laundry—chores that no self-respecting man of a generation ago would have done. Has Dad's ego suffered? Maybe. But possibly, just possibly, his sense of being part of a family unit, not just the breadwinner and disciplinarian, has increased. Because he is now forced to deal with his children on a less exalted level, he may find that he is closer to them and they to him. Certainly, both parent and child will be affected by this more active fathering.

5 So now we have Dad helping with the household chores and with the children. What about meals? Again, Dad may be

asked to help out, but many men (and women) still feel the kitchen is the woman's domain. Enter time-saving appliances, such as the microwave oven and convenience foods such as boil-in-the-bag frozen entrees. Mom simply doesn't have the time or the energy to prepare traditional meals, including apple pie and home-baked bread. Instant meals are no longer considered a luxury and the food industry is cashing in on the demand. Even old standby items on the grocery shelves now proclaim that they are microwavable, a fact that is not hurting their sales one bit. However, even with quickie meals Mom is sometimes just too tired to cook. At those times fast-food restaurants enjoy the family's business. They offer no fuss, no muss, and someone to clean up after the meal. And "clean up" the restaurants have. At a time when food prices were rising almost daily and supermarket sales were dropping, fast-food restaurants were enjoying even higher sales. Maybe part of the reason was that women were beginning to realize that their time was valuable too, and if food prices were high anyway, they reasoned, they might as well eat out and not have to spend their few precious hours at home in the kitchen.

6 How does the family feel about Mom as a late bloomer? Dad may feel somewhat threatened, especially if he was raised to believe that a woman's place is in the home. He may resent her working even more when the financial need is severe because he feels it announces to the world that he cannot provide for his family. Sometimes in marriages that are not solid to begin with, this perceived loss of dominance by the husband may even lead to divorce.

7 Yes, the two-income family has played havoc with our lifestyles but it hasn't been all bad. There are problems that must be solved, changes that are difficult to accept, priorities that must be rearranged. However, with increased pressure from the growing number of two-income families, these problems will be addressed. Hopefully, society in general and individual families in particular will find even better ways to deal with these changes regarding how we raise our children, how we care for our homes, and how we view our marriages and ourselves.

WORKING TOGETHER

OUTLINING AN ESSAY

1. Imagine yourself in the following situation: You and your classmates are guidance counselors in a high school. You have been asked to produce a brochure that will be entitled, "When a Young Person Quits School." This brochure is intended for students who are thinking of dropping out of school. You and the other counselors meet to brainstorm on the topic. Divide into groups. Each group will choose a method of brainstorming: clustering, mapping, or listing. Work for 15 minutes or so, and then come together again as a class. Discuss what brainstorming method you chose and then on the board make a final grouping of the ideas for this topic.

2. In groups, or as a class, use the information gathered in the brainstorming activity above to construct an outline for the brochure "When a Young Person Quits School." Organize the information into main points and supporting details. Use the traditional framework (shown below) to construct your outline. *Roman numerals* (I, II, etc.) indicate main sections or different paragraphs of the piece of writing. *Capital letters* (A, B, etc.) indicate supporting points that will be contained in those sections.

I. ______________________________

  A. ______________________________

  B. ______________________________

II. ______________________________

  A. ______________________________

  B. ______________________________

  C. ______________________________

  D. ______________________________

III. ______________________________

  A. ______________________________

  B. ______________________________

continued on next page

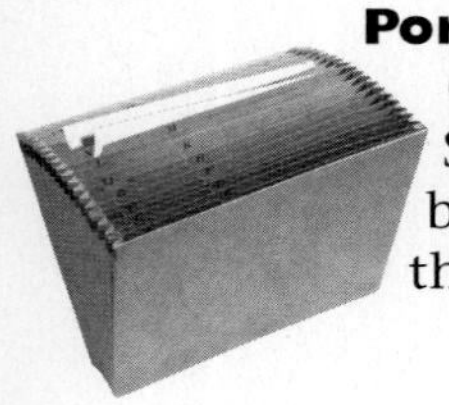

Portfolio Suggestion

Gather a few brochures from different offices on campus. (Five or six may be sufficient.) Study them carefully. What are the differences among the brochures? What makes one brochure more attractive, more effective, more impressive than another? Write an article that gives advice on how to produce an effective brochure.

Online Activity

For statistics on high school dropouts, go to:

http://www.ameristat.org/edu/dropouts.htm
http://nces.ed.gov/pubs98/condition98/C9824a01.html

Chapter 27 Writing an Essay Using Examples, Illustrations, or Anecdotes

Preview

- Explore the topic: the fear of AIDS.
- Read and analyze a model essay.
- Use the writing process to develop your own essay using *examples*.

Key Term

Example

Charts

Transitions commonly used in *example*
Guidelines for revision
Checklist for the final copy
Checklist for proofreading

Exploring the Topic: The Fear of AIDS

For nearly twenty years, one of our most serious medical situations has been the presence of AIDS in our society. The disease, which has affected every part of American life, has caused enormous suffering. This chapter is devoted to an essay on the subject of AIDS, a piece of writing that has been developed by using different kinds of examples. As you preview the essay by answering the following questions, you will be preparing to write an essay of your own, complete with examples that will illustrate and support the points you will be making.

1. Based upon what you have heard and what you have read, do people feel more educated about AIDS, and therefore less fearful, than they did in previous years? What other illnesses carry with them an unusual degree of fear?

____

____

____

____

2. When you speak with other people about AIDS, do you find that they are aware of proper precautions to be taken against AIDS?

3. People have varying attitudes toward AIDS victims, ranging from sympathy to hostility. Have these attitudes been changing?

4. Scientists have been working, with limited success, to find a cure for AIDS. Some people have been critical of these efforts, arguing that the money spent on this research could be used to fight other illnesses. What is your opinion on this aspect of the AIDS issue?

Reading a Model Essay to Discover Examples, Illustrations, and Anecdotes

AIDS: An Epidemic of Fear

Margaret O. Hyde and Elizabeth H. Forsyth, M.D.

The cure for AIDS remains to be found. The disease is an epidemic that has caused widespread misery and death. In the following essay, two prominent writers on medical subjects show us another aspect of the disease we know as AIDS: the pervasive fear that accompanies the very mention of its name and the immediate unthinking reaction some people have when they find themselves near someone who has been stricken by the virus.

1 Some people are so frightened by AIDS that they shun all homosexuals. Many customers have changed hairdressers because they suspected that the ones they frequented were gay. They now insist on women doing their hair. Actresses have refused to be made up by men who might be homosexual. One couple visiting New Orleans was so concerned about the numerous gay waiters in the French Quarter restaurants that they stopped going out to eat. They bought food in supermarkets and ate it in their hotel room. A woman who was given a book purchased at a gay-lesbian book store called the store and asked if she could safely open the package without getting AIDS. Even

people who do not think they know a homosexual person have expressed fear of the disease. All of these people were acting on unfounded fears.

2 The epidemic of fear has been evident in many places. Some television technicians refused to work on a program in which an AIDS patient was to be interviewed. Fourteen people asked to be excused from jury duty in the trial of a man who had AIDS and was accused of murder. The sheriff's deputies who had to walk with this murder suspect were so concerned about contracting the disease that they wore rubber gloves and other protective clothing when they escorted him into the courtroom.

3 There have been reports that funeral homes refused to handle the bodies of AIDS patients without using elaborate precautions. In one case, it was alleged that a funeral home charged a family an extra two hundred dollars for the gloves and gowns used to handle an AIDS patient's body, and another funeral home tried to sell a family an expensive "germ-free" coffin. A Baltimore man, Don Miller, who is concerned about the rights of homosexuals, reported that he called ninety-nine funeral homes to see what response they gave when he told them he had AIDS and was making funeral arrangements in advance. Ten refused to deal with him, and about half of them said they would require special conditions such as no embalming and/or a sealed casket. Some groups have been working toward establishing guidelines for embalming and burying people who had AIDS.

4 Children with AIDS and those whose parents have AIDS have been the victims of the epidemic of fear that spread throughout the country. Prospective foster parents often shy away from children whose mothers died from infectious diseases because of AIDS, even though the children do not have the disease. For example, one little boy lived at Jackson Memorial Hospital in Miami, Florida, for two years after he was born because his mother had AIDS before she died. He showed no indication of having the virus.

5 While some babies die quickly after birth, others live well into school age. In a number of places, hospitals have begun day care programs for children with AIDS, and a California monastery has opened its doors to unwanted infants born with AIDS who might otherwise have to spend their lives in hospitals. For many children with AIDS, life outside the hospital is one in which they are shunned by friends, neighbors, and even relatives because of the fear that still surrounds the disease.

6 Controversies about whether or not children with AIDS should be permitted to attend school have reached far and wide. The case of Ryan White of Russiaville, Indiana, was well publicized. A hemophiliac, he contracted AIDS from a blood transfusion he received in December 1984. At one point, Ryan was forced to monitor classes at home by telephone because of a restraining order obtained by parents of the other children. In the fall of 1986, Ryan started school with his class for the first time in two years, after the parents who fought his return dropped their lawsuit because of legal costs. Ryan's school had been picketed in the past, but by 1986, some students just took the attitude that they did not mind his being in school as long as he did not sit near them. Ryan was assigned his own bathroom and was given disposable utensils in the cafeteria, even though scientists believe this precaution to be unnecessary. School staff members were instructed in handling any health emergencies that arose.

7 In New York City, when school opened in late August of 1985, the fear of AIDS created a great deal of excitement. Whether or not a child who had

AIDS could attend public school in New York City was determined by a panel made up of health experts, an educator, and a parent. One child with AIDS had been attending school for three years and was identified only as a second grader. The child was said to have been born with AIDS but was in good health, the disease being in remission. She had received all the inoculations necessary for school admission, and had recovered from a case of chicken pox, managing to fight off this childhood illness uneventfully.

8 In Hollywood, many people were near hysteria after Rock Hudson's announcement that he was suffering from AIDS. Some actresses who had kissed people with AIDS were especially concerned, while others refused to work with anyone considered to be gay. After one actor became sick, makeup artists burned the brushes they had used on him. But Hollywood stars have been outstanding in their support of care for persons with AIDS and research on AIDS. Shortly before he died, Rock Hudson sent a brief message to a benefit dinner, "I am not happy that I am sick. I am not happy that I have AIDS. But if that is helping others, I can, at least, know that my own misfortune has had some positive worth."

9 Only through education and further research can one strike a balance between fear of the disease, sensible precautions, and concern for people who suffer from AIDS. Fear makes people "block out" information. We need more campaigns which emphasize the lack of danger from casual contact since polls show that people are simply not listening.

Analyzing the Writers' Strategies

1. **In the first paragraph of the essay, the writers choose a variety of examples to introduce their subject. Examine each sentence of the paragraph and underline each example. How do these different examples show the variety of the AIDS experience in our society?**
2. **One of the points the writers make throughout their essay is that AIDS is a nationwide problem. Review each paragraph and note the area of the country mentioned in the paragraph. How do the contents of the different paragraphs confirm the idea that AIDS is a widespread problem?**
3. **Throughout the essay, the writers use a number of short examples. They also use extended examples. Review the essay and find at least two paragraphs that contain several short examples. Then find at least two paragraphs that each contain one more fully developed example.**
4. **One method writers use to make their work more memorable is to be very specific when they use examples. Choose one paragraph in the essay and judge each example in that paragraph. How have the writers made a good example even better by being specific?**
5. **Can you find an anecdote in this essay? (An anecdote tells a brief story in order to illustrate a point.)**

EXPLORING ONLINE

For more information about essays developed with examples and illustrations, see

http://www.powa.org/thesfrms.htm

Writing an Essay Using Examples, Illustrations, or Anecdotes

Of the many ways writers choose to support their ideas, none is more useful or appreciated than the ***example.*** All of us have ideas in our minds, but these ideas will not become real for our readers until we use examples to make our concepts clear, concrete, and convincing. Writers who use good examples will be able to hold the attention of their readers.

> **Illustration or example** is a method of developing ideas by providing one or more instances of the idea, making the abstract idea more concrete, clarifying the idea, or making the idea more convincing.

The following terms are closely related:

Example: a specific instance of something being discussed

Extended example: an example which is developed at some length, often taking up one or more complete paragraphs

Illustration: an example used to clarify or explain

Anecdote: a brief story used to illustrate a point

Choose a Topic and Controlling Idea for the Thesis Statement

Here is a list of possible topics that could lead to an essay using *example* as the main method of development. The section that follows this list will help you work through the various stages of the writing process.

1. Doctors I Have Encountered
2. The Quality of Medical Care
3. Crises Children Face
4. What Makes a Class Exciting
5. Features to Look for When Buying a ________
6. The World's Worst Habits
7. The Lifestyles of College Students Today
8. The Increasing Problem of Homelessness
9. People I Have Admired
10. The Top Five Best Recording Artists

Using this list or ideas of your own, jot down two or three topics that appeal to you.

____

____

____

From these topics, select the one you think would give you the best opportunity for writing. About which one do you feel strongest? About which one are you the most expert? Which one is most likely to interest your readers? Which one is best suited to being developed into a college essay containing examples?

Selected Topic: ______________________________

Your next step is to decide what your controlling idea should be. What is the point you want to make about the topic you have chosen? For instance, if you choose to write about "Doctors I Have Encountered," your controlling idea may be "compassionate," or it may be "egotistical."

Controlling idea: ______________________________

Now put your topic and controlling idea together into your thesis statement.

Thesis statement: ______________________________

____

Gather the Information (Use Brainstorming Techniques)

Take at least fifteen minutes to jot down every example you can think of that you could use in your essay. If your topic is not of a personal nature, you might form a group to help each other think of examples, anecdotes, and illustrations. Later, you may want to refer to material from magazines or newspapers if you feel your examples need to be improved. If you do use outside sources, be sure to take notes, checking the correct spelling of names and the accuracy of dates and facts.

____

____

____

____

____

____

____

____

____

____

____

____

Select and Organize Material

Review your list of examples, crossing out any ideas that are not useful. Do you have enough material to develop three body paragraphs? This might mean using three extended examples, some anecdotes, or several smaller examples that could be organized into three different groups. Decide the order in which you want to present your examples. Do you have any ideas for how you might want to write the introduction? On the lines that follow, show your plan for organizing your essay. You may want to make an outline that will show major points with supporting details under each major point.

____

____

____

____

____

____

____

____

____

____

____

____

Write the Rough Draft

Now you are ready to write your rough draft. Approach the writing with the attitude that you are going to write down all your thoughts on the subject without worrying about mistakes of any kind. It is important that your mind is relaxed enough to allow your thoughts to flow freely, even if you do not follow your plan exactly. Just get your thoughts on paper. You are free to add ideas, drop others, or rearrange the order of your details at any point. Sometimes a period of freewriting leads to new ideas, ideas that could be better than the ones you had in your brainstorming session. Once a writer has something on paper, he or she usually feels a great sense of relief, even though it is obvious there are revisions ahead.

Achieve Coherence

Keep in mind that in a paragraph with several examples, the order of these examples usually follows some logical progression. This could mean that you would start with the less serious and then move to the more serious, or you might start with the simpler one and move to the more complicated. If your examples consist of events, you might begin with examples from the more distant past and move forward to give examples from the present day. Whatever logical progression you choose, you will find it helpful to signal your examples by using some of transitional expressions that follow.

TRANSITIONS COMMONLY USED IN *EXAMPLE*

the following illustration
to illustrate this
as an illustration
for example
for instance
specifically
an example of this is
such as
one such case
a typical case
To illustrate my point, let me tell you a story.
Let me prove my point with a story.

Revise the Rough Draft

As you work on your rough draft, you may revise alone, with a group, with a peer tutor, or directly with your instructor. Here are some of the basic questions you should consider at this most important stage of your work:

GUIDELINES FOR REVISION

1. Does the rough draft satisfy the conditions for the essay form? Is there an introductory paragraph? Are there at least three well-developed paragraphs in the body of the essay? Do each of these paragraphs have at least one example? Is there a concluding paragraph? Remember that one sentence is not usually considered an acceptable paragraph. (Many journalistic pieces do not follow this general rule because they often have a space limitation and are not expected to develop every idea.)
2. Have you used ***example*** as your major method of development? Could you make your examples even better by being more specific or by looking up statistics or facts that would lend more authority to your point of view? Could you quote an expert on the subject?
3. What is the basis for the ordering of your examples? Whenever appropriate, did you use transitions to signal the beginning of an example?
4. Is any important part missing? Are there any parts that seem irrelevant or out of place?
5. Are there words or expressions that could have been better choices? Is there any place where you have been repetitious?
6. Find at least two verbs (usually some form of the verb "to be") that could be replaced with more descriptive verbs. Add at least two adjectives that will provide better sensory images for the reader.
7. Find at least one place in the draft where you can add a sentence or two that will make an example better.
8. Can you think of a more effective way to begin or end?
9. Show your draft to two other readers and ask each one to give you at least one suggestion for improvement.

Prepare the Final Copy, Print, and Proofread

The typing of the final version should follow the traditional rules for an acceptable submission.

CHECKLIST FOR THE FINAL COPY

Use only 8½-by-11–inch paper (never paper torn out of a spiral-bound notebook).

Type on one side of the paper only.

Double-space.

Leave approximately 1½-inch margins on each side of the paper.

Center the title at the top of the page. Do not put quotation marks around the title and do not underline it.

Do not hyphenate a word at the end of a line unless you are willing to consult a dictionary to check on the acceptable division of the word into syllables.

You may put your name, the date, and the title of your paper on a separate title page. Ask your instructor for specific advice on what information to include.

Indent each paragraph five spaces.

Leave two spaces after each period.

If your paper is more than one page, number the pages and staple the pages together so they will not get lost.

Do not forget to make a copy before you submit the paper.

Note: In most cases, college teachers will not accept handwritten work. However, if you are submitting handwritten work, you must be sure to write on every other line and have good legible handwriting. Begin today to learn to type on the computer. You will be at a disadvantage if you cannot use the current technology.

Once you have typed your final version and printed it out, an important step still remains. This step can often mean the difference of an entire letter grade. You must *proofread* your paper. Even if you have used a spellcheck feature available on your word processing program, there still could be errors in your paper. The spellcheck feature only finds groupings of letters that are not words. For example, if you typed the word *van* when you meant to type *ban,* the spellcheck would not catch this error.

The secret of good proofreading is to look at each word and sentence construction by itself without thinking about the paper's contents.

CHECKLIST FOR PROOFREADING

Study each sentence: One way to proofread is to read backwards, starting with the last sentence and examining every sentence, one at a time. First, check that the sentence is really complete and not a fragment or a run-on. Then check the punctuation. Go on to the next sentence and do the same. In this way, you will develop a critical eye for spotting any problems with sentence level errors.

Study each word: Read the paper again, this time studying each word in every sentence. Look at the letters of the words. Have you transposed any letters or have you left off an ending such as the *-ed* or the *-s?* If there are any words you are not sure how to spell, do not forget to check for the correct spelling. Is there any word you have omitted?

WORKING TOGETHER

BRAINSTORMING FOR EXAMPLES

Topic: Why Do Some Employees Fail to Get Ahead in Their Jobs?

Sometimes, without being aware of it, people act in such a way at work that they are prevented from getting good performance evaluations. These evaluations are important in order to obtain permanent positions, salary increases, and job promotions. People's bad evaluations can even result in their being fired.

Work in groups for at least twenty minutes to develop a list of examples that illustrate this kind of behavior. Your list should be made up of things workers do that make their employers (and their fellow workers) think less of them.

Then come together as a class and share your lists. Put the examples on the board. Can class members think of specific incidents they have observed that would illustrate these examples?

Portfolio Suggestion

Use this list to write an essay in which you incorporate some of the examples provided by members of your class. If you wish, you could do more research on this work-related topic in order to develop your essay into a longer research paper.

Online Activity

Review and discuss an actual form for evaluating employee performance:

http://www.smartbiz.com/sbs/arts/cbf2.htm

Chapter 28 Writing an Essay Using Narration

Preview

- Explore the topic: a painful childhood memory.
- Read and analyze a model essay.
- Use the writing process to develop your own essay using *narration*.

Key Term

Narration

Charts

Transitions commonly used in *narration*
Guidelines for revision
Checklist for the final copy
Checklist for proofreading

Exploring the Topic: A Painful Childhood Memory

For most of us, childhood holds a mixture of happy and painful memories. The memory that the author Audré Lorde writes about in the selection you are about to read is the humiliation and agony of being the target of racist practices. The essay you will write in this chapter will be a narrative essay, based on a painful experience you have had as a child, perhaps an incident in which you were treated unfairly. As you answer the following questions, and as you read the narrative selection, think about what childhood experience you might want to choose.

1. What are some of the painful experiences that nearly all children go through?

____

____

____

____

2. What are some of the painful experiences that only some children are forced to endure?

____

____

____

____

3. How has society tried to protect children from cruel and unjust treatment?

____

____

____

____

4. How can individuals survive injustices that they have suffered?

____

____

____

____

Reading a Model Essay to Discover Narrative Elements

The Fourth of July

Audré Lorde

Audré Lorde (1934–1992) was born and raised in New York City. Her career included teaching at the City University of New York (CUNY), autobiographical writing, and the creation of some memorable poetry. In 1991, she was named the official poet for New York State.

The following selection, taken from her 1982 memoir *Zami: A New Spelling of My Name,* tells us the story of a trip the thirteen-year-old Audré took with her family to Washington, D.C. The account also provides us with a portrait of the state of our nation in the late 1940s.

1 The first time I went to Washington, D.C., was on the edge of the summer when I was supposed to stop being a child. At least that's what they said to us all at graduation from the eighth grade. My sister Phyllis graduated at the same time from high school. I don't know what she was supposed to stop being. But as graduation presents for us both, the whole family took a Fourth of July trip to Washington, D.C., the fabled and famous capital of our country.

2 It was the first time I'd ever been on a railroad train during the day. When I was little, and we used to go to the Connecticut shore, we always went at night on the milk train, because it was cheaper.

3 Preparations were in the air around our house before school was even over. We packed for a week. There were two very large suitcases that my father carried, and a box filled with food. In fact, my first trip to Washington was a mobile feast; I started eating as soon as we were comfortably ensconced in our seats, and did not stop until somewhere after Philadelphia. I remember it was Philadelphia because I was disappointed not to have passed by the Liberty Bell.

4 My mother had roasted two chickens and cut them up into dainty bite-size pieces. She packed slices of brown bread and butter and green pepper and carrot sticks. There were little violently yellow iced cakes with scalloped edges called "marigolds," that came from Cushman's Bakery. There was a spice bun and rock-cakes from Newton's, the West Indian bakery across Lenox Avenue from St. Mark's School, and iced tea in a wrapped mayonnaise jar. There were sweet pickles for us and dill pickles for my father, and peaches with the fuzz still on them, individually wrapped to keep them from bruising. And, for neatness, there were piles of napkins and a little tin box with a washcloth dampened with rosewater and glycerine for wiping sticky mouths.

5 I wanted to eat in the dining car because I had read all about them, but my mother reminded me for the umpteenth time that dining car food always cost too much money and besides, you never could tell whose hands had been playing all over that food, nor where those same hands had been just before. My mother never mentioned that Black people were not allowed into railroad dining cars headed south in 1947. As usual, whatever my mother did not like and could not change, she ignored. Perhaps it would go away, deprived of her attention.

6 I learned later that Phyllis's high school senior class trip had been to Washington, but the nuns had given her back her deposit in private, explaining to her that the class, all of whom were white, except Phyllis, would be staying in a hotel where Phyllis "would not be happy," meaning, Daddy explained to her, also in private, that they did not rent rooms to Negroes. "We will take you to Washington, ourselves," my father had **avowed,** "and not just for an overnight in some measly fleabag hotel."

avowed
promised

7 American racism was a new and crushing reality that my parents had to deal with every day of their lives once they came to this country. They handled it as a private woe. My mother and father believed that they could best protect their children from the realities of race in America and the fact of American racism by never giving them name, much less discussing their nature. We were told we must never trust white people, but *why* was never explained, nor the nature of their ill will. Like so many other vital pieces of information in my childhood, I was supposed to know without being told. It always seemed like a very strange injunction coming from my mother, who looked so much like one of those people we were never supposed to trust. But something always warned me not to ask my mother why she wasn't white, and why Auntie Lillah and Auntie Etta weren't, even though they were all that same problematic color so different from my father and me, even from my sisters, who were somewhere in-between.

8 In Washington, D.C., we had one large room with two double beds and an extra cot for me. It was a back-street hotel that belonged to a friend of my father's who was in real estate, and I spent the whole next day after Mass

Marian Anderson *internationally famous African American singer*
the D.A.R. *The Daughters of the American Revolution*

squinting up at the Lincoln Memorial where **Marian Anderson** had sung after **the D.A.R.** refused to allow her to sing in their auditorium because she was Black. Or because she was "Colored," my father said as he told the story. Except that what he probably said was "Negro," because for his times, my father was quite progressive.

9 I was squinting because I was in that silent agony that characterized all of my childhood summers, from the time school let out in June to the end of July, brought about by my dilated and vulnerable eyes exposed to the summer brightness.

corona *a hazy light*

10 I viewed Julys through an agonizing **corona** of dazzling whiteness and I always hated the Fourth of July, even before I came to realize the travesty such a celebration was for Black people in this country.

11 My parents did not approve of sunglasses, nor of their expense.

12 I spent the afternoon squinting up at monuments to freedom and past presidencies and democracy, and wondering why the light and heat were both so much stronger in Washington, D.C., than back home in New York City. Even the pavement on the streets was a shade lighter in color than back home.

13 Late that Washington afternoon my family and I walked back down Pennsylvania Avenue. We were a proper caravan, mother bright and father brown, the three of us girls step-standards in-between. Moved by our historical surroundings and the heat of the early evening, my father decreed yet another treat. He had a great sense of history, a flair for the quietly dramatic and the sense of specialness of an occasion and a trip.

14 "Shall we stop and have a little something to cool off, Lin?"

15 Two blocks away from our hotel, the family stopped for a dish of vanilla ice cream at a Breyer's ice cream and soda fountain. Indoors, the soda fountain was dim and fan-cooled, deliciously relieving to my scorched eyes.

mottled *having spots of different colors*

16 Corded and crisp and pinafored, the five of us seated ourselves one by one at the counter. There was I between my mother and father, and my two sisters on the other side of my mother. We settled ourselves along the white **mottled** marble counter, and when the waitress spoke at first no one understood what she was saying, and so the five of us just sat there.

17 The waitress moved along the line of us closer to my father and spoke again. "I said I kin give you to take out, but you can't eat here. Sorry." Then she dropped her eyes looking very embarrassed, and suddenly we heard what it was she was saying all at the same time, loud and clear.

Bataan *a major World War II battle*

18 Straight-backed and indignant, one by one, my family and I got down from the counter stools and turned around and marched out of the store, quiet and outraged, as if we had never been Black before. No one would answer my emphatic questions with anything other than a guilty silence. "But we hadn't done anything!" This wasn't right or fair! Hadn't I written poems about **Bataan** and freedom and democracy for all?

19 My parents wouldn't speak of this injustice, not because they had contributed to it, but because they felt they should have anticipated it and avoided it. This made me even angrier. My fury was not going to be acknowledged by a like fury. Even my two sisters copied my parents' pretense that nothing unusual and anti-American had occurred. I was left to write

my angry letter to the president of the United States all by myself, although my father did promise I could type it out on the office typewriter next week, after I showed it to him in my copybook diary.

20 The waitress was white, and the counter was white, and the ice cream I never ate in Washington, D.C., that summer I left childhood was white, and the white heat and the white pavement and the white stone monuments of my first Washington summer made me sick to my stomach for the whole rest of that trip and it wasn't much of a graduation present after all.

Analyzing the Writer's Strategies

1. Explain how the first paragraph establishes the setting for the story by telling us who, what, where, when, and why.
2. Narration uses transitions of time to move the story along. Go through the story and find these transitions.
3. Go through the story and find the places where the author uses quotations to set off the exact words a person used. Who are the persons Audré Lorde has chosen to quote, and why do you think she selected those people?
4. Throughout the story, Audré Lorde provides a number of details that reveal how her family lived. Choose five details and explain how each detail reveals something about their lives.
5. Point out each instance in the selection where the writer mentions her problems with eyesight. How does her difficulty in *seeing* relate to her ability to *see* (in the sense of understanding) the injustice she and her family have suffered?

EXPLORING ONLINE

Review and discuss six students' narrative essays:

http://www.tp.ac.sg/content/lcd/cillmatters/Matters_98/TELLS1_98/tells.htm

Writing the Essay Using Narration

Narration is the oldest and best-known form of verbal communication. It is, quite simply, the telling of a story.

Choose a Story and Your Point for that Story

1. A terrible classroom experience
2. A parent who wasn't sensitive
3. The pain of growing up being shy
4. The pain of not fitting in

5. The difficulty of moving to a new neighborhood
6. Losing a loved one
7. The pain of being in a family that doesn't get along together
8. A time of loneliness
9. An accident that affected my childhood
10. Having to endure discrimination

Using the above list of suggested topics to start you thinking, jot down two or three powerful memories you have from your own childhood. These are possible topics for your writing.

____

____

____

From these two or three topics, select the one you think would give you the best opportunity for writing an interesting story. Which one do you feel strongest about? Which one is most likely to interest your readers? Which topic is most suitable for a college essay?

____

____

____

Selected topic: ______________________________

Good narration should have a point. Think about your story. What is the point you could make by telling this story? In a story, a writer does not always come right out and state the point of the story, but the reader should understand the point by the time he or she reaches the end.

Point of your story: ______________________________

____

____

____

The introductory paragraph for a story usually sets the scene. What will be the time (time of year, time of day), place, and mood that you would like to set in your introductory paragraph?

Time: ______________________________

Place: ______________________________

Mood: ______________________________

Gather the Information (Use Brainstorming Techniques)

Take at least fifteen minutes to jot down the sequence of events for your story as you remember it. Try to remember the way things looked at the time, how people reacted (what they did, what they said), and what you thought as the event was happening. If you can go to the actual spot where the event took place, you might go there and take notes of the details of the place. Later on you can sort through the material and pick out what you want to use.

Select and Organize Material

Review your brainstorming list and cross out any details that are not appropriate. Prepare to build on the ideas that you like. Put these remaining ideas into an order that will serve as your temporary guide.

Write the Rough Draft

Find a quiet place where you will not be interrupted for at least one hour. With the plan for your essay in front of you, sit down and write the story that is in your mind. Do not try to judge what you are putting down as right or wrong. What is important is that you let your mind relax and allow the words to flow freely. Do not worry if you find yourself not following your plan exactly. Keep in mind that you are free to add parts, drop sections of the story, or rearrange details at any point. Sometimes just allowing your thoughts to take you wherever they will lead results in new ideas. You may like these inspirations better than your original plan. Writing a rough draft is a little like setting out on an expedition; there are limitless possibilities, so it is important to be flexible.

Achieve Coherence

Keep in mind that in a narrative essay, details are usually ordered according to a ***time sequence.*** One way to make the time sequence clear is to use transitional words that will signal a time change.

TRANSITIONS COMMONLY USED IN *NARRATION*

A few carefully chosen transitional words will help the reader move smoothly from one part of a story to the next. Here are some examples:

in December of 1980 . . .	after a little while
the following month	then
soon afterward	meanwhile
at once	next, the next day
suddenly	several weeks passed
immediately	later, later on
now, by now	at the same time
in the next month	finally

Revise the Rough Draft

As you work on your rough draft, you may work alone, with a group, with a peer tutor, or directly with your instructor. If you are working on a computer, making changes is so easy that you will feel encouraged to explore alternatives. Unlike making changes using traditional pen and paper, working on a computer to insert or delete material is a simple matter.

Here are some of the basic questions you should consider when the time comes to revise your narration:

GUIDELINES FOR REVISION

1. Does the rough draft satisfy the conditions for the essay form? Is there an introductory paragraph? Are there at least three well-developed paragraphs in the body of the essay? Is there a concluding paragraph? Remember that one sentence is not a developed paragraph. One exception to this rule is when you use dialogue. When you write a story, you often include the conversation between two people. In this case, the writer makes a new paragraph each time a different person speaks. This often means that one sentence could be a separate paragraph.
2. Is your essay a narration? Does it tell the story of one particular incident that takes place in a specific time and location? Sometimes writers make the mistake of talking about incidents in a general way, and commenting on the meaning of the incidents. Be careful. This would not be considered a narration. You must be a storyteller. Where does the action take place? Can the reader see it? What time of day, week, or season is it? What is your main character in the story doing?
3. Have you put the details of the essay in a certain time order? Find the expressions you have used that show the time sequence.
4. Can you think of any part of the story that is missing and should be added? Is there any material that is irrelevant and should be omitted?
5. Are there sentences or paragraphs that seem to be repetitious?
6. Find several places where you can substitute stronger verbs or nouns. Add adjectives to give the reader better sensory images.
7. Find at least three places in your draft where you can add details. Perhaps you might add an entire paragraph that will more fully describe the person or place that is central to your story.
8. Can you think of a more effective way to begin or end?
9. Does your story have a point? If a person just told you everything he did on a certain day, that would not be a good story. A good story needs to have a point.
10. Show your rough draft to at least two other readers and ask for suggestions.

Prepare the Final Copy, Print, and Proofread

The typing of the final version should follow the traditional rules for an acceptable submission.

CHECKLIST FOR THE FINAL COPY

Use only 8½-by-11–inch paper (never paper torn out of a spiral-bound notebook).

Type on one side of the paper only.

Double-space.

Leave approximately 1½-inch margins on each side of the paper.

Center the title at the top of the page. Do not put quotation marks around the title and do not underline it.

Do not hyphenate a word at the end of a line unless you are willing to consult a dictionary to check on the acceptable division of the word into syllables.

You may put your name, the date, and the title of your paper on a separate title page. Ask your instructor for specific advice on what information to include.

Indent each paragraph five spaces.

Leave two spaces after each period.

If your paper is more than one page, number the pages and staple the pages together so they will not get lost.

Do not forget to make a copy before you submit the paper.

Note: In most cases, college teachers will not accept handwritten work. However, if you are submitting handwritten work, be sure to write on every other line and have good legible handwriting. Begin today to learn to type on the computer. You will be at a disadvantage if you cannot use the current technology.

Once you have typed your final version and printed it out, an important step still remains. This step can often mean the difference of an entire letter grade. You must *proofread* your paper. Even if you have used a spellcheck feature available on your word processing program, there still could be errors in your paper. The spellcheck feature only finds groupings of letters that are not words. For example, if you typed the word *van* when you meant to type *ban,* the spellcheck would not catch this error.

The secret of good proofreading is to look at each word and sentence construction by itself without thinking about the paper's contents.

CHECKLIST FOR PROOFREADING

Study each sentence: One way to proofread is to read backwards, starting with the last sentence and examining every sentence, one at a time. First, check that the sentence is really complete and not a fragment or a run-on. Then check the punctuation. Go on to the next sentence and do the same. In this way, you will develop a critical eye for spotting any problems with sentence–level errors.

Study each word: Read the paper again, this time studying each word in every sentence. Look at the letters of the words. Have you transposed any letters or have you left off an ending such as the *-ed* or the *-s?* If there are any words you are not sure how to spell, do not forget to check for the correct spelling. Is there any word you have omitted?

WORKING TOGETHER

SHARING OUR NARRATIVES

Everyone loves a good story, and children are especially fond of being read to by an older person. In this chapter, everyone has already written at least one piece that could be called a narrative or a story. For this Working Together, divide into groups of five or six students; each person should read his or her narrative out loud to the others. As you listen to the narratives, remember to give each person the same careful attention as you would want to have devoted to your work.

After everyone has had a turn reading, use a paper clip to attach a full-sized piece of paper to each essay. Pass the essays around. Each person in the group will now respond to the essay by writing a few sentences on the full-sized piece of paper. Use these questions as your guide:

1. In your opinion, what part of the story did you find most interesting?
2. Was there any part or detail that you found confusing?
3. What is one part you would have liked the writer to explain in more detail?
4. What do you think was the point of the story?

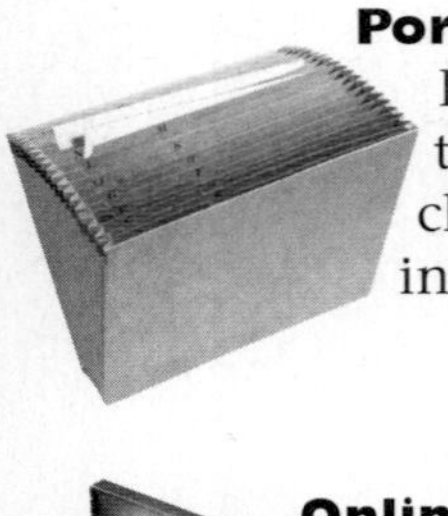

Portfolio Suggestion

Keep all the narratives you have worked on in this chapter in your portfolio. These may be the beginning of a series of stories you could write to capture the memories of your own childhood. You will be surprised how much you can recall when you actually focus on writing about these past events.

Online Activity

Explore the top 100 children's stories listed by the New York Public Library. How many of the titles are familiar to you? Which titles sound interesting?

http://www.nypl.org/branch/kids/100/animal.html

Chapter 29 Writing an Essay Using Process

Preview

- Explore the topic: How to have a successful job interview.
- Read and analyze a model essay.
- Use the writing process to develop your own essay explaining to your readers how to do something.

Key Term

Process

Charts

Transitions commonly used in *process*
Guidelines for revision
Checklist for the final copy
Checklist for proofreading

Exploring the Topic: Preparing for a Job Interview

You are in the market for a job. You have read the newspaper ads, asked your friends for suggestions, made phone calls, and sent out résumés. Now you have a very promising interview coming up next week. What can you do to prepare for this important interview?

Everyone who works, or who is looking for the chance to find work, has been in this situation. Whether we are getting ready for such an interview, or whether we have already gone through the experience, everyone is interested in the all-important process of obtaining a satisfying work situation.

1. If you have ever gone through a job interview, share your experience with the class. What was the best (or worst) aspect of the interview? What questions were you asked? Were you prepared? Did you get the job?

___

___

___

2. Imagine you are a person conducting a job interview. What would you be looking for in a prospective employee?

____

____

____

3. What have you heard that people have done during interviews? What should a person *never* do in a job interview?

____

____

____

4. What are some of the other events in our lives that always benefit from careful planning?

____

____

____

Reading a Model Essay to Discover Steps in a Process

How to Ace a Job Interview

Richard Koonce

In the following essay, Richard Koonce takes us through the stages of the interview process, giving valuable pointers to job seekers. Whether we are heading toward an interview ourselves or advising a friend who is looking for a job, the following essay is filled with practical wisdom about what it takes to have a successful job interview.

1 Next to public speaking, most people think that enduring a job interview is one of the most stressful human experiences.

2 I wouldn't quibble with that. However, a lot of people not only manage to master the art of effective interviewing as they go about job searches, but actually grow to enjoy the interview experience.

3 Good thing! Job interviews are something we all have to deal with from time to time in our careers. So, it pays to know how to handle yourself effectively when you're sitting across the desk from a prospective employer. Indeed, knowing how to navigate the terrain of job interviews can pay off big time for your career, land you a better job than the one you initially interview for, and position you for the job success and satisfaction you deserve.

4 How do you ace a job interview? Here are some tips.

5 Recognize that when you interview for a job, employers are looking for evidence of four things: your ability to do the job, your motivation, your

compatibility with the rest of the organization, and your self-confidence. If you understand how all those things play into an interviewer's questions (and an employer's hiring decisions), you'll have a better chance of getting hired.

6 Often the first thing an employer wants to know is, "Will you fit in?" Presuming a company has seen your resume ahead of time and invited you for an interview, it may assume you have certain skills. Now they want to know, "Will you be compatible with everyone else that works here?"

7 Fitting in is a real hot button for employers. That's because it's expensive to go through the rehiring process if someone doesn't work out.

8 Along with determining compatibility, employers want to know that you're motivated to do a job. And, they want to know why you want to work for their organization. So be ready with career highlights that illustrate why hiring you would be a good decision for the organization. Showcase your talents as an instructional designer for example, or tell the interviewer about the process improvement efforts you've put in place in your current job that ensure continuous refinement of training courses. Concise oral vignettes like these can make a great impression on interviewers.

9 Throughout the interview, breathe deeply, speak slowly, and focus on projecting yourself confidently. This is important. Employers want to see self-confidence in job seekers. A lot of job seekers are too modest. They downplay their accomplishments. Don't embellish or exaggerate, but don't be a shrinking violet either. Rehearse ahead of time the answers to key questions that you expect to be asked, especially that all-time favorite: "Tell me about yourself."

10 Some other points to keep in mind:

11 Before the interview, do some research on the company you're interviewing with. That will enable you to demonstrate knowledge of the company when you meet the interviewer. It may also prompt questions that you'll want to get answers to, even as questions are being asked of you.

12 There are lots of research options. You can tap into the Internet and pull down everything from company profiles to *Dun and Bradstreet* financial reports. You can talk to friends or coworkers that may know something about the organization. And don't forget to watch the paper for late-breaking developments about the company. (If you read in the paper the day of your interview that your prospective employer is about to file Chapter 11, you may want to think twice about working there!)

13 Arrive for the interview early enough to go to the restroom to check yourself out. The last thing you want is to arrive for your interview beaded with sweat, having just sprinted there from the subway stop two blocks away.

14 Once in the interview, concentrate on making a pleasant and strong first impression. Eighty percent of the first impression an interviewer gets of you is visual—and it's formed in the first two minutes of the meeting! So, men, wear a well-made suit, crisply starched white or blue shirt, and polished shoes. Women, you can get away with more color than men, but dress conservatively in dresses, or jacket and skirt combinations. Wearing a colorful scarf is a good way to weave in color, but keep jewelry to a minimum.

15 As you answer questions, be sure to emphasize as often as you can the reasons why your skills, background, and experience make you a good fit for the job that you're interviewing for.

16 After the interview, immediately send a thank-you note to the interviewer. This is a critical point of interview etiquette. Many job candidates eliminate themselves from competition for a job because they don't do this.

17 Finally, learn from every job interview you have. Don't be hard on yourself if things don't go your way. Even job interviews that don't go well can be great learning experiences. And in my own life, I can look back on interviews where I'm glad I didn't get the job!

Analyzing the Writer's Strategies

1. How many paragraphs comprise the introduction?
2. What are the four pieces of information employers want to know about a prospective employee?
3. The stages in this process consist of the following: (1) what you should know before the interview, (2) how you should prepare for the interview, (3) what to do upon arrival at the interview, (4) how you should conduct yourself during the interview, and (5) what you should do after the interview. What is the author's advice at each of these stages?
4. From your own experience, can you think of any other advice that should have been included?
5. How does the writer's last paragraph provide a useful conclusion to the essay?

Writing the Essay Using Process (How to . . .)

> **Process,** a method of developing ideas, gives a step-by-step explanation of how to do something (directional process) or how something works (informational process).

The "how to" section of every library and bookstore is usually a busy area. People come to find books that will help them perform thousands of different tasks—from plumbing to flower arranging. If you want to learn how to cook Chinese dishes, assemble a child's bicycle, start your own business, or even remodel your bathroom, you can find a book that will tell you how to do it. Thousands of books and articles have been written that promise to help people accomplish their goals in life. What do you think are the best selling "how to" books in America? Perhaps you have guessed the answer: how to lose weight! In the essay that you write, be sure to choose a process with which you are already familiar.

Choose a Topic and the Purpose of the Information for the Thesis Statement

1. How to get good grades in college
2. How to prepare for a driver's test
3. How to plan a budget
4. How to buy a used car
5. How to study for a test
6. How to change a tire
7. How to redecorate a room
8. How to buy clothes on a limited budget
9. How to find the right place to live
10. How to make new friends

Using the above list of ten topics or using ideas of your own, jot down two or three processes with which you are familiar.

____

____

____

____

____

From these two or three topics, select the one you think would give you the best opportunity for writing. Which process do you feel strongest about? Which one is most likely to interest your readers? For which topic do you have the most first-hand experience?

Selected topic: ______________________________________

Your next step is to decide your purpose in writing. Which of the two types of process writing will you be doing? Do you want to give directions on how to carry out each step in a process so that your readers can do this process themselves? For instance, would you provide directions on how to change a tire, perhaps suggesting that your readers keep these directions in the glove compartments of their cars? On the other hand, do you want to provide information as to how a certain process works because you think your readers might find the process interesting? For instance, you might explain the process involved in getting an airplane off the ground. Not many of us understand how this works, and very few of us will actually ever pilot a plane. Perhaps you know a lot about an unusual process that might amuse or entertain readers.

Directional __________ or informational __________

Now put your topic and controlling idea together into your thesis statement.

Thesis statement: ______________________________________

____

Gather the Information (Use Brainstorming Techniques)

Take at least fifteen minutes to list as many steps or stages in the process as you can. If the process is one that others in your class or at home already know, consult with them for any additional steps that you may have overlooked. You may also need to think of the precise vocabulary words associated with the process (such as the names of tools used for building or repairing something). The more specific you can be, the more helpful and interesting the process will be for your readers. List the steps or stages in the process:

Select and Organize Material

Review your brainstorming list and ask yourself if you now have a complete list. Have you left out any step that someone who is unfamiliar with this process might need to know? Is there some extra information you could provide along the way that would be helpful and encouraging? Do you have a special warning about something that the reader should *not* do? You might consider telling your readers exactly where in the process most people are likely to make mistakes.

Make an outline giving each stage a heading. Underneath each heading, list all of the different ideas or vocabulary words that you should keep in mind as you begin to write. In a process essay, the most essential elements for judging its success are the order, the accuracy, and the completeness of all the steps.

____

____

____

____

____

____

Write the Rough Draft

Follow your outline and write your rough draft, keeping in mind that this outline is only a guide. As you write, you will find yourself reevaluating the logic of your ideas, a perfectly natural step that may involve making some changes from your outline. You may think of some special advice that would help the reader, and if you do, feel free to add these details. Your main goal is to get the process down on paper as completely and accurately as possible.

Achieve Coherence

When you buy a product and read the instructions that go with it, the form of writing in those instructions usually consists of a list of numbered items, each telling you what to do. In an essay, you do not usually number the steps. Instead, you can signal the movement from one step to another by changing to a new paragraph and/or by using a transitional expression. As in other methods for developing ideas, *process* has its own special words and expressions that can be used to signal movement from one step to the next.

TRANSITIONS COMMONLY USED IN *PROCESS*

the first step	while you are	the last step
in the beginning	as you are	the final step
to start with	next	finally
to begin with	then	at last
first of all	the second step	eventually
	after you have	

Revise the Rough Draft

A space of time is very helpful to allow you to think about your written ideas; this allows you to judge your work more objectively than you can immediately after writing. Therefore, if you can put aside your draft for a day or two before you need to revise it, your work will benefit.

When you revise, you may work alone, with a group, with a peer tutor, or directly with your instructor. Here are some of the basic questions you should consider during this most important stage of your work:

GUIDELINES FOR REVISION

1. Does the rough draft satisfy all the conditions for the essay form? Is there an introductory paragraph? Are there at least three well-developed paragraphs in the body of the essay? Have you written a concluding paragraph? Remember that a single sentence is not a developed paragraph.
2. Does the essay describe the process, one that is either directional or informational?
3. Are the steps in the process in the correct order? In a process essay, the sequence of the steps is crucial. A step that is placed out of order could result in a disaster of major proportions.
4. Are the directions accurate and complete? Check more than once that no important piece of information has been left out. Have you considered the points where some special advice might be helpful? Are there any special tools that would be useful?
5. Is any of the material not relevant?
6. Are there sentences or words that seem to be repetitious?
7. Find several places where you can substitute more specific verbs, nouns or adjectives. Always try to use vocabulary that is appropriate for the process being described.
8. Can you think of a more effective way to begin or end?
9. Does the essay flow logically from one idea to the next? Could you improve this flow with better use of transitional expressions?
10. Show your draft to at least two other readers and ask for suggestions.

Prepare the Final Copy, Print, and Proofread

The typing of the final version should follow the traditional rules for an acceptable submission.

CHECKLIST FOR THE FINAL COPY

Use only 8½-by-11–inch paper (never paper torn out of a spiral-bound notebook).

Type on one side of the paper only.

Double-space.

Leave approximately 1½-inch margins on each side of the paper.

Center the title at the top of the page. Do not put quotation marks around the title and do not underline it.

Do not hyphenate a word at the end of a line unless you are willing to consult a dictionary to check on the acceptable division of the word into syllables.

You may put your name, the date, and the title of your paper on a separate title page. Ask your instructor for specific advice on what information to include.

Indent each paragraph five spaces.

Leave two spaces after each period.

If your paper is more than one page, number the pages and staple the pages together so they will not get lost.

Do not forget to make a copy before you submit the paper.

Note: In most cases, college teachers will not accept handwritten work. However, if you are submitting handwritten work, you must be sure to write on every other line and have good legible handwriting. Begin today to learn to type on the computer. You will be at a disadvantage if you cannot use the current technology.

Once you have typed your final version and printed it out, an important step still remains. This step can often mean the difference of an entire letter grade. You must *proofread* your paper. Even if you have used a spellcheck feature available on your word processing program, there still could be errors in your paper. The spellcheck feature only finds groupings of letters that are not words. For example, if you typed the word *van* when you meant to type *ban,* the spellcheck would not catch this error.

The secret of good proofreading is to look at each word and sentence construction by itself without thinking about the paper's contents.

CHECKLIST FOR PROOFREADING

Study each sentence: One way to proofread is to read backwards, starting with the last sentence and examining every sentence, one at a time. First, check that the sentence is really complete and not a fragment or a run-on. Then check the punctuation. Go on to the next sentence and do the same. In this way, you will develop a critical eye for spotting any problems with sentence level errors.

Study each word: Read the paper again, this time studying each word in every sentence. Look at the letters of the words. Have you transposed any letters or have you left off an ending such as the *-ed* or the *-s?* If there are any words you are not sure how to spell, do not forget to check for the correct spelling. Is there any word you have omitted?

WORKING TOGETHER

DEAR ABBY

Dear Abby: I work for a cable television company as a computer operator. Lately, every morning when I sign in on my computer I find suggestive messages from the man I relieve from the night shift.

I am a single mother. I am also dating another man and have no interest in this co-worker. Should I report him to my supervisor? Someone in my office suggested that I file a sexual harassment charge. —*Harassed*

ABIGAIL VAN BUREN

SEXUAL HARASSMENT IN THE WORKPLACE

Being harassed at work can create very complicated issues on the job. In many cases, it comes down to one person's word against that of another. In addition, the person in the less powerful position is often afraid to report a more powerful person to outside authorities. Fear of losing one's job is a strong incentive to remain silent. However, a person should not have to endure unacceptable behavior. Consider the specific example described in the letter to Dear Abby. Divide into groups and discuss the following questions concerning the woman who wrote the letter:

a) Should she confront the man who is harassing her?
b) Should she go to her supervisor? Should she have told her coworkers about the problem?
c) Should she share her problem with the man she is dating?
d) Should she avoid the problem and quit her job?
e) How important is evidence for a person in this situation? How and when should she gather documentation for a possible formal action?
f) Does she need a lawyer? Does she need to consider the consequences of a formal action?

Portfolio Suggestion

Write a process essay in which you outline the steps a person should take if he or she is being harassed on the job.

The discussion of this issue may remind you of other problems that arise in the workplace. If so, you may want to start gathering ideas on some of these other problems that are of interest to you. Your examination of these issues could relate directly to other subject areas you might study, such as psychology, sociology, business ethics, or business management.

Online Activity

Read a definition of sexual harassment in the workplace:

http://www.uakron.edu/lawrev/robert1.html

Chapter 30 Writing an Essay Using Comparison/Contrast

Preview

- Explore the topic: The computer and the brain.
- Read and analyze a model essay.
- Use the writing process to develop your own essay using comparison/contrast.

Key Term

Comparison/contrast

Charts

Transitions commonly used in *comparison/contrast*
Guidelines for revision
Checklist for the final copy
Checklist for proofreading

Exploring a Topic: Computers and the Human Brain

Computer technology is advancing so rapidly that scientists are already discussing the possibility of creating *artificial intelligence*—a computer that will be able to duplicate the thinking process of the human mind. Scientists in this country and abroad are making progress in designing such a computer. While many people are skeptical that any machine could ever replace a person's mind, many jobs are certainly changing or disappearing because of the work that computers are now able to do.

1. What are some of the jobs computers can already do better and faster than human beings can?

____

____

____

2. **What are some of the jobs you have to do now that you would like a computer to do for you? How many of these jobs do you think a computer will take over in your lifetime?**

____

____

____

3. **Do you think a computer could ever be programmed to be as creative as the human mind? Why or why not?**

____

____

____

4. **In your opinion, what are the dangers in the sophisticated computer technology we see today?**

____

____

____

Reading a Model Essay to Discover How a Writer Uses Comparison/Contrast to Develop a Topic

The Computer and the Brain

Isaac Asimov

In the following selection from his book *Please Explain,* science writer Isaac Asimov compares the workings of the modern computer with the workings of the human mind.

1 The difference between a brain and a computer can be expressed in a single word: complexity.

mammalian *having the characteristics of animals that produce milk for their young*

2 The large **mammalian** brain is the most complicated thing, for its size, known to us. The human brain weighs three pounds, but in that three pounds are ten billion neurons and a hundred billion smaller cells. These many billions of cells are interconnected in a vastly complicated network that we can't begin to unravel as yet.

intricacy *having complex parts*

3 Even the most complicated computer man has yet built can't compare in **intricacy** with the brain. Computer switches and components number in the thousands rather than in the billions. What's more, the computer switch is just an on-off device, whereas the brain cell is itself possessed of a tremendously complex inner structure.

4 Can a computer think? That depends on what you mean by "think." If solving a mathematical problem is "thinking," then a computer can "think"

and do so much faster than a man. Of course, most mathematical problems can be solved quite mechanically by repeating certain straightforward processes over and over again. Even the simple computers of today can be geared for that.

5 It is frequently said that computers solve problems only because they are "programmed" to do so. They can only do what men have them do. One must remember that human beings also can only do what they are "programmed" to do. Our genes "program" us the instant the fertilized ovum is formed, and our potentialities are limited by that "program."

6 Our "program" is so much more enormously complex, though, that we might like to define "thinking" in terms of the creativity that goes into writing a great play or composing a great symphony, in conceiving a brilliant scientific theory or a profound ethical judgment. In that sense, computers certainly can't think and neither can most humans.

7 Surely, though, if a computer can be made complex enough, it can be as creative as we. If it could be made as complex as a human brain, it could be the equivalent of a human brain and do whatever a human brain can do.

8 To suppose anything else is to suppose that there is more to the human brain than the matter that composes it. The brain is made up of cells in a certain arrangement and the cells are made up of atoms and molecules in certain arrangements. If anything else is there, no signs of it have ever been detected. To duplicate the material complexity of the brain is therefore to duplicate everything about it.

9 But how long will it take to build a computer complex enough to duplicate the human brain? Perhaps not as long as some think. Long before we approach a computer as complex as our brain, we will perhaps build a computer that is at least complex enough to design another computer more complex than itself. This more complex computer could design one still more complex and so on and so on and so on.

10 In other words, once we pass a certain critical point, the computers take over and there is a "complexity explosion." In a very short time thereafter, computers may exist that not only duplicate the human brain—but far surpass it.

11 Then what? Well, mankind is not doing a very good job of running the earth right now. Maybe, when the time comes, we ought to step gracefully aside and hand over the job to someone who can do it better. And if we don't step aside, perhaps Supercomputer will simply move in and push us aside.

Analyzing the Writer's Strategies

1. An essay of comparison usually emphasizes the similarities between two subjects, while an essay of contrast emphasizes the differences. With this in mind, is the essay you have just read an essay of comparison or contrast?
2. How does this essay help to explain why a human can still beat a computer in a game of chess?
3. Does the writer provide an equal number of details that relate to both computers and the human brain or does he concentrate mostly on one part of the two-part topic? Go through the essay and underline each comparison or contrast that is made.

4. Specifically, how does the writer demonstrate the complexity of a computer and the complexity of the human brain?
5. Study the conclusion. How serious is the author's final suggestion?

EXPLORING ONLINE

For further reading about comparison/contrast essays, go to

http://www.wuacc.edu/services/zzcwwctr/org-comp.wm.txt

Writing the Essay Using Comparison/Contrast

Comparison/Contrast, a method for developing ideas, is the careful examination of similarities and/or differences between people, objects, or ideas, in order to arrive at a judgment or conclusion.

Choose a Topic and Controlling Idea for the Thesis Statement

1. High school classes and college classes
2. Studying with a friend or studying alone
3. Male and female stereotypes
4. Your best friend in childhood with your best friend now
5. Using public transportation versus using a car
6. Our current president with any previous chief executive
7. Two items you have compared when shopping
8. Two apartments or houses where you have lived
9. Cooking dinner at home versus eating out
10. Watching television versus reading a book

Using the above list of ten topics or using ideas of your own, jot down a few two-part topics that appeal to you.

____

____

____

From your list of two-part topics, select the one you think would give you the best opportunity for writing. Which one of these do you feel most strongly about? Which one is most likely to interest your readers? For which topic do you have the greatest firsthand experience?

Selected topic: ______________________________

Your next step is to decide what your controlling idea should be. What is your main purpose in comparing or contrasting these two topics? Do you want to show that although people think two topics are similar, they actually differ in important ways? Do you want to show one topic is better in some ways than the other topic? Do you want to analyze how something has changed over the years (a "then-and-now" essay)?

Controlling idea: ______________________________

At this point, combine your two-point topic and controlling idea into one thesis statement.

Thesis statement: ______________________________

____

Gather the Information (Use Brainstorming Techniques)

Take at least fifteen minutes to brainstorm (use listing or clustering) as many comparison or contrasting points as you can on your chosen topic. You will probably want to think of at least three or four points. Under each point, brainstorm as many details as come to mind. For instance, if you are comparing two friends and the first point concerns the interests you have in common, recall as much as you can about the activities you share together. If you are brainstorming a topic that other classmates or family members might know something about, ask them to help you think of additional points to compare. If any special vocabulary comes to mind, jot that down as well. The more specific you can be, the more helpful and interesting you will make your comparison or contrast for your readers.

Points to Compare or Contrast	*Topic One*	*Topic Two*
Point 1		
Point 2		
Point 3		
Point 4		
Point 5		

Select and Organize Material

As a method of developing ideas, comparison/contrast involves a two-part topic. For instance, you might compare the school you attend now with a school you attended in the past. Often we need to make choices or judgments, and we can make better decisions if we can compare and/or contrast the two items in front of us. Since this is a two-part topic, there is a choice in organizing the essay:

1. **The block method:** This is when you write entirely about one item or idea, and then in a later paragraph or paragraphs you write entirely about the other topic. If you choose this method, you must be sure to bring up the same points and keep the same order as when you discussed the first topic.
2. **The point-by-point method:** This is when you discuss one point and show both topics relating to this in one paragraph. Then, in a new paragraph, you discuss the second point and relate it to both topics, and so forth.

Which method will be best for the topic you have selected—the block method or the point-by-point method?

At this stage, review your brainstorming list and ask yourself if you have a list that is complete. Have you left out any point that might need to be considered? Do you have at least three points, and do you have enough material to develop both parts of the topic? You do not want the comparison or contrast to end up one-sided with all the content about only one part of the topic.

Make an outline, choosing one of the formats below, depending on whether you selected the block method or point-by-point method.

The example shown is the contrast between high school classes and college classes.

Outline for Block Method

I. Topic 1	High School Classes
A. First Point	meet 5 days a week
B. Second Point	daily homework
C. Third Point	no research papers
D. Fourth Point	disciplinary problems in the class
II. Topic 2	College Classes
A. First Point	meet only 2 or 3 days a week
B. Second Point	long-term assignments
C. Third Point	research papers required
D. Fourth Point	no discipline problems

Outline for Point-by-Point Method

I. First Point	How often classes meet
A. Topic 1	high school classes
B. Topic 2	college classes
II. Second Point	Homework
A. Topic 1	high school classes
B. Topic 2	college classes
III. Third Point	Research papers
A. Topic 1	high school classes
B. Topic 2	college classes

IV. Fourth Point	Discipline
A. Topic 1	high school classes
B. Topic 2	college classes

Write the Rough Draft

Follow your outline and write your rough draft. Remember the outline is a guide. Most writers find new ideas occur to them at this time, so if you have new thoughts, you should feel free to explore these ideas along the way. As you write, you will be constantly re-evaluating the logic of your ideas.

Achieve Coherence

As in other methods of developing ideas, the comparison/contrast essay has its particular words and expressions which can be used to signal the movement from one point to the next.

TRANSITIONS COMMONLY USED IN COMPARISON/CONTRAST

Transitions for Comparison	*Transitions for Contrast*	
similar to	on the contrary	though
similarly	on the other hand	unlike
like	in contrast with	even though
likewise	in spite of	nevertheless
just like	despite	however
just as	instead of	but
furthermore	different from	otherwise
moreover	whereas	except for
equally	while	and yet
again	although	still
also		
too		
so		

Revise the Rough Draft

If you can have an interval of time between the writing of the rough draft and your work on revising it, you will be able to look at your work with a greater objectivity. Ideally, you should put aside your first draft for a day or two before you approach it again for revision.

When you revise, you may work alone, with a group, with a peer tutor, or directly with your instructor. Here are some of the basic questions you should consider during this most important stage of your work:

GUIDELINES FOR REVISION

1. Does the rough draft satisfy the conditions for the essay form? Is there an introductory paragraph? Are there at least three well-developed paragraphs in the body of the essay? Is there a concluding paragraph? Remember that one sentence is not a developed paragraph.
2. Does the essay compare or contrast a two-part topic and come to some conclusion about the comparison or contrast?
3. Did you use either the point-by-point method or the block method to organize the essay?
4. Is any important point omitted? Is any of the material included irrelevant?
5. Are there sentences or paragraphs that are repetitious?
6. Find several places where you can substitute more specific verbs, nouns, or adjectives. Try to use the vocabulary appropriate for the topic being discussed.
7. Can you think of a more effective way to begin or end?
8. Does the essay flow logically from one idea to the next? Could you improve this flow with better use of transitional devices?
9. Show your draft to at least two other readers and ask for suggestions.

Prepare the Final Copy, Print, and Proofread

The typing of the final version should follow the traditional rules for an cceptable submission.

CHECKLIST FOR THE FINAL COPY

Use only 8½-by-11–inch paper (never paper torn out of a spiral-bound notebook).

Type on one side of the paper only.

Double-space.

Leave approximately 1½-inch margins on each side of the paper.

Center the title at the top of the page. Do not put quotation marks around the title and do not underline it.

Do not hyphenate a word at the end of a line unless you are willing to consult a dictionary to check on the acceptable division of the word into syllables.

You may put your name, the date, and the title of your paper on a separate title page. Ask your instructor for specific advice on what information to include.

Indent each paragraph five spaces.

Leave two spaces after each period.

If your paper is more than one page, number the pages and staple the pages together so they will not get lost.

Do not forget to make a copy before you submit the paper.

Note: In most cases, college teachers will not accept handwritten work. However, if you are submitting handwritten work, you must be sure to write on every other line and have good legible handwriting. Begin today to learn to type on the computer. You will be at a disadvantage if you cannot use the current technology.

Once you have typed your final version and printed it out, an important step still remains. This step can often mean the difference of an entire letter grade. You must *proofread* your paper. Even if you have used a spellcheck feature available on your word processing program, there still could be errors in your paper. The spellcheck feature only finds groupings of letters that are not words. For example, if you typed the word *van* when you meant to type *ban,* the spellcheck would not catch this error.

The secret of good proofreading is to look at each word and sentence construction by itself without thinking about the paper's contents.

CHECKLIST FOR PROOFREADING

Study each sentence: One way to proofread is to read backwards, starting with the last sentence and examining every sentence, one at a time. First, check that the sentence is really complete and not a fragment or a run-on. Then check the punctuation. Go on to the next sentence and do the same. In this way, you will develop a critical eye for spotting any problems with sentence level errors.

Study each word: Read the paper again, this time studying each word in every sentence. Look at the letters of the words. Have you transposed any letters or have you left off an ending such as the *-ed* or the *-s?* If there are any words you are not sure how to spell, do not forget to check for the correct spelling. Is there any word you have omitted?

WORKING TOGETHER

The Top Ten Sources of Calories in the American Diet

Whole Milk

Cola

Margarine

White Bread

Rolls
(commercial ready-to-serve)

Sugar

2% Milk

Ground Beef
(broiled medium)

Wheat Flour

Pasteurized Process American Cheese

SOURCE:
U.S. DEPARTMENT OF AGRICULTURE

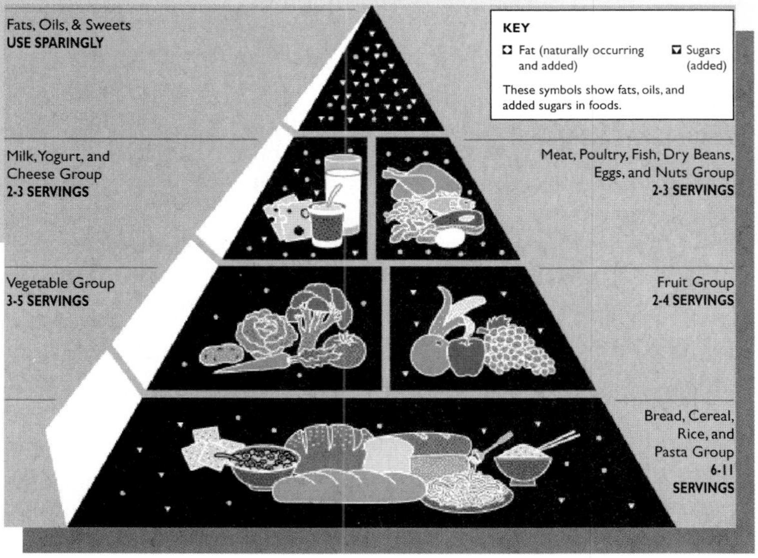

USING OUTSIDE SOURCES

Topic: Comparing the ideal diet with an actual diet

The two charts show (1) the well-known food pyramid that the U.S. government has developed and (2) to the left, a dietary chart provided by the U.S. Department of Agriculture. The first source tells us what we should be eating according to government research. The second tells us what the diets of most Americans are really like.

Divide into groups and discuss how you could plan an essay on the topic of people's eating habits using the information in these charts as well as facts about your own diet. Consider the following questions as you plan your presentation of information:

1. First outline your own diet. You might list typical foods eaten at each meal of the day or you might be very scientific and make an exact list of everything eaten for one week to see what patterns emerge. Don't forget to include snacks.
2. What do you think the ideal diet should look like?
3. Is your own diet closer to the ideal, or is it closer to the diet of most Americans?

continued on next page

Discuss these issues with other members of your group. Take notes on information gained from the ideas of others.

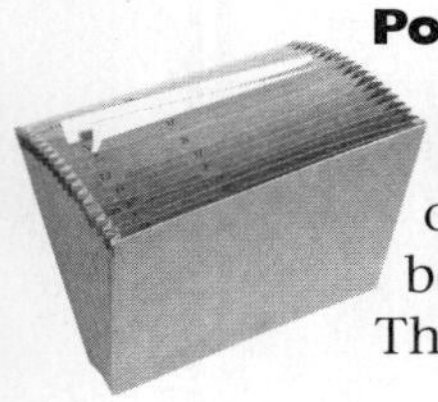

Portfolio Suggestion

Write your own outline on how you might compare the ideal diet with that of your own actual diet. Will you use the block method or the point-by-point method? Then, using your outline, compose an essay that examines your own diet and compares it to what you should be eating.

Three related subjects that may be of interest to you for future writing projects include:

- Why don't most people follow a healthier diet?
- What are some of the results of poor eating habits?
- How can parents instill in their children healthy eating habits?

Online Activity

Compare the Asian Diet Pyramid to its American counterpart:

http://www.news.cornell.edu/science/Dec95/st.asian.pyramid.html

Chapter 31 Writing an Essay Using Persuasion

Preview

- Study the guidelines for writing the *persuasive essay*
- Read and analyze a model persuasive essay on the topic of *euthanasia* before writing a persuasive essay on a related topic
- Read and analyze a model persuasive essay on the topic of *censorship* before writing a persuasive essay on a related topic
- Use research material provided to develop your own persuasive essays on the topics of *violence in the media* and *affirmative action*
- Additional topics for writing persuasive essays

Key Term

Essay of persuasion

Charts

Transitions commonly used to signal the parts of the persuasive essay
Checklist for the final copy
Checklist for proofreading

What Is Persuasion?

From one point of view, all writing is persuasion since the main goal of any writer is to convince a reader to see, think, or believe in a certain way. There is, however, a more formal understanding of persuasive writing. Anyone who has ever been a member of a high school debate team knows there are techniques that the effective speaker or writer uses to present a case successfully. Learning how to recognize these techniques of persuasion and discovering how to use them in your own writing is the subject of this chapter.

An essay of **persuasion** presents evidence intended to convince the reader that the writer's viewpoint is valid.

Guide to Writing the Persuasive Essay

1. **State a clear thesis.** Use words such as *must, ought,* or *should.* Study the following three sample thesis statements:

   The United States must reform its prison system.

   All states ought to have the same legal drinking age.

   We should not ban all handguns.

2. **Give evidence or reasons for your beliefs.** Your evidence is the heart of the essay. You must show the wisdom of your logic by providing the best evidence available.
3. **Use examples.** Well-chosen examples are among the best types of evidence for an argument. People can identify with a specific example from real life in a way that is not possible with an abstract idea. Without examples, essays of persuasion would be flat, lifeless, and unconvincing.
4. **Use opinions from recognized authorities to support your points.** One of the oldest methods of supporting an argument is to use one or more persons of authority to support your particular position. People will usually believe what well-known experts claim. However, be sure that your expert is someone who is respected in the area you are discussing. For example, if you are arguing that we must end ocean dumping, your argument will be stronger if you quote a respected scientist who can accurately predict the consequences of this approach to waste disposal. A famous movie star giving the same information might be more glamorous and get more attention, but he or she would not be as great an authority as the scientist.
5. **Be careful to avoid faulty logic.**

   a) *Do not appeal to fear or pity.*

   Example: If we don't double the police force, innocent children will die.

   b) *Do not make sweeping or false generalizations.*

   Example: All women belong in the kitchen.

   c) *Do not oversimplify with an either–or presentation.*

   Example: A woman should either stay home and take care of her children or go to work but have no children.

   d) *Do not give misleading or irrelevant support to your argument.*

   Example: Don't hire that man; his wife is blind.

6. **Answer your critics in advance.** When you point out, beforehand, what your opposition is likely to say in answer to your argument, you will be writing from a position of strength. You are letting your reader know that there is another side to the argument you are making. By pointing out this other side and then answering its objections in advance, you are strengthening your own position.
7. **Point out the results.** Here, you help your reader see what will happen if your argument is (or is not) believed or acted upon as you think it should be. You should be very specific and very rational when you point out results, making sure that you avoid exaggerations of any kind. For example, if you are arguing against the possession of handguns, it would be an exaggeration to say that if we don't ban handguns, "everyone will be murdered."

Achieving Coherence

As in other methods of developing the essay, the essay using persuasion has its own special words that signal parts of the argument. The chart on page 538 can help you choose transitional expressions that will move you from one part of your argument to the next.

TRANSITIONS COMMONLY USED TO SIGNAL THE PARTS OF A *PERSUASIVE ESSAY*

To signal the thesis of an argument
- I agree (disagree) that . . .
- I support (do not support) the idea that . . .
- I am in favor of (not in favor of) . . .
- I propose . . .
- ___________ must be (must not be) changed
- ___________ should be (should not be) adopted

To signal a reason
- because, just because, since, for
- in the first place
- in view of
- can be shown
- The first reason is . . .
- An additional reason is . . .
- Another reason is . . .
- The most convincing piece of evidence is . . .

To admit an opponent's point of view
- Most people assume that . . .
- One would think that . . .
- We have been told that . . .
- Popular thought is that . . .
- Some may claim . . .
- The opposition would have you believe . . .

To signal a conclusion
- therefore, thus, consequently, so
- as a result
- We can conclude that . . .
- This proves that . . .
- This shows that . . .
- This demonstrates that . . .
- This suggests that . . .
- This leads to the conclusion that . . .
- It follows that . . .

It's Time We Helped Patients Die

Dr. Howard Caplan

Howard Caplan is a medical doctor who specializes in geriatrics, that branch of medicine that deals with the care of older people. He is also the medical director of three nursing homes in Los Angeles, California.

As you read Dr. Caplan's essay, look for all of the elements of an effective argument. Where does the writer give his thesis statement? Where are his major examples? At what point does he use authorities to support his point of view? In addition, look for the paragraphs where he answers those who do not agree with him and be sure to find that section of the essay where he predicts the future of euthanasia, commonly known as "mercy killing." As you read the essay, do you see any weaknesses in the writer's argument?

aneurysm *a sac formed by the swelling of a vein or artery*

astrocytoma *a tumor made up of nerve cells*

nasogastric *relating to a tube inserted through the nose and into the stomach*

1 For three years, the husband of one of my elderly patients watched helplessly as she deteriorated. She'd burst an **aneurysm** and later had an **astrocytoma** removed from her brain. Early in the ordeal, realizing that she'd never recover from a vegetative state, he'd pleaded with me to pull her **nasogastric** tube.

2 I'd refused, citing the policy of the convalescent hospital. I told him I could do it only if he got a court order. But he couldn't bring himself to start such proceedings, although the months dragged by with no signs of improvements in his wife's condition. He grieved as her skin broke down and she developed terrible bedsores. She had to have several courses of antibiotics to treat the infections in them, as well as in her bladder, which had an indwelling catheter.

3 Finally I got a call from a lawyer who said he'd been retained by the family to force me to comply with the husband's wishes.

4 "I'm on your side," I assured him. "But you'll have to get that court order just the same."

5 I went on to suggest—though none too hopefully—that we ask the court to do more than just let the patient starve to death. "If the judge will agree to let her die slowly, why won't he admit that he wants death to happen? Let's ask for permission to give her an injection and end her life in a truly humane manner."

6 The lawyer had no answer except to say, "Aw, come on, Doc—that's euthanasia!"

7 Frankly, I'd have been surprised at any other reaction. Although most states have enacted living-will laws in the past decade, none has yet taken the next logical step—legalizing euthanasia. But I believe it's time they did. Ten years of practice in geriatrics have convinced me that a proper death is a humane death, either in your sleep or being *put* to sleep.

8 I see appropriate patients every day in the extended-care facilities at which I practice. About 50 of the 350 people under my care have already ended their biographical lives. They've reached the stage in life at which there's no more learning, communicating, or experiencing pleasure. They're now simply existing in what is left of their biological lives.

demented *having lost normal brain function*

9 Most of these patients are the elderly **demented.** A typical case is that of a woman in her 80s or 90s, who speaks only in gibberish and doesn't recognize her family. She has forgotten how to eat, so she has a feeding tube coming from her nose. She is incontinent, so she has an indwelling catheter. She can no longer walk, so she is tied into a wheelchair. She's easily agitated, so she gets daily doses of a major tranquilizer. Why shouldn't I, with the concurrence of her family and an independent medical panel, be allowed to quickly and painlessly end her suffering?

aphasic triplegic
a person who has lost the ability to express or comprehend language, and who has paralysis of three limbs

10 I think of another patient, a woman in her 50s, with end-stage multiple sclerosis, unable to move a muscle except for her eyeballs and her tongue. And younger patients: I have on my census a man in his early 40s, left an **aphasic triplegic** by a motorcycle accident when he was 19. For nearly a quarter of a century, while most of us were working, raising children, traveling, reading, and otherwise going about our lives, he's been vegetating. His biographical life ended with that crash. He can't articulate—only make sounds to convey that he's hungry or wet. If he were to become acutely ill, I would prefer not to try saving him. I'd want to let pneumonia end it for him.

11 Of my remaining 300 patients, there are perhaps 50 to 100 borderline functional people who are nearing the end of their biographical lives and—were euthanasia legal—would probably tell me: "I'm ready to go. My bags are packed. Help me."

12 Anyone who's had front-line responsibility for the elderly has been asked if there wasn't "something you can give me" to end life. Such requests are made by patients who clearly see the inevitability of their deterioration and dread having to suffer through it. For these people, there is no more pleasure, let alone joy—merely misery. They want out.

13 What is their fate? Chances are they'll be referred for psychiatric consultation on the grounds that they must be seriously depressed. The psychiatrist, usually decades younger than the patient, does indeed diagnose depression and recommends an antidepressant.

anesthesiologist
a medical specialist who administers anesthesia, or pain killers, to people about to undergo operations

14 But if such patients lived in the Netherlands, odds are they'd get assistance in obtaining a release from the slow dying process to which our modern technology condemns them. While euthanasia is not yet legal there, it's openly practiced. On a segment of the CBS show "60 Minutes" not long ago, I heard a Dutch **anesthesiologist** describe how doctors in his country help 5,000 terminal patients slip away peacefully each year. Isn't that a promising indication of how well euthanasia would work in this country?

15 I realize that there are those who vigorously oppose the idea. And there are moral issues to confront—how much suffering is too much, the one-in-several-million chance that a person given no hope of improving will beat the odds. But it's time for society to seriously reconsider whether it is immoral to take the life of someone whose existence is nothing but irreversible suffering. Euthanasia ought to be treated the same way the abortion issue has been treated: People who believe it a sin to take a life even for merciful reasons would not be forced to do so. What I'm pleading for is that doctors and their patients at least have the choice.

16 I doubt that we'll get congressional action on such an emotionally charged issue during my lifetime. Action may have to come at the state level. Ideally, legislatures should permit each hospital and each nursing home to have a panel that would approve candidates for euthanasia. Or it might be more practical to have one panel serve several hospitals and nursing homes in a geographic area. Made up of one or two physicians and a lawyer or judge, plus the attending doctor, the panel would assess the attending's findings and recommendations, the patient's wishes, and those of the immediate family. This would ensure that getting a heart-stopping injection was truly in the patient's best interests, and that there was no ulterior motive—for example, trying to hasten an insurance payout. Needless to say, members of the board would be protected by law from liability claims.

17 Then, if the patient had made it known while of sound mind that under certain circumstances he wanted a deadly substance administered, the process would be easy for everyone. But in most cases, it would be up to the attending to raise the question of euthanasia with the patient's relatives.

18 I'd start with those who've been part of the patient's recent life. If there are relatives who haven't seen the patient for years, it really shouldn't be any of their business. For instance, I'd try involving a son who's just kept in touch by phone. I'd say to him, "If you really want to stop this from happening, then you'd better come out here to see firsthand what's going on."

19 However, if he said, "Well, I can't really get away, Doctor, but I violently disagree," my answer would be, "Well, not violently enough. Everyone here can see what shape your mother's in. We're quite sure what she'd want if she could tell us, and we're going to help her."

20 Before any of this can happen, though, there's going to have to be widespread public education. The media will have to do a better job of discussing the issues than it has with living wills. Among my patients who are nearing death, there aren't more than a half-dozen with living wills attached to their charts. Patients' families often haven't even heard of them, and even when large institutions encourage families to get these things taken care of while the patient is still alert, it's hardly ever done.

21 Not knowing about living wills, unaware of no-code options, many families plunge their loved ones—and themselves—into unwanted misery. How many rapidly deteriorating patients are rushed from a nursing home to a hospital to be intubated, simply because that's the facility's rigid policy? How many families impoverish themselves to keep alive someone who's unaware of himself and his surroundings?

22 For that matter, how many people themselves suffer heart attacks or ulcers—not to mention divorces or bankruptcies—from the stresses involved in working to pay where Medicare and Medicaid leave off?

23 Every day in my professional life, I encounter illogical, irrational, and inhumane regulations that prevent me, and those with whom I work, from doing what we know in our souls to be the right thing. Before high technology, much of this debate was irrelevant. There was little we could do, for example, when a patient **arrested.** And what we could do rarely worked.

arrested
died

24 But times have changed. Now we have decisions to make. It helps to understand that many of the elderly infirm have accepted the inevitability—and, indeed, the desirability—of death. We who are younger must not mistake this philosophical position for depression. We need to understand the natural acceptance of death when life has lost its meaning.

25 About 28 percent of our huge Medicare budget is spent providing care during the last year of life. Far too little of that money goes to ensure that dying patients' last months are pain-free and comfortable. Far too much is wasted on heroic, pain-inducing measures that can make no difference. It's time to turn that ratio around—and to fight for the right to provide the ultimate assistance to patients who know their own fight to prolong life is a losing one.

Analyzing the Writer's Strategies

Because Dr. Caplan deals with a very sensitive subject, many people might find his position to be dangerous and even frightening. Even before we examine his essay, the title of the piece and the writer's medical background gain our attention. When a doctor writes on matters of life and death, we tend to pay more attention than we ordinarily might; the fact that Dr. Caplan works so closely with older people tends to give his views even more authority. For example, the facts and figures he gives in paragraphs eight and eleven go a long way toward strengthening his point of view. In addition, the writer uses both his own experience and his close observation of people in other countries to convince us that his stand on this controversial topic is a valid one.

The writer's position is also supported by the fact that he is so precise in paragraphs three to seven, when he deals with the law; almost from the beginning, Dr. Caplan is seen as a careful and caring professional. We notice too that in paragraphs twelve and thirteen he points out what happens under our present system, and in paragraphs sixteen to eighteen he gives practical suggestions that would help put his own system into operation. Finally, we see that in paragraph fifteen he pays attention to the other side's arguments and then answers those same arguments.

It is clear that Dr. Caplan's argument is carefully written and complete; it has all of the parts needed for a good argument. After you have studied each part of the essay, are you able to find any weaknesses in the writer's presentation?

Responding to the Writer's Argument

Take a position either for or against one of the following topics and write an argumentative essay supporting your position. Use the "Guide to Writing the Persuasive Essay" (pages 536–537) to help construct the essay. Be sure to include all of the important points needed for a good argument.

1. All medical care should be free in our society.
2. Doctors should not be burdened by outrageously high malpractice insurance payments.
3. If a person wishes to commit suicide, for any reason, society should not try to interfere with that decision.
4. Doctors should always work to preserve life; they must never cooperate in any effort to end a life.
5. New medical technology has created more problems than it has solved.
6. Permitting euthanasia would create a dangerous precedent that could easily lead to government-sponsored murder of people it considers "undesirable."
7. People should always leave instructions (a living will) as to what should be done if they are terminally ill and are unable to respond to their surroundings.
8. A person's family has the responsibility to support decisions for life, not death, when a person is gravely ill, no matter how much money and effort it might cost that family.
9. In the case of a hopeless medical situation, no human being—including the person who is ill—has the right to make decisions that would lead to immediate death (euthanasia).

10. A husband or wife who helps a terminally ill spouse die should not be prosecuted by the law.

Censorship or Common Sense?

Roxana Robinson

Roxana Robinson, a professional writer, produced the following essay as a response to a controversial issue. Advocates of free speech objected when some libraries blocked unlimited Internet access for children. The writer's position is unmistakable: children are not adults, and we should shield our children from material that is clearly inappropriate. As you read the essay, note each section where the writer reports her position and each section where she reports the opposing point of view.

1 A 5-year-old is not ready to confront the world. This should be obvious, but it doesn't seem that way to many free-speech advocates, who are angry that some libraries around the country have installed software on their computers to block out Internet material that's unsuitable for children.

2 The objections are coming from some usual sources: the American Civil Liberties Union, for example, and Web publishers. But even the American Library Association has opposed the use of filtering software.

3 Traditionally, the library has been a safe place for children. And librarians have long been the guardians of public virtue. While they have been firm supporters of the First Amendment, they haven't generally interpreted it to mean that they should acquire large holdings of published pornography and make such materials available to children.

4 Librarians have always acquired books according to their own discrimination and their sense of what is appropriate to their neighborhoods. They generally refuse to buy, among other things, pornography. This isn't censorship; it's common sense.

5 If a library were to have a section of pornographic books, would we want these to be printed in large, colorfully illustrated, lightweight volumes, shelved near the floor where they were easily available to children? Probably not. But we have gone to a great deal of trouble to insure that computers are user friendly, with brightly colored graphics and easily accessible information.

6 Material on the Internet is not only uncensored but also unedited. Adults can be expected to make their own evaluations of what they find. Children, who lack experience and knowledge, cannot.

7 The debate over the filtering of the Internet is a bit like the debate over grants given out by the National Endowment for the Arts. It's all tangled up in false cries of censorship. Censorship is a legal term; it refers to government action prohibiting material from being circulated. This is very different from a situation in which a museum or an arts panel decides not to use public money to finance an exhibition or an artist.

8 Commendably, our society defends freedom of speech with great vigor. But there is a difference between allowing everything to be said and allowing everyone to hear it. We should know this by now, having seen the effects that exposure to television and movie violence has on children.

9 The A.C.L.U. and the American Library Association say that the use of filtering software in computers is censorship because it blocks access to constitutionally protected speech. But these cries are baffling and unfounded. The only control libraries are asserting is over a small portion of the audience, not over the material itself. Moreover, this control has a powerful historical precedent: parental guidance is even older than the Constitution.

10 The protection of children should be instinctive. A man may have the right to stand on the street and spew obscenities at passers-by, but he would be ordered to leave a kindergarten classroom.

11 It is absurd to pretend that adults and children are the same audience, and it is shameful to protect the child pornographer instead of the child.

Analyzing the Writer's Strategies

The use of the Internet in our schools, libraries, and homes brings a world of knowledge and information. It also brings in such abuses as pornography, and many observers were alarmed when it became clear that children had almost unlimited access to this inappropriate material.

Roxana Robinson begins her essay by considering the position of those who argue for unlimited information directed at children; these are the groups that oppose censorship of any kind. The writer's own position is almost immediately apparent, as she comes down on the side of what she calls "common sense." She refers to a lesson from history when she observes in paragraph 3 that librarians have traditionally been the ones to keep sensitive material away from children—actions that were considered common sense, not censorship.

This is the writer's own approach for the rest of the essay, as she judges the difference between what adults should be able to absorb, and what children are exposed to every day, thanks to modern technology. Children, the author concludes, are in a special situation when it comes to these sensitive materials. In fact, she concludes, it is wrong for a society to be more concerned about the rights of a pornographer than with the protection of our children.

As you study the essay, decide if the writer indulges in any faulty logic in making her case. In what paragraph is her thesis statement? Who are the opposing in the groups she names in her essay?

Responding to the Writer's Argument

Take a position either for or against one of the following topics and write an argumentative essay supporting your position. Use the "Guide to Writing the Persuasive Essay" (pages 536–537) to help you construct your essay. Be sure to include all of the important parts needed for a good argument.

1. Dictionaries should (or should not) be banned from elementary schools because some of the definitions include sexually explicit information.
2. A Nazi should be permitted (or denied) the right to speak at a public meeting.
3. Certain novels should (or should not) be banned because they are clearly pornographic.
4. Anyone who wants to view pornography should (or should not) be allowed to do so.

5. Pornography helps (or does not help) people deal with their frustrations without having to commit crimes or engage in other antisocial activities.
6. The United States government was right (or was wrong) when, in 1983, newspaper and television reporters were not told we would invade the Caribbean island of Grenada.
7. It is (or is not) the job of the public schools to teach morality and ethics.
8. Violent video games should (or should not) be banned.

EXERCISE 1

Using Research Material to Write the Persuasive Essay

The following pieces of information are on the controversial topic of **violence in movies, on television, and in videos.** To what extent do you believe the violence we see in the media is responsible for the level of violence in our society? You may select as many of the following items as you want for supporting evidence in your essay, or you may research on your own to obtain other evidence for your point of view.

1. Over 900 research studies on violent entertainment give overwhelming evidence that violent films and other programs are having a harmful effect on the American people.
2. In some years, more than half of the films produced by Hollywood have intensely violent content.
3. The National Coalition on Television Violence estimates that up to half of all violence in our country comes from the violent entertainment we are exposed to every day.
4. In June, 1999, shortly after the school massacre in Littleton, Colorado, legislation was proposed in Congress to make it a felony to expose children to books, movies, and video games that contain explicit sex or violence. The legislation failed to pass.
5. Three surgeons general of the United States have publicly declared that violent entertainment is a serious health problem that contributes to the level of violence and number of rapes in our society.
6. On television, 55 percent of the characters in prime-time programs are involved in violent confrontations at least once a week.
7. Cartoons on television have become increasingly violent, averaging 48 acts of violence per hour.
8. In a single year, the average child between four and eight will see over 250 war-related cartoons and over 1,000 commercials for war toys, time equal to more than three weeks of school.
9. Lt. Col. Dave Grossman, a psychologist and army ranger, claims that video games function like firing ranges. These games use the same type of conditioning that was used to train soldiers to kill during the Vietnam War.
10. The National Coalition on Television Violence claims that children in homes with cable TV and/or a VCR will view 32,000 murders and 40,000 attempted murders by the time they reach 18 years of age.

EXERCISE 2 **Using Research Material to Write the Persuasive Essay**

Affirmative action continues to be an issue that is either passionately supported or just as passionately denounced. Sharply different views deal with this approach to correcting past wrongs against people who have been disadvantaged in our society. The following pieces of information could be used in an essay of persuasion that takes a stand for or against the use of affirmative action in our institutions.

1. The University of Michigan faces two separate lawsuits from white students who were denied admission to the university and say that they were discriminated against by the admittance of less qualified minorities.
2. Courts in Texas and Georgia have reversed university affirmative action plans.
3. Voters in California and the state of Washington have voted to ban affirmative action in state government, including state institutions of higher learning.
4. Frederick Douglass was quoted as saying that "equality of numbers has nothing to do with equality of attainments."
5. In 1978, Americans of African, Asian, Hispanic, and Native American descent made up about 20 percent of the population. Today, it is 28 percent; by the middle of this century, it is expected to reach 48 percent.
6. Web sites, such as the Minority Online Information Service at www.sciencewise.com/molis, offer help on prospects for affirmative action opportunities in colleges.
7. The University of Iowa provides $5,000 a year to each student from underrepresented populations who meets certain academic requirements, such as a SAT score of at least 1,110 and a ranking in the top 30 percent of his or her class.
8. Texas A&M recently launched a "Century Scholars" program for underrepresented students in the top 10 percent of their class at 10 Houston-area high schools. Recipients get an aid package that covers the entire cost of their college education.
9. In 1871, African American writer and activist Frederick Douglass described a black nationalist's demand for quotas in government jobs as "absurd."
10. New York City police-hiring requirements have changed over the last 30 years. In order to recruit more minorities as officers, the physical requirements for strength and physique have become less demanding, and lower written test marks are selected over those of other candidates, if a certain percentage of minorities are not represented on the force. What is the more important goal: having a police force that requires a traditionally high standard or one that has a gender/racially correct number of people?

Writing the Persuasive Essay: Additional Topics

Choose one of the fifteen topics listed and write an essay of at least five paragraphs. Use the seven points discussed on pages 536–537 and repeated below as a guide for your writing.

- Write a strong thesis statement.
- Give evidence for your beliefs.
- Provide examples for each of your reasons.
- Use at least one authority to support your thesis.
- Avoid faulty logic.
- Admit that others may have a different point of view.
- Indicate the results, predictions, or your solution in the conclusion.

Essay topics

Argue for or against:

1. Legalized prostitution
2. Gambling casinos
3. Stricter immigration laws
4. Prayer in the public schools
5. Abortion
6. Tax exemption for religious organizations
7. Capital punishment
8. Single-parent adoption
9. Continuation of the manned space program
10. Females playing on male sports teams
11. Required courses in college
12. Tenure for teachers
13. Expense accounts for businesspeople
14. Suspending a driver's license for drunk driving
15. Random drug testing in the workplace

EXPLORING ONLINE

For more information about writing argumentative essays, see:

http://www.dartmouth.edu/~compose/student/ac-paper/write.html#arrangement

WORKING TOGETHER

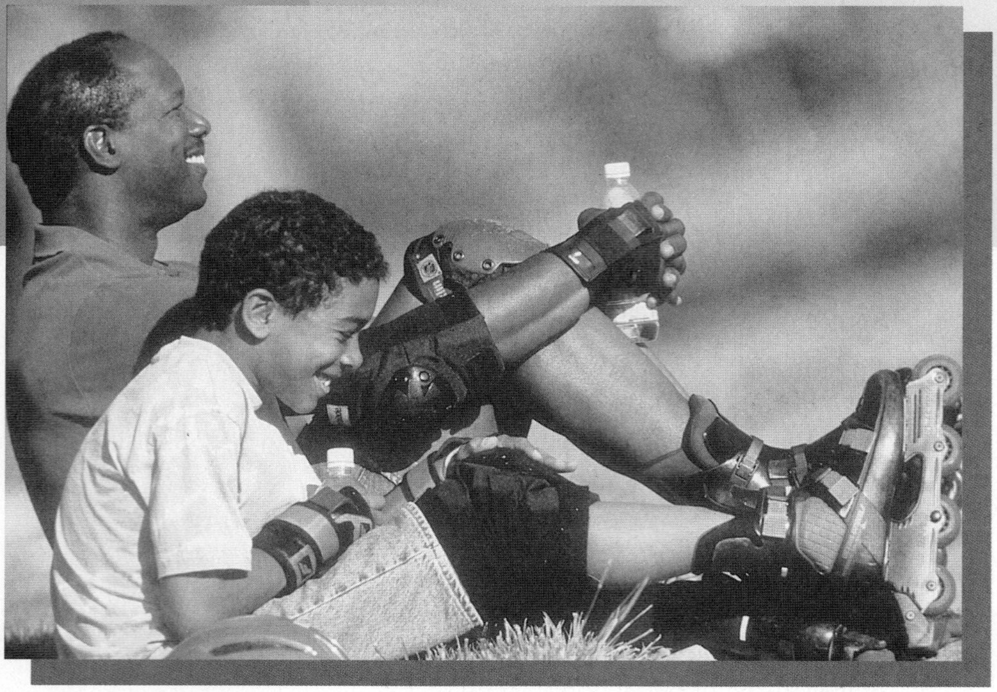

ANALYZING A NEWSPAPER EDITORIAL

The following editorial appeared in the *Chicago Tribune* on June 18, 1995.

Where Have All the Fathers Gone?

1 Today is Father's Day, so let's talk about dads. Not the ones who cheer their sons and daughters at baseball and soccer games or the ones who fix dinner for the family every night or the ones who come home dead tired after a day at the **Merc** or McDonald's but still have time for a little family conversation.

Merc *The Chicago Mercantile Exchange*

2 No, let's talk about the invisible dads, the ones who don't marry mom, don't support their kids and don't hang around for hugs, kisses and helping with homework. There are millions of them in the United States, and their numbers are growing.

3 In 1950, 14 of every 1,000 unmarried women had babies. By 1992, 45 of every 1,000 did. In fact, almost one-third of the children born in the United States in 1992 were born to unwed parents, a 54 percent increase over 1980, according to figures released this month by the National Center for Health Statistics.

4 And though the figures generally are compiled in terms of unmarried women and the resulting handwringing is done in the name of unwed mothers, the facts of life are that for every one of those unmarried mothers there is an unmarried father.

5 The moms are a lot more visible though, because in the overwhelming number of cases, they are the ones raising the kids. So who's the real problem here? And why should we care?

6 We *must* care because the social and financial costs of children growing up in households without fathers is immense. Many of the country's most troublesome social problems—poverty, poor performance in schools, gang activity, juvenile crime, mounting welfare costs—have their roots in families where a father has abdicated responsibility for his children.

7 Women who do not marry before having their first child are three times more likely to wind up on welfare for 10 years or more than those who do marry. And census figures indicate that an intact mother-father household has a far better chance for financial security than a single-parent family.

8 Moreover, children who have little or no contact with their fathers are robbed of a crucial role model for fashioning their own lives.

9 What's to be done? For starters, parents, grandparents, churches and schools must hammer home the lesson that a man who conceives a child without marrying and being prepared to support the child for 18 years unfairly burdens his family and his community. He must understand that his action will be met by community disapprobation, not the respect and awe of his peers.

10 And while government can't legislate morality, it can encourage responsibility. Legislators should make that a priority by providing tax incentives for couples to marry and by requiring every woman to name her child's father on the birth certificate. Law enforcement officers can (and are beginning to) go after the fathers for child support.

11 Fatherhood, like motherhood, is its own reward—as most dads have found. Sadly, for the others, the invisible ones, it is a gift foolishly squandered.

Read the editorial out loud. Then divide into groups and discuss the following questions:

1. What is the thesis of the editorial?
2. What supporting evidence for the thesis is given in the editorial?
3. Were any outside sources used to support the thesis? If so, indicate the sources.
4. Does the editor say what will or will not happen if nothing is done?
5. Does the editorial propose a solution to the problem?
6. Does the editorial seem reasonable to you?
7. State whether or not you believe this is an effective argument.

When the members of your group are satisfied with the answers to these questions, each person should write his or her own answer (in compete sentences, of course) to each question. Your instructor will want to collect these answers at the end of the class period, so be sure to allow twenty minutes for students to write their own answers to these questions.

Portfolio Suggestion

For many readers, the editorial page is the best part of the newspaper. It is on this paper that writers argue, passionately at times, about issues that are of great importance to them. Look at the editorial section of a newspaper at least once a week and clip editorials that are about

continued on next page

subjects that interest you. This is one way to gradually develop a feeling for argumentative or persuasive writing. You can learn from editorials that are outrageous in their points of view as well as from those that are logical and convincing.

On this subject of the deadbeat dad, you might want to use one of the following ideas for a piece of writing to add to your portfolio:

1. Write a letter to a "vanished" father. Try to persuade him to become involved in the lives of his children.
2. Imagine you have gathered ten of these "vanished" fathers in a room. What do you think would be some of their arguments for not participating in the raising of their children?

Online Activity

Search online newspapers for letters to the editor on a current issue. Are the arguments convincing? Why or why not?

Chapter 32 Writing under Pressure

Preview

Most people prefer to do their writing when they are not under the pressure of a time limit. However, many situations demand that a piece of writing be finished by a certain time. One situation is writing for a newspaper where a deadline is a daily reality. Another pressured situation is writing an essay exam that must be handed in by the end of a class period. This chapter will review some of the techniques for writing successful essays under pressure.

- Coming to the exam well prepared
- Strategies for answering in-class essay questions
- Picking out methods of development and parts of a question
- Using a thesis statement

Key Terms

Definition (and analysis)
Comparison/contrast
Narration
Summary
Discussion
Classification
Cause and effect

How to Write Well under Pressure

The first rule of doing well in any test is to come to the test well rested and well prepared. Research proves that reviewing notes and reading assignments systematically throughout the semester is much more effective than cramming for a test the night before. You'll be greatly satisfied if you learn to use your time efficiently and wisely.

Coming to an Exam Well Prepared

1. **Study the textbook chapters and your notes. In your textbook, review headings and words in boldface type as well as information you have highlighted or underlined. Look for both chapter reviews and summaries at the ends of chapters. If you have already made an outline, study that too.**
2. **Avoid having to face any surprises when the exam is distributed. When the test is first announced in class, ask if it will include material from the textbook in addition to notes taken in class. Also, find out the format of the test: how many essay questions**

there will be, and how many points each question is worth. Ask how much time you will have to complete the test.

3. Form a study group if you can. One way a study group can work is the following: Each person comes to the study group prepared to present at least one major question that he or she thinks the instructor will ask and then provides the information that will be needed for answering that question. The other students take notes and add whatever additional information they can. Each person in turn presents a different question along with the information needed for the answer. Members of the group can quiz each other on the information that is to be covered by the exam. For an essay exam, some material needs to be memorized. If you are unable to be part of a study group, you should still try to predict what questions will be on the exam. Prepare an outline for study and then memorize your outline.

Remember that an essay test, unlike a multiple-choice test, requires more than simply recognizing information. In an essay exam, you must be able to recall ideas and specific details and present them quickly in your own words. This ability to memorize both concepts and factual information is quite demanding.

Strategies for Answering Timed In-Class Essay Questions

The smart test taker does not begin to answer the first question immediately. Instead, he or she takes a few moments to look over the test and form a strategy for the best way to tackle it. The following pointers will help you become "test smart."

1. When you receive the exam, *read over each essay question twice.* How many points is each question worth? The way in which you budget your time will depend heavily on the importance of each question. A well-written test should tell you how many points each question is worth. If, for example, one essay question is worth 50 points, you should spend approximately half your time planning and answering this question. However, if the test consists of ten shorter essay questions and you have a class period of 100 minutes, you should spend no more than ten minutes on each question, keeping a careful watch on your time. Tests composed of several shorter essays can be disastrous to people who do not watch their time. Students often write too much for the first four or five questions and then panic because they have very little time left to answer the final questions.
2. When you read an essay question, ask yourself *what method of development is being asked for.* We all know stories of people who failed tests because they misunderstood the question.
3. *Use key words from the test question itself* to compose your thesis statement, which in a test should be your first sentence. Don't try to be too clever on a test. State your points as directly and clearly as possible.
4. Answer the question by stating your basic point and then *use as many specific details as you have time or knowledge to give.* The

more specific names, dates, and places (all spelled correctly) that you can provide, the more points will be added to your grade.

5. **Since a question can have more than one part, be sure you *answer all the parts.* Check over the question to be sure your answer includes all parts.**

Study the question to determine exactly what is being asked for.

Sample essay question

What were the changes that contributed to the rise of the feminist movement in the 1960s in the United States? Be specific.

If the question given were one of ten short essay questions on a ninety-minute final examination, the following answer would probably be adequate.

Sample essay question answer

The feminist movement grew out of many changes happening in the 1960sin the United States. In 1961, the President's Commission on the Status of Women documented discrimination against women in the workforce. The result of the Commission's report was a growing public awareness which soon led to the enactment of two pieces of legislation: the Equal Pay Act of 1963 and the Civil Rights Act of 1964. In addition, the development of the birth-control pill brought the discussion of sexuality out into the open. It also lowered the birthrate, leaving more women looking to the world of work. A high divorce rate as well as delayed marriages further contributed to more women being concerned with feminist issues. Finally, in 1966 the National Organization for Women was formed which encouraged women to share their experiences with each other and to organize in an effort to lobby for legislative change.

Notice that the first sentence uses the key words from the question to state the thesis. The answer gives not one but four examples of the changes that were taking place in the 1960s. Moreover, the answer is very specific, naming legislation or an organization and giving dates whenever significant. Can you spot the transitional expressions the writer uses to signal the movement from one example to the next?

Frequently Used Terms in Essay Questions

Definition: A definition is the precise meaning of a word or term. When you define something in an essay you usually write an *extended definition,* in which you select an appropriate example or examples to illustrate the meaning of a term.

Comparison/Contrast: When you *compare* two people or things, you point out the similarities between them. When you *contrast* two items, you point out the differences. Sometimes you may find yourself using both comparison and contrast in an essay.

Narration: Narration is the telling of a story by the careful use of a sequence of events. The events are usually (but not always) told in chronological order.

Summary: When you write a summary, you are supplying the main ideas of a longer piece of writing.

Discussion: This is a general term that encourages you to analyze a subject at length. Inviting students to discuss some aspect of a topic is a widely used method of asking examination questions.

Classification: When you *classify* items of any kind, you place them into separate groups so that large amounts of material can be more easily understood.

Cause and Effect: When you deal with causes, you answer the question *why;* when you deal with effects you show *results* or *consequences.*

EXERCISE 1 **Methods of Development**

Each of the following college essay questions deals with the single topic of computers. Use the previous list of terms to decide which method of development is being called for in each case. In the space provided after each question, identify the method being required.

1. Trace the development of the computer, beginning in 1937. Be sure to include all significant developments discussed in class.

   Method of development: ______________________

2. Choose two of the word-processing programs practiced in class and discuss the similarities and differences you encountered. What in your opinion were the advantages and disadvantages of each?

   Method of development: ______________________

3. Explain the meaning of each of the following terms: *hard disk, memory, directory, menu,* and *software.*

   Method of development: ______________________

4. We have discussed many of the common business applications for the computer. Select ten applications and group them according to the functions they perform.

   Method of development: ______________________

5. Discuss the problems that have resulted in the typical office as a result of computer technology.

   Method of development: ______________________

EXERCISE 2 **Methods of Development/Parts of a Question**

Each of the following is an example of a possible essay question that could be asked in a college course. In the spaces provided after each question, indicate: (a) what method of development (definition, comparison or contrast, narration, summary, or discussion) is being called for; (b) how many parts there are to the question. This indicates how many parts there will be in your answer.

1. What does the term *sociology* mean? Include in your answer at least four different meanings the term *sociology* has had since this area of study began.

   Method of development: ______________________

   The different parts of the question: ______________________

   ____

   ____

2. Compare and contrast the reasons the United States entered the Korean War with the reasons it entered the Vietnam War.

Method of development: ____________________

The different parts of the question: ____________________

____

____

3. Trace the history of our knowledge of the planet Jupiter, from the time it was first discovered until the present day. Include in your answer at least one nineteenth-century discovery and three of the most recent discoveries that have been made about Jupiter through the use of unmanned space vehicles sent near that planet.

Method of development: ____________________

The different parts of the question: ____________________

____

____

4. In view of the dramatic increase in cases of contagious diseases, describe the types of precautions now required for medical personnel. What changes are likely to be required in the future?

Method of development: ____________________

The different parts of the question: ____________________

____

____

5. Explain the three effects of high temperatures on space vehicles as they reenter the earth's atmosphere.

Method of development: ____________________

The different parts of the question: ____________________

____

____

6. What was the complete process of restoring the Statue of Liberty to its original condition? Include in your answer six different aspects of the restoration, from the rebuilding of the inside supports to the treatment of the metal surface.

Method of development: ____________________

The different parts of the question: ____________________

____

____

7. Trace the history of the English language from its beginning to the present day. Divide the history of the language into at least three different parts, using Old English, Middle English, and Modern English as your main divisions.

Method of development: ______________________________

The different parts of the question: ______________________________

____

____

8. Discuss the events that led up to World War II. Be sure to include both the political and social problems of the time that directly and indirectly led to the war.

Method of development: ______________________________

The different parts of the question: ______________________________

____

____

9. Summarize the four theories that have been proposed as to why dinosaurs became extinct 65 million years ago.

Method of development: ______________________________

The different parts of the question: ______________________________

____

____

10. Define the term *monarchy* and discuss the relevance or irrelevance of this form of government in today's world.

Method of development: ______________________________

The different parts of the question: ______________________________

____

____

Using the Thesis Statement in Timed In-Class Essay Questions

One of the most effective ways to begin an essay answer is to write a thesis statement. Your thesis statement should include the important parts of the question and should also give a clear indication of the approach you intend to take in your answer. Writing your opening sentence in this way gives you a real advantage: as your professor begins to read your work, it is clear what you are going to write about and how you are going to treat your subject.

For example, suppose you were going to write an essay on the following topic:

> Agree or disagree that doctors should be allowed to use germ-line gene therapy to alter a woman's egg, a man's sperm, or an embryo just a few days old in order to eliminate inherited diseases.

An effective way to write your opening sentence would be to write the following thesis sentence:

A strong argument exists to support the view that doctors should be allowed to use germ-line therapy to alter the egg, the sperm, or the embryo if the purpose is to eliminate an inherited disease.

The reader would then know that this was indeed the topic you had chosen and would also know how you intended to approach that topic.

EXERCISE 3

Writing Thesis Statements

Rewrite each of the following essay questions in thesis statement form. Read each question carefully and underline the important words or phrases in it. Then decide on the approach you would take in answering that question. An example has been done for you.

Essay question: How does one learn another language?

Thesis statement: The process of learning another language is complicated but usually follows four distinct stages.

1. Essay Questions: Discuss Thorstein Veblen's theory of the leisure class.

   Thesis statement: ______________________________

   ____

2. Essay Question: What are the effects of television violence on children?

   Thesis statement: ______________________________

   ____

3. Essay Question: Trace the development of portrait painting from the Middle Ages to today.

   Thesis statement: ______________________________

   ____

4. Essay Question: What are the major causes for the economic crisis facing the African nations today?

   Thesis statement: ______________________________

   ____

5. Essay Question: What have we recently learned from ocean exploration, and what remains to be done?

   Thesis statement: ______________________________

   ____

6. Essay Question: What are the problems when a couple adopts a child from one culture and raises that child in another culture?

   Thesis statement: ______________________________

   ____

7. Essay Question: In what ways does the new Japan differ from the old Japan?

   Thesis statement: ______________________________

   ____

8. Essay Question: What four countries depend on tourism for the major part of their national income and why is this so?

Thesis statement: ______________________________

____

9. Essay Question: What factors should a college use when judging the merits of a particular student for admission?

Thesis statement: ______________________________

____

10. Essay Question: What is Alzheimer's disease, its sequence of characteristic symptoms, and what are the current methods of treatment?

Thesis statement: ______________________________

____

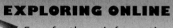

EXPLORING ONLINE

For further information about essay exams, see: http://www.as.ttu.edu/uwc/tablecontents.html Click on "Suggestions for Writing Essay Exams."

WORKING TOGETHER

PREPARING FOR TESTS

The following information is taken from a computer textbook. The material is found at the end of the final chapter in the book.

Chapter Title: Computers—The Future and You

REVIEW OF KEY POINTS

- We are gradually becoming an information-based society rather than an agricultural or industrial one; the reduction of "information float" will accelerate this movement.
- Careers in computer-related fields have a bright future with an expanding need for workers.
- The seven major areas in computer careers are operations, analysis and programming, information management, repair and service, sales and marketing, instruction, and engineering.
- Computers will continue to become smaller and faster through the increase in the number of transistors on each chip and the eventual use of gallium arsenide and photonic switches.
- Internal and external storage capacities will also continue to grow, with internal capacities on personal computers possibly exceeding 1 Mbyte.
- The use of video disks for external storage appears to be a strong possibility in the near future.
- Supercomputers will continue to grow more powerful through the use of parallel processing and pipelining.
- The markets for mainframe computers and personal computers are growing at about the same rate. The use of minicomputers may decline in the future.
- The use of robots in assembly line operations is expected to grow dramatically in the future, with negative effects on some human workers.

continued on next page

- Software will have to become easier to use if new users are to be enticed into the computer market.
- "Softer" software will include voice input, natural languages, expert systems, and other forms of artificial intelligence.
- Telecommunications may be the most rapidly expanding computer-related field in the future.
- Electronic funds transfer makes it unnecessary to leave the home or office to handle financial matters.

—Patrick G. McKeown, *Living with Computers*

1. After you have read through the review material, divide into groups. Each group should do the following:
   a. Construct four essay questions that you believe would be fair questions for a test covering the material in the chapter.
   b. From the "Review of Key Points," make a list of key terms in this chapter. (Students would have to memorize the definitions of these terms in order to be prepared for a test on this material.)
2. Come together as a class and put some of these questions on the board to be analyzed. Use the following checklist to analyze the questions:
   a. Does the question seem to be fair? (Some questions might be too vague or too general to be a fair test of what the student has learned.)
   b. How many parts does the question have?
   c. Does the question call for a specific method of development (for example, definition and analysis)?
   d. What are the key terms that should be used in the answer?
   e. What would be an effective opening sentence for the answer?

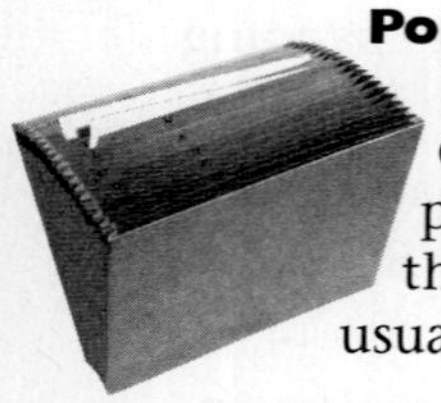

Portfolio Suggestion

Write about test anxiety. What can be done to help students who feel under pressure at exam time? In one paragraph, discuss what students can do to help themselves. In another paragraph, discuss what teachers can do to help students reduce their level of anxiety. In a third paragraph, suggest what the college could do to help those students who become unusually tense when taking exams.

Online Activity

Read about essay test–taking strategies at

http://www.yorku.ca/admin/cdc/lsp/ep/exam5.htm

Appendix A Parts of Speech

Words can be divided into categories called ***parts of speech.*** Understanding these categories will help you work with language more easily, especially when it comes to revising your own writing.

Nouns

A **noun** is a word that names a person, place, or thing.

Common Nouns	**Proper Nouns**
officer	Michael Johnson
station	Grand Central Station
magazine	*Newsweek*

Nouns are said to be ***concrete*** if you can see or touch them.

window
paper
river

Nouns are said to be ***abstract*** if you cannot see or touch them. These words can express concepts, ideas, or qualities.

marriage
democracy
honesty

To test for a noun, it may help to ask one or more of these questions.

- Can I make the word plural? (Most nouns have a plural form.)
- Can I put the article *the* in front of the word?
- Is the word used as the subject or object of the sentence?

Pronouns

A **pronoun** is a word that takes the place of a noun. Just like a noun, it is used as the subject or object of a sentence.

Pronouns can be divided into several classes. Here are some of them:

PRONOUNS

1. Personal Pronouns	Subjective		Objective		Possessive	
	Singular	*Plural*	*Singular*	*Plural*	*Singular*	*Plural*
1st person	I	we	me	us	my (mine)	our (ours)
2nd person	you	you	you	you	your (yours)	your (yours)
3rd person	he	they	him	them	his (his)	their (theirs)
	she		her		her (hers)	
	it		it		its (its)	

2. Relative Pronouns (can introduce noun clauses and adjective clauses)	3. Demonstrative Pronouns (can point out the antecedent)	4. Indefinite Pronouns (refer to nonspecific persons or things)			
		Singular			
who, whom, whose	this	someone	anyone	no one	
which	that everyone	everybody	somebody	anybody	nobody
that	these	everything	something	anything	nothing
what	those	each	another	either	neither
whoever		*Singular* or *Plural* (depending on meaning)			
whichever		all	more	none	
whatever		any	most	some	
		Plural			
		both	few	many	several

Adjectives

An **adjective** is a word that modifies a noun or pronoun. Adjectives usually come before the nouns they modify, but they can also come in the predicate.

The adjective comes directly in front of the noun it modifies:

The *unusual* package was placed on my desk.

The adjective occurs in the predicate but refers back to the noun it modifies:

The package felt *cold*.

Verbs

A **verb** is a word that shows action or expresses being. It can also change form in order to show the time (past, present, or future) of that action or being.

Verbs can be divided into three classes:

1. *Action Verbs*

Action verbs tell us what the subject is doing and when the subject does that action.

The action takes place in the present:

The athlete *runs* five miles every morning.

The action takes place in the past:

The crowd *cheered* for the oldest runner.

2. *Linking Verbs*

A **linking verb** joins the subject of a sentence to one or more words that describe or identify the subject.

The linking verb *was* identifies *He* with the noun *dancer:*

He *was* a dancer in his twenties.

The linking verb *seemed* describes *She* as *disappointed:*

She *seemed* disappointed with her job.

COMMON LINKING VERBS	
be (am, is, are, was, were, have been)	
act	grow
appear	look
become	seem
feel	taste

3. ***Helping Verbs*** **(also called "auxiliaries")**

A **helping verb** is any verb used just before the main verb.

The helping verb could show the ***tense*** of the verb:

It *will* rain tomorrow.

The helping verb could show the ***passive voice:***

The new civic center *has been* finished.

The helping verb could give a ***special meaning*** to the verb:

Ricky Martin *may be* singing here tonight.

COMMON HELPING VERBS

can, could
may, might, must
shall, should
will, would
forms of the irregular verbs *be, have,* and *do*

Adverbs

An **adverb** is a word that modifies a verb, an adjective, or another adverb. It often ends in -ly, but a better test is to ask yourself if the word answers one of the questions *how, when,* or *where.*

The adverb could modify a ***verb:***

The student walked *happily* into the classroom.

The adverb could modify an ***adjective:***

It will be *very* cold tomorrow.

The adverb could modify another ***adverb:***

Winter has come *too* early.

Learn to recognize the following common adverbs:

COMMON ADVERBS	
Adverbs of Frequency	*Adverbs of Degree*
often	even
never	extremely
sometimes	just
seldom	more
always	much
ever	only
	quite
	surely
	too
	very

Prepositions

A **preposition** is a word used to relate a noun or pronoun to some other word in the sentence. The preposition with its noun or pronoun is called a **prepositional phrase.**

The letter is *from* my father.

The envelope is addressed *to* my sister.

Read through the following list of prepositions several times so that you will be able to recognize them. Your instructor may ask you to memorize them.

COMMON PREPOSITIONS			
about	below	in	since
above	beneath	inside	through
across	beside	into	to
after	between	like	toward
against	beyond	near	under
along	by	of	until
among	down	off	up
around	during	on	upon
at	except	outside	with
before	for	over	within
behind	from	past	without

Conjunctions

A **conjunction** is a word that joins or connects words, phrases, or clauses.

A conjunction connecting *two words:*

Sooner *or* later, you will have to pay.

A conjunction connecting *two phrases:*

The story was on the radio *and* in the newspaper.

A conjunction connecting *two clauses:*

Dinner was late *because* I had to work overtime.

CONJUNCTIONS

Coordinating Conjunctions	*Subordinating Conjunctions*	
and	after	provided that
but	although	since
or	as, as if, as though	unless
nor	because	until
for (meaning *because*)	before	when, whenever
yet	how	where, wherever
so	if, even if	while

Correlative Conjunctions	*Adverbial Conjunctions (also known as* conjunctive adverbs*)*	
either . . . or	To add an idea:	furthermore
neither . . . nor		moreover
both . . . and		likewise
not only . . . but also	To contrast:	however
		nevertheless
	To show results:	consequently
		therefore
	To show an alternative:	otherwise

Interjections

An **interjection** is a word that expresses a strong feeling and is not connected grammatically to any other part of the sentence.

Oh, I forgot my keys.

Well, that means I'll have to sit here all day.

Study the Context

Since one word can function differently or have different forms or meanings, you must often study the context in which the word is found to be sure of its part of speech.

for functioning as a preposition:

The parent makes sacrifices *for* the good of the children.

for functioning as a conjunction, meaning *because:*

The parent worked two jobs, *for* her child needed a good education.

Appendix B Irregular Verbs

Alphabetical Listing of Principal Parts of Irregular Verbs

Base Form	Past Tense	Past Participle
arise	arose	arisen
bear	bore	borne
beat	beat	beat or beaten
become	became	become
begin	began	begun
bend	bent	bent
bet	bet	bet
bind	bound	bound
bite	bit	bitten, bit
bleed	bled	bled
blow	blew	blown
break	broke	broken
breed	bred	bred
bring	brought	brought
build	built	built
burst	burst	burst
buy	bought	bought
cast	cast	cast
catch	caught	caught
choose	chose	chosen
cling	clung	clung
come	came	come
cost	cost	cost
creep	crept	crept
cut	cut	cut
deal	dealt	dealt
dig	dug	dug
dive	dived, dove	dived
do	did	done
draw	drew	drawn
drink	drank	drunk
drive	drove	driven
eat	ate	eaten
fall	fell	fallen
feed	fed	fed
feel	felt	felt
fight	fought	fought
find	found	found
fit	fit	fit
flee	fled	fled

Base Form	Past Tense	Past Participle
fling	flung	flung
fly	flew	flown
forbid	forbade, forbad	forbidden
forget	forgot	forgotten
forgive	forgave	forgiven
freeze	froze	frozen
get	got	gotten
give	gave	given
go	went	gone
grind	ground	ground
grow	grew	grown
hang	*hung, hanged	hung, hanged
have	had	had
hear	heard	heard
hide	hid	hidden
hit	hit	hit
hold	held	held
hurt	hurt	hurt
keep	kept	kept
kneel	knelt	knelt
know	knew	known
lay (to put)	laid	laid
lead	led	led
leave	left	left
lend	lent	lent
let	let	let
lie (to recline)	lay	lain
lose	lost	lost
make	made	made
mean	meant	meant
meet	met	met
mistake	mistook	mistaken
pay	paid	paid
plead	pleaded	pleaded
prove	proved	proved, proven
put	put	put
quit	quit	quit
read	†read	†read
ride	rode	ridden
ring	rang	rung
rise	rose	risen
run	ran	run
say	said	said
see	saw	seen
seek	sought	sought
sell	sold	sold
send	sent	sent
set	set	set
sew	sewed	sewn, sewed

*See the dictionary to clarify usage.

†Pronunciation changes in past and past participle forms.

Base Form	Past Tense	Past Participle
shake	shook	shaken
shave	shaved	shaved, shaven
shed	shed	shed
shine	shone	shone
shoot	shot	shot
show	showed	shown, showed
shrink	shrank, shrunk	shrunk, shrunken
shut	shut	shut
sing	sang	sung
sink	sank	sunk
sit	sat	sat
slay	slew	slain
sleep	slept	slept
slide	slid	slid
sling	slung	slung
slink	slunk	slunk
slit	slit	slit
sow	sowed	sown, sowed
speak	spoke	spoken
speed	sped, speeded	sped, speeded
spend	spent	spent
spin	spun	spun
spit	spat	spat
split	split	split
spread	spread	spread
spring	sprang	sprung
stand	stood	stood
steal	stole	stolen
stick	stuck	stuck
sting	stung	stung
stink	stank, stunk	stunk
stride	strode	stridden
strike	struck	struck
string	strung	strung
swear	swore	sworn
sweep	swept	swept
swim	swam	swum
swing	swung	swung
take	took	taken
teach	taught	taught
tear	tore	torn
tell	told	told
think	thought	thought
throw	threw	thrown
wake	woke, waked	woken, waked
wear	wore	worn
weave	wove	woven
weep	wept	wept
wet	wet	wet
win	won	won
wind	wound	wound
wring	wrung	wrung
write	wrote	written

Appendix C Spelling

I. Forming the Plurals of Nouns

Almost all nouns can be made plural by simply adding *-s* to the singular form:

girl / girls
dinner / dinners

However, each of the following groups of words has its own special rules for forming the plural.

1. Words ending in *-y:*

In words ending in *-y* preceded by a *consonant,* change the *-y* to *-i* and add *-es.*

la*dy* / lad*ies*
ceremo*ny* / ceremon*ies*

Words ending in *-y* preceded by a *vowel* form their plurals in the regular way by just adding *-s.*

d*ay* / day*s*
monk*ey* / monkey*s*
vall*ey* / valley*s*

2. Words ending in *-o:*

Most words ending in *-o* preceded by a *consonant* add *-es* to form the plural.

he*ro* / hero*es*
pota*to* / potato*es*
ec*ho* / echo*es*

However, musical terms or names of musical instruments add only *-s.*

pian*o* / piano*s*
sol*o* / solo*s*
sopran*o* / soprano*s*

Words ending in *-o* preceded by a *vowel* add *-s*.

pat*io* /	patio*s*
rad*io* /	radio*s*
rod*eo* /	rodeo*s*

Some words ending in *-o* may form their plural with *-s* or *-es*.

memento /	memento*s*	or	memento*es*
pinto /	pinto*s*	or	pinto*es*
zero /	zero*s*	or	zero*es*

If you are uncertain about the plural ending of a word ending in *-o,* it is best to use the dictionary. The dictionary gives all the endings of irregular plurals. If no plural form is given, you know the word will form its plural in the regular way by adding only *-s*.

3. Words ending in *-ch, -sh, -s, -x,* and *-z:*

For words ending in *-ch, -sh, -s, -x,* and *-z,* add *-es*.

witch*es*	dress*es*	buzz*es*
dish*es*	tax*es*	

4. Words ending in *-fe* or *-f:*

Some words ending in *-fe* or *-f* change the *f* to *v* and add *-es*. You can hear the change from the *f* sound to the *v* sound in the plural.

wi*fe* /	wi*ves*
lea*f* /	lea*ves*

Other words ending in *-fe* or *-f* keep the *f* and just add *-s*.

sherif*f* /	sheriff*s*
belie*f* /	belief*s*

Again, you can hear that the *f* sound is kept in the plural. Some words can form their plural either way. If so, the dictionary will give the preferred way first.

5. Foreign words:

Some words borrowed from other languages keep the plurals from those other languages to form the plural in English.

cris*is* /	cris*es*
phenomen*on* /	phenomen*a*
alumn*us* (masc.) /	alumn*i*
alumn*a* (fem.) /	alumn*ae*
alg*a* /	alg*ae*

6. Compound nouns:

Compound nouns form their plurals by putting the *-s* on the end of the main word.

brother-in-law /	brothers-in-law
passer-by /	passers-by

7. Irregular plurals:

Some nouns in English have irregular plurals.

Singular	*Plural*
child	children
deer	deer
foot	feet
goose	geese
man, woman	men, women
moose	moose
mouse	mice
ox	oxen
sheep	sheep
tooth	teeth

II. Words Ending in y

1. When a *y* at the end of a word is preceded by a consonant, change *y* to *i* and add the ending.

Word		**Ending**		**New Word**
carry	+	er	=	carr*ier*
merry	+	ment	=	merr*iment*
funny	+	er	=	________________
busy	+	ness	=	________________
vary	+	es	=	________________

Exceptions: Do not change the *y* to *i* if the ending starts with an *i*. In English we seldom have two *i's* together.

stu*dy*	+	ing	=	stud*ying* not studiing
rea*dy*	+	ing	=	________________

Some long words drop the *y* when adding the ending. You can hear that the *y* syllable is missing when you pronounce the word correctly.

milita*ry*	+	ism	=	milita*rism*
accomp*any*	+	ist	=	________________

2. When *y* at the end of a word is preceded by a vowel, do *not* change the *y* when adding the ending. Simply add the ending.

surv*ey*	+	s	=	surv*eys*
enj*oy*	+	ment	=	________________

III. Learning to Spell *ie* or *ei* Words

Use this rhyme to help you remember how to spell most *ie* and *ei* words:

i before *e*
except after *c*
or when sounded like *ā*
as in *n**ei**ghbor* or *w**ei**gh.*

i before *e:*
The majority of all the *ie* or *ei* words use *ie.*

believe	friend	yield
chief	shriek	

except after *c:*

ceiling	conceive	receive
conceit	receipt	

or when sounded like *ā* as in *n**ei**ghbor* or *w**ei**gh:*

beige	reins	vein
eight	sleigh	

EXCEPTIONS TO THE *ie* OR *ei* RULE

Once you have learned the rhyme, concentrate on learning the following groups of words that are the exceptions to this rhyme.

caffeine	leisure	ancient
codeine	seizure	conscience
protein	seize	efficient
		sufficient
neither	height	
either	Fahrenheit	
sheik	counterfeit	
stein	foreign	
their		
weird		

IV. When Should the Final Consonant of a Word Be Doubled?

When you add an ending that begins with a vowel *(-ed, -er, -est, -ing)* to a word, how do you know if you should double the final consonant of that word?

The answer to this question involves the most complicated spelling rule. However, the rule is well worth learning because once you know it, you will suddenly be able to spell scores of words correctly.

Can you explain why the word *trap* doubles its *p* but the word *turn* does not double its *n* in the examples below?

The final *p* doubles: trap + ing = tra*pp*ing

Since *rap* in the word *trap* is a consonant-vowel-consonant combination, this one-syllable word will double the final consonant (when adding an ending beginning with a vowell).

The final *n* does not double: turn + ing = tur*n*ing

Since the last three letters *urn* in the word *turn* are a vowel-consonant-consonant combination, this one-syllable word does not double the final consonant (when adding an ending beginning with a vowel).

RULE FOR DOUBLING ONE-SYLLABLE WORDS

Double the final consonant of a one-syllable word when adding an ending that begins with a vowel only if the last three letters of the word end with a consonant-vowel-consonant combination.

PRACTICE

Study the list of words that follows. For each of these one-syllable words, decide if the word will or will not double the final consonant (when adding an ending beginning with a vowel).

One-Syllable Word	Consonant-Vowel-Consonant Combination?	Double?	Add -ing Ending
d*rag*	________	________	________
dr*ain*	________	________	________
slip	________	________	________
crack	________	________	________
broil	________	________	________
win	________	________	________

Note: In words with *qu* like *quit* or *quiz,* think of the *qu* as a consonant. The *u* does have a consonant *w* sound.) *quit* + ing = qui*t*ting

RULE FOR DOUBLING WORDS OF MORE THAN ONE SYLLABLE

For words of more than one syllable, the rule adds one more condition: If the first syllable is accented in the newly formed word, you do not double the final consonant.

pre fer´ + ed = pre ferred´

(The new word *preferred* maintains the accent on the second syllable. Therefore, the final *r* is doubled.)

but

pre fer´ + ence = pref´ er ence

(In the new word *preference,* the accent is on the first syllable. The final consonant *r* is therefore not doubled.)

V. Is It One Word or Two?

There is often confusion about whether or not certain word combinations should be joined together to form compound words. Study the following three groups of words to avoid this common confusion.

These words are always written as one word:

another	grandmother	playroom
bathroom	nearby	schoolteacher
bedroom	nevertheless	southeast, northwest, etc.
bookkeeper	newspaper	roommate
cannot	good-bye, goodbye, or good-by	yourself
downstairs		

These words are always written as two words:

a lot	living room	high school
all right	no one	good night
dining room		

These words are written as one or two words depending on their use:

all ready *(pronoun* and *adjective)* — completely prepared
already *(adverb)* — previously; before

He was ______________ there by the time I arrived.

I have ______________ read that book.

We were ______________ for the New Year's Eve party.

all together *(pronoun* and *adjective)* — in a group
altogether *(adverb)* — completely

Our family was ______________ at Thanksgiving.

I am ______________ too upset to concentrate.

Have you gathered your papers ______________?

all ways *(adjective* and *noun)* — every road or path
always *(adverb)* — on every occasion

Be sure to check ______________ before you cross that intersection.

______________ look both ways before you cross that intersection.

She ______________ figures out the homework.

any one *(adjective* and *pronoun)* — one person or thing in a specific group
anyone *(indefinite pronoun)* — any person at all

Did ______________ ever find my gloves?

She will talk to ______________ who will listen to her.

I would choose ______________ of those sweaters if I had the money.

every one *(adjective* and *pronoun)* — every person or thing in a specific group
everyone *(indefinite pronoun)* — all of the people

______________ of the books we wanted was out of stock.

______________ was so disappointed.

______________ of the workers disapproved of the new rules.

may be *(verb)* — might be
maybe *(adverb)* — perhaps

The news broadcast said that there ______________ a storm tomorrow.

If it's bad, ______________ I won't go to work.

______________ my car won't start.

VI. Learning to Spell Commonly Mispronounced Words

Several common English words are often mispronounced or pronounced in such a way that the result is incorrect spelling. Below are sixty common words that are often misspelled. As you study them, be careful to spell each of the underlined syllables correctly.

I. The Common Omission of Vowels

1. Remember the *a* in each of the underlined syllables:

accidentally	literature
basically	miniature
boundary	separate
extraordinary	temperament
incidentally	temperature

2. Remember the *e* in each of the underlined syllables:

considerable	mathematics
difference	numerous
funeral	scenery
interesting	

Notice, however, that each word in column 1 that ends in *er,* drops the *e* when it changes to the new form in column 2.

disaster /	disastrous
enter /	entrance
hinder /	hindrance
hunger /	hungry
launder /	laundry
monster /	monstrous
remember /	remembrance

3. Remember the *i* in each of the underlined syllables:

aspirin family similar

4. Remember the *o* in each of the underlined syllables:

chocolate	humorous
environment	laboratory
favorite	sophomore

5. Remember the *u* in each of the underlined syllables:

luxury accuracy

6. Remember the *y* in each of the underlined syllables:

studying carrying

II. Remember the underlined consonant in each of the following words:

1. **b**
   probably
2. **c**
   arctic
3. **d**
   candidate
   handkerchief
   supposed to
   used to
4. **g**
   recognize
5. **n**
   government
6. **r**
   February
   library
   surprise
7. **t**
   authentic
   identical
   partner
   promptly
   quantity

III. Do not add an extra *e* after the *th:*

athlete athletic

IV. Do not transpose the underlined letters:

tragedy	
persuade	prefer
perform	prescription

VII. Spelling 200 Tough Words

WORD LIST 1: SILENT LETTERS

b	***h***	***p***
crum*b*	ex*h*ibit	*p*neumonia
clim*b*	r*h*etoric	*p*sychology
de*b*t	r*h*ythm	***s***
dou*b*t	sc*h*edule	ai*s*le
c	***l***	i*s*land
indi*c*t	co*l*onel	debri*s*
d	***n***	***t***
knowle*d*ge	autum*n*	depo*t*
We*d*nesday	colum*n*	lis*t*en
	condem*n*	mor*t*gage
		w
		ans*w*er

WORD LIST 2: DOUBLE LETTERS

a*cc*identa*ll*y	a*rr*angement	nece*ss*ary
a*cc*o*mm*odate	co*mm*i*tt*ee	o*cc*asiona*ll*y
acro*ss*	exa*gg*erate	po*ss*e*ss*ion
a*nn*ual	fina*ll*y	prefe*rr*ed
a*pp*arently	guarant*ee*	questio*nn*aire
reco*mm*end	su*gg*est	tomo*rr*ow
su*cc*e*e*d	su*mm*arize	wri*tt*en (but: wri*t*ing)
su*cc*e*ss*		

WORD LIST 3: *-able* OR *-ible*

-able Usually, when you begin with a complete word, the ending is *-able*.

acceptable	agreeable

These words keep the *e* when adding the ending:

peaceable	manageable
noticeable	knowledgeable

These words drop the *e* when adding the ending:

conceivable	indispensable
desirable	inevitable
imaginable	irritable

-ible Usually, if you start with a root that is not a word, the ending is *-ible*.

audible	irresistible
compatible	permissible
eligible	plausible
feasible	possible
illegible	sensible
incredible	susceptible
inexhaustible	tangible

WORD LIST 4: *de-* OR *di-*

de-	***di-***
decide	dilemma
decision	dilute
delinquent	discipline
descend	discuss
describe	disease
despair	disguise
despicable	dispense
despise	dispute
despite	dissent
despondent	divide
destructive	division
develop	divine
device	

WORD LIST 5: THE *-er* SOUND

Most words ending with the *-er* sound are spelled with *-er,* as in the words *prisoner, customer,* and *hunger.* Words that are exceptions to this should be learned carefully.

-ar	***-or***
beggar	actor
burglar	author
calendar	bachelor
cellar	doctor
dollar	emperor
grammar	governor
pillar	humor
polar	labor
similar	motor
vulgar	neighbor
-ur	professor
murmur	sailor
-yr	scissors
martyr	

WORD LIST 6: *-ance* OR *-ence*

Most words with the *-ence* sound at the end are spelled *-ence.* Here are a few examples:

audience	intelligence
correspondence	presence
excellence	reference
existence	

Learn these exceptions:

-ance	
allowance	nuisance
ambulance	observance
appearance	resistance
assistance	significance
attendance	tolerance
balance	***-ense***
dominance	license
guidance	***-eance***
ignorance	vengeance

WORD LIST 7: PROBLEMS WITH *s, c, z, x,* AND *k*

absence	criticize	medicine
alcohol	ecstasy	muscle
analyze	emphasize	prejudice
auxiliary	especially	recede
awkward	exceed	sincerely
biscuit	exercise	supersede
complexion	fascinate	vacillate
concede	magazine	vicious
consensus		

WORD LIST 8: TWENTY-FIVE DEMONS

acquire	extremely	occurred
argument	frightening	occurrence
benefit	grateful	privilege
cafeteria	inoculate	ridiculous
cemetery	judgment	secretary
category	lightning	truly
conquer	ninety	until
corroborate	ninth	village
courageous		

Appendix D Transitions

Transitions are words or phrases that take the reader from one idea to another. Here are some of the most commonly used transitional expressions. They are especially useful when we want to make the connections between ideas clear to our readers.

Transitions for Description—to Show Place

above, on top of
beneath, under
ahead, in front of, in the distance
behind, in back of
toward, away from
to the left, to the right,
beside, near, close by, at hand, next to
across from, nearby, in the neighborhood
between, in the middle, in the center

Transitions for Narration—to Show a Shift in Time

recently
previously
earlier
in the past
a few days ago
a hundred years ago
now, by now
at once
suddenly
immediately
meanwhile
at the same time
within a few minutes
soon, soon afterward
later, later on
after a little while
then
next, the next day
several weeks later
the following month
finally
eventualy
in the end

Transitions to Show Examples

for example
another example is . . .
to illustrate
an illustration of this is . . .
a case in point is . . .
one such case
a typical case
take the case of . . .
specifically
for instance
such as

Transitions for Process

the first step
in the beginning
to start with
to begin with
first of all
while you are . . .
as you are . . .
next
then
the second step
after you have . . .
the last step
the final step
finally
at last
eventually

Transitions for Comparison

similar to
similarly
likein contrast with
likewise
just like, just as
again
furthermore
moreover
equally
so though
also
too

Transitions for Contrast

on the contrary
on the other hand
even though
in spite of
despite
instead of
different from
whereas
while
still
contrary to current thinking
though
unlike

nevertheless
however
but
otherwise
except for
and yet

Transitions for Cause

because
caused by
results from
the reason is that
since

Transitions for Effect

accordingly
as a result, resulted in
consequently
for this reason
so, so that
then, therefore, thus

Transitions for Classification

divisions, divided into
categories, categorized by
types, kinds
groups, groupings, grouped into
areas, fields

Transitions for Definition

is defined as
is understood to be
means that
is sometimes thought to be
signifies

Transitions for Persuasion

To signal the thesis

I agree (disagree)
I support (do not support)
I am in favor of
(not in favor of)
. . . should be changed
. . . should be adopted
I propose

To admit an opponent's viewpoint

while it is true
although there are those who . . .
the opposition would have
you believe . . .
of course,
some may claim
we have been told that . . .
popular thought is that . . .
most people assume that . . .

To signal a reason

a convincing piece of
evidence
an additional reason
because, since
in view of this fact

To signal a conclusion

therefore
consequently
as a result

Index

Photo Credits

Page 21 © Walter Hodges/Stone

Page 31 © Scott Robinson/Stone

Page 71 Courtesy of the authors

Page 94 Bankers Trust Company

Page 112 AP/Wide World Photos

Page 132 © Beryl Goldberg

Page 146 © Robert Torrez/Stone

Page 201 © Terry Vince/Stone

Page 242 UN/DPI Photo

Page 282 © Walter Hodges/Stone

Page 304 © Kathleen Duxbury Yeaw

Page 318 © NY Times Pictures/Jeff Topping

Page 337 © Beryl Goldberg

Page 398 © Stewart Cohen/Stone

Page 423 © 2000 Gigi Cohen/Network Photographers

Page 423 © 2000 Gigi Cohen/Network Photographers

Page 441 © Corbis-Bettmann

Page 453 Courtesy of the authors

Page 474 Tom Toles in the *Buffalo News* © 1967

Page 499 UN/DPI Photo

Page 512 UN/DPI Photo

Page 522 Taken from the DEAR ABBY column by Abigail Van Buren. © UNIVERSAL PRESS SYNDICATE. Reprinted with permission. All rights reserved.

Page 548 © Lori Adamski Peek/Stone

Page 559 UN/DPI Photo

Literary Credits

Page 132 "A Hard Lesson Learned Door to Door" by Anita Santiago written with Julie Dunn. July 16, 2000. © 2000 The New York Times. Reprinted by permission.

Page 162 "Princess Must Face Immigration Charges" July 18, 2000. © 2000 The New York Times. Reprinted by permission.

Page 423 Arthur Lidz. Reprinted with permission.

Page 441 "Rosa Parks" by Ruth Edmonds Hill from *Notable Black American Women,* Editor Jessie Carney Smith. Copyright © 1996 Gale Research. Reprinted by permission of The Gale Group.

Page 485 "Goodbye Mom's Apple Pie" by Colleen Brosnan. Permission of Colleen Brosnan.

Page 490 "AIDS: An Epidemic of Fear" from *Aids: What Does It Mean to You?* Copyright © 1994 by Margaret O. Hyde and Elizabeth Forsyth. Reprinted by permission of Walker and Company, 435 Hudson Street, New York, New York 10014, 1-800-289-2553. All Rights Reserved.

Page 502 "The Fourth of July" by Audre Lorde. Reprinted with permission from *Zami: A New Spelling of My Name* © 1982 by Audre Lorde. Published by The Crossing Press, Freedom, California.

Page 514 "How to Ace a Job Interview" by Richard Koonce. Copyright March 1997, Training & Development, ASTD - www.astd.org. Reprinted with permission. All rights reserved.

Page 524 "The Difference Between a Brain and A Computer," from *Please Explain.* Copyright 1973 by Isaac Asimov. Reprinted by permission of Houghton Mifflin Co. All rights reserved.

Page 538 "It's Time We Helped Patients Die" from *Medical Economics,* June 8, 1987. Copyright © 1987 by Medical Economics Company. Reprinted with permission from *Medical Economics* magazine.

Page 543 "Censorship or Common Sense?" by Roxana Robinson, October 19, 1998. Copyright 1998 The New York Times. Reprinted by permission.

Page 548 "Where Have All the Fathers Gone?" editorial June 18, 1995 © Copyrighted 1995 Chicago Tribune Company. All rights reserved. Used with permission.